Part III

DOM

Chapter 9

The Document Object Model

The *Document Object Model, DOM* for short, is an abstract data structure that represents XML documents as trees made up of nodes. Various interfaces in the `org.w3c.dom` package represent elements, attributes, parsed character data, comments, and processing instructions. All of these are subinterfaces of the common `Node` interface, which provides basic methods for navigating and pruning the tree.

The root of the tree is a `Document` object that represents a complete, well-formed document. A parser reads an XML document from a stream and builds a `Document` object representing that XML document. The client program calls the methods of `Document` and the other DOM interfaces to navigate the tree and extract information from the document. Programs can also manipulate the tree in memory to add, delete, move, or change its nodes. Programs can even create completely new documents from scratch in memory, and these new documents are then written into an XML file.

DOM is defined in the Interface Definition Language (IDL); therefore, it is language neutral. DOM bindings exist for most object-oriented languages, including Java, JavaScript, C++, Python, and Perl. However, since this is a book about Java, I will deal exclusively with the Java implementation.

The Evolution of DOM

The first version of DOM, sometimes called DOM Level 0, wasn't an official specification but merely the object model that Netscape Navigator 3 and Internet Explorer 3 browsers implemented. (These were actually two different object models only marginally compatible with each other.)

DOM Level 0 applied only to HTML documents and only in the context of JavaScript. Nonetheless, both the usefulness of JavaScript and the growing incompatibility between the two browser object models underscored the need for something more standard. Hence, the W3C launched the W3C DOM Activity and began work on DOM Level 1. DOM1 was an attempt to devise a specification as quickly as possible that would codify existing practice and also achieve some level of compatibility across browsers. Given the constraints under which the working group labored, DOM1 is a surprisingly good specification. Although the naming conventions feel wrong to a Java developer, DOM1 does provides a solid core of functionality that covers maybe 75 percent of what developers want to do when processing XML.

DOM Level 2 cleaned up the DOM1 interfaces. The big change was namespace support in the `Element` and `Attr` interfaces. In addition, DOM2 added a number of supplementary interfaces for events, traversal, ranges, views, and stylesheets. I'll address these in upcoming chapters. In 2002, all significant XML parsers that support DOM support DOM2. There's not a lot of reason to worry about the difference between DOM1 and DOM2. From this point forward, I'm just going to teach DOM2.

DOM Level 3 is visible not far up the road. Parts of it are just beginning to be supported by bleeding-edge parsers, most especially Xerces 2. In the core, DOM3 just adds a few missing pieces needed to allow DOM to fully support all XML Information Set (Infoset) properties. This includes the original encoding and base URI of the document. However, DOM3 will also provide some crucial functionality missing from DOM2. In particular, DOM2 doesn't provide a parser-independent means to create a new `Document` object, either by parsing a file or by building one from scratch in memory. DOM3 will provide standard ways of doing both. DOM3 will also add a lot more support for DTDs and schemas. But despite all its new features and functionality, DOM3 will not replace DOM2. Everything that works today in DOM2 will continue to work the same way in DOM3. DOM3 extends the DOM into new territory, but it doesn't change what has gone before it.

DOM Modules

DOM2 is divided into fourteen modules organized in eight different packages. DOM1 roughly corresponds to the Core and XML modules. The other twelve modules are new in DOM2.

Core: `org.w3c.dom`
The basic interfaces that can be used to represent any SGML-like, hierarchical, tree-structured document, including `DOMException`, `DOMImplementation`, `DocumentFragment`, `Document`, `Node`, `NodeList`, `NamedNodeMap`, `CharacterData`, `Attr`, `Element`, `Text`, and `Comment`.

XML: `org.w3c.dom`
The additional subinterfaces of `Node` just for XML documents, including `CDATASection`, `DocumentType`, `Notation`, `Entity`, `EntityReference`, and `ProcessingInstruction`. An HTML DOM might not implement these.

HTML: `org.w3c.dom.html`
Interfaces designed specifically to represent the parts of an HTML document, such as `HTMLHtmlElement`, `HTMLHeadElement`, and `HTMLParagraphElement`. These are all subinterfaces of core interfaces like `Node` and `Element`. These aren't normally relevant to processing XML documents, but if you have a DOM-aware HTML parser, you can apply the techniques described in this book to HTML as well as XML.

Views: `org.w3c.dom.views`
The `AbstractView` and `DocumentView` interfaces used to associate different views with one document. For example, applying two stylesheets to one XML document could produce two views. This is not supported by most XML parsers.

StyleSheets: `org.w3c.dom.stylesheets`
Some basic interfaces for representing stylesheets, including `StyleSheet`, `StyleSheetList`, `MediaList`, `LinkStyle`, and `DocumentStyle`.

CSS: `org.w3c.dom.css`
Interfaces that specifically represent CSS style sheets including `CSSStyleSheet`, `CSSRuleList`, `CSSRule`, `CSSStyleRule`, `CSSMediaRule`, `CSSFontFaceRule`, `CSSPageRule`, `CSSImportRule`, `CSSCharsetRule`, `CSSUnknownRule`, `CSSStyleDeclaration`, `CSSValue`, `CSSPrimitiveValue`, `CSSValueList`, `RGBColor`, `Rect`, `Counter`, `ViewCSS`, `DocumentCSS`, `DOMImplementationCSS`, and `ElementCSSInlineStyle`.

CSS2: `org.w3c.dom.css`
The `CSS2Properties` class, which provides shortcut methods for setting all of the different CSS2 style properties.

Events: `org.w3c.dom.events`
The interfaces in these classes establish a system that allows event listeners to be attached to nodes. Events nodes can respond to include user interface events, such as mouse clicks, structure modification events like document edits, and anything else the implementation wants to support. The next four modules define specific kinds of events. However, applications can define their own as well. In practice, events are more relevant to JavaScript and other browser-based script systems than they are to most XML programs; nonetheless, events can be useful when an XML document is displayed in a browser or otherwise shown to a user.

UIEvents: `org.w3c.dom.events`
The `UIEvent` interface signals when a node represented on the screen in some form of GUI has received the focus, lost the focus, or been activated.

MouseEvents: `org.w3c.dom.events`
The `MouseEvent` interface signals when, where, and with which keys pressed the user has clicked the mouse, pressed the mouse button, released the mouse button, moved the mouse, or moved the cursor into or out of an element's graphical representation.

MutationEvents: `org.w3c.dom.events`
The `MutationEvent` interface signals that Cerebro has detected a new mutant of exceptional power. (Sorry about that one, I couldn't help myself.) Really, it signals that a node has been added, removed, or modified in the document.

HTMLEvents: `org.w3c.dom.events`
The HTML events module doesn't define any new interfaces. Instead it uses the base `DOMEvent` interface to report a dozen events specific to web browsers, including load, unload, abort, error, select, change, submit, reset, focus, blur, resize, and scroll.

Traversal: `org.w3c.dom.traversal`
This package provides simple utility classes for performing common operations on a tree, such as walking the entire tree or filtering out nodes that meet certain conditions. Chapter 12 discusses it in depth.

Range: `org.w3c.dom.ranges`
This optional module extends DOM to cover sections of documents that don't neatly match element boundaries. For example, it would be useful for indicat-

ing the section of text that the user has selected with the mouse. It also could be used for XPointer ranges.

Aside from the core and XML modules, not all DOM implementations support all of these modules, or all parts of the modules that they do support. Most Java implementations do support the traversal module; the events module is not uncommon; and the range module is occasionally supported. As far as I know, only Xerces supports the HTML module. So far I haven't found any parsers that support the views, StyleSheets, or CSS modules.

The `hasFeature()` method in the `DOMImplementation` interface can tell you whether that implementation supports a particular feature. Just pass in the name and version of the feature you're looking for. For DOM2 the version is `"2.0"`.

```
public boolean hasFeature (String name, String version)
```

In addition to the standard modules, implementations and application-specific DOMs may define additional feature name strings. These nonstandard features use a reversed domain name, much like a Java package name, to clearly indicate who is responsible for the feature. For example, SVG 1.0 uses the feature name `"org.w3c.dom.svg"` and the version number `"1.0"` to indicate support for some part of the SVG DOM. It uses the feature strings `"org.w3c.dom.svg.static"`, `"org.w3c.dom.svg.animation"`, or `"org.w3c.dom.svg.dynamic"` to indicate support for specific parts of the SVG DOM.

Different DOM implementations use different concrete classes to implement the standard interfaces. For example, in Xerces, the `org.apache.xerces.dom.DOMImplementationImpl` singleton class implements the `DOMImplementation` interface. In the Oracle XML Parser for Java, `XMLDOMImplementation` implements the `DOMImplementation` interface. This class has a simple no-args constructor. Example 9.1 uses this class and constructor to check for the standard features in Oracle.

Example 9.1 Which Modules Does Oracle Support?

```
import oracle.xml.parser.v2.XMLDOMImplementation;
import org.w3c.dom.DOMImplementation;

public class OracleModuleChecker {

  public static void main(String[] args) {

    // parser dependent
```

```
    DOMImplementation implementation = new XMLDOMImplementation();
    String[] features = {"Core", "XML", "HTML", "Views",
     "StyleSheets", "CSS", "CSS2", "Events", "UIEvents",
     "MouseEvents", "MutationEvents", "HTMLEvents", "Traversal",
     "Range"};

    for (int i = 0; i < features.length; i++) {
      if (implementation.hasFeature(features[i], "2.0")) {
        System.out.println("Oracle supports " + features[i]);
      }
      else {
        System.out.println("Oracle does not support "
         + features[i]);
      }
    }

  }

}
```

Following is the output from Version 9.0.1.1.0A Production of the Oracle XML Parser for Java. Notice that Oracle only supports the XML, events, traversal, and range modules. The reported lack of support for core is almost certainly just an oversight. The "Core" feature string was only added in the final draft of DOM2 and was not present in earlier drafts. The core module is a prerequisite for all the other modules. It's hard to believe Oracle really doesn't support it.

```
D:\books\XMLJAVA\examples\09>java OracleModuleChecker
Oracle does not support Core
Oracle supports XML
Oracle does not support HTML
Oracle does not support Views
Oracle does not support StyleSheets
Oracle does not support CSS
Oracle does not support CSS2
Oracle supports Events
Oracle does not support UIEvents
Oracle does not support MouseEvents
Oracle does not support MutationEvents
Oracle does not support HTMLEvents
Oracle supports Traversal
Oracle supports Range
```

Application-Specific DOMs

A number of XML applications have built useful application-specific DOMs by extending the standard DOM interfaces. XML applications with their own custom DOMs include HTML and XHTML, the Wireless Markup Language (WML), Scalable Vector Graphics (SVG), and MathML.

Whereas the generic DOM would use an `Element` object, a WML-specific DOM might use a `WMLOptionElement`, or a `WMLPElement`, or a `WMLPostfieldElement` object, as appropriate for the actual type of element it represents. These custom subclasses and subinterfaces have all the methods and properties of the standard interfaces, as well as other methods and properties appropriate only for their type. For example, a WML `p` element has `align`, `mode`, and `xml:lang` attributes, like this:

```
<p align="center" mode="wrap" xml:lang="en">
  Hello!
</p>
```

Therefore, the `WMLPElement` interface has getter and setter methods for those three attributes:

```
public void setMode (String mode)
public void setAlign (String align)
public void setXMLLang (String lang)
public String getMode()
public String getAlign()
public String getXMLLang()
```

An application-specific DOM can enforce application-specific rules such as, "The `mode` attribute must have one of the values `wrap` or `nowrap`," though currently this practice is uncommon.

Of course, because `WMLPElement` extends `Element`, which extends `Node`, it also has the usual methods of any DOM node. When processing a WML document, you can use the generic DOM interfaces if you prefer, or you can use the more specific WML subclasses and subinterfaces.

The big issue for most application-specific DOMs is parser support. To read these documents, you not only need a custom DOM; you also need a custom parser that knows how to generate the application-specific DOM. That's a little harder to come by. With some effort, you can configure the Xerces DOM parser to produce HTML DOM `Document` objects for well-formed HTML and XHTML. The XML

Apache Project's open source Batik *[http://xml.apache.org/batik/domapi.html]* includes an SVG parser that can produce SVG DOM `Document` objects. For other application-specific DOMs, the pickings are a little slim right now.

It's somewhat easier to create new WML, SVG, MathML, or similar documents in a particular vocabulary using an application-specific DOM. However, you do still need a concrete implementation of that DOM's abstract interfaces. Xerces includes HTML and WML implementations. Batik includes one for SVG. For other models, you'll have to roll your own.

Trees

DOM is based on an implicit data model, which is similar to but not quite the same as the data models used by other XML technologies such as XPath, the XML Infoset, and SAX. Before we delve too deeply into the nitty-gritty details of the DOM API, it's helpful to have a higher level understanding of just what DOM thinks an XML document is.

According to DOM, an XML document is a tree made up of nodes of several types. The tree has a single root node, and all nodes in this tree except for the root have a single parent node. Furthermore, each node has a list of child nodes. In some cases, this list of children may be empty, in which case the node is called a leaf node.

There can also be nodes that are not part of the tree structure. For example, each attribute node belongs to one element node but is not considered to be a child of that element. Furthermore, nodes can be removed from the tree or created but not inserted in the tree. Thus a full DOM document is composed of the following:

- A tree of nodes
- Various nodes that are somehow associated with other nodes in the tree but are not themselves part of the tree
- A random assortment of disconnected nodes

DOM trees are not red-black trees, binary trees, B-trees, or any other sort of special-purpose trees. From a data-structures point of view, they are just plain-vanilla trees. Recursion works very well on DOM data structures, as it does on any tree. You can use all of the techniques you learned for processing trees in Data Structures 201. Breadth-first search, depth-first search, inorder traversal, preorder traversal, postorder traversal, and so on all work with DOM data structures.

In addition to its tree connections, each node has a local name, a namespace URI, and a prefix; although for several kinds of nodes, these may be null. For example, the local name, namespace URI, and prefix of a comment are always null. Each node also has a *node name*. For an element or attribute, the node name is the prefixed name. For other named things such as notations or entities, the node name is the name of the thing. For nodes without names, such as text nodes, the node name is the value from the following list that matches the node type:

- #document
- #comment
- #text
- #cdata-section
- #document-fragment

Finally each node has a string value. For text-like things such as text nodes and comments, this tends to be the text of the node. For attributes, it's the normalized value of the attribute. For everything else, including elements and documents, the value is null.

DOM divides nodes into twelve types, seven of which can potentially be part of a DOM tree:

- Document nodes
- Element nodes
- Text nodes
- Attribute nodes
- Processing instruction nodes
- Comment nodes
- Document type nodes
- Document fragment nodes
- Notation nodes
- CDATA section nodes
- Entity nodes
- Entity reference nodes

Of these twelve, the first seven are by far the most important; and often a tree built by an XML parser will contain only the first seven.

Document Nodes

Each DOM tree has a single root document node. This node has children. Because all documents have exactly one root element, a document node always has exactly one element-node child. If the document has a document type declaration, then it also has one document-type-node child. If the document contains any comments or processing instructions before or after the root element, then these are also child nodes of the document node. The order of all children is maintained. Consider the simple XML-RPC document shown in Example 9.2.

Example 9.2 An XML-RPC Request Document

```
<?xml version="1.0"?>
<?xml-stylesheet type="text/css" href="xml-rpc.css"?>
<!-- It's unusual to have an xml-stylesheet processing
     instruction in an XML-RPC document but it is legal, unlike
     SOAP where processing instructions are forbidden. -->
<!DOCTYPE methodCall SYSTEM "xml-rpc.dtd">
<methodCall>
  <methodName>getQuote</methodName>
  <params>
    <param>
      <value><string>RHAT</string></value>
    </param>
  </params>
</methodCall>
```

The document node representing the root of this document has four child nodes in this order:

1. A processing instruction node for the `xml-stylesheet` processing instruction
2. A comment node for the comment
3. A document type node for the document type declaration
4. An element node for the root `methodCall` element

The XML declaration, the DOCTYPE declaration, and the white space between these nodes are not included in the tree. The document type node is available as a separate property of the document node. However, it is not a child and is not included in the list of the document's children. The XML declaration (including the version, standalone, and encoding declarations) and the white space are removed by the parser. They are not part of the model.

Element Nodes

Each element node has a name, a local name, a namespace URI (which may be null if the element is not in any namespace), and a prefix (which may also be null). The string also contains children. For example, consider this `value` element:

```
<value><string>RHAT</string></value>
```

When represented in DOM, it becomes a single element node with the name `value`. This node has a single element-node child for the `string` element. The string also has a single text-node child containing the text `RHAT`.

Or consider this `para` element:

```
<db:para xmlns:db="http://www.example.com/"
  xmlns="http://namespaces.cafeconleche.org/">
  Or consider this <markup>para</markup> element:
</db:para>
```

In DOM it's represented as an element node with the name `db:para`, the local name `para`, the prefix `db`, and the namespace URI `http://www.example.com/`. It has three children:

1. A text node containing the text `Or consider this`
2. An element node with the name `markup`, the local name `markup`, the namespace URI `http://namespaces.cafeconleche.org/`, and a null prefix
3. Another text node containing the text `element:`

White space is included in text nodes, even if it's ignorable. For example, consider this `methodCall` element:

```
<methodCall>
  <methodName>getQuote</methodName>
  <params>
    <param>
      <value><string>RHAT</string></value>
    </param>
  </params>
</methodCall>
```

It is represented as an element node with the name `methodCall` and five child nodes:

1. A text node containing only white space
2. An element node with the name `methodName`
3. A text node containing only white space
4. An element node with the name `params`
5. A text node containing only white space

Of course, these element nodes also have their own child nodes.

In addition to containing element and text nodes, an element node may contain comment and processing instruction nodes. Depending on how the parser behaves, an element node might also contain some CDATA section nodes, entity reference nodes, or both. However, many parsers resolve these automatically into their component text and element nodes, and do not report them separately.

Attribute Nodes

An attribute node has a name, a local name, a prefix, a namespace URI, and a string value. The value is normalized as required by the XML 1.0 specification. That is, entity and character references in the value are resolved, and all white space characters are converted to a single space. If the attribute has any type other than CDATA, then leading and trailing white space is stripped from its value, and all other runs of white space are converted to a single space. An attribute node also has children, all of which are text and entity reference nodes forming the value of the attribute. However, it's unusual to access these directly instead of by the value.

If a validating parser builds an XML document from a file, then default attributes from the DTD are included in the DOM tree. If the parser supports schemas, then default attributes can be read from the schema as well. DOM does not provide the type of the attribute as specified by the DTD or schema, or the list of values available for an enumerated type attribute. This is a major shortcoming.

Attributes are *not* considered to be children of the element to which they are attached. Instead they are part of a separate set of nodes. For example, consider this `Quantity` element:

```
<Quantity amount="17" />
```

This element has no children, but it does have a single attribute with the name `amount` and the value `17`.

Attributes that declare namespaces do not receive special treatment in DOM. They are reported by DOM parsers in the same way as any other attribute. Furthermore, DOM always provides the fully qualified names and namespace URIs for all element and attribute nodes.

Leaf Nodes

Only document, element, attribute, entity, and entity reference nodes can have children. The remaining node types are much simpler.

Text Nodes

Text nodes contain character data from the document stored as a `String`. Any characters like 𝄢 from outside Unicode's Basic Multilingual Plane are represented as surrogate pairs. Characters like & and < that are represented in the document by predefined entity or character references are replaced by the actual characters they represent. If these nodes are written out again to an XML document, these characters need to be re-escaped.

When a parser reads an XML document to form a DOM `Document`, it puts as much text as possible into each text node before being interrupted by non-predefined entities, comments, tags, CDATA section delimiters, or other markup. Thus no text node immediately follows any other text node, as there is always an intervening nontext node. However, if a DOM is created or modified in memory, then the client program may divide text between immediately adjacent text nodes. As a result, it's not always guaranteed that each text node contains the maximum possible contiguous run of text, just that this is the case immediately after a document is parsed.

Comment Nodes

A comment node has a name (which is always #comment), a string value (the text of the comment) and a parent (the node that contains it). That's all. For example, consider this comment:

```
<!-- Don't forget to fix this! -->
```

The value of this node is `Don't forget to fix this!` The white space at either end is included.

Processing Instruction Nodes

A processing instruction node has a name (the target of the processing instruction), a string value (the data of the processing instruction), and a parent (the node that contains it). That's all. For example, consider this processing instruction:

```
<?xml-stylesheet type="text/css" href="xml-rpc.css"?>
```

The name of this node is `xml-stylesheet`. The value is `type="text/css" href="xml-rpc.css"`. The white space between the target and the data is not included, but the white space between the data and the closing ?> is included. Even if the processing instruction uses a pseudo-attribute format as this one does, it is not considered to have attributes or children. Its data is just a string that happens to have some equal signs and quote marks in suggestive positions.

CDATA Section Nodes

A CDATA section node is a special text node that represents the contents of a CDATA section. Its name is #cdata-section. Its value is the text content of the section. For example, consider this CDATA section:

```
<![CDATA[<?xml-stylesheet type="text/css" href="xml-rpc.css"?>]]>
```

Its name is #cdata-section and its value is `<?xml-stylesheet type="text/css" href="xml-rpc.css"?>`.

Entity Reference Nodes

When a parser encounters a general entity reference such as `Æ` or `©right_notice;`, it may or may not replace it with the entity's replacement text. Validating parsers always replace entity references. Nonvalidating parsers may do so at their option.

If a parser does not replace entity references, then the DOM tree will include entity reference nodes. Each entity reference node has a name, and if the parser has read the DTD, then you should be able to look up the public and system IDs for this entity reference using the map of entity nodes available on the document type node. Furthermore, the child list of the entity will contain the replacement text for this entity reference. However, if the parser has not read the DTD and resolved external entity references, then the child list may be empty.

If a parser does replace entity references, then the DOM tree may or may not include entity reference nodes. Some parsers resolve all entity reference nodes completely and leave no trace of them in the parsed tree. Other parsers instead include entity reference nodes in the DOM tree that have a list of children. The child list contains text nodes, element nodes, comment nodes, and so forth, representing the replacement text of the entity.

For example, suppose an XML document contains this element:

```
<para>&AElig;lfred is a very nice XML parser.</para>
```

If the parser is not resolving entity references, then the `para` element node contains two children—an entity reference node with the name AElig and a text node containing the text “lfred is a very nice XML parser.” The AElig entity reference node will not have any children.

Now suppose the parser is resolving entity references, and the replacement text for the AElig entity reference is the single ligature character Æ. Now the parser has a choice: It can represent the children of the `para` element as a single text node containing the full sentence, “Ælfred is a very nice XML parser.” Alternately, it can represent the children of the `para` element as an entity reference node with the name AElig followed by a text node containing the text, “lfred is a very nice XML parser.” If it chooses the second option, then the AElig entity reference node contains a single read-only text-node child containing single ligature character Æ.

DOM never includes entity reference nodes for the five predefined entity references: `&`, `<`, `>`, `'`, and `"`. These are simply replaced by their respective characters and included in a text node. Similarly, character references such as ` ` and ` ` are not specially represented in DOM as any kind of node. The characters they represent are simply added to the relevant text node.

Document Type Nodes

A document type node has a name (the name the document type declaration specifies for the root element), a public ID (which may be null), a system ID (required), an internal DTD subset (which may be null), a parent (the document that contains it), and lists of the notations and general entities declared in the DTD. The value of a document type node is always null. For example, consider this document type declaration:

```
<!DOCTYPE mml:math PUBLIC "-//W3C//DTD MathML 2.0//EN"
 "http://www.w3.org/TR/MathML2/dtd/mathml2.dtd" [
  <!ENTITY % MATHML.prefixed "INCLUDE">
  <!ENTITY % MATHML.prefix "mml">
]>
```

The name of the corresponding node is `mml:math`. The public ID is `-//W3C//DTD MathML 2.0//EN`. The system ID is `http://www.w3.org/TR/MathML2/dtd/mathml2.dtd`. The internal DTD subset is the complete text between `[` and `]`.

Nontree Nodes

There are four kinds of DOM nodes that are part of the document but not the document's tree: attribute nodes, entity nodes, notation nodes, and document fragment nodes. You've already seen that attribute nodes are attached to element nodes but are not children of those nodes. Entity and notation nodes are available as special properties of the type node. Document fragment nodes are used only when building DOM trees in memory, not when reading them from a parsed file.

Entity Nodes

Entity nodes (not to be confused with entity reference nodes) represent the parsed and unparsed entities declared in the document's DTD. If the parser reads the DTD, then it will attach a map of entity nodes to the document type node. Because this map is indexed by the entity names, you can use it to match entity reference nodes to entity nodes.

Each entity node has a name and a system ID. It can also have a public ID if one was used in the DTD. Furthermore, if the parser reads the entity, then the entity node has a list of children containing the replacement text of the entity. However, these children are read-only and cannot be modified, unlike children of similar type elsewhere in the document. For example, suppose the following entity declaration appeared in the document's DTD:

```
<!ENTITY AElig "&#x00C6;">
```

If the parser read the DTD, then it would create an entity node with the name AElig. This node would have a null public and system ID (because the entity would be purely internal) and one child, a read-only text node containing the single character Æ.

For another example, suppose this entity declaration appeared in the document's DTD:

```
<!ENTITY Copyright SYSTEM "copyright.xml">
```

If the parser read the DTD, then it would create an entity node with the name Copyright, the system ID copyright.xml, and a null public ID. The children of this node would depend on what was found at the relative URL copyright.xml. Suppose that document contained the following content:

```
<copyright>
  <year>2002</year>
  <person>Elliotte Rusty Harold</person>
</copyright>
```

Then the child list of the Copyright entity node would contain a single read-only element child with the name copyright. The element would contain its own read-only element and text node children.

Notation Nodes

Notation nodes represent the notations declared in the document's DTD. If the parser reads the DTD, then it will attach a map of notation nodes to the document type node. This map is indexed by the notation name. You can use it to look up the notation for each entity node that corresponds to an unparsed entity, or the notations associated with particular processing instruction targets.

In addition to its name, each notation node has a public ID or a system ID, whichever was used to declare it in the DTD. Notation nodes do not have any children. For example, suppose this notation declaration for PNG images was included in the DTD:

```
<!NOTATION PNG SYSTEM "http://www.w3.org/TR/REC-png">
```

This would produce a notation node with the name PNG and the system ID http://www.w3.org/TR/REC-png. The public ID would be null.

For another example, suppose this notation declaration for TeX documents was included in the DTD:

```
<!NOTATION TEX PUBLIC
    "+//ISBN 0-201-13448-9::Knuth//NOTATION The TeXbook//EN">
```

This would produce a notation node with the name TEX and the public ID +//ISBN 0-201-13448-9::Knuth//NOTATION The TeXbook//EN. The system ID would be null. (XML doesn't allow notations to have both public and system IDs.)

Document Fragment Nodes

The document fragment node is an alternative root node for a DOM tree. It can contain anything an element can contain (for example, element nodes, text nodes, processing instruction nodes, comment nodes, and so on). Although a parser will never produce such a node, your own programs may create one when extracting part of an XML document in order to move it elsewhere.

In DOM, the nonroot nodes never exist alone. That is, there's never a text node or an element node or a comment node that's not part of a document or a document fragment. They may be temporarily disconnected from the main tree, but they always know which document or fragment they belong to. The document fragment node enables you to work with pieces of a document that are composed of more than one node.

What Is and Isn't in the Tree

Table 9.1 summarizes the DOM data model with the name, value, parent, and possible children for each kind of node. One thing to keep in mind is the parts of the XML document that are not exposed in this data model:

- The XML declaration, including the version, standalone declaration, and encoding declaration. These will be added as properties of the document node in DOM3, but current parsers do not provide them.
- Most information from the DTD and/or schema, including element and attribute types and content models, is not provided.
- Any white space outside the root element.
- Whether or not each character was provided by a character reference. Parsers may provide information about entity references but are not required to do so.

Table 9.1 Node Properties

Node Type	Name	Value	Parent	Children
Document	#document	Null	Null	Comment, processing instruction, one element, zero or one document type
Document type	Root element name specified by the DOCTYPE declaration	Null	Document	None
Element	Prefixed name	Null	Element, document, or document fragment	Comment, processing instruction, text, element, entity reference, CDATA section
Text	#text	Text of the node	Element, attribute, entity, or entity reference	None
Attr	Prefixed name	Normalized attribute value	Element	Text, entity reference

Node Type	Name	Value	Parent	Children
Comment	#comment	Text of the comment	Element, document, or document fragment	None
Processing instruction	Target	Data	Element, document, or document fragment	None
Entity Reference	Name	Null	Element or document fragment	Comment, processing instruction, text, element, entity reference, CDATA section
Entity	Entity name	Null	Null	Comment, processing instruction, text, element, entity reference, CDATA section
CDATA section	#cdata-section	Text of the section	Element, entity, or entity reference	None
Notation	Notation name	Null	Null	None
Document fragment	#document-fragment	Null	Null	Comment, processing instruction, text, element, entity reference, CDATA section

A DOM program cannot manipulate any of these constructs. It cannot, for example, read in an XML document and then write it out again in the same encoding as in the original document, because it doesn't know what encoding the original document used. It cannot treat `$var` differently from `$var`, because it doesn't know which was originally written.

DOM Parsers for Java

DOM is defined almost completely in terms of interfaces rather than classes. Different parsers provide their own custom implementations of these standard interfaces. This offers a great deal of flexibility. Generally you do not install the DOM interfaces on their own. Instead they come bundled with a parser distribution that provides the detailed implementation classes. DOM isn't quite as broadly supported as SAX, but most of the major Java parsers provide it, including Crimson, Xerces, XML for Java, the Oracle XML Parser for Java, and GNU JAXP.

DOM is not complete to itself. Almost all significant DOM programs need to use some parser-specific classes. DOM programs are not too difficult to port from one parser to another, but a recompile is normally required. You can't just change a system property to switch from one parser to another, as you can with SAX. In particular, DOM2 does not specify how one parses a document, creates a new document, or serializes a document into a file or onto a stream. These important functions are all performed by parser-specific classes.

JAXP, the Java API for XML Processing, fills in a few of the holes in DOM by providing standard parser-independent means to parse existing documents, create new documents, and serialize in-memory DOM trees to XML files. Most current Java parsers that support DOM2 also support JAXP 1.1. JAXP is a standard part of Java 1.4. Although JAXP is not included in earlier versions of Java, it does work with Java 1.1 and later and is bundled with most parser class libraries. DOM3 promises to fill the same holes that JAXP fills (that is, parsing, serializing, and bootstrapping), but it is not yet finished and not yet supported in a large way by any parsers.

Because DOM depends so heavily on parser classes, its performance characteristics vary widely from one parser to the next. Speed is something of a concern, but memory consumption is a much bigger issue for most applications. All DOM implementations I've seen use more space for the in-memory DOM tree than the actual file on the disk occupies. Generally the in-memory DOM trees range from three to ten times as large as the actual XML text. Some parsers including Xerces offer a "lazy DOM" that leaves most of the document on the disk and reads into memory only those parts of the document that the client actually requests.

Another distinguishing factor between different DOM implementations is the extra features the parser provides. Most parsers provide methods to parse XML documents and serialize DOM trees to XML. Other useful features include schema

Measuring DOM Size

To test the memory usage of various implementations, I wrote a simple program that loaded the second edition of the XML 1.0 specification into a DOM `Document` object. The specification's text format is 197K (not including the DTD, which adds another 56K but isn't really modeled by DOM at all). Following is the approximate amount of memory that various parsers used to build `Document` objects from this file:

- Xerces-J 2.0.1: 1489K
- Crimson 1.1.3 (JDK 1.4 default): 1230K
- Oracle XML Parser for Java 9.2.0.2.0: 2500K

I used a couple of different techniques to measure the memory used. In one case, I used OptimizeIt and the Java Virtual Machine Profiling Interface (JVMPI) to check the heap size. I ran the program both with and without loading the document. I subtracted the total heap memory used without loading the document from the memory used when the document was loaded to get the numbers reported above. In the other test, I used the `Runtime` class to measure the total memory and the free memory before and after the `Document` was created. In both cases, I garbage collected before taking the final measurements. The results from the separate tests were within 15 percent of each other. I performed all tests in Sun's JDK 1.4.0 using Hotspot on Windows NT 4.0SP6.

I don't claim these numbers to be exact, and I certainly don't think this one test document justifies any claims whatsoever about the relative efficiency of the different DOM implementations. The difference between Crimson and Xerces is well within my margin of error. A more serious test would have to look at how the different implementations scale with the size of the initial document, and perhaps graph the curves of memory size versus file size. For example, it's possible that each of these requires a minimum of 1024K per document, but grows relatively slowly after that point. I did run the same tests on a minimal document that contained a single empty element. The results ranged from 3K to 131K for this document. However, these numbers were extremely sensitive to exactly when and how garbage was collected. I wouldn't claim the results are accurate to better than ±300K. However, I do think that together these tests demonstrate just how inefficient DOM is.

validation, database access, XInclude, XSLT, XPath, support for different character sets, and application-specific DOMs like the MathML, SVG, and WML DOMs.

For example, the Oracle and Xerces parsers provide schema validation. Ælfred and Crimson don't. Ælfred has partial support for XInclude. The other three don't. The Oracle XML parser can produce a DOM `Document` object from a SQL query against a relational database or a JDBC `ResultSet` object. The other three can't. The Oracle XML parser can decode the WAP binary XML format. The other three can't. Xerces has specialized DOMs for HTML and WML documents. The other three don't. These are all nonstandard features; but if they're useful to you, that would be a good reason to choose one parser over another. Table 9.2 summarizes parser support for various useful features.

Table 9.2 DOM Parser Features

	Xerces	Ælfred	Oracle	Crimson
DTDs	X	X	X	X
Schemas	X		X	
Namespaces	X	X	X	X
Lazy DOM	X			
HTML DOM	X			
Views				
Stylesheets				
CSS				
CSS2				
Events	X	X	X	
UI events		X		
Mouse events				
Mutation events	X	X		
HTML events		X		
Traversal	X	Partial	X	
Range			X	
XSLT/XPath	Via Xalan-J		X	
XInclude		X		

Parsing Documents with a DOM Parser

Unlike SAX, DOM does not have a class or interface that represents the XML parser. Each parser vendor provides its own unique class.

- In Xerces, it's `org.apache.xerces.parsers.DOMParser`.
- In Crimson, it's `org.apache.crimson.jaxp.DocumentBuilderImpl`.
- In Ælfred, it's an inner class, `gnu.xml.dom.JAXPFactory$JAXPBuilder`.
- In Oracle, it's `oracle.xml.parser.v2.DOMParser`.
- In other implementations, it will be something else.

Furthermore, because these classes do not share a common interface or superclass, the methods they use to parse documents vary too. For example, in Xerces the two methods that read XML documents have these signatures:

```
public void parse (InputSource source)
 throws SAXException, IOException

public void parse (String systemID) throws
 SAXException, IOException
```

To get the `Document` object from the parser, you first call one of the `parse` methods and then call the `getDocument()` method.

```
public Document getDocument()
```

In this example, if `parser` is a Xerces `DOMParser` object, then these lines of code load the DOM Core 2.0 specification into a DOM `Document` object named `spec`:

```
parser.parse("http://www.w3.org/TR/DOM-Level-2-Core");
Document spec = parser.getDocument();
```

In Crimson's parser class, by contrast, the `parse()` method returns a `Document` object directly, so that no separate `getDocument()` method is needed. For example,

```
Document spec
 = parser.parse("http://www.w3.org/TR/DOM-Level-2-Core");
```

Furthermore, the Crimson parse() method is five-way overloaded instead of two:

```
public Document parse (InputSource source)
 throws SAXException, IOException

public Document parse (String uri)
 throws SAXException, IOException

public Document parse (File file)
 throws SAXException, IOException

public Document parse (InputStream in)
 throws SAXException, IOException

public Document parse (InputStream in, String systemID)
 throws SAXException, IOException
```

Example 9.3 is a simple program that uses Xerces to check documents for well-formedness. You can see that it depends directly on the org.apache.xerces.parsers.DOMParser class.

Example 9.3 A Program That Uses Xerces to Check Documents for Well-Formedness

```
import org.apache.xerces.parsers.DOMParser;
import org.xml.sax.SAXException;
import java.io.IOException;

public class XercesChecker {

  public static void main(String[] args) {

    if (args.length <= 0) {
      System.out.println("Usage: java XercesChecker URL");
      return;
    }
    String document = args[0];

    DOMParser parser = new DOMParser();
    try {
      parser.parse(document);
      System.out.println(document + " is well-formed.");
    }
```

```
      catch (SAXException e) {
        System.out.println(document + " is not well-formed.");
      }
      catch (IOException e) {
        System.out.println(
         "Due to an IOException, the parser could not check "
         + document
        );
      }

    }

  }
```

It's not hard to port XercesChecker to a different parser such as the Oracle XML Parser for Java, but you do need to change the source code as shown in Example 9.4, and recompile.

Example 9.4 A Program That Uses the Oracle XML Parser to Check Documents for Well-Formedness

```
import oracle.xml.parser.v2.*;
import org.xml.sax.SAXException;
import java.io.IOException;

public class OracleChecker {

  public static void main(String[] args) {

    if (args.length <= 0) {
      System.out.println("Usage: java OracleChecker URL");
      return;
    }
    String document = args[0];

    DOMParser parser = new DOMParser();
    try {
      parser.parse(document);
      System.out.println(document + " is well-formed.");
    }
```

```
      catch (XMLParseException e) {
        System.out.println(document + " is not well-formed.");
        System.out.println(e);

      }
      catch (SAXException e) {
        System.out.println(document + " could not be parsed.");
      }
      catch (IOException e) {
        System.out.println(
         "Due to an IOException, the parser could not check "
         + document
        );
      }

    }

  }
```

Other parsers have slightly different methods still. What all of these have in common is that they read an XML document from a source of text, most commonly a file or a stream, and provide an `org.w3c.dom.Document` object. Once you have a reference to this `Document` object, you can work with it using only the standard methods of the DOM interfaces. There's no further need to use parser-specific classes.

JAXP DocumentBuilder and DocumentBuilderFactory

The lack of a standard means of parsing an XML document is one of the holes that JAXP fills. If your parser implements JAXP, then instead of using the parser-specific classes, you can use the `javax.xml.parsers.DocumentBuilderFactory` and `javax.xml.parsers.DocumentBuilder` classes to parse the documents. The basic approach is as follows:

1. Use the static `DocumentBuilderFactory.newInstance()` factory method to return a `DocumentBuilderFactory` object.
2. Use the `newDocumentBuilder()` method of this `DocumentBuilderFactory` object to return a parser-specific instance of the abstract `DocumentBuilder` class.

3. Use one of the five `parse()` methods of `DocumentBuilder` to read the XML document and return an `org.w3c.dom.Document` object.

Example 9.5 demonstrates with a simple program that uses JAXP to check documents for well-formedness.

Example 9.5 A Program That Uses JAXP to Check Documents for Well-Formedness

```
import javax.xml.parsers.*; // JAXP
import org.xml.sax.SAXException;
import java.io.IOException;

public class JAXPChecker {

  public static void main(String[] args) {

    if (args.length <= 0) {
      System.out.println("Usage: java JAXPChecker URL");
      return;
    }
    String document = args[0];

    try {
      DocumentBuilderFactory factory
       = DocumentBuilderFactory.newInstance();
      DocumentBuilder parser = factory.newDocumentBuilder();
      parser.parse(document);
      System.out.println(document + " is well-formed.");
    }
    catch (SAXException e) {
      System.out.println(document + " is not well-formed.");
    }
    catch (IOException e) {
      System.out.println(
       "Due to an IOException, the parser could not check "
       + document
      );
    }
    catch (FactoryConfigurationError e) {
```

```
        // JAXP suffers from excessive brain-damage caused by
        // intellectual in-breeding at Sun. (Basically the Sun
        // engineers spend way too much time talking to each other
        // and not nearly enough time talking to people outside
        // Sun.) Fortunately, you can happily ignore most of the
        // JAXP brain damage and not be any the poorer for it.

        // This, however, is one of the few problems you can't
        // avoid if you're going to use JAXP at all.
        // DocumentBuilderFactory.newInstance() should throw a
        // ClassNotFoundException if it can't locate the factory
        // class. However, what it does throw is an Error,
        // specifically a FactoryConfigurationError. Very few
        // programs are prepared to respond to errors as opposed
        // to exceptions. You should catch this error in your
        // JAXP programs as quickly as possible even though the
        // compiler won't require you to, and you should
        // never rethrow it or otherwise let it escape from the
        // method that produced it.
        System.out.println("Could not locate a factory class");
      }
      catch (ParserConfigurationException e) {
        System.out.println("Could not locate a JAXP parser");
      }

    }

  }
```

For example, here's the output produced when I ran this program across this chapter's DocBook source code:

```
D:\books\XMLJAVA>java JAXPChecker file:///D:/books/xmljava/dom.xml
file:///D:/books/xmljava/dom.xml is well-formed.
```

How JAXP Chooses Parsers

You may be wondering which parser this program actually uses. JAXP, after all, is reasonably parser independent. The answer depends on which parsers are installed in your class path and how certain system properties are set. The default is to use the class named by the `javax.xml.parsers.DocumentBuilderFactory` system property. For example, if you want to make sure that Xerces is used to parse documents, then you would run JAXPChecker as follows:

```
D:\books\XMLJAVA>java
 -Djavax.xml.parsers.DocumentBuilderFactory=
 org.apache.xerces.jaxp.DocumentBuilderFactory
 JAXPChecker file:///D:/books/xmljava/dom.xml
file:///D:/books/xmljava/dom.xml is well-formed.
```

If the javax.xml.parsers.DocumentBuilderFactory property is not set, then JAXP looks in the lib/jaxp.properties properties file in the JRE directory to determine a default value for the javax.xml.parsers.DocumentBuilderFactory system property. If you want to use a certain DOM parser consistently, for instance gnu.xml.dom.JAXPFactory, then place the following line in that file:

```
javax.xml.parsers.DocumentBuilderFactory=gnu.xml.dom.JAXPFactory
```

If this fails to locate a parser, then JAXP next looks for a META-INF/services/javax.xml.parsers.DocumentBuilderFactory file in all JAR files available to the runtime to find the name of the concrete DocumentBuilderFactory subclass.

Finally, if that fails, then DocumentBuilderFactory.newInstance() returns a default class, generally the parser from the vendor that also provided the JAXP classes. For example, the JDK JAXP classes pick org.apache.crimson.jaxp.DocumentBuilderFactoryImpl by default, but the Ælfred JAXP classes pick gnu.xml.dom.JAXPFactory instead.

Configuring DocumentBuilderFactory

The DocumentBuilderFactory has a number of options that allow you to determine exactly how the parsers it creates behave. Most of the setter methods take a boolean that turns the feature on if true or off if false. However, a couple of the features are defined as confusing double negatives, so read carefully.

Coalescing The following two methods determine whether or not CDATA sections are merged with text nodes. If the coalescing feature is true, then the result tree will not contain any CDATA section nodes, even if the parsed XML document does contain CDATA sections.

```
public boolean isCoalescing()
public void setCoalescing (boolean coalescing)
```

The default is false, but in most situations you should set this to true, especially if you're just reading the document and are not going to write it back out again. CDATA sections should not be treated differently from any other text. Whether or not certain text is written in a CDATA section should be purely a matter of syntax sugar for human convenience, not anything that has an effect on the data model.

Expand Entity References The following two methods determine whether the parsers that this factory produces will expand entity references:

```
public boolean isExpandEntityReferences()

public void setExpandEntityReferences (boolean
 expandEntityReferences)
```

The default is true. If a parser is validating, then it will expand entity references, even if this feature is set to false. That is, the validation feature overrides the expand-entity-references feature. The five predefined entity references—`&`, `<`, `>`, `"`, and `'`—will always be expanded regardless of the value of this property.

Ignore Comments The following two methods determine whether the parsers that this factory produces will generate comment nodes for comments seen in the input document. The default, false, means that comment nodes will be produced. (Watch out for the double negative here. False means include comments, and true means don't include comments. This confused me initially, and I was getting my poison pen all ready to write about the brain damage of throwing away comments even though the specification required them to be included, when I realized that the method was in fact behaving as it should.)

```
public boolean isIgnoringComments()

public void setIgnoringComments (boolean ignoringComments)
```

Ignore Element-Content White Space The following two methods determine whether the parsers that this factory produces will generate text nodes for so-called "ignorable white space"; that is, white space that occurs between tags where the DTD specifies that parsed character data cannot appear.

```
public boolean isIgnoringElementContentWhitespace()

public void setIgnoringElementContentWhitespace (boolean
 ignoreElementContentWhitespace)
```

The default is false; that is, include text nodes for ignorable white space. Setting this to true might well be useful in record-like documents. For this property to make a difference, however, the documents must have a DTD and should be valid or very nearly so. Otherwise the parser won't be able to tell which white space is ignorable and which isn't.

Namespace Aware The following two methods determine whether the parsers that this factory produces will be *namespace aware*. A namespace-aware parser will set the prefix and namespace URI properties of element and attribute nodes that are in a namespace. A non-namespace-aware parser won't.

```
public boolean isNamespaceAware()
public void setNamespaceAware (boolean namespaceAware)
```

The default is false, which is truly the wrong choice. You should always set this to true. For example,

```
DocumentBuilderFactory factory
 = DocumentBuilderFactory.newInstance();
factory.setNamespaceAware(true);
```

Validating These methods determine whether or not the parsers that this factory produces will validate the document against its DTD.

```
public boolean isValidating()
public void setValidating (boolean validating)
```

The default is false; do not validate. If you want to validate your documents, set this property to true. You'll also need to register a SAX `ErrorHandler` with the `DocumentBuilder` using its `setErrorHandler()` method to receive notice of validity errors. Example 9.6 demonstrates with a program that uses JAXP to validate a document named on the command line.

Example 9.6 A Program That Uses JAXP to Check Documents for Well-Formedness

```
import javax.xml.parsers.*; // JAXP
import org.xml.sax.*;
import java.io.IOException;

public class JAXPValidator {
```

```
public static void main(String[] args) {

  if (args.length <= 0) {
    System.out.println("Usage: java JAXPValidator URL");
    return;
  }
  String document = args[0];

  try {
    DocumentBuilderFactory factory
     = DocumentBuilderFactory.newInstance();
    // Always turn on namespace awareness
    factory.setNamespaceAware(true);
    // Turn on validation
    factory.setValidating(true);

    DocumentBuilder parser = factory.newDocumentBuilder();

    // SAXValidator was developed in Chapter 7
    ErrorHandler handler = new SAXValidator();
    parser.setErrorHandler(handler);

    parser.parse(document);
    if (handler.isValid()) {
      System.out.println(document + " is valid.");
    }
    else {
      // If the document isn't well-formed, an exception has
      // already been thrown and this has been skipped.
      System.out.println(document + " is well-formed.");
    }

  }
  catch (SAXException e) {
    System.out.println(document + " is not well-formed.");
  }
  catch (IOException e) {
    System.out.println(
     "Due to an IOException, the parser could not check "
      + document
    );
  }
```

```
      catch (FactoryConfigurationError e) {
        System.out.println("Could not locate a factory class");
      }
      catch (ParserConfigurationException e) {
        System.out.println("Could not locate a JAXP parser");
      }

    }

  }
```

Parser-Specific Attributes Many JAXP-aware parsers support various custom features. For example, Xerces has an `http://apache.org/xml/features/dom/create-entity-ref-nodes` feature that lets you choose whether or not to *include* entity reference nodes in the DOM tree. This is not the same as deciding whether or not to expand entity references. That determines whether the entity nodes that are placed in the tree have children representing their replacement text or not.

JAXP allows you to set and get these custom features as objects of the appropriate type using these two methods:

```
public Object getAttribute (String name)
 throws IllegalArgumentException

public void setAttribute (String name, Object value)
 throws IllegalArgumentException
```

For example, suppose you're using Xerces and you don't want to include entity reference nodes. Because they're included by default, you would need to set `http://apache.org/xml/features/dom/create-entity-ref-nodes` to false. You would use `setAttribute()` on the `DocumentBuilderFactory`, like this:

```
DocumentBuilderFactory factory
 = DocumentBuilderFactory.newInstance();
 factory.setAttribute(
  "http://apache.org/xml/features/dom/create-entity-ref-nodes",
  new Boolean(false)
 );
```

The naming conventions for both attribute names and values depend on the underlying parser. Xerces uses URL strings like SAX feature names. Other parsers may do something different. JAXP 1.2 will add a couple of standard attributes related to schema validation.

DOM3 Load and Save

JAXP only works for Java, and it is a Sun proprietary standard. Consequently, the W3C DOM working group is preparing an alternative cross-vendor means of parsing an XML document with a DOM parser. This will be published as part of DOM3. DOM3 is not close to a finished recommendation at the time of this writing and is not yet implemented by any parsers, but I can give you an idea of what the interface is likely to look like.

Parsing a document with DOM3 will require four steps:

1. Load a `DOMImplementation` object by passing the feature string `"LS-Load 3.0"` to the `DOMImplementationRegistry.getDOMImplementation()` factory method. (This class is also new in DOM3.)
2. Cast this `DOMImplementation` object to `DOMImplementationLS`, the subinterface that provides the extra methods you need.
3. Call the implementation's `createDOMBuilder()` method to create a new `DOMBuilder` object. This is the new DOM3 class that represents the parser. The first argument to `createDOMBuilder()` is a named constant that specifies whether the document is parsed synchronously or asynchronously. The second argument is a URL identifying the type of schema to be used during the parse, "http://www.w3.org/2001/XMLSchema" for W3C XML Schemas, "http://www.w3.org/TR/REC-xml" for DTDs. You can pass null to ignore all schemas.
4. Pass the document's URL to the builder object's `parseURI()` method to read the document and return a `Document` object.

Example 9.7 demonstrates with a simple program that uses DOM3 to check documents for well-formedness.

Example 9.7 A Program That Uses DOM3 to Check Documents for Well-Formedness

```
import org.w3c.dom.*;
import org.w3c.dom.ls.*;

public class DOM3Checker {

  public static void main(String[] args) {

    if (args.length <= 0) {
      System.out.println("Usage: java DOM3Checker URL");
```

```
      return;
    }
    String document = args[0];

    try {
      DOMImplementationLS impl = (DOMImplementationLS)
       DOMImplementationRegistry
       .getDOMImplementation("LS-Load 3.0");
      DOMBuilder parser = impl.createDOMBuilder(
       DOMImplementationLS.MODE_SYNCHRONOUS,
       "http://www.w3.org/TR/REC-xml");
    // ^^^^^^^^^^^^^^^^^^^^^^^^^^^^^^^^
    // Use DTDs when parsing
      Document doc = parser.parseURI(document);
      System.out.println(document + " is well-formed.");
    }
    catch (NullPointerException e) {
      System.err.println("The current DOM implementation does"
       + " not support DOM Level 3 Load and Save");
    }
    catch (DOMException e) {
      System.err.println(document + " is not well-formed");
    }
    catch (IOException e) {
      System.out.println(
       "Due to an IOException, the parser could not check "
       + document
      );
    }
    catch (Exception e) {
      // Probably a ClassNotFoundException,
      // InstantiationException, or IllegalAccessException
      // thrown by DOMImplementationRegistry.getDOMImplementation
      System.out.println("Probable CLASSPATH problem.");
      e.printStackTrace();
    }

  }

}
```

For the time being, JAXP's DocumentBuilderFactory is the obvious choice because it works today and is supported by almost all DOM parsers written in Java. Longer term, DOM3 will provide a number of important capabilities JAXP does not, including parse progress notification and document filtering. Because these APIs are far from ready for prime time just yet, for the rest of this book I'm mostly going to use JAXP without further comment.

The Node Interface

Once you've parsed the document and formed an org.w3c.dom.Document object, you can forget about the differences among the various parsers and just work with the standard DOM interfaces.[1]

All of the nodes in the tree are represented by instances of the Node interface summarized in Example 9.8.

Example 9.8 The Node Interface

```
package org.w3c.dom;

public interface Node {

  // Node type constants
  public static final short ELEMENT_NODE                = 1;
  public static final short ATTRIBUTE_NODE              = 2;
  public static final short TEXT_NODE                   = 3;
  public static final short CDATA_SECTION_NODE          = 4;
  public static final short ENTITY_REFERENCE_NODE       = 5;
  public static final short ENTITY_NODE                 = 6;
  public static final short PROCESSING_INSTRUCTION_NODE = 7;
  public static final short COMMENT_NODE                = 8;
  public static final short DOCUMENT_NODE               = 9;
  public static final short DOCUMENT_TYPE_NODE          = 10;
  public static final short DOCUMENT_FRAGMENT_NODE      = 11;
  public static final short NOTATION_NODE               = 12;

  // Node properties
```

1. At least until you want to write the document back out to a file again. Then you have to consider parser-specific classes or JAXP once more.

```
  public String   getNodeName();
  public String   getNodeValue() throws DOMException;
  public void     setNodeValue(String nodeValue)
   throws DOMException;
  public short    getNodeType();
  public String   getNamespaceURI();
  public String   getPrefix();
  public void     setPrefix(String prefix) throws DOMException;
  public String   getLocalName();

  // Navigation methods
  public Node         getParentNode();
  public boolean      hasChildNodes();
  public NodeList     getChildNodes();
  public Node         getFirstChild();
  public Node         getLastChild();
  public Node         getPreviousSibling();
  public Node         getNextSibling();
  public Document     getOwnerDocument();
  public boolean      hasAttributes();
  public NamedNodeMap getAttributes();

  // Manipulator methods
  public Node insertBefore(Node newChild, Node refChild)
   throws DOMException;
  public Node replaceChild(Node newChild,  Node oldChild)
   throws DOMException;
  public Node removeChild(Node oldChild) throws DOMException;
  public Node appendChild(Node newChild) throws DOMException;

  // Utility methods
  public Node cloneNode(boolean deep);
  public void normalize();
  public boolean isSupported(String feature, String version);

}
```

You can do quite a lot with just this interface alone. You can add, move, remove, and copy nodes in the tree. You can walk the tree while reading the names and values of everything in the tree. This interface can be roughly divided into five sections:

1. Node type constants
2. Methods to set and get node properties
3. Methods to navigate the DOM tree
4. Methods to add and remove children of a node
5. A few utility methods.

Let's take them in that order.

Node Types

There are 12 constants—1 for each of the 12 named node types defined in the DOM core—and a method that returns the type of the current node using one of these constants. To a Java developer, these are just weird all around. First of all, you'd probably expect to use `instanceof`, `getClass()`, and class names to test for types when necessary, instead of short constants and a `getNodeType()` method. And even if for some strange reason you did use named constants, you'd probably use the type-safe enum pattern if you were familiar with it, or ints if you weren't. Either way, a short constant is just plain weird.

What's going on here is that DOM is not designed in or for Java. It is written in IDL and intended for all object-oriented languages, including C++, Python, Perl, JavaScript, and more. And it has to make a lot of compromises to support the broad range of capabilities of those different languages. For example, AppleScript doesn't have any equivalent to Java's `instanceof` operator that allows it to test whether a variable is an instance of a particular class. Prior to version 1.4, JavaScript didn't have one either. Some older C++ compilers don't support runtime type information (RTTI) and no C compilers do. Consequently, DOM can't rely on these features because it has to work in those languages. Therefore, it has to reinvent things Java already has.

> **Note**
>
> Using a `getNodeType()` method also allows a single class to implement more than one of the standard interfaces, which is possible because Java supports multiple interface inheritance. For example, an implementation might use a single `NodeImpl` class for all 12 different subinterfaces of `Node`. Then, an object could simultaneously be an instance of `Comment`, `Element`, `Text`, and all the other things besides. I've seen exactly one DOM implementation that does this. The Saxon XSLT processor (discussed in Chapter 16) uses its `NodeImpl` class to represent all nondocument and nonelement nodes. However, all of the general-purpose DOM implementations I've encountered use a separate class for each separate node type.

The issue of the short constants is a little different. Here, DOM has simply chosen to implement idioms from a language other than Java. In this case, it's following the C++ conventions, where shorts and short constants are much more common than they are in Java. As for using integers instead of type-safe enums, I suspect that the DOM group simply felt that type-safe enums were too complicated to implement in IDL (if they considered the possibility at all). After all, this whole set of node types is really just a hack for languages whose reflection isn't as complete as Java's.

Example 9.9 is a simple utility class that uses the `getNodeType()` method and these constants to return a string specifying the node type. In itself, it isn't very interesting, but I'll need it for a few of the later programs.

Example 9.9 Changing Short Type Constants to Strings

```
import org.w3c.dom.Node;

public class NodeTyper {

   public static String getTypeName(Node node) {

    int type = node.getNodeType();
    /* Yes, getNodeType() returns a short, but Java will
       almost always upcast this short to an int before
       using it in any operation, so we might as well just go
       ahead and use the int in the first place. */

    switch (type) {
      case Node.ELEMENT_NODE: return "Element";
      case Node.ATTRIBUTE_NODE: return "Attribute";
      case Node.TEXT_NODE: return "Text";
      case Node.CDATA_SECTION_NODE: return "CDATA Section";
      case Node.ENTITY_REFERENCE_NODE: return "Entity Reference";
      case Node.ENTITY_NODE: return "Entity";
      case Node.PROCESSING_INSTRUCTION_NODE:
       return "Processing Instruction";
      case Node.COMMENT_NODE: return "Comment";
      case Node.DOCUMENT_NODE: return "Document";
      case Node.DOCUMENT_TYPE_NODE:
       return "Document Type Declaration";
      case Node.DOCUMENT_FRAGMENT_NODE:
       return "Document Fragment";
```

```
        case Node.NOTATION_NODE: return "Notation";
        default: return "Unknown Type";
      /* It is possible for the default case to be
        reached. DOM only defines 12 kinds of nodes, but other
        application-specific DOMs can add their own as well.
        You're not likely to encounter these while parsing an
        XML document with a standard parser, but you might
        encounter such things with custom parsers designed for
        non-XML documents. DOM Level 3 XPath does define a
        13th kind of node, XPathNamespace. */
      }

    }

  }
```

Node Properties

The next batch of methods allows you to get and, in a couple of cases, set the common node properties. Although all nodes have these methods, they don't necessarily return a sensible value for every kind of node. For example, only element and attribute nodes have namespace URIs. `getNamespaceURI()` returns null when invoked on any other kind of node. The `getNodeName()` method returns the complete name for nodes that have names, and *`#node-type`* for nodes that don't have names; that is, `#document`, `#text`, `#comment`, and so on.

```
public String getNodeName()
public String getNodeValue() throws DOMException
public String setNodeValue (String value) throws DOMException
public short getNodeType()
public String getNamespaceURI()
public String getPrefix()
public void setPrefix (String prefix) throws DOMException
public String getLocalName()
```

Example 9.10 demonstrates another simple utility class that accepts a `Node` as an argument and prints out the values of its non-null properties. Again, I'll be using this class shortly in another program.

Example 9.10 A Class to Inspect the Properties of a Node

```
import org.w3c.dom.*;
import java.io.*;

public class PropertyPrinter {

  private Writer out;

  public PropertyPrinter(Writer out) {
    if (out == null) {
      throw new NullPointerException("Writer must be non-null.");
    }
    this.out = out;
  }

  public PropertyPrinter() {
    this(new OutputStreamWriter(System.out));
  }

  private int nodeCount = 0;

  public void writeNode(Node node) throws IOException {

    if (node == null) {
      throw new NullPointerException("Node must be non-null.");
    }
    if (node.getNodeType() == Node.DOCUMENT_NODE
     || node.getNodeType() == Node.DOCUMENT_FRAGMENT_NODE) {
      // starting a new document, reset the node count
      nodeCount = 1;
    }

    String name      = node.getNodeName(); // never null
    String type      = NodeTyper.getTypeName(node); // never null
    String localName = node.getLocalName();
    String uri       = node.getNamespaceURI();
    String prefix    = node.getPrefix();
    String value     = node.getNodeValue();
```

```
      StringBuffer result = new StringBuffer();
      result.append("Node " + nodeCount + ":\r\n");
      result.append("  Type: " + type + "\r\n");
      result.append("  Name: " + name + "\r\n");
      if (localName != null) {
        result.append("  Local Name: " + localName + "\r\n");
      }
      if (prefix != null) {
        result.append("  Prefix: " + prefix + "\r\n");
      }
      if (uri != null) {
        result.append("  Namespace URI: " + uri + "\r\n");
      }
      if (value != null) {
        result.append("  Value: " + value + "\r\n");
      }

      out.write(result.toString());
      out.write("\r\n");
      out.flush();

      nodeCount++;

    }

  }
```

The writeNode() method operates on a Node object without any clue what its actual type is. It prints the properties of the node onto the configured Writer in the following form:

```
Node 16:
  Type: Text
  Name: #text
  Value: RHAT
```

The format changes depending on what kind of node is passed to it.

There are also two methods in the Node interface that can change a node. First, the setPrefix() method changes a node's namespace prefix. Trying to use an illegal or reserved prefix throws a DOMException. This method has no effect on anything except an element or an attribute node.

Second, the `setValue()` method changes the node's string value. It can be used on comment, text, processing instruction, and CDATA section nodes. It has no effect on other kinds of nodes. It throws a `DOMException` if the node you're setting is read-only (as a text node might be inside an entity node).

The remaining properties cannot be set from the `Node` interface. To change names, URIs, and such you have to use the more specific interfaces, such as `Element` and `Attr`. Most of the time, you're better off using the more detailed subinterfaces if you're trying to change a tree, anyway.

Navigating the Tree

The third batch of methods allow you to navigate the tree by finding the parent, first child, last child, previous and next siblings, and attributes of any node. Because not all nodes have children, you should test for their presence with `hasChildren()` before calling the `getFirstChild()` and `getLastChild()` methods. You should also be prepared for any of these methods to return null in the event that the requested node doesn't exist. Similarly, you should check `hasAttributes()` before calling the `getAttributes()` method.

Example 9.11 demonstrates with a simple program that recursively traverses the tree in a preorder fashion. As each node is visited, its name and value is printed using the previous section's `PropertyPrinter` class. Once again, `Node` is the only DOM class used. That's the power of polymorphism. You can do quite a lot without knowing exactly what you're doing it to.

Example 9.11 Walking the Tree with the Node Interface

```
import javax.xml.parsers.*;  // JAXP
import org.w3c.dom.Node;
import org.xml.sax.SAXException;
import java.io.IOException;

public class TreeReporter {

  public static void main(String[] args) {

    if (args.length <= 0) {
      System.out.println("Usage: java TreeReporter URL");
      return;
    }
```

```
    TreeReporter iterator = new TreeReporter();
    try {
      // Use JAXP to find a parser
      DocumentBuilderFactory factory
       = DocumentBuilderFactory.newInstance();
      // Turn on namespace support
      factory.setNamespaceAware(true);
      DocumentBuilder parser = factory.newDocumentBuilder();

      // Read the entire document into memory
      Node document = parser.parse(args[0]);

      // Process it starting at the root
      iterator.followNode(document);

    }
    catch (SAXException e) {
      System.out.println(args[0] + " is not well-formed.");
      System.out.println(e.getMessage());
    }
    catch (IOException e) {
      System.out.println(e);
    }
    catch (ParserConfigurationException e) {
      System.out.println("Could not locate a JAXP parser");
    }

  } // end main

  private PropertyPrinter printer = new PropertyPrinter();

  // note use of recursion
  public void followNode(Node node) throws IOException {

    printer.writeNode(node);
    if (node.hasChildNodes()) {
      Node firstChild = node.getFirstChild();
      followNode(firstChild);
    }
```

```
      Node nextNode = node.getNextSibling();
      if (nextNode != null) followNode(nextNode);

    }

  }
```

Following is the beginning of the output produced by running this program across Example 9.2:

```
% java TreeReporter getQuote.xml
Node 1:
  Type: Document
  Name: #document

Node 2:
  Type: Processing Instruction
  Name: xml-stylesheet
  Value: type="text/css" href="xml-rpc.css"

Node 3:
  Type: Comment
  Name: #comment
  Value:  It's unusual to have an xml-stylesheet processing
     instruction in an XML-RPC document but it is legal, unlike
     SOAP where processing instructions are forbidden.

Node 4:
  Type: Document Type Declaration
  Name: methodCall

Node 5:
  Type: Element
  Name: methodCall
  ...
```

The key to this program is the `followNode()` method. It first writes the node using the `PropertyPrinter`, then recursively invokes `followNode()` on the current node's first child and then its next sibling. This is equivalent to XPath document order (in which children come before siblings). The `hasChildNodes()` method tests whether there actually are children before asking for the first child node. For siblings, we have to retrieve the next sibling whether there is one or not, and then check to see whether it's null before de-referencing it.

`TreeReporter` is actually very raw. As you'll see, DOM provides a lot of helper classes that make operations such as this much simpler to code. However, it never hurts to keep in mind what all those helper classes are doing behind the scenes, which in fact is very much like this.

Modifying the Tree

The `Node` interface has four methods that change the tree by inserting, removing, replacing, and appending children at points specified by nodes in the tree:

```
public Node insertBefore (Node toBeInserted,
 Node toBeInsertedBefore) throws DOMException

public Node replaceChild (Node toBeInserted, Node toBeReplaced)
 throws DOMException

public Node removeChild (Node toBeRemoved) throws DOMException

public Node appendChild (Node toBeAppended) throws DOMException
```

Any of these four methods will throw a `DOMException` if you try to use it to make a document malformed; for instance, by removing the root element or appending a child to a text node. All four methods return the node being inserted/replaced/removed/appended.

The only use for these methods is to move nodes around in the same document. Although `removeChild()` and `replaceChild()` disconnect nodes from a document's tree, they do not change those nodes' owner document. The disconnected nodes cannot be placed in a different document. Nodes can only be placed in the document where they begin their life. Moving a node from one document to another requires importing it, a technique that I'll take up in Chapter 10.

It's hard to come up with a plausible example of these methods until I've shown you how to create new nodes, also in Chapter 10. In the meantime, Example 9.12 is a program that moves all processing instruction nodes from inside the root element to before the root element, and all comment nodes from inside the root element to after the root element. For example, this document:

```
<?xml version="1.0"?>
<document>
  Some data
  <!-- first comment -->
```

```
  <?example first processing instruction ?>
  Some more data
  <!-- second comment -->
  <?example second processing instruction ?>
  <empty/>
</document>
```

would become this document:

```
<?xml version="1.0" encoding="utf-8"?>
<?example first processing instruction ?>
<?example second processing instruction ?><document>
  Some data


  Some more data



  <empty/>
</document><!-- first comment --><!-- second comment -->
```

I don't actually think this is a sensible thing to do. In particular, it inaccurately implies that comments and processing instructions can be removed and reordered willy-nilly without changing anything significant, which is not true in general. This is just the best example of these methods I could come up with without using too many classes and interfaces we haven't yet covered.

Example 9.12 A Method That Changes a Document by Reordering Nodes

```
import org.w3c.dom.*;

public class Restructurer {

  // Since this method only operates on its argument and does
  // not interact with any fields in the class, it's
  // plausibly made static.
  public static void processNode(Node current)
   throws DOMException {

    // I need to store a reference to the current node's next
```

```
        // sibling before we delete the node from the tree, in which
        // case it no longer has a sibling
        Node nextSibling = current.getNextSibling();

        int nodeType = current.getNodeType();
        if (nodeType == Node.COMMENT_NODE
         || nodeType == Node.PROCESSING_INSTRUCTION_NODE) {

          Node document = current.getOwnerDocument();
          // Find the root element by looping through the children of
          // the document until we find the only one that's an
          // element node. There's a quicker way to do this once we
          // learn more about the Document class in the next chapter.
          Node root = document.getFirstChild();
          while (!(root.getNodeType() == Node.ELEMENT_NODE )) {
            root = root.getNextSibling();
          }

          Node parent = current.getParentNode();
          parent.removeChild(current);
          if (nodeType == Node.COMMENT_NODE) {
            document.appendChild(current);
          }
          else if (nodeType == Node.PROCESSING_INSTRUCTION_NODE) {
            document.insertBefore(current, root);
          }

        }
        else if (current.hasChildNodes()) {
          Node firstChild = current.getFirstChild();
          processNode(firstChild);
        }

        if (nextSibling != null) {
          processNode(nextSibling);
        }

      }

    }
```

This program walks the tree, calling the `removeChild()` method every time a comment or processing instruction node is spotted, and then inserting the processing instruction nodes before the root element with `insertBefore()` and the comment nodes after the root element with `appendChild()`. Both references to the document node, the root element node, and the nearest parent element node have to be stored at all times. The `Document` object is modified in place.

This program does not provide any means of outputting the changed document to a file where you can look at it. That too is coming.

Utility Methods

Finally, there are three assorted utility methods:

```
public Node cloneNode (boolean deep)
public void normalize()
public void isSupported (String feature, String version)
```

normalize()

The `normalize()` method descends the tree from the given node, merges all adjacent text nodes, and deletes empty text nodes. This operation makes DOM roughly equivalent to an XPath data model in which each text node contains the maximum contiguous run of text not interrupted by markup. However, `normalize()` does not merge CDATA section nodes, which XPath would require.

The easiest approach is to invoke `normalize()` on the `Document` object as soon as you get it. For example,

```
Document document = parser.parse(document);
document.normalize();
```

cloneNode()

The `cloneNode()` method makes a copy of the given node. If the `deep` argument is true, then the copy contains the full contents of the node including all of its descendants. If the `deep` argument is false, then the clone does not contain copies of the original node's children. The cloned node is disconnected; that is, it is not a child of the original node's parent. However, it does belong to the original node's document, even though it doesn't have a position in that document's tree. It can be added via `insertBefore()`, or `appendNode()`, or `replaceNode()`. Conversely, the clone cannot be inserted into a different document. To make a copy for a different document, you would instead use the `importNode()` method in the `Document` interface. We'll look at this in Chapter 10.

isSupported()

The `isSupported()` method determines whether or not this node provides a given feature. For example, you can pass the string `"Events"` to this method to find out whether or not this one node supports the events module. The version number for all DOM2 features is 2.0.

The `isSupported()` method isn't used much, since there's little point to asking for the features an individual node supports. A similar method named `hasFeature()` in the `DOMImplementation` interface is more useful.

The NodeList Interface

DOM stores the lists of children of each node in `NodeList` objects. Example 9.13 illustrates this very basic indexed list. Indexes start from 0 and continue to the length of the list minus 1, just like Java arrays.

Example 9.13 The NodeList Interface

```
package org.w3c.dom;

public interface NodeList {

  public Node item(int index);
  public int  getLength();

}
```

Instances of this interface are returned by the `getChildNodes()` method in the `Node` interface, as well as by various methods in its subinterfaces that we'll encounter in Chapter 10.

The actual data structure that backs this interface can be a linked list, an array, or something else. Details vary from implementation to implementation. Whatever the concrete data structure is, you can use node lists to simplify operations that iterate over children. For example, the `followNode()` method in Example 9.11 could be rewritten using `NodeList` instead of `getNextSibling()` like this:

```
public void followNode(Node node) throws IOException {

  printer.writeNode(node);
```

```
      // Process the children
      NodeList children = node.getChildNodes();
      for (int i = 0; i < children.getLength(); i++) {
        Node child = children.item(i);
        followNode(child); // recursion
      }

    }
```

This still walks the tree such as in several of the earlier programs; however, the algorithm is somewhat more obvious because it uses more list iteration and less recursion. (Recursion is still necessary to descend the tree but not to move from one sibling to the next.)

Whether or not this variant is more efficient than the original version that only uses the `Node` interface depends on the concrete implementation. It may indeed be faster if the implementation classes store children in arrays. It may not be faster if the implementation classes use linked lists. Either way the difference is unlikely to be significant. Using the approach that feels more natural to you is a lot more important than the marginal speed you might gain by picking one over the other.

Node lists are *live*. That is, if you add or delete a node from the list, the change is reflected in the document and vice versa. This can make it a little tricky to keep track of where you are in the list, as the length can keep changing, and nodes can move from one place in the list to another.

Node lists (and pretty much everything else in DOM) are *not* thread safe. If one thread is writing to or modifying a `NodeList` while another thread is reading from it, data corruption is almost guaranteed. Because node lists are live, code can be unsafe even when no other thread has a reference to that particular node list, as long as some other thread has a reference to the `Document` from which the `NodeList` was built.

JAXP Serialization

Although DOM is a read-write API in memory, it's sorely lacking when it comes to moving its in-memory data structure back out onto a disk, a network socket, or some other stream. Eventually, this omission will be rectified in DOM3. In the meantime, you have the choice of using either implementation-specific serialization classes or JAXP. The implementation-specific serialization classes generally provide more customization and features, but JAXP is sufficient for basic uses.

JAXP doesn't include a serialization package, but you can hack basic output through the `javax.xml.transform` package by conveniently "forgetting" to install a transform. :-) The pattern is the same as parsing a document with JAXP. The basic steps are as follows:

1. Use the static `TransformerFactory.newInstance()` factory method to return a `javax.xml.transform.TransformerFactory` object.
2. Use the `newTransformer()` method of this `TransformerFactory` object to return an implementation-specific instance of the abstract `javax.xml.transform.Transformer` class.
3. Construct a new `javax.xml.transform.dom.DOMSource` object from your DOM `Document` object.
4. Construct a new `javax.xml.transform.stream.StreamResult` object connected to the `OutputStream` you want to write the document onto.
5. Pass both the source and the result objects to the `transform()` method of the `Transformer` object created in step 2.

We can use this procedure to write a simple driver program for Example 9.12. Example 9.14 first uses JAXP to build a DOM `Document` object from a URL, then passes this object to the `Restructurer.processNode()` method, and finally serializes the whole document onto `System.out`.

Example 9.14 Using JAXP to Read and Write an XML Document

```
import javax.xml.parsers.*; // JAXP
import javax.xml.transform.*; // JAXP
import javax.xml.transform.dom.DOMSource; // JAXP
import javax.xml.transform.stream.StreamResult; // JAXP
import org.xml.sax.SAXException;
import org.w3c.dom.Document;
import java.io.IOException;

public class RestructureDriver {

  public static void main(String[] args) {

    if (args.length <= 0) {
      System.out.println("Usage: java RestructureDriver URL");
      return;
    }
    String url = args[0];
```

```
try {
  // Find a parser
  DocumentBuilderFactory factory
   = DocumentBuilderFactory.newInstance();
  factory.setNamespaceAware(true);
  DocumentBuilder parser = factory.newDocumentBuilder();

  // Read the document
  Document document = parser.parse(url);

  // Modify the document
  Restructurer.processNode(document);

  // Write it out again
  TransformerFactory xformFactory
   = TransformerFactory.newInstance();
  Transformer idTransform = xformFactory.newTransformer();
  Source input = new DOMSource(document);
  Result output = new StreamResult(System.out);
  idTransform.transform(input, output);

}
catch (SAXException e) {
  System.out.println(url + " is not well-formed.");
}
catch (IOException e) {
  System.out.println(
   "Due to an IOException, the parser could not read " + url
  );
}
catch (FactoryConfigurationError e) {
  System.out.println("Could not locate a factory class");
}
catch (ParserConfigurationException e) {
  System.out.println("Could not locate a JAXP parser");
}
catch (TransformerConfigurationException e) {
  System.out.println("This DOM does not support transforms.");
}
catch (TransformerException e) {
  System.out.println("Transform failed.");
```

```
    }

  }

}
```

You'll learn how to actually use these classes for their intended purposes of XSLT transformation in Chapter 17.

DOMException

You've probably noticed that many of the methods so far have been declared to throw a `DOMException`. This class shown in Example 9.15 is the generic exception for essentially anything that can go wrong while working with DOM—from logical errors like making an element one of its own children to implementation bugs. Although it is a runtime exception that does not have to be caught, I nonetheless recommend that you always catch it or declare that your method throws it. Conceptually, this should be a checked exception; however, many languages that DOM supports, including C++ and Python, don't have checked exceptions, so DOM uses runtime exceptions in order to keep the semantics of the various methods as similar as possible across languages.

Example 9.15 The DOMException Class

```
package org.w3c.dom;

public class DOMException extends RuntimeException {

  public DOMException(short code, String message);

  public short code;

  public static final short INDEX_SIZE_ERR              = 1;
  public static final short DOMSTRING_SIZE_ERR          = 2;
  public static final short HIERARCHY_REQUEST_ERR       = 3;
  public static final short WRONG_DOCUMENT_ERR          = 4;
  public static final short INVALID_CHARACTER_ERR       = 5;
  public static final short NO_DATA_ALLOWED_ERR         = 6;
  public static final short NO_MODIFICATION_ALLOWED_ERR = 7;
  public static final short NOT_FOUND_ERR               = 8;
```

```
    public static final short NOT_SUPPORTED_ERR           = 9;
    public static final short INUSE_ATTRIBUTE_ERR         = 10;
    public static final short INVALID_STATE_ERR           = 11;
    public static final short SYNTAX_ERR                  = 12;
    public static final short INVALID_MODIFICATION_ERR    = 13;
    public static final short NAMESPACE_ERR               = 14;
    public static final short INVALID_ACCESS_ERR          = 15;

}
```

DOMException is the *only* exception that DOM standard methods throw. DOM methods don't throw IOException, IllegalArgumentException, SAXException, or any other exceptions you may be familiar with from Java. In a few cases, the implementation classes may throw a different exception, especially NullPointer-Exception; and methods in non-DOM support classes such as org.apache.xerces.parser.DOMParser or javax.xml.transform.dom.DOMResult can most certainly throw these exceptions. However, the DOM methods themselves don't throw them.

Not only do DOM methods only throw DOMExceptions. They don't even throw any subclasses of DOMException. Here, DOM is following C++ conventions rather than Java conventions. Whereas Java tends to differentiate related exceptions through many different subclasses,[2] DOM uses named short constants to identify the different problems that can arise. This is also useful for languages like AppleScript in which exceptions aren't even classes. The exception code is exposed through DOMException's public code field. The codes are defined as follows:

DOMException.DOMSTRING_SIZE_ERR
Something tried to put more than 2 billion characters into one string, not too likely in Java. (If you're trying to stuff that much text into one string, you're going to have other problems long before DOM complains.) This exception is really meant for other languages with much smaller maximum string sizes.

DOMException.HIERARCHY_REQUEST_ERR
An attempt was made to add a node where it can't go; for example, making an element a child of a text node, making an attribute a child of an element, adding a second root element to a document, or trying to make an element its own grandpa.

2. In Java 1.4, there are more than 50 different subclasses of IOException alone.

DOMException.INDEX_SIZE_ERR
A rare exception thrown by the `splitText()` method of a `Text` object resulting from an attempt to split the text before the beginning or after the end of the node.

DOMException.INUSE_ATTRIBUTE_ERR
An attempt was made to add an existing `Attr` to a new element without removing it from the old element first.

DOMException.INVALID_ACCESS_ERR
The class that implements the DOM interface does not support the requested method, even though you'd normally expect it to.

DOMException.INVALID_CHARACTER_ERR
A Unicode character was used where it isn't allowed; for example, an element name contained a dollar sign or a text node value contained a formfeed. Many DOM implementations miss at least some problems that can occur with invalid characters. This exception is not thrown as often as it should be.

DOMException.INVALID_MODIFICATION_ERR
The class that implements the DOM interface cannot change the object in the requested way, even though you'd normally expect it to; for example, it ran out of space for more child nodes.

DOMException.INVALID_STATE_ERR
The implementation class that backs the DOM interface being used has gotten confused and cannot perform the requested operation. This would generally indicate a bug in the implementation.

DOMException.NAMESPACE_ERR
The namespace prefixes or URIs specified are somehow incorrect; for example, the qualified name contains multiple colons, or the qualified name has a prefix but the namespace URI is null, or it has the prefix `xml` but the namespace URI is not `http://www.w3.org/XML/1998/namespace`.

DOMException.NOT_FOUND_ERR
A referenced node is not present in the document; for example, an attempt was made to remove an attribute the element does not have, or to insert a node before another node that is no longer in the document.

DOMException.NOT_SUPPORTED_ERR
The implementation does not support the requested object type; for example, an attempt was made to create a CDATA section node using an HTML document implementation.

`DOMException.NO_DATA_ALLOWED_ERR`
An attempt was made to set the value of an element, document, document fragment, document type, entity, entity reference, or notation node. These kinds of nodes always have null values.

`DOMException.NO_MODIFICATION_ALLOWED_ERR`
An attempt was made to change a read-only node. The most common reason for a node to be read-only is that it's a descendant of an entity reference node.

`DOMException.SYNTAX_ERR`
An attempt was made to set a value to a string that's illegal in context; for example, a comment value that contains the double hyphen `--` or a CDATA section that contains the CDATA section end delimiter `]]>`. In practice, most implementations do not watch for these sorts of syntax errors and do not throw this exception.

`DOMException.WRONG_DOCUMENT_ERR`
An attempt was made to insert or add a node into a document other than its *owner* (the document that originally created the node). DOM does not allow nodes to change documents. Instead it's necessary to use the `importNode()` method in the new `Document` to make a copy of the node you want to move.

Although there's no way for DOM to prevent programs from using error codes other than those listed here, the W3C has reserved all possible error codes for its own use. If you need something not listed here, I recommend writing your own exception class or subclass `DOMException`. (Just because DOM doesn't make full use of an object-oriented exception mechanism for reasons of compatibility with languages less object-oriented than Java doesn't mean you shouldn't do this in your pure Java code.)

Choosing between SAX and DOM

The single biggest factor in deciding whether to code your programs with SAX or with DOM is personal preference. SAX and DOM are very different APIs. Whereas SAX models the parser, DOM models the XML document. Most developers find the DOM approach more to their taste, at least initially. Its *pull model* (in which the client program extracts the information it wants from a document by invoking various methods on that document) is much more familiar than SAX's *push model* (in which the parser tells you what it reads when it reads it, whether you're ready for that information or not).

However, SAX's push model, unfamiliar as it is, can be much more efficient. SAX programs can be much faster than their DOM equivalents, and they almost always use far less memory. In particular, SAX works extremely well when documents are streamed, and the individual parts of each document can be processed in isolation from other parts. If complicated processes can be broken down into serial filters, then SAX is hard to beat. SAX lends itself to assembly-line-like automation wherein different stations perform small operations on just the parts of the document they have at hand right at that moment. By contrast, DOM is more like a factory in which each worker operates only on an entire car. Every time the worker receives a new car off the line, he or she must take the entire car apart to find the piece needed to work with, then do his or her job, then put the car back together again before moving it along to the next worker. This system is inefficient if there's more than one station. DOM lends itself to monolithic applications in which one program does everything. SAX works better when the program can be divided into small bits of independent work.

In particular, the following characteristics indicate that a program should probably use a streaming API such as SAX, XNI, or XMLPULL.

- Documents will not fit into available memory. This is the only rule that really mandates one or the other. If your documents are too big for available memory, then you must use a streaming API such as SAX, painful though it may be. You really have no other choice.
- You can process the document in small contiguous chunks of input. The entire document does not need to be available before you can do useful work. A slightly weaker variant of this is if the decisions you make depend only on preceding parts of the document, never on what comes later.
- Processing can be divided up into a chain of successive operations.

On the other hand, if the problem matches this next set of characteristics, the program should probably use DOM or perhaps another of the tree-based APIs such as JDOM.

- The program needs to access widely separated parts of the document at the same time. Even more so, it needs access to multiple documents at the same time.
- The internal data structures are almost as complicated as the document itself.
- The program must modify the document repeatedly.
- The program must store the document for a significant amount of time through many method calls, not just process it once and forget it.

On occasion, it's possible to use both SAX and DOM. In particular, you can parse the document using a SAX XMLReader attached to a series of SAX filters, then use the final output from that process to construct a DOM Document. Working in reverse, you can traverse a DOM tree while firing off SAX events to a SAX ContentHandler.

The approach is the same Example 9.14 used earlier to serialize a DOM Document onto a stream. You can use JAXP to perform an identity transform from a source to a result. JAXP supports SAX, DOM, and streams as sources and results. For example, the following code fragment reads an XML document from the InputStream in and parses it with the SAX XMLReader named saxParser. Then it transforms this input into the equivalent DOMResult from which the DOM Document is extracted.

```
XMLReader saxParser = XMLReaderFactory.createXMLReader();
Source input = new SAXSource(saxParser, in);
Result output = new DOMResult();
TransformerFactory xformFactory
 = TransformerFactory.newInstance();
Transformer idTransform = xformFactory.newTransformer();
idTransform.transform(input, output);
Node document = idTransform.getNode();
```

To go in the other direction, from DOM to SAX, you can just use a DOMSource and a SAXResult. The DOMSource is constructed from a DOM Document object, and the SAXResult is configured with a ContentHandler:

```
Source input = new DOMSource(document);
ContentHandler handler = new MyContentHandler();
Result output = new SAXResult(handler);
TransformerFactory xformFactory
 = TransformerFactory.newInstance();
Transformer idTransform = xformFactory.newTransformer();
idTransform.transform(input, output);
Node document = idTransform.getNode();
```

The transform will walk the DOM tree, firing off events to the SAX ContentHandler.

Although TrAX is the most standard, parser-independent means of passing documents back and forth between SAX and DOM, many implementations of these APIs also provide their own utility classes for crossing the border between the APIs. For example, GNU JAXP has the gnu.xml.pipeline.DomConsumer class for building DOM `Document` objects from SAX event streams, and the `gnu.xml.util.DomParser` class for feeding a DOM `Document` into a SAX program. The Oracle XML Parser for Java provides the `oracle.xml.parser.v2.DocumentBuilder`, which is a SAX `LexicalHandler/ContentHandler/DeclHandler` that builds a DOM `Document` from a SAX `XMLReader`.

Summary

The Document Object Model, DOM, is a W3C standard API for reading and writing XML and HTML documents represented as trees. DOM is defined in IDL, but there are standard bindings for Java. In DOM, an XML document is represented as a connected tree of `Node` objects. The root of the tree is a `Document` object. Other kinds of nodes found in the tree include `Element`, `Text`, `Comment`, `ProcessingInstruction`, and several more. The basic `Node` interface provides generic methods to navigate the tree, as well as to get the names, values, local names, prefixes, types, and namespace URIs of each node. Because not all of these properties really make sense for all kinds nodes, many of these methods can return null.

DOM Level 2 does not provide any standard way to parse an existing document, serialize a document onto a stream, or load the parser's `DOMImplementation`. Sun's Java API for XML Processing (JAXP) fills these holes. DOM Level 3 will also add this functionality as a standard part of DOM.

Chapter 10

Creating XML Documents with DOM

DOM is a read-write API. DOM documents are created not only by parsing text files, but also by creating new documents in memory out of nothing at all. These documents can then be serialized onto a stream or into a file. The abstract factory interface that creates new `Document` objects is called `DOMImplementation`. The `Document` interface has a dual purpose: First, it represents XML documents themselves and provides access to their contents, document type declaration, and other properties. Second, it too is an abstract factory responsible for creating the nodes that go in the document: elements, text, comments, processing instructions, and so on. Each such node belongs exclusively to the document that created it and cannot be moved to a different document.

DOMImplementation

The `DOMImplementation` interface, shown in Example 10.1, is an abstract factory that is responsible for creating two things—new `Document` and `DocumentType` objects. It also provides the `hasFeature()` method discussed in Chapter 9 that tells you what features this implementation supports.

Example 10.1 The DOMImplementation Interface

```
package org.w3c.dom;

public interface DOMImplementation {

  public DocumentType createDocumentType(
   String rootElementQualifiedName,
   String publicID, String systemID) throws DOMException;
  public Document createDocument(String rootElementNamespaceURI,
   String rootElementQualifiedName, DocumentType doctype)
   throws DOMException;
  public boolean hasFeature(String feature, String version);

}
```

For example, given a DOMImplementation object named impl, the following chunk of code creates a new DocumentType object named svgDOCTYPE pointing to the Scalable Vector Graphics (SVG) DTD:

```
DocumentType svgDOCTYPE = impl.createDocumentType("svg",
 "-//W3C//DTD SVG 1.0//EN",
 "http://www.w3.org/TR/2001/REC-SVG-20010904/DTD/svg10.dtd");
```

If the DTD does not have a public ID, you can simply pass null for the second argument.

You can use this DocumentType object when constructing a new SVG Document object:

```
Document svgDoc = impl.createDocument(
 "http://www.w3.org/2000/svg", "svg", svgDOCTYPE
);
```

If svgDoc were serialized into a text file, it would look something like this (modulo insignificant white space):

```
<?xml version="1.0" encoding="UTF-8"?>
<!DOCTYPE svg PUBLIC "-//W3C//DTD SVG 1.0//EN"
 "http://www.w3.org/TR/2001/REC-SVG-20010904/DTD/svg10.dtd">
<svg xmlns="http://www.w3.org/2000/svg"/>
```

Of course not all XML documents have document type declarations or namespace URIs. If the document is merely well-formed, then you simply can pass null for the `doctype` argument. If the document root element is not in a namespace, you also can pass null for the namespace URI. This code fragment creates an XML-RPC document with neither a document type declaration nor a namespace URI:

```
Document xmlrpc = impl.createDocument(null, "methodCall", null);
```

These `Document` objects, with or without document type declarations, are not yet complete. In particular, they do not yet have any content beyond an empty root element. For that, you'll have to use the methods of the `Document` interface to create nodes, and use the methods of the `Node` interface to add these newly created nodes to the tree.

Locating a DOMImplementation

So far, I've deliberately avoided the crucial question of how one creates a `DOMImplementation` object in the first place. Because `DOMImplementation` is an interface, not a class, it cannot be instantiated directly through its own constructor. Instead you have to build it in one of three ways:

- Construct the implementation-specific class.
- Use the JAXP `DocumentBuilder` factory class.
- Use the DOM3 `DOMImplementationRegistry` factory class.

Implementation-Specific Class

Directly constructing an instance of the vendor class that implements `DOMImplementation` is the simplest of the three alternatives. However, the name of this class and how it's created vary from one implementation to the next. For example, in Xerces the `org.apache.xerces.dom.DOMImplementationImpl` singleton class implements the `DOMImplementation` interface. The singleton object is retrieved via the `getDOMImplementation()` factory method as follows:

```
DOMImplementation impl
 = DOMImplementationImpl.getDOMImplementation();
```

However, if you were to switch to a different implementation, you would need to change your source code and recompile. For example, in the Oracle XML Parser for Java, `oracle.xml.parser.v2.XMLDOMImplementation` class implements the `DOMImplementation` interface, and instances of this class are created with a no-args constructor, as follows:

```
DOMImplementation impl = new XMLDOMImplementation();
```

In both cases, the implementation-specific object is assigned to a variable of type `DOMImplementation`. This enables the compiler to ensure that you don't accidentally use any implementation-specific methods in the object, or tie the code too tightly to one vendor. The implementation-dependent code should be limited to this one line.

JAXP DocumentBuilder

The JAXP `DocumentBuilder` class introduced in Chapter 9 has a `getDOMImplementation()` method that can locate a local `DOMImplementation` class.

```
public abstract DOMImplementation getDOMImplementation()
```

For example, this code fragment uses JAXP to create a new SVG `Document` object in memory:

```
try {
  DocumentBuilderFactory factory
   = DocumentBuilderFactory.newInstance();
  DocumentBuilder builder = factory.newDocumentBuilder();
  DOMImplementation impl = builder.getDOMImplementation();

  DocumentType svgDOCTYPE = impl.createDocumentType("svg",
   "-//W3C//DTD SVG 1.0//EN",
   "http://www.w3.org/TR/2001/REC-SVG-20010904/DTD/svg10.dtd");
  Document svgDoc = impl.createDocument(
   "http://www.w3.org/2000/svg", "svg", svgDOCTYPE
  );
  // work with the document...
}
catch (FactoryConfigurationError e) {
  System.out.println(
   "Could not locate a JAXP DocumentBuilderFactory class");
}
```

```
catch (ParserConfigurationException e) {
  System.out.println(
   "Could not locate a JAXP DocumentBuilder class");
}
```

If you only want to create a new `Document`, then `DocumentBuilder` also has a `newDocument()` method that shortcuts the `DOMImplementation` class:

```
public abstract Document newDocument()
```

However, this method does not properly set a root element. Thus the documents created by `newDocument()` are at least initially malformed; therefore, I recommend that you don't use this method. Just use JAXP to retrieve a `DOMImplementation` object and use its `createDocument()` method instead.

The specific implementation that JAXP chooses is determined in the same way as described for locating a parser in Chapter 9. That is, JAXP reads first the *javax.xml.parsers.DocumentBuilderFactory* system property, then the `lib/jaxp.properties` file, then the `META-INF/services/javax.xml.parsers.DocumentBuilderFactory` file in all JAR files available to the runtime, and then finally a fallback class hardcoded into the JAXP implementation.

DOM3 DOMImplementationRegistry

The final option for locating the `DOMImplementation` is new in DOM3 and only supported by Xerces-2 so far. This is the `DOMImplementationRegistry` class shown in Example 10.2.

Example 10.2 The DOMImplementationRegistry Class

```
package org.w3c.dom;

public class DOMImplementationRegistry  {

  // The system property that specifies DOMImplementationSource
  // class names.
  public static String PROPERTY
   = "org.w3c.dom.DOMImplementationSourceList";

  public static DOMImplementation getDOMImplementation(
   String features) throws ClassNotFoundException,
   InstantiationException, IllegalAccessException;
```

```
    public static void addSource(DOMImplementationSource s)
     throws ClassNotFoundException, InstantiationException,
     IllegalAccessException;

}
```

The getDOMImplementation() method returns a DOMImplementation object that supports the features given in the argument, or null if no such implementation can be found. For example, the following code fragment requests a DOMImplementation that supports XML DOM1, any version of the traversal module, and DOM2 events:

```
try {
  DOMImplementation impl = DOMImplementationRegistry
   .getDOMImplementation("XML 1.0 Traversal Events 2.0");
  if (impl != null) {
    DocumentType svgDOCTYPE = impl.createDocumentType("svg",
     "-//W3C//DTD SVG 1.0//EN",
     "http://www.w3.org/TR/2001/REC-SVG-20010904/DTD/svg10.dtd");
    Document svgDoc = impl.createDocument(
     "http://www.w3.org/2000/svg", "svg", svgDOCTYPE
    );
    // work with the document...
  }
}
catch (Exception e) {
  System.out.println(e);
}
```

Be sure to check whether the implementation returned is null before using it. Many installations may not be able to support all the features you want.

DOMImplementationRegistry searches for DOMImplementation classes by looking at the value of the *org.w3c.dom.DOMImplementationSourceList* Java system property. This property should contain a white-space-separated list of DOMImplementationSource classes on the local system. Example 10.3 summarizes this interface.

Example 10.3 The DOMImplementationSource Interface

```
package org.w3c.dom;

public interface DOMImplementationSource {

  public DOMImplementation getDOMImplementation(String features);

}
```

DOMImplementationRegistry.getDOMImplementation() queries each source for its DOMImplementation. The double indirection (listing DOMImplementationSource classes rather than DOMImplementation classes) is necessary to allow DOMImplementationRegistry.getDOMImplementation() to return different classes of objects depending on which combination of features are requested.

The three exceptions that getDOMImplementation() throws—ClassNotFoundException, InstantiationException, and IllegalAccessException—shouldn't be very common. The only way that any of these can be thrown is if the *org.w3c.dom.DOMImplementationSourceList* system property includes the name of a class that can't be found or one that is not a conforming instance of DOMImplementationSource.

Remember, like the other DOM3 material discussed in this book, all of this is on the wrong side of the bleeding edge and cannot be expected to work in most existing implementations.

The Document Interface as an Abstract Factory

The Document interface, summarized in Example 10.4, serves two purposes in DOM:

1. As an abstract factory, it creates instances of other nodes for that document.
2. It is the representation of the document node.

Example 10.4 The Document Interface

```
package org.w3c.dom;

public interface Document extends Node {
```

```
  public Element createElement(String tagName)
   throws DOMException;
  public Element createElementNS(String namespaceURI,
   String qualifiedName) throws DOMException;
  public Text createTextNode(String data);
  public Comment createComment(String data);
  public CDATASection createCDATASection(String data)
   throws DOMException;
  public ProcessingInstruction createProcessingInstruction(
   String target, String data) throws DOMException;
  public Attr createAttribute(String name) throws DOMException;
  public Attr createAttributeNS(String namespaceURI,
   String qualifiedName) throws DOMException;
  public DocumentFragment createDocumentFragment();
  public EntityReference createEntityReference(String name)
   throws DOMException;

  public DocumentType      getDoctype();
  public DOMImplementation getImplementation();
  public Element           getDocumentElement();
  public Node              importNode(Node importedNode,
                               boolean deep) throws DOMException;
  public NodeList          getElementsByTagName(String tagname);
  public NodeList          getElementsByTagNameNS(
                          String namespaceURI, String localName);
  public Element           getElementById(String elementId);

}
```

Remember that in addition to the methods listed here, each `Document` object has all the methods of the `Node` interface discussed in Chapter 9. These are key parts of the functionality of the class.

I'll begin with the use of the `Document` interface as an abstract factory. You'll notice that the `Document` interface has nine separate `create`*`XXX`*`()` methods for creating seven different kinds of node objects. (There are two methods each for creating element and attribute nodes, because you can create these with or without namespaces.) For example, given a `Document` object `doc`, the following code fragment creates a new processing instruction and a comment:

```
ProcessingInstruction xmlstylesheet
 = doc.createProcessingInstruction("xml-stylesheet",
 "type=\"text/css\" href=\"standard.css\"");
Comment comment = doc.createComment(
 "An example from Chapter 10 of Processing XML with Java");
```

Although these two nodes are associated with the document, they are not yet parts of its tree. To add them, it's necessary to use the `insertBefore()` method of the `Node` interface that `Document` extends. Specifically, I'll insert each of these nodes before the root element of the document, which can be retrieved via `getDocumentElement()`:

```
Node rootElement = doc.getDocumentElement();
doc.insertBefore(comment, rootElement);
doc.insertBefore(xmlstylesheet, rootElement);
```

To add content inside the root element, it's necessary to use the `Node` methods on the root element. For example, the following code fragment adds a `desc` child element to the root element:

```
Element desc
 = doc.createElementNS("http://www.w3.org/2000/svg", "desc");
rootElement.appendChild(desc);
```

Each node is created by the owner document, but it is inserted using the parent node. For example, the following code fragment adds a text-node child containing the phrase "An example from Processing XML with Java" to the previous `desc` element node:

```
Text descText
 = doc.createTextNode("An example from Processing XML with Java");
desc.appendChild(descText);
```

Example 10.5 puts this all together to create a program that builds a complete, albeit very simple, SVG document in memory using DOM. JAXP loads the `DOMImplementation` so that the program is reasonably parser independent. The JAXP ID-transform hack introduced in Chapter 9 dumps the document on `System.out`.

Example 10.5 Using DOM to Build an SVG Document in Memory

```
import javax.xml.parsers.*;
import javax.xml.transform.*;
import javax.xml.transform.stream.StreamResult;
import javax.xml.transform.dom.DOMSource;
import org.w3c.dom.*;


public class SimpleSVG {

  public static void main(String[] args) {

    try {
      // Find the implementation
      DocumentBuilderFactory factory
       = DocumentBuilderFactory.newInstance();
      factory.setNamespaceAware(true);
      DocumentBuilder builder = factory.newDocumentBuilder();
      DOMImplementation impl = builder.getDOMImplementation();

      // Create the document
      DocumentType svgDOCTYPE = impl.createDocumentType(
       "svg", "-//W3C//DTD SVG 1.0//EN",
       "http://www.w3.org/TR/2001/REC-SVG-20010904/DTD/svg10.dtd"
      );
      Document doc = impl.createDocument(
       "http://www.w3.org/2000/svg", "svg", svgDOCTYPE);

      // Fill the document
      Node rootElement = doc.getDocumentElement();
      ProcessingInstruction xmlstylesheet
       = doc.createProcessingInstruction("xml-stylesheet",
       "type=\"text/css\" href=\"standard.css\"");
      Comment comment = doc.createComment(
       "An example from Chapter 10 of Processing XML with Java");
      doc.insertBefore(comment, rootElement);
      doc.insertBefore(xmlstylesheet, rootElement);
      Node desc = doc.createElementNS(
       "http://www.w3.org/2000/svg", "desc");
```

```
      rootElement.appendChild(desc);
      Text descText = doc.createTextNode(
       "An example from Processing XML with Java");
      desc.appendChild(descText);

      // Serialize the document onto System.out
      TransformerFactory xformFactory
       = TransformerFactory.newInstance();
      Transformer idTransform = xformFactory.newTransformer();
      Source input = new DOMSource(doc);
      Result output = new StreamResult(System.out);
      idTransform.transform(input, output);

    }
    catch (FactoryConfigurationError e) {
      System.out.println("Could not locate a JAXP factory class");
    }
    catch (ParserConfigurationException e) {
      System.out.println(
        "Could not locate a JAXP DocumentBuilder class"
      );
    }
    catch (DOMException e) {
      System.err.println(e);
    }
    catch (TransformerConfigurationException e) {
      System.err.println(e);
    }
    catch (TransformerException e) {
      System.err.println(e);
    }

  }

}
```

When this program is run, it produces the following output:

```
C:\XMLJAVA>java SimpleSVG
<?xml version="1.0" encoding="utf-8"?><!--An example from Chapter
10 of Processing XML with Java--><?xml-stylesheet type="text/css"
```

```
href="standard.css"?><svg><desc>An example from Processing XML
with Java</desc></svg>
```

I've inserted line breaks to make the output fit on this page, but the actual output doesn't have any. In the prolog, that's because the JAXP ID transform doesn't include any. In the document, that's because the program did not add any text nodes containing only white space. Many parser vendors include custom serialization packages that allow you to more closely manage the placement of white space and other syntax sugar in the output. In addition, this will be a standard part of DOM3. We'll explore these options for prettifying the output in Chapter 13.

Note

The lack of namespace declarations and possibly the lack of a document type declaration is a result of bugs in JAXP implementations. I've reported the problem to several XSLT processor/XML parser vendors and am hopeful that at least some of them will fix this bug before the final draft of this book. As of July 2002, GNU JAXP and Oracle include the namespace declaration, whereas Xerces 2.0.2 leaves it out. So far no implementation I've seen includes the document type declaration. You can work around the problem by explicitly adding namespace declaration attributes to the tree.

The same techniques can be used for all of the nodes in the tree: text, comments, elements, processing instructions, and entity references. But because attributes are not children, attribute nodes can only be set on element nodes and only by using the methods of the `Element` interface. I'll take that up in Chapter 11. `Attr` objects, on the other hand, are created by `Document` objects, just like all the other DOM node objects.

DOM is not picky about whether you work from the top down or the bottom up. You can start at the root and add its children, then add the child nodes to these nodes, and continue down the tree. Alternately, you can start by creating the deepest nodes in the tree, and then create their parents, and then create the parents of the parents, and so on back up to the root. Or you can mix and match as seems appropriate in your program. DOM really doesn't care as long as there's always a root element.

Each node created is firmly associated with the document that created it. If document A creates node X, then node X cannot be inserted into document B. A copy of node X can be imported into document B, but node X itself is always attached only to document A.

We're now in a position to repeat some examples from Chapter 3, this time using DOM to create the document rather than just writing strings onto a stream.

Among other advantages, this means that many well-formedness constraints are automatically satisfied. Furthermore, the programs will have a much greater object-oriented feel to them.

I'll begin with the simple Fibonacci problem of Example 3.3. That program produced documents that look like this:

```
<?xml version="1.0"?>
<Fibonacci_Numbers>
  <fibonacci>1</fibonacci>
  <fibonacci>1</fibonacci>
  <fibonacci>2</fibonacci>
  <fibonacci>3</fibonacci>
  <fibonacci>5</fibonacci>
  <fibonacci>8</fibonacci>
  <fibonacci>13</fibonacci>
  <fibonacci>21</fibonacci>
  <fibonacci>34</fibonacci>
  <fibonacci>55</fibonacci>
</Fibonacci_Numbers>
```

This is a straightforward element-based hierarchy that does not use namespaces or document type declarations. Although simple, these sorts of documents are important. XML-RPC is just one of many real-world applications that does not use anything more than element, text, and document nodes.

Example 10.6 is a DOM-based program that generates documents of this form. It is at least superficially more complex than the equivalent program from Chapter 3, but it has some advantages over that program. In particular, well-formedness of the output is almost guaranteed. It's a lot harder to produce incorrect XML with DOM than by simply writing strings on a stream. Furthermore, the data structure is a lot more flexible. Here, the document is written more or less from beginning to end, but if this were part of a larger program that ran for a longer time, then nodes could be added and deleted in almost random order anywhere in the tree at any time. It's not necessary to know all of the information that will ever go into the document before you begin writing it. The downside is that DOM programs tend to eat substantially more RAM than the streaming equivalents because they must keep the entire document in memory at all times. This can be a significant problem for large documents.

Example 10.6 A DOM Program That Outputs the Fibonacci Numbers as an XML Document

```
import org.w3c.dom.*;
import javax.xml.parsers.*;
import javax.xml.transform.*;
import javax.xml.transform.dom.DOMSource;
import javax.xml.transform.stream.StreamResult;
import java.math.BigInteger;


public class FibonacciDOM {

  public static void main(String[] args) {

    try {

      // Find the implementation
      DocumentBuilderFactory factory
       = DocumentBuilderFactory.newInstance();
      factory.setNamespaceAware(true);
      DocumentBuilder builder = factory.newDocumentBuilder();
      DOMImplementation impl = builder.getDOMImplementation();

      // Create the document
      Document doc = impl.createDocument(null,
       "Fibonacci_Numbers", null);

      // Fill the document
      BigInteger low  = BigInteger.ONE;
      BigInteger high = BigInteger.ONE;

      Element root = doc.getDocumentElement();

      for (int i = 0; i < 10; i++) {
        Element number = doc.createElement("fibonacci");
        Text text = doc.createTextNode(low.toString());
        number.appendChild(text);
        root.appendChild(number);
```

```
            BigInteger temp = high;
            high = high.add(low);
            low = temp;
          }

          // Serialize the document onto System.out
          TransformerFactory xformFactory
           = TransformerFactory.newInstance();
          Transformer idTransform = xformFactory.newTransformer();
          Source input = new DOMSource(doc);
          Result output = new StreamResult(System.out);
          idTransform.transform(input, output);

        }
        catch (FactoryConfigurationError e) {
          System.out.println("Could not locate a JAXP factory class");
        }
        catch (ParserConfigurationException e) {
          System.out.println(
            "Could not locate a JAXP DocumentBuilder class"
          );
        }
        catch (DOMException e) {
          System.err.println(e);
        }
        catch (TransformerConfigurationException e) {
          System.err.println(e);
        }
        catch (TransformerException e) {
          System.err.println(e);
        }

      }

    }
```

As usual, this code contains the four main tasks for creating a new XML document with DOM:

1. Locate a `DOMImplementation`.
2. Create a new `Document` object.

3. Fill the `Document` with various kinds of nodes.
4. Serialize the `Document` onto a stream.

Most DOM programs that create new documents follow this structure. They may hide parts in different methods, or use DOM3 to serialize instead of JAXP; but they all must locate a `DOMImplementation`, use that to create a `Document` object, fill the document with other nodes created by the `Document` object, and finally serialize the result. (A few programs may skip the serialization step.)

The only part that really changes from one program to the next is how the document is filled with content. This naturally depends on the structure of the document. A program that reads tables from a database to get the data will naturally look very different from a program like this one, which algorithmically generates numbers. And both of these will look very different from a program that asks the user to type in information. However, all three and many more besides will use the same methods of the `Document` and `Node` interfaces to build the structures they need.

Here is the output when this program is run:

```
C:\XMLJAVA>java FibonacciDOM
<?xml version="1.0" encoding="utf-8"?><Fibonacci_Numbers>
<fibonacci>1</fibonacci><fibonacci>1</fibonacci><fibonacci>2
</fibonacci><fibonacci>3</fibonacci><fibonacci>5</fibonacci>
<fibonacci>8</fibonacci><fibonacci>13</fibonacci><fibonacci>21
</fibonacci><fibonacci>34</fibonacci><fibonacci>55</fibonacci>
</Fibonacci_Numbers>
```

Notice once again that the white space is not quite what was expected. One way to fix this is to add the extra text nodes that represent the white space. For example,

```
for (int i = 0; i < 10; i++) {
  Text space = doc.createTextNode("\n  ");
  root.appendChild(space);
  Element number = doc.createElement("fibonacci");
  Text text = doc.createTextNode(low.toString());
  number.appendChild(text);
  root.appendChild(number);

  BigInteger temp = high;
  high = high.add(low);
  low  = temp;
}
Text lineBreak = doc.createTextNode("\n");
root.appendChild(lineBreak);
```

An alternate approach is to use a more sophisticated serializer and tell it to add the extra white space. I prefer this approach because it's much simpler and does not clutter up the code with basically insignificant white space, as I'll demonstrate in Chapter 13. Of course, if you really do care about white space, then you need to manage the white-space-only text nodes explicitly and tell whichever serializer you use to leave the white space alone.

Adding namespaces or a document type declaration pointing to an external DTD subset is not significantly harder. For example, suppose you want to generate valid MathML, as in Example 10.7.

Example 10.7 A Valid MathML Document That Contains Fibonacci Numbers

```
<?xml version="1.0"?>
<!DOCTYPE math PUBLIC "-//W3C//DTD MathML 2.0//EN"
 "http://www.w3.org/TR/MathML2/dtd/mathml2.dtd">
<math xmlns:mathml="http://www.w3.org/1998/Math/MathML">
  <mrow><mi>f(1)</mi><mo>=</mo><mn>1</mn></mrow>
  <mrow><mi>f(2)</mi><mo>=</mo><mn>1</mn></mrow>
  <mrow><mi>f(3)</mi><mo>=</mo><mn>2</mn></mrow>
  <mrow><mi>f(4)</mi><mo>=</mo><mn>3</mn></mrow>
  <mrow><mi>f(5)</mi><mo>=</mo><mn>5</mn></mrow>
  <mrow><mi>f(6)</mi><mo>=</mo><mn>8</mn></mrow>
  <mrow><mi>f(7)</mi><mo>=</mo><mn>13</mn></mrow>
  <mrow><mi>f(8)</mi><mo>=</mo><mn>21</mn></mrow>
  <mrow><mi>f(9)</mi><mo>=</mo><mn>34</mn></mrow>
  <mrow><mi>f(10)</mi><mo>=</mo><mn>55</mn></mrow>
</math>
```

The markup is somewhat more complex, but the Java code is not significantly more so. You simply need to use the implementation to create a new `DocumentType` object, and include both that and the namespace URL in the call to `createDocument()`. Example 10.8 demonstrates.

Example 10.8 A DOM Program That Outputs the Fibonacci Numbers as a MathML Document

```
import org.w3c.dom.*;
import javax.xml.parsers.*;
import javax.xml.transform.*;
```

```
import javax.xml.transform.dom.DOMSource;
import javax.xml.transform.stream.StreamResult;
import java.math.BigInteger;


public class FibonacciMathMLDOM {

  public static void main(String[] args) {

    try {

      // Find the implementation
      DocumentBuilderFactory factory
       = DocumentBuilderFactory.newInstance();
      factory.setNamespaceAware(true);
      DocumentBuilder builder = factory.newDocumentBuilder();
      DOMImplementation impl = builder.getDOMImplementation();

      // Create the document
      DocumentType mathml = impl.createDocumentType("math",
       "-//W3C//DTD MathML 2.0//EN",
       "http://www.w3.org/TR/MathML2/dtd/mathml2.dtd");
      Document doc = impl.createDocument(
       "http://www.w3.org/1998/Math/MathML", "math", mathml);

      // Fill the document
      BigInteger low  = BigInteger.ONE;
      BigInteger high = BigInteger.ONE;

      Element root = doc.getDocumentElement();

      for (int i = 1; i <= 10; i++) {
        Element mrow = doc.createElement("mrow");

        Element mi = doc.createElement("mi");
        Text function = doc.createTextNode("f(" + i + ")");
        mi.appendChild(function);

        Element mo = doc.createElement("mo");
        Text equals = doc.createTextNode("=");
        mo.appendChild(equals);
```

```
        Element mn = doc.createElement("mn");
        Text value = doc.createTextNode(low.toString());
        mn.appendChild(value);

        mrow.appendChild(mi);
        mrow.appendChild(mo);
        mrow.appendChild(mn);

        root.appendChild(mrow);

        BigInteger temp = high;
        high = high.add(low);
        low = temp;
      }

      // Serialize the document onto System.out
      TransformerFactory xformFactory
       = TransformerFactory.newInstance();
      Transformer idTransform = xformFactory.newTransformer();
      Source input = new DOMSource(doc);
      Result output = new StreamResult(System.out);
      idTransform.transform(input, output);

    }
    catch (FactoryConfigurationError e) {
      System.out.println("Could not locate a JAXP factory class");
    }
    catch (ParserConfigurationException e) {
      System.out.println(
        "Could not locate a JAXP DocumentBuilder class"
      );
    }
    catch (DOMException e) {
      System.err.println(e);
    }
    catch (TransformerConfigurationException e) {
      System.err.println(e);
    }
    catch (TransformerException e) {
      System.err.println(e);
    }
```

```
    }

}
```

Internal DTD subsets are a little harder, and not really supported at all in DOM2. For example, let's suppose you want to use a namespace prefix on your MathML elements but still want to have the document be valid MathML. The MathML DTD is designed in such a way that you can change the prefix and whether or not prefixes are used by redefining the `MATHML.prefixed` and `MATHML.prefix` parameter entities. Example 10.9 uses the prefix `math`.

Example 10.9 A Valid MathML Document That Uses Prefixed Names

```
<?xml version="1.0"?>
<!DOCTYPE math:math PUBLIC "-//W3C//DTD MathML 2.0//EN"
 "http://www.w3.org/TR/MathML2/dtd/mathml2.dtd" [
  <!ENTITY % MATHML.prefixed "INCLUDE">
  <!ENTITY % MATHML.prefix "math">
]>
<math:math xmlns:mathml="http://www.w3.org/1998/Math/MathML">
  <math:mrow>
    <math:mi>f(1)</math:mi>
    <math:mo>=</math:mo>
    <math:mn>1</math:mn>
  </math:mrow>
  <math:mrow>
    <math:mi>f(2)</math:mi>
    <math:mo>=</math:mo>
    <math:mn>1</math:mn>
  </math:mrow>
  <math:mrow>
    <math:mi>f(3)</math:mi>
    <math:mo>=</math:mo>
    <math:mn>2</math:mn>
  </math:mrow>
  <math:mrow>
    <math:mi>f(4)</math:mi>
    <math:mo>=</math:mo>
    <math:mn>3</math:mn>
  </math:mrow>
</math:math>
```

Using prefixed names in DOM code is straightforward enough, but there's no way to override the entity definitions in the DTD to tell it to validate against the prefixed names. DOM does not provide any means to create a new internal DTD subset or change an existing one. In order for the document you generate to be valid, therefore, it must use the same prefix the DTD does.

There are some hacks that can work around this. Some of the concrete classes that implement the `DocumentType` interface such as Xerces' `org.apache.xerces.dom.DocumentTypeImpl` include a nonstandard `setInternalSubset()` method. Or instead of pointing to the normal DTD, you can point to an external DTD that overrides the namespace parameter entity references and then imports the usual DTD. You could even generate this DTD on the fly using a separate output stream that writes strings containing entity declarations into a file. However, the bottom line is that the internal DTD subset just isn't well supported by DOM, and any program that needs access to it should use a different API.

The Document Interface as a Node Type

In addition to the factory methods and the methods common to all nodes, the `Document` interface has unique methods that perform operations relevant only to document nodes. These include

- Getter methods
- Methods to find elements
- A method to copy nodes from other documents

Getter Methods

The `Document` interface has three methods that simply return particular parts of the document:

```
public Element getDocumentElement()
public DocumentType getDoctype()
public DOMImplementation getImplementation()
```

These are fairly self-explanatory. You've already seen the `getDocumentElement()` method used several times. It returns the `Element` object that represents the root element of the document. Similarly, the `getDoctype()` method returns the document's `DocumentType` object, or null if the document does not have a document type declaration. The `getImplementation()` method returns the `DOMImplementation` object that created this document.

Several pieces are missing. In particular, no part of the XML declaration is available: not version, not encoding, not standalone status. Other useful information that's missing from DOM2 includes the actual encoding of the document (which is usually but not always the same as the encoding declared in the XML declaration) and the base URI of the document against which relative URIs in the document should be resolved. DOM3 will add several more getter and setter methods to the `Document` interface to make these available:

```
public String getActualEncoding()
public void setActualEncoding (String actualEncoding)
public String getEncoding()
public void setEncoding (String encoding)
public boolean getStandalone()
public void setStandalone (boolean standalone)
public String getVersion()
public void setVersion (String version)
public void setBaseURI (String baseURI) throws DOMException
```

The obvious `getBaseURI()` method is not really missing. It's just included in the `Node` super-interface rather than directly in the `Document` interface. Thus you can find out the base URI for any kind of node. This is important because XML documents can be built from multiple entities, and different nodes may come from different files.

```
public String getBaseURI()
```

Finally, DOM3 adds one more setter/getter pair that, strictly speaking, doesn't describe the document so much as the implementation. These two methods determine how draconian DOM is about checking for errors as the document is built in memory:

```
public boolean getStrictErrorChecking()
public void setStrictErrorChecking (boolean strictErrorChecking)
```

If the strict error-checking property is false, then the implementation may not make every test it could possibly make. For example, it might allow namespace prefixes that are not mapped to namespace URIs, or make a text node a child of the document element. This can be faster, but it is also dangerous, because other code may fail when presented with a `Document` object that does not satisfy all of the usual constraints. Strict error checking is enabled by default. Even if strict error checking is false, however, some error checking may still be done. The purpose of these methods is to allow implementations to skip some of the tedious checking they normally do and thus improve performance. The purpose is not to allow malformed documents, although that may be the effect in some cases.

These properties are experimentally supported in Xerces 2.0.2. No other parsers support them at the time of this writing. The detailed signatures are still subject to change, however, and you should not rely on them.

Example 10.10 is a simple program that parses a document from a URL passed through the command line and prints the values of these various properties. Because Xerces is currently the only parser to support the DOM3 properties, I used its implementation classes explicitly rather than the more generic JAXP.

Example 10.10 The Properties of a Document Object

```
import org.apache.xerces.parsers.DOMParser;
import org.apache.xerces.dom.DocumentImpl;
import org.w3c.dom.*;
import org.xml.sax.SAXException;
import java.io.IOException;

public class DocumentProperties {

  public static void main(String[] args) {

    if (args.length <= 0) {
      System.out.println("Usage: java DocumentProperties URL");
      return;
    }
    String url = args[0];

    DOMParser parser = new DOMParser();
    try {
      parser.parse(url);
      DocumentImpl document = (DocumentImpl) parser.getDocument();

      // DOM2 properties
      System.out.println("Implementation: " +
       document.getImplementation());
```

```
        System.out.println("Root element: " +
         document.getDocumentElement());
        System.out.println("DOCTYPE: " + document.getDoctype());

        // DOM3 Properties
        System.out.println("Version: " + document.getVersion());
        System.out.println("Standalone: " +
         document.getStandalone());
        System.out.println("Declared encoding: " +
         document.getEncoding());
        System.out.println("Strict error checking: " +
         document.getStrictErrorChecking());

        System.out.println("Actual encoding: " +
         document.getActualEncoding());
        System.out.println("Base URI: " + document.getBaseURI());

      }
      catch (SAXException e) {
        System.out.println(url + " is not well-formed.");
      }
      catch (IOException e) {
        System.out.println(
         "Due to an IOException, the parser could not read " + url
        );
      }

    }

  }
```

Running this program against the DocBook source code for this chapter produced the following ouput:

```
$java DocumentProperties ch10.xml
Implementation: org.apache.xerces.dom.DOMImplementationImpl@ef9f1d
Root element: [chapter: null]
DOCTYPE: [chapter: null]
Version: 1.0
Standalone: false
Declared encoding: UTF-8
Strict error checking: true
```

```
Actual encoding: UTF-8
Base URI: file: ///home/elharo/books/xmljava/ch10.xml
```

In this case, the detailed output for the DOM2 properties depends on what the `toString()` method for each of the implementation classes does. A more serious application would use the methods of each interface (`Document`, `Doctype`, and `Element`) to provide more complete output.

Tip
If a non-Xerces DOM implementation precedes Xerces in your class path, then this program won't compile. You need to make sure Xerces is the first DOM the compiler and runtime find. This is particularly problematic in Java 1.4, which includes a DOM implementation that does not support the DOM3 properties used here. However, in Java 1.4 you can use the **`java`** interpreter's `-Xbootclasspath/p:` option to prepend JAR archives to the boot class path, so that they will be preferred to the ones bundled with Java.

Finding Elements

Some of the most useful methods in the `Document` interface are those that retrieve all of the elements with certain names or IDs in the document, irrespective of where in the document they may actually be. When you're only really interested in certain elements, this can avoid a lot of tedious and complex tree-walking. These three methods are

```
public NodeList getElementsByTagName (String tagName)
public NodeList getElementsByTagNameNS (String namespaceURI,
 String localName)
public Element getElementByID()
```

The first two methods return a `NodeList` of the elements with the specified name or local name/namespace URI pair. This list is in document order. You can use the asterisk (*) to match all names or all namespace URIs. The third method returns the single element with the specified ID value, or null if no such element is present in the document. The ID is given by an ID-type attribute on that element.

As a demonstration, let's develop an XML-RPC servlet that generates Fibonacci numbers. (This actually was on the other side of the clients in Chapter 3 and Chapter 5.) Recall that the request document looks like Example 10.11. The server needs to find the integer value of the single `param`. Because we know there's

Caution

It is possible though invalid for multiple elements in one document to share the same ID. In this case, this method's behavior is undefined. For maximum safety, you may want to limit this method to provably valid documents.

exactly one `int` element in the request, it's easy to use `getElementsByTagName()` to find it.

Example 10.11 An XML-RPC Request Document

```
<?xml version="1.0"?>
<methodCall>
  <methodName>calculateFibonacci</methodName>
  <params>
    <param>
      <value><int>23</int></value>
    </param>
  </params>
</methodCall>
```

The server needs to calculate the result based on the input transmitted by the client, wrap that up in a response document like the one shown in Example 10.12, and transmit that document back to the client.

Example 10.12 An XML-RPC Response Document

```
<?xml version="1.0"?>
<methodResponse>
  <params>
    <param>
      <value><double>28657</double></value>
    </param>
  </params>
</methodResponse>
```

Example 10.13 demonstrates the complete servlet. It extends `HttpServlet` and implements `SingleThreadModel`. This interface notifies the servlet container that this servlet is not thread safe, and it should use a different instance of this class for each concurrent thread. However, one instance may be used for successive threads. This was necessary here because the JAXP `DocumentBuilder` and `Transformer` classes and possibly the class that implements `DOMImplementation` are not thread safe. You could make the servlet thread safe by loading new instances of these interfaces inside `doPost()` rather than sharing instances created in `init()`. However, in a potentially high-volume server environment, the resource cost for that feels disturbingly large. A better alternative would be to manually synchronize access to these objects inside `doPost()`. But because proper synchronization is notoriously difficult, I prefer to leave the work to the server.

Example 10.13 A DOM-Based XML-RPC Servlet

```
import javax.servlet.*;
import javax.servlet.http.*;
import java.io.*;
import java.math.BigInteger;
import org.w3c.dom.*;
import org.xml.sax.SAXException;
import javax.xml.parsers.*;
import javax.xml.transform.*;
import javax.xml.transform.dom.DOMSource;
import javax.xml.transform.stream.StreamResult;

public class FibonacciXMLRPCDOMServlet extends HttpServlet
 implements SingleThreadModel {

  // Fault codes
  public final static int MALFORMED_REQUEST_DOCUMENT = 1;
  public final static int INVALID_REQUEST_DOCUMENT   = 2;
  public final static int INDEX_MISSING              = 3;
  public final static int NON_POSITIVE_INDEX         = 4;
  public final static int BAD_INTEGER_FORMAT         = 5;
  public final static int UNEXPECTED_PROBLEM         = 255;

  private DocumentBuilder   parser;
  private DOMImplementation impl;
  private Transformer       idTransform;

  // Load a parser, transformer, and implementation
  public void init() throws ServletException {
```

```
    try {
      DocumentBuilderFactory factory
       = DocumentBuilderFactory.newInstance();
      this.parser = factory.newDocumentBuilder();
      this.impl   = parser.getDOMImplementation();
    }
    catch (Throwable t) {
      // It's unusual to catch a generic Throwable instead of an
      // exception. Here I'm specifically worried about
      // FactoryConfigurationErrors and
      // ParserConfigurationExceptions, both of which are real
      // possibilities in a servlet environment because of the
      // weird ways servlet containers arrange classpaths.
      throw new ServletException(
       "Could not locate a JAXP parser", t);
    }

    try {
      TransformerFactory xformFactory
       = TransformerFactory.newInstance();
      this.idTransform = xformFactory.newTransformer();
    }
    catch (Throwable t) {
      throw new ServletException(
       "Could not locate a JAXP transformer", t);
    }

  }

  // Respond to an XML-RPC request
  public void doPost(HttpServletRequest servletRequest,
   HttpServletResponse servletResponse)
   throws ServletException, IOException {

  servletResponse.setContentType("text/xml; charset=UTF-8");
    PrintWriter out = servletResponse.getWriter();
    InputStream in  = servletRequest.getInputStream();

    Document request;
    Document response;
    try {
      request = parser.parse(in);
```

```
    NodeList ints = request.getElementsByTagName("int");
    if (ints.getLength() == 0) {
      // XML-RPC allows i4 as an alias for int.
      ints = request.getElementsByTagName("i4");
    }
    Node input = ints.item(0); // throws NullPointerException
    String generations = getFullText(input);
    int numberOfGenerations = Integer.parseInt(generations);
    BigInteger result = calculateFibonacci(numberOfGenerations);
    response = makeResponseDocument(result);
  }
  catch (SAXException e) {
    response = makeFaultDocument(MALFORMED_REQUEST_DOCUMENT,
     e.getMessage());
  }
  catch (NullPointerException e) {
    response = makeFaultDocument(INDEX_MISSING, e.getMessage());
  }
  catch (NumberFormatException e) {
    response = makeFaultDocument(BAD_INTEGER_FORMAT,
     e.getMessage());
  }
  catch (IndexOutOfBoundsException e) {
    response = makeFaultDocument(NON_POSITIVE_INDEX,
     e.getMessage());
  }
  catch (Exception e) {
    response = makeFaultDocument(UNEXPECTED_PROBLEM,
     e.getMessage());
  }

  // Transform onto the OutputStream
  try {
    Source input = new DOMSource(response);
    Result output = new StreamResult(out);
    idTransform.transform(input, output);
    servletResponse.flushBuffer();
    out.flush();
    out.println();
  }
  catch (TransformerException e) {
```

```
      // If we get an exception at this point, it's too late to
      // switch over to an XML-RPC fault.
      throw new ServletException(e);
    }

  }


  // Given a node that does not contain any Element children,
  // accumulate all its text content from both text nodes and
  // CDATA sections (but not comments or processing instructions)
  // and return it as a single string.
  private static String getFullText(Node node) {

    StringBuffer result = new StringBuffer();

    NodeList children = node.getChildNodes();
    for (int i = 0; i < children.getLength(); i++) {
      Node child = children.item(i);
      int type = child.getNodeType();
      if (type == Node.TEXT_NODE
       || type == Node.CDATA_SECTION_NODE) {
        result.append(child.getNodeValue());
      }
      else if (type == Node.ENTITY_REFERENCE_NODE) {
        // The JAXP spec is unclear about whether or not it's
        // possible for entity reference nodes to appear in the
        // tree. Just in case, let's expand them recursively:
        result.append(getFullText(child));
        // Validity does require that if they do appear their
        // replacement text is pure text, no elements.
      }
    }

    return result.toString();

  }

  // If performance is an issue, this could be pre-built in the
  // init() method and then cached. You'd just change one text
  // node each time.  This would only work in a SingleThreadModel
```

```
// servlet.
public Document makeResponseDocument(BigInteger result) {

  Document response
   = impl.createDocument(null, "methodResponse", null);

  Element methodResponse = response.getDocumentElement();
  Element params         = response.createElement("params");
  Element param          = response.createElement("param");
  Element value          = response.createElement("value");
  Element doubleElement  = response.createElement("double");
  Text    text = response.createTextNode(result.toString());

  methodResponse.appendChild(params);
  params.appendChild(param);
  param.appendChild(value);
  value.appendChild(doubleElement);
  doubleElement.appendChild(text);

  return response;

}

public Document makeFaultDocument(int faultCode,
 String faultString) {

  Document faultDoc
   = impl.createDocument(null, "methodResponse", null);

  Element methodResponse = faultDoc.getDocumentElement();

  Element fault         = faultDoc.createElement("fault");
  Element value         = faultDoc.createElement("value");
  Element struct        = faultDoc.createElement("struct");
  Element memberCode    = faultDoc.createElement("member");
  Element nameCode      = faultDoc.createElement("name");
  Text    nameCodeText  = faultDoc.createTextNode("faultCode");
  Element valueCode     = faultDoc.createElement("value");
  Element intCode       = faultDoc.createElement("int");
  String  codeString    = String.valueOf(faultCode);
  Text    textCode      = faultDoc.createTextNode(codeString);
```

```
    Element doubleElement = faultDoc.createElement("double");
    Element memberString  = faultDoc.createElement("member");
    Element nameString    = faultDoc.createElement("name");
    Text    nameText      = faultDoc.createTextNode("faultString");
    Element valueString   = faultDoc.createElement("value");
    Element stringString  = faultDoc.createElement("string");
    Text    textString    = faultDoc.createTextNode(faultString);

    methodResponse.appendChild(fault);
    fault.appendChild(value);
    value.appendChild(struct);
    struct.appendChild(memberCode);
    struct.appendChild(memberString);
    memberCode.appendChild(nameCode);
    memberCode.appendChild(valueCode);
    memberString.appendChild(nameString);
    memberString.appendChild(valueString);
    nameCode.appendChild(nameCodeText);
    nameString.appendChild(nameText);
    valueCode.appendChild(intCode);
    valueString.appendChild(stringString);
    intCode.appendChild(textCode);
    stringString.appendChild(textString);

    return faultDoc;

  }

  public static BigInteger calculateFibonacci(int generations)
   throws IndexOutOfBoundsException {

    if (generations < 1) {
      throw new IndexOutOfBoundsException(
       "Fibonacci numbers are not defined for " + generations
       + "or any other number less than one.");
    }
    BigInteger low  = BigInteger.ONE;
    BigInteger high = BigInteger.ONE;
    for (int i = 2; i <= generations; i++) {
      BigInteger temp = high;
      high = high.add(low);
```

```
          low = temp;
        }
        return low;

    }

}
```

To compile FibonacciXMLRPCDOMServlet, you will need to install the Java Servlet API somewhere in your class path. This is not included in the base distribution of the JDK. To get it to run in most servlet containers, therefore, you'll need to add the JAR files for the DOM and JAXP implementations to the servlet's library. In Tomcat, that directory is $TOMCAT_HOME/lib. Note that it is not enough to have these files in the virtual machine's default ext directory because most servlet engines do not load classes from there (details are in Chapter 3).

The servlet is divided into six methods: init() doPost(), getFullText(), makeResponseDocument(), makeFaultDocument(), and calculateFibonacci(). The init() method, the servlet substitute for a constructor, is responsible for finding a DOMImplementation class and loading a parser and a transformer engine. There's no reason to waste time creating new DOMImplementations for each request.

doPost() is the standard servlet method for responding to HTTP POST. Each POST to this servlet represents a separate XML-RPC request. This method first uses getElementsByTagName() to find the single int element in this request. Then it extracts the text content of this element and converts it to a Java int. This is more involved than you might expect because of the possibility that this text might not be part of a single node. For example, any of these three legal elements would give the int element multiple children:

```
<int>12<!-- Why is this comment here? -->34</int>
<int><?target data?>1234</int
<int>12<![CDATA[34]]></int>
```

Admittedly these are unusual cases, but they must be handled because they are legal. Comments and CDATA sections could be eliminated at parse time with the DocumentBuilderFactory's setCoalescing(true) and setIgnoringComments(true) methods, but that still leaves the possibility of a processing instruction.

There are also a lot of illegal things we aren't handling. For example, nothing notices if the methodName element is missing or if the root element isn't methodCall. The proper way to handle this is to write a schema and validate the document against it before processing. Example 2.14 demonstrated an XML-RPC schema, but actually validating against this requires resorting to parser-specific classes. If you're using Xerces, the following code would do the trick:

```
DOMParser parser = new DOMParser();
parser.setErrorHandler(YourErrorHandler);
parser.setFeature(
 "http://apache.org/xml/features/validation/schema", true);
parser.setProperty(
 "http://apache.org/xml/properties/schema/"
 + "external-noNamespaceSchemaLocation",
 "http://example.com/schemas/xmlrpc.xsd");
parser.parse(in);
Document doc = parser.getDocument();
// Work with the parser as before
```

YourErrorHandler is an instance of some `org.xml.sax.ErrorHandler` implementation that throws a `SAXException` on detecting a validity error. Other schema-validating parsers such as the Oracle XML Parser for Java have slightly different APIs for checking a document against a known schema. Neither JAXP nor DOM2 provides a standard way to do this. When finished and implemented, DOM3 should allow you to perform schema validation in a parser-independent fashion.

Assuming that the request document is valid, the next step is to calculate the requested Fibonacci number with the `calculateFibonacci()` method. There's nothing new here, just math. This method doesn't have to know anything about XML, DOM, or XML-RPC. If the original XML-RPC request contained a nonpositive integer, then this method detects it and throws an `IndexOutOfBoundsException`. This will be caught in the `doPost()` method and converted into an XML-RPC fault response.

Once the result has been calculated, the `makeResponseDocument()` method wraps it up in properly formatted XML-RPC. If at any point something goes wrong—for example, the request document is missing the required `int` element—then an exception is thrown. This is caught, and instead of the normal response, `makeFaultDocument()` is called to produce a proper XML-RPC fault response document.

Finally, a JAXP identity transform copies the finished result document onto the servlet's output `Writer`. There's not a lot we can do about an exception at this point, so any `TransformerExceptions` caught during the transform are converted into a `ServletException`, with the original exception kept available as the root cause of the `ServletException`. We can't just let the `TransformerException` exception bubble up because `doPost()` in the superclass is not declared to throw it.

The SOAP servlet is similar in structure. But because namespaces are significant in SOAP, `getElementsByTagNameNS()` and other namespace-aware methods should be used. Example 10.14 demonstrates.

Example 10.14 A DOM-Based SOAP Servlet

```
import javax.servlet.*;
import javax.servlet.http.*;
import java.io.*;
import java.math.BigInteger;
import org.w3c.dom.*;
import org.xml.sax.SAXException;
import javax.xml.parsers.*;
import javax.xml.transform.*;
import javax.xml.transform.dom.DOMSource;
import javax.xml.transform.stream.StreamResult;

public class FibonacciSOAPDOMServlet extends HttpServlet
  implements SingleThreadModel {

  // Fault codes
  public final static String MALFORMED_REQUEST_DOCUMENT
   = "MalformedRequest";
  public final static String INVALID_REQUEST_DOCUMENT
   = "InvalidRequest";
  public final static String INDEX_MISSING
   = "IndexMissing";
  public final static String NON_POSITIVE_INDEX
   = "NonPositiveIndex";
  public final static String BAD_INTEGER_FORMAT
  = "BadIntegerFormat";
  public final static String UNEXPECTED_PROBLEM
  = "UnexpectedProblem";

  private DocumentBuilder   parser;
  private DOMImplementation impl;
  private Transformer       idTransform;

  // Load a parser, transformer, and implementation
  public void init() throws ServletException {
```

```
    try {
      DocumentBuilderFactory factory
       = DocumentBuilderFactory.newInstance();
      // Always turn on namespace awareness
      factory.setNamespaceAware(true);

      this.parser = factory.newDocumentBuilder();
      this.impl   = parser.getDOMImplementation();

    }
    catch (Throwable t) {
      throw new ServletException(
       "Could not locate a JAXP parser", t);
    }

    try {
      TransformerFactory xformFactory =
       TransformerFactory.newInstance();
      this.idTransform = xformFactory.newTransformer();
    }
    catch (Throwable t) {
      throw new ServletException(
       "Could not locate a JAXP transformer", t);
    }

  }

  public void doPost(HttpServletRequest servletRequest,
   HttpServletResponse servletResponse)
   throws ServletException, IOException {

    servletResponse.setContentType("text/xml; charset=UTF-8");
    PrintWriter out = servletResponse.getWriter();
    InputStream in  = servletRequest.getInputStream();

    Document request;
    Document response;
    String generations ="here";
    try {
      request = parser.parse(in);
```

```
    NodeList ints = request.getElementsByTagNameNS(
     "http://namespaces.cafeconleche.org/xmljava/ch3/",
     "calculateFibonacci");
    Node input = ints.item(0);
    generations = getFullText(input);
    int numberOfGenerations = Integer.parseInt(generations);
    BigInteger result = calculateFibonacci(numberOfGenerations);
    response = makeResponseDocument(result);
  }
  catch (SAXException e) {
    response = makeFaultDocument(MALFORMED_REQUEST_DOCUMENT,
     e.getMessage());
  }
  catch (NullPointerException e) {
    response = makeFaultDocument(INDEX_MISSING,
     e.getMessage());
  }
  catch (NumberFormatException e) {
    response = makeFaultDocument(BAD_INTEGER_FORMAT,
     generations + e.getMessage());
  }
  catch (IndexOutOfBoundsException e) {
    response = makeFaultDocument(NON_POSITIVE_INDEX,
     e.getMessage());
  }
  catch (Exception e) {
    response = makeFaultDocument(UNEXPECTED_PROBLEM,
     e.getMessage());
  }

  // Transform onto the OutputStream
  try {
    Source input = new DOMSource(response);
    Result output = new StreamResult(out);
    idTransform.transform(input, output);
    servletResponse.flushBuffer();
    out.flush();

    out.println();
  }
  catch (TransformerException e) {
```

```
      // If we get an exception at this point, it's too late to
      // switch over to a SOAP fault
      throw new ServletException(e);
    }

  }

  private static String getFullText(Node node) {

    StringBuffer result = new StringBuffer();

    NodeList children = node.getChildNodes();
    for (int i = 0; i < children.getLength(); i++) {
      Node child = children.item(i);
      int type = child.getNodeType();
      if (type == Node.TEXT_NODE
       || type == Node.CDATA_SECTION_NODE) {
        result.append(child.getNodeValue());
      }
    }

    return result.toString();

  }

  // The details of the formats and namespace URIs are likely to
  // change when SOAP 1.2 is released.
  public Document makeResponseDocument(BigInteger result) {

    Document response
     = impl.createDocument(
      "http://schemas.xmlsoap.org/soap/envelope/",
      "SOAP-ENV:Envelope", null);

    Element envelope = response.getDocumentElement();
    Element body = response.createElementNS(
     "http://schemas.xmlsoap.org/soap/envelope/",
     "SOAP-ENV:Body");
    envelope.appendChild(body);

    Element Fibonacci_Numbers = response.createElementNS(
```

```
     "http://namespaces.cafeconleche.org/xmljava/ch3/",
     "Fibonacci_Numbers");
    body.appendChild(Fibonacci_Numbers);

    Element fibonacci = response.createElementNS(
     "http://namespaces.cafeconleche.org/xmljava/ch3/",
     "fibonacci");
    Fibonacci_Numbers.appendChild(fibonacci);

    Text text = response.createTextNode(result.toString());
    fibonacci.appendChild(text);

    return response;

  }

  public Document makeFaultDocument(String code, String message){

    Document faultDoc = impl.createDocument(
      "http://schemas.xmlsoap.org/soap/envelope/",
      "SOAP-ENV:Envelope", null);

    Element envelope = faultDoc.getDocumentElement();

    Element body = faultDoc.createElementNS(
     "http://schemas.xmlsoap.org/soap/envelope/",
     "SOAP-ENV:Body");
    envelope.appendChild(body);

    Element fault = faultDoc.createElementNS(
     "http://schemas.xmlsoap.org/soap/envelope/", "Fault");
    body.appendChild(fault);

    Element faultCode = faultDoc.createElement("faultcode");
    fault.appendChild(faultCode);

    Element faultString = faultDoc.createElement("faultstring");
    fault.appendChild(faultString);

    Text textCode = faultDoc.createTextNode(code);
    faultCode.appendChild(textCode);
```

```
      Text textString = faultDoc.createTextNode(message);
      faultString.appendChild(textString);

      return faultDoc;

    }

    public static BigInteger calculateFibonacci(int generations)
     throws IndexOutOfBoundsException {

      if (generations < 1) {
        throw new IndexOutOfBoundsException(
         "Fibonacci numbers are not defined for " + generations
         + "or any other number less than one.");
      }
      BigInteger low  = BigInteger.ONE;
      BigInteger high = BigInteger.ONE;
      for (int i = 2; i <= generations; i++) {
        BigInteger temp = high;
        high = high.add(low);
        low = temp;
      }
      return low;

    }

  }
```

This example has the same basic structure as the XML-RPC version (Example 10.13). That is, the `init()` method loads the parser, DOM implementation, and identity transform. The `doPost()` method reads the request data and delegates building the request to the `makeResponseDocument()` method. If anything goes wrong, `makeFaultDocument()` is called to produce a properly formatted SOAP fault response. Finally, a JAXP ID transform serializes the response onto the network stream. The formats of the request and response are a little different, but the program flow is the same.

I did structure the building of the two response documents (success and fault) a little differently. `FibonacciXMLRPCServlet` built all of the nodes first and then connected them. Here I added them to the tree as soon as they were created. There's not a lot of reason to choose one way over the other—just use whichever seems more natural to you.

The details can be a little opaque. In a real-world program, I'd definitely add some comments containing an example of the documents that each method builds. If you're building a lot of XML-RPC or SOAP documents with varying parameters, then it wouldn't hurt to either develop a more generic library, or buy or borrow a third-party library such as Apache SOAP *[http://xml.apache.org/soap/docs/index.html]*. Behind the scenes, they're doing something very similar to what I've done in Example 10.13 and Example 10.14.

Transferring Nodes between Documents

In DOM, every node belongs to exactly one document at all times. It cannot exist independently of a `Document`, and it cannot be part of more than one `Document` at the same time. This is why the `Document` interface serves as the factory for creating node objects of various kinds. Furthermore, in DOM2, a node cannot be detached from its original document and placed in a new document, although this restriction is loosened somewhat in DOM3.

Copying Nodes

The `importNode()` method makes a copy of a node found in another document. The copy can then be inserted in the importing document's tree using the usual methods, such as `insertBefore()` and `appendChild()`. The document from which the node is imported is not changed in any way.

```
public Node importNode (Node toBeImported, boolean deep)
 throws DOMException
```

The *deep* argument determines whether or not all of the node's descendants are copied with it. If true, they are; if false, they aren't.

Document and document type nodes cannot be imported. Trying to import one will throw a `DOMException`. Entity and notation nodes can be imported but cannot be added as children of the importing document's document type node. Thus there's little reason to import them.

Most of the other kinds of nodes can be imported with pretty much the results you'd expect. (Just remember to pass true for the second argument. This is almost always what you want.) The only really tricky ones are entity reference nodes. Even if *deep* is true, the children of the entity reference node are not copied. Instead the replacement text (node list) of the imported entity reference depends on what the importing document's DTD says it is, not the original replacement text.

Moving Nodes

DOM3 adds an `adoptNode()` method that moves a node from one document to another. That is, it deletes the node from the original document and inserts it into the new document:

```
public Node adoptNode (Node adoptee) throws DOMException
```

Adopted nodes are always moved with all of their descendants intact. Otherwise, this method behaves pretty much like `importNode`. That is, document nodes, document type nodes, notation nodes, and entity nodes cannot be adopted. All other kinds can be. Descendants of entity reference nodes are deleted from the original document but not copied into the new document.

As usual with DOM3 methods, this is beyond the bleeding edge. The latest versions of Xerces support it, but no other parsers do. There also remain a lot of unresolved issues concerning the behavior of this method, so I wouldn't rely on it. For the time being, it's better to use a two-step procedure in which a node is first copied into the new document with `importNode()` and then deleted from the original document with `removeChild()`.

Normalization

Implementations have quite a bit of leeway in exactly how they parse and serialize any given document. For example, a parser may represent CDATA sections as `CDATASection` objects, or it may merge them into neighboring `Text` objects. A parser may include entity reference nodes in the tree, or it may instead include the nodes corresponding to each entity's replacement text. A parser may include comments, or it may ignore them. DOM3 adds four methods to the `Document` interface to control exactly how a parser makes these choices:

```
public void normalizeDocument()

public boolean canSetNormalizationFeature (String name,
 boolean state)

public void setNormalizationFeature (String name, boolean state)

public boolean getNormalizationFeature (String name)
```

The `canSetNormalizationFeature()` method tests whether the implementation supports the desired value (true or false) for the named feature. The `setNormalizationFeature()` method sets the value of the named feature. It throws a `DOMException` with the error code `NOT_FOUND_ERR` if the implementation does not support the feature at all. It throws a `DOMException` with the error code `NOT_SUPPORTED_ERR` if the implementation does not support the requested value for the feature (for example, if you try to set to true a feature that must have the value false). Finally, after all of the features have been set, client code can invoke the `normalizeDocument()` method to modify the tree in accordance with the current values for all of the different features.

> **Caution**
> These are very bleeding-edge ideas from the latest DOM3 Core Working Draft. Xerces 2.0.2 is the only parser that supports any of this so far.

The DOM3 specification defines 13 standard features:

normalize-characters, optional, default false
If true, document text should be normalized according to the W3C Character Model. For example, the word *resumé* would be represented as the six-character string *r e s u m é* rather than the seven-character string *r e s u m e combining_'*. Implementations are only required to support a false value for this feature.

split-cdata-sections, required, default true
If true, CDATA sections containing the CDATA section end delimiter `]]>` are split into pieces, and the `]]>` is included in a raw text node. If false, such a CDATA section is not split.

entities, optional, default true
If false, entity reference nodes are replaced by their children. If true, they're not.

whitespace-in-element-content, optional, default true
If true, all white space is retained. If false, text nodes containing only white space are deleted if the parent element's declaration from the DTD/schema does not allow #PCDATA to appear at that point.

discard-default-content, required, default true
If true, the implementation throws away any nodes whose presence can be inferred from the DTD or schema; for example, default attribute values.

canonical-form, optional, default false
If true, the document is arranged according to the rules of the canonical XML specification, at least within the limits of what can be represented in a DOM implementation. For example, `EntityReference` nodes are replaced by their

content, and `CDATASection` objects are converted to `Text` objects. However, there's no way in DOM to control everything that the canonical XML specification requires. For instance, a DOM `Element` does not know the order of its attributes or whether an empty element will be written as a single empty-element tag or start-tag/end-tag pair. Thus, full canonicalization has to be deferred to serialization time.

namespace-declarations, optional, default true
If false, then all `Attr` nodes representing namespace declarations are deleted from the tree. Otherwise they're retained. This has no effect on the namespaces associated with individual elements and attributes.

validate, optional, default false
If true, then the document's schema or DTD is used to validate the document as it is being normalized. Any validation errors that are discovered are reported to the registered error handler. (Both validation and error handlers are new features in DOM3.)

validate-if-schema, optional, default false
If true and the validation feature is also true, then the document is validated if and only if it has a some kind of schema (for example, DTD, W3C XML Schema Language schema, or RELAX NG schema).

datatype-normalization, required, default false
If true, datatype normalization is performed according to the schema. For example, an element declared to have type `xsd:boolean` and represented as `<state>1</state>` could be changed to `<state>true</state>`.

cdata-sections, optional, default true
If false, all `CDATASection` objects are changed into `Text` objects and merged with any adjacent `Text` objects. If true, each CDATA section is represented as its own `CDATASection` object.

comments, required, default true
If true, comments are included in the `Document`; if false, they're not.

infoset, optional
If true, the `Document` only contains information provided by the XML Infoset. This is the same as setting namespace-declarations, validate-if-schema, entities, and cdata-sections to false; and datatype-normalization, whitespace-in-element-content, and comments to true.

In addition, vendors are allowed to define their own nonstandard features. Feature names must be XML 1.0 names and should use a vendor-specific prefix such as `apache:` or `oracle:`.

For an example of how these could be useful, consider the SOAP servlet in Example 10.14. It needed to locate the `calculateFibonacci` element in the request document and extract its full text content. This had to work even if that element contained comments and CDATA sections. The `getFullText()` method that accomplished this wasn't too hard to write. Nonetheless, in DOM3 it's even easier. Set the create-cdata-nodes and comments features to false and call `normalizeDocument()` as soon as the document is parsed. Once this is done, the `calculateFibonacci` element contains only one text-node child.

```
try {
    Document request = parser.parse(in);
    request.setNormalizationFeature("create-cdata-nodes", false);
    request.setNormalizationFeature("comments", false);
    request.normalizeDocument();

    NodeList ints = request.getElementsByTagNameNS(
      "http://namespaces.cafeconleche.org/xmljava/ch3/",
      "calculateFibonacci");
    Node calculateFibonacci = ints.item(0);
    Node text = calculateFibonacci.getFirstChild();
    String generations = text.getNodeValue();
    // ...
}
catch (DOMException e) {
  // The create-cdata-nodes features is true by default and
  // parsers aren't required to support a false value for it, so
  // you should be prepared to fall back on manual normalization
  // if necessary. The comments feature, however, is required.
}
```

This wouldn't work for the XML-RPC case, however, because XML-RPC documents can contain processing instructions, and there's no feature to turn off processing instructions.

Summary

DOM is designed around the abstract-factory design pattern. The DOMImplementation interface is the abstract factory that creates implementation-specific instances of the Document and DocumentType interfaces. A vendor-specific DOMImplementation object can be retrieved by JAXP, by vendor-specific classes, or by the DOMImplementationRegistry class in DOM3.

The Document interface is in turn an abstract factory that creates implementation-specific instances of Element, Text, Comment, Attr, ProcessingInstruction, EntityReference, CDATASection, and DocumentFragment. Each instance of these classes can only be part of the Document that created it. However, the Document interface also has an importNode() method that copies a node from one document to another.

The Document interface is also DOM's representation of the root node of the tree. It provides methods to get the implementation that created the Document object, get the root element of the document, get the DOCTYPE of the document, import nodes into the document from other documents, and find elements by name, namespace, and ID. This last capability is often enough for many simple search applications.

Finally, don't forget that Document is a subinterface of Node and has all of the methods of that interface discussed in Chapter 9. This is crucial for adding content to documents and removing content from documents, especially at the top level outside the root element.

Chapter 11

The DOM Core

Chapters 9 and 10 considered a DOM document as primarily a tree of nodes—that is, as composed of instances of the `Node` interface. Indeed, for many purposes this is all you need to know. But not all nodes are the same. Elements have properties that attributes don't have. Attributes have properties that processing instructions don't have. Processing instructions have properties that comments don't have, and so forth. In this chapter, we look at the unique properties and methods of the individual interfaces that make up an XML document.

The Element Interface

The `Element` interface is perhaps the most important of all the DOM component interfaces. After all, it's possible to write XML documents without any comments, processing instructions, attributes, CDATA sections, entity references, or even text nodes. By contrast, every XML document has at least one element, and most XML documents have many more. Elements, more than any other component, define the structure of an XML document.

Example 11.1 summarizes the `Element` interface. This interface includes methods to get the prefixed name of the element, manipulate the attributes on the element, and select from the element's descendants. Of course, `Element` objects also have all the methods of the `Node` superinterface, such as `appendChild()` and `getNamespaceURI()`.

Example 11.1 The Element Interface

```
package org.w3c.dom;

public interface Element extends Node {

  public String  getTagName();

  public boolean hasAttribute(String name);
  public boolean hasAttributeNS(String namespaceURI,
   String localName);
  public String  getAttribute(String name);
  public void    setAttribute(String name, String value)
   throws DOMException;
  public void    removeAttribute(String name)
   throws DOMException;
  public Attr    getAttributeNode(String name);
  public Attr    setAttributeNode(Attr newAttr)
   throws DOMException;
  public Attr    removeAttributeNode(Attr oldAttr)
   throws DOMException;
  public String  getAttributeNS(String namespaceURI,
   String localName);
  public void    setAttributeNS(String namespaceURI,
   String qualifiedName, String value) throws DOMException;
  public void    removeAttributeNS(String namespaceURI,
   String localName) throws DOMException;
  public Attr    getAttributeNodeNS(String namespaceURI,
   String localName);
  public Attr    setAttributeNodeNS(Attr newAttr)
   throws DOMException;

  public NodeList getElementsByTagName(String name);
  public NodeList getElementsByTagNameNS(String namespaceURI,
   String localName);

}
```

The aesthetics of this interface are seriously marred by DOM's requirement to avoid method overloading. The differences in the argument lists are redundantly repeated in the method names. For example, if DOM had been written in pure

Java, then there would probably be three setAttribute() methods with these signatures:

```
public void setAttribute (String name, String value)
 throws DOMException

public void setAttribute (String namespaceURI, String localName,
 String value) throws DOMException

public void setAttribute (Attr attribute) throws DOMException
```

Instead, Element has these four methods with slightly varied names:

```
public void setAttribute (String name, String value)
 throws DOMException

public void setAttributeNS (String namespaceURI, String localName,
 String value) throws DOMException

public void setAttributeNode (Attr attribute) throws DOMException

public void setAttributeNodeNS (Attr attribute)
 throws DOMException
```

The distinction between setAttributeNode() and setAttributeNodeNS is unnecessary. setAttributeNode() is used only with attributes in no namespace, whereas setAttributeNodeNS() is used only with attributes in a namespace. The only motivation I can imagine for this is symmetry with the getter methods, where the distinction is relevant because the argument lists are different. For the setter methods, however, this is frankly a mistake. Attr objects include their own namespace information. There's no need for separate methods to set nodes with and without namespaces.

Extracting Elements

The getElementsByTagName() and getElementsByTagNameNS() methods behave the same as the similarly named methods in the Document interface discussed in Chapter 10. The only difference is that they search through a single element rather than the entire document. These methods return a NodeList that contains all of the elements with the specified name.

An asterisk (*) can be passed as either argument to indicate that all names or namespaces are desired. This is particularly useful for the local name passed to getElementsByTagNameNS(). For example, the following NodeList would contain all RDF elements that are descendants of element:

```
NodeList rdfs = element.getElementsByTagNameNS(
 "http://www.w3.org/1999/02/22-rdf-syntax-ns#", "*");
```

The list returned is sorted in document order. In other words, elements are arranged in order of the appearance of their start-tags. If the start-tag for element A appears earlier in the document than the start-tag for element B, then element A comes before element B in the list.

The next example was inspired by the source code for this very book. Prior to publication, I needed to extract all of the code examples from the source text and put them in separate directories by chapter. That is, the examples from Chapter 1 went into examples/1; the examples from Chapter 2 went into examples/2; and so forth. XSLT 1.0 isn't quite up to this task, but DOM and Java are more powerful.[1]

The source code for this book is structured as follows:

```
<book>
  ...
  <chapter>
    ...
    <example id="filename.java">
      <title>Some Java Program</title>
      <programlisting>import javax.xml.parsers;
        // more Java code...
      </programlisting>
    </example>
    ...
    <example id="filename.xml">
      <title>Some XML document</title>
      <programlisting><![CDATA[<?xml version="1.0"?>
<root>
  ...
</root>]]></programlisting>
     </example>
    ...
  </chapter>
  more chapters...
</book>
```

At least, that's the part which is relevant to this example. The advantage to `getElementsByTagName()` and `getElementsByTagNameNS()` is that a program can extract just the parts that interest it very straightforwardly and without explicitly walking the entire tree.[2] These methods effectively flatten the hierarchy to just the

1. XSLT 2.0 could handle this, and many XSLT engines include extension functions that could pull this off in XSLT 1.0. But I needed the example. :-)

elements of interest. In this case, those elements are `chapter` and `example`. Inside each `example`, the complete structure is somewhat more relevant; therefore, the normal tree-walking methods of `Node` are indicated.

The program follows these steps:

1. Parse the entire book into a `Document` object.
2. Use `Document`'s `getElementsByTagName()` method to retrieve a list of all `chapter` elements in the document. (DocBook doesn't use namespaces, so `getElementsByTagName()` is chosen over `getElementsByTagNameNS()`.)
3. For each element in that list, use `Element`'s `getElementsByTagName()` method to retrieve a list of all `example` elements in that chapter.
4. From each element in that list, extract its `programlisting` child element.
5. Write the text content of that `programlisting` element into a new file named by the ID of the `example` element.

This example is quite specific to one XML application, DocBook. Indeed it won't even work with all DocBook documents because it relies on various private conventions of this specific DocBook document, in particular that the `id` attribute of each `example` element contains a file name. But that's all right. Most programs you write will be designed to process only certain XML documents in certain situations.

To increase robustness, I do require that the DocBook document be valid, and the parser does validate the document. If validation fails, this program aborts without extracting the examples, because it can't be sure whether the document meets the preconditions. Example 11.2 demonstrates.

Example 11.2 Extracting Examples from DocBook

```
import javax.xml.parsers.*;
import org.w3c.dom.*;
import org.xml.sax.*;
import java.io.*;
```

2. A naive DOM implementation probably would implement `getElementsByTagName()` and `getElementsByTagNameNS()` by walking the tree or subtree, but there also exist more efficient implementations based on detailed knowledge of the data structures that implement the various interfaces. For example, a DOM that sits on top of a native XML database might have access to an index of all the elements in the document.

```
public class ExampleExtractor {

  public static void extract(Document doc) throws IOException {

    NodeList chapters = doc.getElementsByTagName("chapter");

    for (int i = 0; i < chapters.getLength(); i++) {

      Element chapter = (Element) chapters.item(i);
      NodeList examples = chapter.getElementsByTagName("example");

      for (int j = 0; j < examples.getLength(); j++) {

        Element example = (Element) examples.item(j);
        String fileName = example.getAttribute("id");
        // All examples should have id attributes, but it's safer
        // not to assume that
        if (fileName == null) {
          throw
           new IllegalArgumentException("Missing id on example");
        }
        NodeList programlistings
         = example.getElementsByTagName("programlisting");
        // Each example is supposed to contain exactly one
        // programlisting, but we should verify that
        if (programlistings.getLength() != 1) {
          throw new
           IllegalArgumentException("Missing programlisting");
        }
        Element programlisting = (Element) programlistings.item(0);

        // Extract text content; this is a little tricky because
        // these often contain CDATA sections and entity
        // references which can be represented as separate nodes,
        // so we can't just ask for the first text node child of
        // each program listing.
        String code = getText(programlisting);

        // write code into a file
        File dir = new File("examples2/" + i);
```

```
        dir.mkdirs();
        File file = new File(dir, fileName);
        System.out.println(file);
        FileOutputStream fout = new FileOutputStream(file);
        Writer out = new OutputStreamWriter(fout, "UTF-8");
        // Buffering almost always helps performance a lot
        out = new BufferedWriter(out);
        out.write(code);
        // Remember to flush and close your streams
        out.flush();
        out.close();

      } // end examples loop

    } // end chapters loop

  }

  public static String getText(Node node) {

    // We need to retrieve the text from elements, entity
    // references, CDATA sections, and text nodes; but not
    // comments or processing instructions
    int type = node.getNodeType();
    if (type == Node.COMMENT_NODE
     || type == Node.PROCESSING_INSTRUCTION_NODE) {
       return "";
    }

    StringBuffer text = new StringBuffer();

    String value = node.getNodeValue();
    if (value != null) text.append(value);
    if (node.hasChildNodes()) {
      NodeList children = node.getChildNodes();
      for (int i = 0; i < children.getLength(); i++) {
        Node child = children.item(i);
        text.append(getText(child));
      }
    }
```

```
    return text.toString();

  }

  public static void main(String[] args) {

    if (args.length <= 0) {
      System.out.println("Usage: java ExampleExtractor URL");
      return;
    }
    String url = args[0];

    try {
      DocumentBuilderFactory factory
       = DocumentBuilderFactory.newInstance();
      factory.setValidating(true);

      DocumentBuilder parser = factory.newDocumentBuilder();
      parser.setErrorHandler(new ValidityRequired());

      // Read the document
     Document document = parser.parse(url);

     // Extract the examples
     extract(document);

    }
    catch (SAXException e) {
      System.out.println(e);
    }
    catch (IOException e) {
      System.out.println(
       "Due to an IOException, the parser could not read " + url
      );
      System.out.println(e);
    }
    catch (FactoryConfigurationError e) {
      System.out.println("Could not locate a factory class");
    }
    catch (ParserConfigurationException e) {
      System.out.println("Could not locate a JAXP parser");
    }
```

```
    } // end main

  }

  // Make validity errors fatal
  class ValidityRequired implements ErrorHandler {

    public void warning(SAXParseException e)
      throws SAXException {
      // ignore warnings
    }

    public void error(SAXParseException e)
     throws SAXException {
      // Mostly validity errors. Make them fatal.
      throw e;
    }

    public void fatalError(SAXParseException e)
     throws SAXException {
      throw e;
    }

  }
```

Because `ExampleExtractor` is fairly involved, I've factored it into several relatively independent pieces. The `main()` method builds the document and parses the document as usual. The nonpublic class `ValidityRequired` more or less converts all errors into fatal errors by rethrowing the exception passed to it. Assuming validation succeeds, the document is then passed to the `extract()` method.

The `extract()` method iterates through all the `chapters` and `examples` in the book using `getElementsByTagName()`. Each `example` is supposed to have an `id` attribute and a single `programlisting` child element, but because this is just a convention for this one document rather than a rule enforced by the DTD, the code checks to make sure that's true. If it isn't true, then the code throws an `IllegalArgumentException`.

Next comes one of the trickiest parts of working with elements in DOM. I need to extract the text content of the `programlisting` element. This sounds simple enough, except that there's no method in either `Element` or `Node` that performs this routine task. You might expect `getNodeValue()` to do this, especially if you're accustomed to XPath. But in DOM, unlike XPath, the value of an element is null. Only its children have values. Thus I need to descend recursively through the children of the `programlisting` element, accumulating the values of all text nodes, entity references, CDATA sections, and other elements as I go. The `getText()` method accomplishes this.

Once I have the actual example code from the `programlisting` element, it can be written into a file. The file location is relative to the current working directory and the chapter number. The file name is read from the `id` attribute. UTF-8 works well as the default encoding.

Attributes

Although DOM has an `Attr` interface, the `Element` interface is the primary means of reading and writing attributes. Because each element can have no more than one attribute with the same name, attributes can be stored and retrieved just by their names. There's no need to manage complex list structures, as there is with other kinds of nodes.

Here are a few tips that help explain how the attribute methods work in DOM:

- Most attributes are not in any namespace. In particular, unprefixed attributes are never in any namespace. For these attributes, simply use the name and value.
- When setting attributes that are in a namespace, specify the prefixed name and URI. Specify the local name and the namespace URI when getting them.
- Getting the value of a nonexistent attribute returns the empty string.
- Setting an attribute that already exists changes the value of the existing attribute.

With these few principles in mind, it's not complicated to write programs that read attributes. I'll demonstrate by revising the Fibonacci program from Example 10.6. That example just used elements. Now I'll add an `index` attribute to each `fibonacci` element, as shown in Example 11.3.

Example 11.3 A Document That Uses Attributes

```
<?xml version="1.0"?>
<Fibonacci_Numbers>
  <fibonacci index="1">1</fibonacci>
  <fibonacci index="2">1</fibonacci>
  <fibonacci index="3">2</fibonacci>
  <fibonacci index="4">3</fibonacci>
  <fibonacci index="5">5</fibonacci>
  <fibonacci index="6">8</fibonacci>
  <fibonacci index="7">13</fibonacci>
  <fibonacci index="8">21</fibonacci>
  <fibonacci index="9">34</fibonacci>
  <fibonacci index="10">55</fibonacci>
</Fibonacci_Numbers>
```

This is quite simple to implement. You just need to calculate a string name and value for the attribute and call `setAttribute()` in the right place. Example 11.4 demonstrates.

Example 11.4 A DOM Program That Adds Attributes

```
import org.w3c.dom.*;
import javax.xml.parsers.*;
import javax.xml.transform.*;
import javax.xml.transform.dom.DOMSource;
import javax.xml.transform.stream.StreamResult;
import java.math.BigInteger;


public class FibonacciAttributeDOM {

  public static void main(String[] args) {

    try {

      // Find the implementation
      DocumentBuilderFactory factory
       = DocumentBuilderFactory.newInstance();
```

```
      factory.setNamespaceAware(true);
      DocumentBuilder builder = factory.newDocumentBuilder();
      DOMImplementation impl = builder.getDOMImplementation();

      // Create the document
      Document doc = impl.createDocument(null,
       "Fibonacci_Numbers", null);

      // Fill the document
      BigInteger low  = BigInteger.ONE;
      BigInteger high = BigInteger.ONE;

      Element root = doc.getDocumentElement();

      for (int i = 0; i < 10; i++) {
        Element number = doc.createElement("fibonacci");
        String value = Integer.toString(i);
        number.setAttribute("index", value);
        Text text = doc.createTextNode(low.toString());
        number.appendChild(text);
        root.appendChild(number);

        BigInteger temp = high;
        high = high.add(low);
        low = temp;
      }

      // Serialize the document onto System.out
      TransformerFactory xformFactory
       = TransformerFactory.newInstance();
      Transformer idTransform = xformFactory.newTransformer();
      Source input = new DOMSource(doc);
      Result output = new StreamResult(System.out);
      idTransform.transform(input, output);

    }
    catch (FactoryConfigurationError e) {
      System.out.println("Could not locate a JAXP factory class");
    }
    catch (ParserConfigurationException e) {
      System.out.println(
```

```
          "Could not locate a JAXP DocumentBuilder class"
        );
      }
      catch (DOMException e) {
        System.err.println(e);
      }
      catch (TransformerConfigurationException e) {
        System.err.println(e);
      }
      catch (TransformerException e) {
        System.err.println(e);
      }

    }

  }
```

The NamedNodeMap Interface

If for some reason you want all the attributes of an element or you don't know their names, you can use the `getAttributes()` method to retrieve a `NamedNodeMap` inherited from the `Node`.[3] The `NamedNodeMap` interface, summarized in Example 11.5, has methods to get and set the various named nodes as well as to iterate through the nodes as a list. Here it's used for attributes, but soon you'll see it used for notations and entities as well.

Example 11.5 The NamedNodeMap Interface

```
package org.w3c.dom;

public interface NamedNodeMap {

  // for iterating through the map as a list
  public Node item(int index);
  public int  getLength();
```

3. Why `getAttributes()` is in `Node` instead of `Element` I have no idea. Elements are the only kind of node that can have attributes. For all other types of node, `get-Attributes()` returns null.

```
  // For working with particular items in the list
  public Node getNamedItem(String name);
  public Node setNamedItem(Node arg) throws DOMException;
  public Node removeNamedItem(String name)
   throws DOMException;
  public Node getNamedItemNS(String namespaceURI,
   String localName);
  public Node setNamedItemNS(Node arg) throws DOMException;
  public Node removeNamedItemNS(String namespaceURI,
   String localName) throws DOMException;

}
```

I'll demonstrate with an XLink spider program like the one in Chapter 6—this time implementing the program on top of DOM rather than SAX. You can judge for yourself which one is more natural.

Recall that XLink is an attribute-based syntax for denoting connections between documents. The element that is the link has an `xlink:type` attribute with the value `simple`, and an `xlink:href` attribute whose value is the URL of the remote document. For example, the following `book` element points to this book's home page:

```
<book xlink:type="simple"
      xlink:href="http://www.cafeconleche.org/books/xmljava/"
      xmlns:xlink="http://www.w3.org/1999/xlink">
  Processing XML with Java
</book>
```

The customary prefix `xlink` is bound to the namespace URI `http://www.w3.org/1999/xlink`. It's usually advisable to depend on the URI and not the prefix, which may change.

Relative URLs are relative to the nearest ancestor `xml:base` attribute if one is present, or the location of the document otherwise. For example, the `book` element in this `library` element also points to *http://www.cafeconleche.org/books/xmljava/*.

```
<library xml:base="http://www.cafeconleche.org/"
         xmlns:xlink="http://www.w3.org/1999/xlink">
  <book xlink:type="simple" xlink:href="books/xmljava/">
    Processing XML with Java
  </book>
</library>
```

The prefix `xml` is bound to the namespace URI `http://www.w3.org/XML/1998/namespace`. This is a special case, however. The `xml` prefix cannot be changed, and it does not need to be declared.

Attributes provide all of the information needed to process the link. Consequently, a spider can follow XLinks without knowing any details about the rest of the markup in the document. Example 11.6 is such a program. Currently this spider does nothing more than follow the links and print their URLs. It would not be hard to add code to load the discovered documents into a database or perform some other useful operation, however. You would simply subclass `DOMSpider` while overriding the `process()` method.

Example 11.6 An XLink Spider That Uses DOM

```
import org.xml.sax.SAXException;
import javax.xml.parsers.*;
import java.io.*;
import java.util.*;
import java.net.*;
import org.w3c.dom.*;


public class DOMSpider {

  public static String XLINK_NAMESPACE
   = "http://www.w3.org/1999/xlink";

  // This will be used to read all the documents. We could use
  // multiple parsers in parallel. However, it's a lot easier
  // to work in a single thread, and doing so puts some real
  // limits on how much bandwidth this program will eat.
  private DocumentBuilder parser;

  // Builds the parser
  public DOMSpider() throws ParserConfigurationException {

    try {
      DocumentBuilderFactory factory
       = DocumentBuilderFactory.newInstance();
      factory.setNamespaceAware(true);
      parser = factory.newDocumentBuilder();
    }
```

```
  catch (FactoryConfigurationError e) {
    // I don't absolutely need to catch this, but I hate to
    // throw an Error for no good reason.
    throw new ParserConfigurationException(
     "Could not locate a factory class");
  }

}

// store the URLs already visited
private Vector visited = new Vector();

// Limit the amount of bandwidth this program uses
private int maxDepth = 5;
private int currentDepth = 0;

public void spider(String systemID) {
  currentDepth++;
  try {
    if (currentDepth < maxDepth) {
      Document document = parser.parse(systemID);
      process(document, systemID);

      Vector toBeVisited = new Vector();
      // search the document for URIs,
      // store them in vector, and print them
      findLinks(document.getDocumentElement(),
       toBeVisited, systemID);

      Enumeration e = toBeVisited.elements();
      while (e.hasMoreElements()) {
        String uri = (String) e.nextElement();
        visited.add(uri);
        spider(uri);
      }

    }

  }
  catch (SAXException e) {
    // Couldn't load the document,
```

```
      // probably not well-formed XML, skip it
    }
    catch (IOException e) {
      // Couldn't load the document,
      // likely network failure, skip it
    }
    finally {
      currentDepth--;
      System.out.flush();
    }

  }

  public void process(Document document, String uri) {
    System.out.println(uri);
  }

  // Recursively descend the tree of one document
  private void findLinks(Element element, List uris,
   String base) {

    // Check for an xml:base attribute
    String baseAtt = element.getAttribute("xml:base");
    if (!baseAtt.equals(""))  base = baseAtt;

    // look for XLinks in this element
    if (isSimpleLink(element)) {
      String uri
       = element.getAttributeNS(XLINK_NAMESPACE, "href");
      if (!uri.equals("")) {
        try {
          String wholePage = absolutize(base, uri);
          if (!visited.contains(wholePage)
           && !uris.contains(wholePage)) {
            uris.add(wholePage);
          }
        }
        catch (MalformedURLException e) {
          // If it's not a good URL, then we can't spider it
          // anyway, so just drop it on the floor.
        }
```

```
      } // end if
    } // end if

    // process child elements recursively
    NodeList children = element.getChildNodes();
    for (int i = 0; i < children.getLength(); i++) {
      Node node = children.item(i);
      int type = node.getNodeType();
      if (type == Node.ELEMENT_NODE) {
        findLinks((Element) node, uris, base);
      }
    } // end for

  }

  // If you're willing to require Java 1.4, you can do better
  // than this with the new java.net.URI class
  private static String absolutize(String context, String uri)
   throws MalformedURLException {

    URL contextURL = new URL(context);
    URL url = new URL(contextURL, uri);
    // Remove fragment identifier if any
    String wholePage = url.toExternalForm();
    int fragmentSeparator = wholePage.indexOf('#');
    if (fragmentSeparator != -1) {
      // There is a fragment identifier
      wholePage = wholePage.substring(0, fragmentSeparator);
    }
    return wholePage;

  }

  private static boolean isSimpleLink(Element element) {

    String type
     = element.getAttributeNS(XLINK_NAMESPACE, "type");
    if (type.equals("simple")) return true;
    return false;

  }
```

```
    public static void main(String[] args) {

      if (args.length == 0) {
        System.out.println("Usage: java DOMSpider topURL");
        return;
      }

      // start parsing...
      try {
        DOMSpider spider = new DOMSpider();
        spider.spider(args[0]);
      }
      catch (Exception e) {
        System.err.println(e);
        e.printStackTrace();
      }

    } // end main

  } // end DOMSpider
```

There are two levels of recursion here. The `spider()` method recursively spiders documents. The `findLinks()` method recursively searches through the elements in a document looking for XLinks. It adds the URLs found in these links to a list of unvisited pages. As each of these documents is finished, the next document is retrieved from the list and processed in turn. If it's an XML document, then it is parsed and passed to the `process()` method. Non-XML documents found at the end of XLinks are ignored.

I tested this program by pointing it at the Resource Directory Description Language (RDDL) *[http://www.rddl.org/]* specification, which is one of the few real-world documents I know of that uses XLinks. I was surprised to find out just how much XLinked XML there is out there, although as of yet most of it is simply more XML specifications. This must be what the Web felt like circa 1991. Here's a sample of the more interesting output:

```
D:\books\XMLJAVA>java DOMSpider http://www.rddl.org/
http://www.rddl.org/
http://www.rddl.org/purposes
http://www.rddl.org/purposes/software
http://www.rddl.org/rddl.rdfs
http://www.rddl.org/rddl-integration.rxg
```

```
http://www.rddl.org/modules/rddl-1.rxm
...
http://www.w3.org/2001/XMLSchema
http://www.w3.org/2001/XMLSchema.xsd
http://www.examplotron.org
http://www.examplotron.org/compile.xsl
http://www.examplotron.org/examplotron.xsd
http://www.examplotron.org/0/1/
http://www.examplotron.org/0/2/
http://www.examplotron.org/0/3/
http://webns.net/rdfs/
http://www.w3.org/2000/01/rdf-schema
http://webns.net/rdfs/?format=rdf
http://webns.net/foaf/
http://xmlns.com/foaf/0.1/
http://webns.net/foaf/?format=rdf
http://webns.net/dc/
http://purl.org/dc/elements/1.1/
http://webns.net/dc/?format=rdf
http://openhealth.org/XSet
http://xsltunit.org/0/1/
http://xsltunit.org/0/1/xsltunit.xsl
http://xsltunit.org/0/1/tst_library.xsl
http://xsltunit.org/0/1/library.xml
http://xsltunit.org/0/1/library.xsl
http://venetica.com/venicebridgecontent/
http://www.venetica.com/VeniceBridgeContent
http://www.venetica.com/VeniceBridgeContent/
 VeniceBridgeContent40.xsd
http://www.venetica.com/VeniceBridgeContent/VeniceBridgeContent.biz
http://www.venetica.com/VeniceBridgeContent/rddl30.html
http://www.w3.org/TR/xhtml-basic
http://www.w3.org/TR/xml-infoset/
http://www.w3.org/TR/xhtml-modularization/
```

The CharacterData Interface

The CharacterData interface is a generic superinterface for nodes that are composed mostly of text, including Text, CDATASection, and Comment. The CharacterData interface is almost never used directly. Rather, it is used as an instance of one of these three subinterfaces. But you almost always work with text, CDATA section, and comment nodes using the methods of the CharacterData interface.

Example 11.7 summarizes the CharacterData interface. This interface has methods that manipulate the text content of this node. As usual, it also inherits all the methods of its superinterface Node such as getParentNode() and getNodeValue().

Example 11.7 The CharacterData Interface

```
package org.w3c.dom;

public interface CharacterData extends Node {

  public String getData() throws DOMException;
  public void   setData(String data) throws DOMException;
  public int    getLength();
  public String substringData(int offset, int length)
   throws DOMException;
  public void   appendData(String data) throws DOMException;
  public void   insertData(int offset, String data)
   throws DOMException;
  public void   deleteData(int offset, int length)
   throws DOMException;
  public void   replaceData(int offset, int length, String data)
   throws DOMException;

}
```

The getData() method returns a String containing the complete content of the node. Any escaped characters such as & or   are replaced by the actual characters they represent. The setData() method replaces the entire text content of the node. There's no need to escape the string you pass to this method. If the document is written out to a file or a stream, then the serialization code is responsible for escaping these characters. In memory, the type of the object is enough to determine whether a less-than sign is the start of a tag or just a less-than sign.

There are also methods to read and write only parts of the text content. The offsets are all zero based, as in Java's String class. For example, the following code fragment deletes the first six characters from the CharacterData object text:

```
text.delete(0, 6);
```

Java's `String` type is a very good match for DOM strings. Each `char` in a Java `String` is a single UTF-16 code point. That is, most Unicode characters are represented by exactly one Java `char`. However, characters with code points greater than 65,535, such as many musical symbols, are represented by two `char`s each, one for each half of the surrogate pair representing the character in UTF-16. The `getLength()` method in this interface returns the number of UTF-16 code points, not the number of Unicode characters. This is also how the `length()` method in Java's `String` class behaves.

On Usenet, jokes that some people are likely to find offensive are often obscured by rotating the ASCII character set 13 places. That is, the first letter of the alphabet, A, is transformed into the fourteenth letter of the alphabet, N. The second letter of the alphabet, B, is transformed into the fifteenth letter of the alphabet, O, and so forth through M, which becomes Z. Then N is transformed into A, O into B, and so on through Z, which becomes M. It's not a particularly strong cipher, but it's enough to prevent people from accidentally reading something they don't want to read. It has the extra advantage of reversing itself. That is, running the cipher text through the rot-13 algorithm one more time restores the original text.

Example 11.8 is a simple program that obscures text nodes, comments, and CDATA sections by applying the rot-13 algorithm to them. The encoded documents are as well-formed and valid as the original documents. Only the character data gets changed, not the markup.[4] This program can also decode documents that are already encoded.

Example 11.8 Rot-13 Encoder for XML Documents

```
import javax.xml.parsers.*;
import javax.xml.transform.*;
import javax.xml.transform.stream.StreamResult;
import javax.xml.transform.dom.DOMSource;
import org.w3c.dom.*;
import org.xml.sax.SAXException;
import java.io.IOException;


public class ROT13XML {
```

4. `ROT13XML` could also encode attribute values and processing instructions without affecting well-formedness or validity, but because DOM does not represent these nodes as instances of `CharacterData`, I leave this as an exercise for the reader.

```
  // note use of recursion
  public static void encode(Node node) {

    if (node instanceof CharacterData) {
      CharacterData text = (CharacterData) node;
      String data = text.getData();
      text.setData(rot13(data));
    }

    // recurse the children
    if (node.hasChildNodes()) {
      NodeList children = node.getChildNodes();
      for (int i = 0; i < children.getLength(); i++) {
        encode(children.item(i));
      }
    }

  }

  public static String rot13(String s) {

    StringBuffer out = new StringBuffer(s.length());
    for (int i = 0; i < s.length(); i++) {
      int c = s.charAt(i);
      if (c >= 'A' && c <= 'M') out.append((char) (c+13));
      else if (c >= 'N' && c <= 'Z') out.append((char) (c-13));
      else if (c >= 'a' && c <= 'm') out.append((char) (c+13));
      else if (c >= 'n' && c <= 'z') out.append((char) (c-13));
      else out.append((char) c);
    }
    return out.toString();

  }

  public static void main(String[] args) {

    if (args.length <= 0) {
      System.out.println("Usage: java ROT13XML URL");
      return;
    }

    String url = args[0];
```

```
try {
  DocumentBuilderFactory factory
   = DocumentBuilderFactory.newInstance();
  DocumentBuilder parser = factory.newDocumentBuilder();

  // Read the document
  Document document = parser.parse(url);

  // Modify the document
  ROT13XML.encode(document);

  // Write it out again
  TransformerFactory xformFactory
   = TransformerFactory.newInstance();
  Transformer idTransform = xformFactory.newTransformer();
  Source input = new DOMSource(document);
  Result output = new StreamResult(System.out);
  idTransform.transform(input, output);

}
catch (SAXException e) {
  System.out.println(url + " is not well-formed.");
}
catch (IOException e) {
  System.out.println(
  "Due to an IOException, the parser could not encode " + url
  );
}
catch (FactoryConfigurationError e) {
  System.out.println("Could not locate a factory class");
}
catch (ParserConfigurationException e) {
  System.out.println("Could not locate a JAXP parser");
}
catch (TransformerConfigurationException e) {
  System.out.println("Could not locate a TrAX transformer");
}
catch (TransformerException e) {
  System.out.println("Could not transform");
}
```

```
    } // end main

  }
```

The `encode()` method recursively descends the tree, applying the rot-13 algorithm to every `CharacterData` object it finds, whether a `Comment`, `Text`, or `CDATASection`. The algorithm itself is encapsulated in the `rot13()` method. Because both methods merely operate on their arguments but otherwise have no interaction with any state maintained in the class, I made them static. The `main()` method encodes a document at a URL typed on the command line, and then copies the result to `System.out`.

Here's a joke encoded by this program. You'll have to run the program if you want to find out what it says. :-)

```
D:\books\XMLJAVA>java ROT13XML joke.xml
<?xml version="1.0" encoding="utf-8"?><joke>
  Gubhfnaqf bs crbcyr nggraq gur Oheavat Zna srfgviny rirel lrne
  va Arinqn'f Oynpx Ebpx Qrfreg. Guvf vf gur ovt uvccvr srfgviny,
  jurer crbcyr eha nebhaq anxrq, qevax, naq trg fgbarq,
  be nf Trbetr J. Ohfu yvxrf gb pnyy vg,
  trg ernql gb eha sbe cerfvqrag
</joke>
```

The Text Interface

The `Text` interface represents a text node. This can be a child of an element, an attribute, or an entity reference. When a document is built by a parser, each text node will contain the longest possible run of contiguous parsed character data from the document, and thus no text node will be adjacent to any other. By contrast, documents built in memory may contain adjacent text nodes. Invoking the `normalize()` method in the `Node` interface on any ancestor of the text nodes will merge these together.

Example 11.9 summarizes the `Text` interface. In addition to methods such as `setData()` and `getNodeValue()` that `Text` inherits from its superinterfaces, it has one new method that splits a `Text` object into two.

Example 11.9 The Text Interface

```
package org.w3c.dom;

public interface Text extends CharacterData {

  public Text splitText(int offset) throws DOMException;

}
```

The `splitText()` method splits one text node into two by dividing its data at a specified offset. All characters after the split are eliminated from the original node. A new text node is created and returned. Both nodes are included in the tree. If the offset is less than zero or greater than the length of the data, then `splitText()` throws a `DOMException` with the code for `INDEX_SIZE_ERR`.

The main reason to split a text node is so that you can move or delete part of some text, but not the entire node. You also can use it to insert a new node in the middle of a run of text. For example, suppose `date` is an `Element` object representing this element:

```
<date>2002-01-08</date>
```

Now suppose you want to change `date` to represent this element:

```
<date><year>2002</year><month>01</month><day>08</day></date>
```

The following code will do it:

```
Document document = date.getOwnerDocument();
Text yearText = (Text) date.getFirstChild();
Text slash = yearText.splitText(4);
Text monthText = slash.splitText(1);
Text nextSlash = monthText.splitText(2);
Text dayText = nextSlash.splitText(1);

Element year = document.createElement("year");
Element month = document.createElement("month");
Element day = document.createElement("day");
```

```
date.removeChild(slash);
date.removeChild(monthText);
date.removeChild(yearText);
date.removeChild(nextSlash);
date.removeChild(dayText);

year.appendChild(yearText);
month.appendChild(monthText);
day.appendChild(dayText);
date.appendChild(year);
date.appendChild(month);
date.appendChild(day);
```

Much of the time, these operations can be more easily implemented through `String` methods.

Example 11.10 is a simple program that recursively descends a DOM tree and prints all text nodes on `System.out`. This has the effect of stripping out the markup while leaving all text inside the document intact.

Example 11.10 Printing the Text Nodes in an XML Document

```
import javax.xml.parsers.*;
import org.w3c.dom.*;
import org.xml.sax.SAXException;
import java.io.IOException;


public class DOMTextExtractor {

  public void processNode(Node node) {

    if (node instanceof Text) {
      Text text = (Text) node;
      String data = text.getData();
      System.out.println(data);
    }

  }

  // note use of recursion
  public void followNode(Node node) {
```

```
    processNode(node);
    if (node.hasChildNodes()) {
      NodeList children = node.getChildNodes();
      for (int i = 0; i < children.getLength(); i++) {
        followNode(children.item(i));
      }
    }

  }

  public static void main(String[] args) {

    if (args.length <= 0) {
      System.out.println("Usage: java DOMTextExtractor URL");
      return;
    }

    String url = args[0];

    try {
      DocumentBuilderFactory factory
       = DocumentBuilderFactory.newInstance();
      DocumentBuilder parser = factory.newDocumentBuilder();
      // If expandEntityReferences isn't turned off, there
      //  won't be any entity reference nodes in the DOM tree
      factory.setExpandEntityReferences(false);

      // Read the document
      Document document = parser.parse(url);

      // Process the document
      DOMTextExtractor extractor = new DOMTextExtractor();
      extractor.followNode(document);

    }
    catch (SAXException e) {
      System.out.println(url + " is not well-formed.");
    }
    catch (IOException e) {
      System.out.println(
       "Due to an IOException, the parser could not check " + url
```

```
      );
    }
    catch (FactoryConfigurationError e) {
      System.out.println("Could not locate a factory class");
    }
    catch (ParserConfigurationException e) {
      System.out.println("Could not locate a JAXP parser");
    }

  } // end main

}
```

Here is the result of running the XML specification through this program:

```
D:\books\XMLJAVA>java DOMTextExtractor   http://www.w3.org/TR/
 2000/REC-xml-20001006.xml






Extensible Markup Language (XML)


1.0 (Second Edition)


REC-xml-20001006


W3C Recommendation


6
October
2000
...
```

Notice that white space is included in text nodes and is significant. Text inside entity references is also found, one way or another. If the DOM parser is producing entity reference nodes, then the replacement text of the entity becomes children of the entity reference nodes. Otherwise, the replacement text of the entity is simply resolved into the surrounding text nodes.

The CDATASection Interface

The `CDATASection` interface, shown in Example 11.11, is a subinterface of `Text` that specifically represents CDATA sections. It has no unique methods of its own, but when a `CDATASection` is serialized into a file, the text of the node may be wrapped inside CDATA section markers. As a result, characters such as ampersand and the less-than sign do not need to be escaped as `&` and `<`.

Example 11.11 The CDATASection Interface

```
package org.w3c.dom;

public interface CDATASection extends Text {

}
```

CDATA sections are convenient syntax sugar for documents that will sometimes be read or authored by human beings in source code form. The source code for this book uses them frequently for examples. Please don't use CDATA sections for more than that. With the possible exception of editors, all programs that process XML documents should treat CDATA sections as identical to the same text with all the less-than signs changed to `<` and all the ampersands changed to `&`. In particular, *do not* use CDATA sections as a sort of pseudo-element to hide HTML in your XML documents, like this:

```
<Product>
  <Name>Brass Ship's Bell</Name>
  <Quantity>1</Quantity>
  <Price currency="USD">144.95</Price >
  <Discount>.10</Discount>
  <![CDATA[<html><body>
    <b>Happy Father&rsquo;s Day to a great Dad!<P></b>
```

```
    <i>Love,<br>
    Sam and Beatrice<body></html>]]>
</Product>
```

Instead, write well-formed HTML inside an appropriate element, like this:

```
<Product>
  <Name>Brass Ship's Bell</Name>
  <Quantity>1</Quantity>
  <Price currency="USD">144.95</Price >
  <Discount>.10</Discount>
  <GiftMessage><html><body>
    <p><b>Happy Father's Day to a great Dad!</b></p>

    <i>Love,<br />
    Sam and Beatrice</i></body></html>
  </GiftMessage>
</Product>
```

The second example is much more flexible and much more robust. DOM parsers are not required to report CDATA sections, and other processes are even less likely to maintain them, so you should not use CDATA sections as a substitute for elements.

The `normalize()` method in the `Node` interface does not combine CDATA sections with adjacent text nodes or other CDATA sections. Example 11.12 provides a static utility method that does do this. A `Node` is passed in as an argument. All `CDATASection` descendants of this node are converted to simple `Text` objects, and then all adjacent `Text` objects are merged. The argument is modified in place. Thus the method returns void.

Example 11.12 Merging CDATA Sections with Text Nodes

```
import org.w3c.dom.*;


public class CDATAUtility {

  // Recursively descend the tree converting all CDATA sections
  // to text nodes and merging them with adjacent text nodes.
  public static void superNormalize(Node parent) {
```

```
    // We'll need this to create new Text objects
    Document factory = parent.getOwnerDocument();

    Node current = parent.getFirstChild();
    while (current != null) {

      int type = current.getNodeType();
      if (type == Node.CDATA_SECTION_NODE) {
        // Convert CDATA section to a text node
        CDATASection cdata = (CDATASection) current;
        String data = cdata.getData();
        Text newNode = factory.createTextNode(data);
        parent.replaceChild(newNode, cdata);
        current = newNode;
      }

      // Recheck in case we changed type above
      type = current.getNodeType();
      if (type == Node.TEXT_NODE) {
        // If previous node is a text node, then append this
        // node's data to that node, and delete this node
        Node previous = current.getPreviousSibling();
        if (previous != null) {
          int previousType = previous.getNodeType();
          if (previousType == Node.TEXT_NODE) {
            Text previousText = (Text) previous;
            Text currentText = (Text) current;
            String data = currentText.getData();
            previousText.appendData(data);
            parent.removeChild(current);
            current = previous;
          }
        }
      } // end if
      else { // recurse
        superNormalize(current);
      }

      // increment node
      current = current.getNextSibling();
```

```
      } // end while

    } // end superNormalize()

  }
```

More than anything else, superNormalize() is an exercise in navigating the DOM tree. It uses the Node methods getFirstChild(), getNextSibling(), and getPreviousChild() in a while loop instead of iterating through a NodeList in a for loop, because it's constantly changing the contents of the node list. Node lists are live, but keeping the loop counter pointed at the right node as the list changes is tricky (not impossible certainly, just not as straightforward as the approach used here).

The EntityReference Interface

The EntityReference interface represents a general entity reference such as   or ©right_notice;. (It is not used for the five predefined entity references &, <, >, ', and ".)

Example 11.13 summarizes the EntityReference interface. You'll notice it declares exactly zero methods of its own. It inherits all of its functionality from the Node superinterface. In an XML document, an entity reference is just a placeholder for the text that will replace it. In a DOM tree, an EntityReference object merely contains the things that will replace the entity reference.

Example 11.13 The EntityReference Interface

```
package org.w3c.dom;

public interface EntityReference extends Node {

}
```

The name of the entity reference is returned by the getNodeName() method. The replacement text for the entity (assuming that the parser has resolved the entity) can be read through the usual methods of the Node interface, such as getFirstChild(). However, entity references are read only. You cannot change their children using methods such as appendChild() or replaceChild() or change their names using methods such as setNodeName(). An attempt to do so throws a DOMException with the error code NO_MODIFICATION_ALLOWED_ERR.

EntityReference objects do not know their own system ID (URL) or public ID. Using the entity reference's name, however, you can look up this information in the NamedNodeMap of Entity objects returned by the getEntities() method of the DocumentType class. I'll show you an example of this when we get to the Entity interface. In the meantime, let's consider an example that creates new entity references in the tree.

One common complaint about XML is that it doesn't support the entity references like   and é which developers are accustomed to from HTML. Using DOM, it's uncomplicated to replace any inconvenient character with an entity reference, as Example 11.14 proves. This program recursively descends the element tree looking for any nonbreaking space characters (Unicode code point 0xA0). It replaces any it finds with an entity reference with the name nbsp. To do so, it has to split the text node around the nonbreaking space.

Example 11.14 Inserting Entity References into a Document

```
import org.w3c.dom.*;


public class NBSPUtility {

  // Recursively descend the tree replacing all nonbreaking
  // spaces with  
  public static void addEntityReferences(Node node) {

    int type = node.getNodeType();
    if (type == Node.TEXT_NODE) {
                // the only type with attributes
      Text text = (Text) node;
      String s = text.getNodeValue();
      int nbsp = s.indexOf('\u00A0'); // finds the first A0
      if (nbsp != -1) {
        Text middle = text.splitText(nbsp);
        Text end = middle.splitText(1);
        Node parent = text.getParentNode();
        Document factory = text.getOwnerDocument();
        EntityReference ref =
         factory.createEntityReference("nbsp");
        parent.replaceChild(ref, middle);
```

```
          addEntityReferences(end); // finds any subsequent A0s
          System.out.println("Added");
        }
      } // end if

      else if (node.hasChildNodes()) {
        NodeList children = node.getChildNodes();
        for (int i = 0; i < children.getLength(); i++) {
          Node child = children.item(i);
          addEntityReferences(child);
        } // end for
      } // end if

    }  // end addEntityReferences()

}
```

It would be easy enough to make it replace all of the Latin-1 characters, or all of the characters that have standard entity references in HTML, or some such. You'd just need to keep a table of the characters and their corresponding entity references. You could even build such a table from the entities map available from the DTD.

Although this code runs, the documents it produces are not necessarily well-formed. In particular, only entities defined in the DTD should be used. Assuming that's the case, then the child list of the entity will be automatically filled by the entity's replacement text. Unfortunately, however, DOM does not offer any means of defining new entities that are not part of the document's original DTD.

The Attr Interface

Probably 90 percent of the time, everything you need to do with attributes can be done purely through the various attribute methods of the `Element` interface. However, occasionally the `Attr` interface comes in handy. An `Attr` object represents an attribute, whether explicitly included in the document or present by default from the schema.

Example 11.15 summarizes the `Attr` interface. In addition to methods inherited from the `Node` superinterface, `Attr` includes methods to do the following:

- Get the full name of the attribute (including a prefix, if any)
- Determine whether the attribute was specified in the document or merely appears by default from the DTD or schema

- Get the element that contains this attribute
- Get the value of the attribute.

Entity and character references in the value are resolved, but white space is not normalized. There's also a method that can change the value of this attribute. This throws a `DOMException` if the attribute is read only, as it might be if this attribute belonged to an element in a read-only entity reference node.

Example 11.15 The Attr Interface

```
package org.w3c.dom;

public interface Attr extends Node {

  public String  getName();  // Prefixed name
  public String  getValue();
  public Element getOwnerElement();
  public boolean getSpecified();
  public void    setValue(String value) throws DOMException;

}
```

The key thing to watch out for when working with attributes in DOM is that they are not *considered to be children of the elements that contain them. Furthermore, unlike the XPath data model, the elements that contain them are not their parents either.* In DOM, attributes have no parents, so invoking `getParent()` on an `Attr` always returns null.

In DOM terminology, an attribute that is actually placed on the start-tag of an element is called *specified*. An attribute that is present by default from the DTD or schema is not specified. You can tell which is which by invoking the `get-Specified()` method. This is one of the few things you can do with an `Attr` object that you can't do with the owning `Element` object.

Some interoperability problems in XML relate to the fact that some parsers validate and others don't. If validation were only about checking constraints, then this wouldn't be a big problem, but unfortunately validation does more than that. In particular it assigns default attribute values to elements. These attributes may be seen by a validating parser but not by a nonvalidating parser. As an example of this interface, I'm going to write a program that converts unspecified attributes into specified attributes to improve interoperability. Note that an attribute modified or added programmatically in DOM is always specified, even if it has the same value as the default attribute in the DTD. If you delete an attribute for which the DTD provides a default value, then DOM will insert an attribute node with the default value. Thus it's impossible to eliminate a default attribute. Example 11.16 demonstrates.[5]

Example 11.16 Specifying All Attributes

```
import org.w3c.dom.*;


public class AttributeUtility {

  // Recursively descend the tree replacing all unspecified
  // attributes with specified attributes
  public static void specifyAttributes(Node node) {

    int type = node.getNodeType();
    if (type == Node.ELEMENT_NODE) {
               // the only type with attributes
      Element element = (Element) node;
      NamedNodeMap attributes = element.getAttributes();
      Document factory = node.getOwnerDocument();
      for (int i = 0; i < attributes.getLength(); i++) {
        Attr attribute = (Attr) attributes.item(i);
        if (!attribute.getSpecified()) {
          // We can't change the specified property of an
          // attribute in DOM2. However, attributes are specified
          // by default, so if we delete the old attribute and
          // add a new one with the same name and value, or
          // change the attribute's value (even to the same
          // thing), the effect is what we're looking for.
          String name = attribute.getName();
          String value = attribute.getValue();
          Attr specifiedAttribute = factory.createAttribute(name);
          specifiedAttribute.setValue(value);
          element.setAttributeNode(specifiedAttribute);
          // This replaces the old attribute with the same name.
```

5. I admit that this example is a little contrived. Reading each value and writing the same value back out again would be easier.

```
        }
      } // end for
    } // end if

    if (node.hasChildNodes()) {
      NodeList children = node.getChildNodes();
      for (int i = 0; i < children.getLength(); i++) {
        Node child = children.item(i);
        specifyAttributes(child);
      } // end for
    } // end if

  }  // end specifyAttributes()

}
```

This program simply recursively descends the tree beneath a node, looking for elements. It scans each element's attributes. If any of those attributes are not specified, then the attribute is deleted and replaced with a copy.

DOM2 is missing one crucial feature for working with attributes. It cannot tell you the type of the attribute as declared in the DTD. That is, you cannot find out if an attribute is CDATA, ID, IDREF, NMTOKEN, and so forth.

The ProcessingInstruction Interface

The `ProcessingInstruction` interface represents a processing instruction such as `<?xml-stylesheet type="text/css" href="order.css"?>` or `<?php echo "Hello World";?>`.

Example 11.17 summarizes the `ProcessingInstruction` interface. This interface adds methods to get the target and the data of the processing instruction as strings. Even if the data has a pseudo-attribute format, as in `<?xml-stylesheet type="text/css" href="order.css"?>`, DOM doesn't recognize that. For this processing instruction, the target is `xml-stylesheet` and the data is `type="text/css" href="order.css."`

Example 11.17 The ProcessingInstruction Interface

```
package org.w3c.dom;

public interface ProcessingInstruction extends Node {

  public String getTarget();
  public String getData();
  public void   setData(String data) throws DOMException;

}
```

As usual, `ProcessingInstruction` objects also have all the methods of the `Node` superinterface, such as `getNodeName()` and `getNodeValue()`. The value of a processing instruction is its data. Processing instructions do not have children, however, so `Node` methods like `getFirstChild()` return null, and methods such as `appendChild()` throw a `DOMException` with the code `HIERARCHY_REQUEST_ERR`.

As an example, let's extend the earlier `XLinkSpider` program in Example 11.6 so that it respects `robots` processing instructions. Such an instruction looks like this, and appears in the prolog of an XML document:

```
<?robots index="yes" follow="no"?>
```

The semantics of this instruction is deliberately similar to the robots `META` tag in HTML. That is, `follow="yes"` means robots should follow links they find in this page; `follow="no"` means they shouldn't. Similarly, `index="yes"` means search engines should include this page; `index="no"` means they shouldn't.

Like many processing instructions, the syntax is based on pseudo-attributes. DOM doesn't provide any means to parse these, even though it's a very common format for processing instructions. However, you can fake DOM out. I'm going to extract the target and data of the processing instruction and use them to form a string that has this format:

```
<target data/>
```

In other words, a processing instruction such as `<?robots index="yes" follow="no"?>` is going to turn into a `String` like `<robots index="yes" follow="no" />`. This string is in turn a well-formed XML document that can be parsed and its attributes extracted. Admittedly, this approach is very circuitous and probably not optimally efficient. On the other hand, it's a lot easier to code and explain than writing your own mini-parser just to handle pseudo-attributes.

Example 11.18 is a simple utility class that implements this hack. The parsing is completely hidden inside the constructor, so if this is too offensive to your sensibilities, you can replace it with more appropriate code without changing the public interface. Because this class is quite useful in practice, not merely an example for this book, I've placed it in the `com.macfaq.xml` package. Don't forget to configure your class and source paths appropriately when compiling it.

Example 11.18 Reading PseudoAttributes from a ProcessingInstruction

```
package com.macfaq.xml;

import org.w3c.dom.*;
import javax.xml.parsers.*;
import org.xml.sax.*;
import java.io.*;

public class PseudoAttributes {

  private NamedNodeMap pseudo;

  public PseudoAttributes(ProcessingInstruction pi)
   throws SAXException {

    StringBuffer sb = new StringBuffer("<");
    sb.append(pi.getTarget());
    sb.append(" ");
    sb.append(pi.getData());
    sb.append("/>");
    StringReader reader = new StringReader(sb.toString());
    InputSource source = new InputSource(reader);
    try {
      DocumentBuilderFactory factory
       = DocumentBuilderFactory.newInstance();
      DocumentBuilder parser = factory.newDocumentBuilder();

      // This line will throw a SAXException if the processing
      // instruction does not use pseudo-attributes.
      Document doc = parser.parse(source);
      Element root = doc.getDocumentElement();
      pseudo = root.getAttributes();
```

```
      }
      catch (FactoryConfigurationError e) {
        // I don't absolutely need to catch this, but I hate to
        // throw an Error for no good reason.
        throw new SAXException(e.getMessage());
      }
      catch (SAXException e) {
        throw e;
      }
      catch (Exception e) {
        throw new SAXException(e);
      }

    }

    // delegator methods
    public Attr item(int index) {
      return (Attr) pseudo.item(index);
    }

    public int getLength() {
      return pseudo.getLength();
    }

    public String getValue(String name) {
      Attr att = (Attr) pseudo.getNamedItem(name);
      if (att == null) return "";
      return att.getValue();
    }

  }
```

This class makes it easy for the earlier `DOMSpider` program in Example 11.6 to recognize the `robots` processing instruction. I won't repeat the entire program, most of which hasn't changed. The relevant change is in the `spider()` method, which now has to look for a `robots` processing instruction in each document and use that to decide whether or not to call `process()` (`index="yes|no"`) and/or `findLinks()` (`follow="yes|no"`).

```
public void spider(String systemID) {
  currentDepth++;
  try {
    if (currentDepth < maxDepth) {
      Document document = parser.parse(systemID);

      // Look for a robots PI with follow="no"
      boolean index = true;
      boolean follow = true;
      NodeList children = document.getChildNodes();
      for (int i = 0; i < children.getLength(); i++) {
        Node child = children.item(i);
        int type = child.getNodeType();
        if (type == Node.PROCESSING_INSTRUCTION_NODE) {
          ProcessingInstruction pi
           = (ProcessingInstruction) child;
          if (pi.getTarget().equals("robots")) {
             PseudoAttributes pseudo = new PseudoAttributes(pi);
             if (pseudo.getValue("index").equals("no")) {
               index = false;
             }
             if (pseudo.getValue("follow").equals("no")) {
               follow = false;
             }
          }
        }
      } // end for

      if (index) process(document, systemID);

      if (follow) {
        Vector toBeVisited = new Vector();
        // search the document for uris,
        // store them in vector, and print them
        findLinks(
         document.getDocumentElement(), toBeVisited, systemID);

        Enumeration e = toBeVisited.elements();
        while (e.hasMoreElements()) {
          String uri = (String) e.nextElement();
          visited.add(uri);
```

```
              spider(uri);
            } // end while
          } // end if

        }

      }
      catch (SAXException e) {
        // Couldn't load the document,
        // probably not well-formed XML, skip it
      }
      catch (IOException e) {
        // Couldn't load the document,
        // likely network failure, skip it
      }
      finally {
        currentDepth--;
        System.out.flush();
      }

    }
```

The Comment Interface

XML comments don't have a lot of structure. They're really just some undifferentiated text inside <!-- and -->. Therefore, the `Comment` interface, shown in Example 11.19, is a subinterface of `CharacterData` and shares all of its method with that interface. However, your code can use the type to determine that a node is a comment, and treat it appropriately. Serializers will be smart enough to output a `Comment` with the right markup around it.

Example 11.19 The Comment Interface

```
package org.w3c.dom;

public interface Comment extends CharacterData {

}
```

In Example 7.12, I demonstrated a SAX program that reads comments. Now in Example 11.20, you can see the DOM equivalent. The approach is different—actively walking a tree instead of passively receiving events—but the effect is the same, printing the contents of comments and only comments on `System.out`.

Example 11.20 A DOM Program That Prints Comments

```
import javax.xml.parsers.*;
import org.w3c.dom.*;
import org.xml.sax.SAXException;
import java.io.IOException;


public class DOMCommentReader {

  // note use of recursion
  public static void printComments(Node node) {

    int type = node.getNodeType();
    if (type == Node.COMMENT_NODE) {
      Comment comment = (Comment) node;
      System.out.println(comment.getData());
      System.out.println();
    }
    else {
      if (node.hasChildNodes()) {
        NodeList children = node.getChildNodes();
        for (int i = 0; i < children.getLength(); i++) {
          printComments(children.item(i));
        }
      }
    }

  }

  public static void main(String[] args) {

    if (args.length <= 0) {
      System.out.println("Usage: java DOMCommentReader URL");
      return;
    }
```

```
    String url = args[0];

    try {
      DocumentBuilderFactory factory
       = DocumentBuilderFactory.newInstance();
      DocumentBuilder parser = factory.newDocumentBuilder();

      // Read the document
      Document document = parser.parse(url);

      // Process the document
      DOMCommentReader.printComments(document);

    }
    catch (SAXException e) {
      System.out.println(url + " is not well-formed.");
    }
    catch (IOException e) {
      System.out.println(
       "Due to an IOException, the parser could not check " + url
      );
    }
    catch (FactoryConfigurationError e) {
      System.out.println("Could not locate a factory class");
    }
    catch (ParserConfigurationException e) {
      System.out.println("Could not locate a JAXP parser");
    }

  } // end main

}
```

The following is the result of running this program on the XML Schema Datatypes specification:

```
D:\books\XMLJAVA>java DOMCommentReader   http://www.w3.org/TR/
2001/REC-xmlschema-2-20010502/datatypes.xml
  commenting these out means only that they won't show up in the
    stylesheet generated "Revisions from previous draft" appendix
```

```
 Changes before Sept public draft commented out...
<sitem>
19990521: PVB: corrected definition of length and maxLengths
facet for strings to be in terms of <emph>characters</emph>
not <emph>bytes</emph>
</sitem>
<sitem>
19990521: PVB: removed issue "other-date-representations".
We don't want other separators, left mention of aggregate reps
for dates as an ednote.
</sitem>
<sitem>
19990521: PVB: fixed "holidays" example, "-0101" ==> "==0101"
(where == in the correction should be two hyphens, but that would
not allow us to comment out this sitem)
...
```

It's not obvious from this output sample, but there is a big difference in the behavior of the SAX and DOM versions of this program. The SAX version begins producing output almost immediately because it works in streaming mode. By contrast, the DOM version first has to read the entire document from the remote URL, parse it, and only then begin walking the tree to look for comments. The SAX and DOM versions are both limited by the speed of the network connection, so they both take equal amounts of time to run on the same input data. However, the SAX version begins returning results much more quickly than the DOM version, which doesn't present any results until the entire document has been read. This may not be a big concern in a batch-mode application, but it can be very important when there is a human user. The SAX version will feel a lot more responsive.

The DocumentType Interface

The `DocumentType` interface represents a document's document type declaration. That is, it's the in-memory representation of the following construct:

```
<!DOCTYPE mml:math PUBLIC "-//W3C//DTD MathML 2.0//EN"
 "http://www.w3.org/TR/MathML2/dtd/mathml2.dtd" [
  <!ENTITY % MATHML.prefixed "INCLUDE">
  <!ENTITY % MATHML.prefix "mml">
]>
```

Each document type declaration has four parts, three of which are optional:

1. The root element name (`mml:math` in the above example)
2. The public ID (`-//W3C//DTD MathML 2.0//EN` in the above example)
3. The system ID (`http://www.w3.org/TR/MathML2/dtd/mathml2.dtd` in the above example)
4. The internal DTD subset (everything between the `[` and the `]`)

It's important to note that the document type declaration is not the same thing as the document type definition (DTD). The document type declaration points to the DTD, and may sometimes contain the document type definition or part of it as the internal DTD subset. However, the document type declaration and the document type definition are two different things. DOM2 only provides access to the document type declaration; it does not tell you what the document type definition says. The acronym *DTD* is used only for the *document type definition.*

Example 11.21 summarizes DOM's `DocumentType` interface. It has methods to get the root element name, the public ID, the system ID, the internal DTD subset, and maps of the entities and notations declared in the DTD this document type declaration points to.

Example 11.21 The DocumentType Interface

```
package org.w3c.dom;

public interface DocumentType extends Node {

  public String       getName();
  public NamedNodeMap getEntities();
  public NamedNodeMap getNotations();
  public String       getPublicId();
  public String       getSystemId();
  public String       getInternalSubset();

}
```

All of these properties are read only. That is, there are getter methods but no corresponding setter methods. You cannot change the name, public ID, system ID, or anything else about a `DocumentType` object. Once the parser has read it, it's final.

A DocumentType object is created by a DOMImplementation object and assigned to a document when the Document object is created. After that point, a document's DocumentType cannot be changed.

The next two sections will provide some examples of this interface.

The Entity Interface

The Entity interface represents a parsed or unparsed general entity declared in a document's DTD. (DOM does not expose parameter entities.) A map of the entities declared in a document is available from the getEntities() method of the DocumentType interface. However, entities are not part of the tree structure, and the parent of an entity is always null.

An Entity object represents the actual storage unit. It does not represent the entity reference such as Ω or ©right; that appears in the instance document, but rather the replacement text to which that reference points. For parsed entities that the XML parser has resolved, the descendants of the Entity object form a read-only tree containing the XML markup for which the entity reference stands. For unparsed entities and external entities that the XML parser has not read, the Entity object has no children.

Example 11.22 summarizes the Entity interface, which includes methods to get the public ID, system ID, and notation name for the entity. These methods all return null if the property is not applicable to this entity. To get the replacement text of an entity, use the methods Entity inherits from its Node superinterface, such as hasChildNodes() and getFirstChild().

Example 11.22 The Entity Interface

```
package org.w3c.dom;

public interface Entity extends Node {

  public String getPublicId();
  public String getSystemId();
  public String getNotationName();

}
```

In Example 11.23, let's look at a program that walks the document looking for entity references. Every time it sees one, it prints out that reference's name, public

ID, and system ID. To do this, it has to look up the entity reference name in the entities map returned by the `getEntities()` of the `DocumentType` interface. A `java.util.Set` keeps track of which entities have been printed to avoid printing any entity more than once.

Example 11.23 Listing Parsed Entities Used in the Document

```
import javax.xml.parsers.*;
import org.w3c.dom.*;
import org.xml.sax.SAXException;
import java.io.IOException;
import java.util.*;


public class EntityLister {

  // Store the entities that have already been printed
  private Set          printed = new HashSet();
  private NamedNodeMap entities;

  // Recursively descend the tree
  public void printEntities(Document doc) {

    DocumentType doctype = doc.getDoctype();
    entities = doctype.getEntities();
    seekEntities(doc);

  }

  // note use of recursion
  private void seekEntities(Node node) {

    int type = node.getNodeType();
    if (type == Node.ENTITY_REFERENCE_NODE) {
      EntityReference ref = (EntityReference) node;
      printEntityReference(ref);
    }

    if (node.hasChildNodes()) {
      NodeList children = node.getChildNodes();
```

```
      for (int i = 0; i < children.getLength(); i++) {
        seekEntities(children.item(i));
      }
    }

  }

  private void printEntityReference(EntityReference ref) {

    String name = ref.getNodeName();
    if (!printed.contains(name)) {

      Entity entity   = (Entity) entities.getNamedItem(name);
      String publicID = entity.getPublicId();
      String systemID = entity.getSystemId();

      System.out.print(name + ": ");
      if (publicID != null) System.out.print(publicID + " ");
      if (systemID != null) System.out.print(systemID + " ");
      else { // Internal entities do not have system IDs
        System.out.print("internal entity");
      }
      System.out.println();

      printed.add(name);
    }

  }

  public static void main(String[] args) {

    if (args.length <= 0) {
      System.out.println("Usage: java EntityLister URL");
      return;
    }
    String url = args[0];

    try {
      DocumentBuilderFactory factory
       = DocumentBuilderFactory.newInstance();
```

```
      // By default JAXP does not include entity reference nodes
      // in the tree. You have to explicitly request them by
      // telling DocumentBuilderFactory not to expand entity
      // references.
      factory.setExpandEntityReferences(false);
      DocumentBuilder parser = factory.newDocumentBuilder();

      // Read the document
      Document document = parser.parse(url);

      // Print the entities
      EntityLister lister = new EntityLister();
      lister.printEntities(document);

    }
    catch (SAXException e) {
      System.out.println(url + " is not well-formed.");
    }
    catch (IOException e) {
      System.out.println(
       "Due to an IOException, the parser could not read " + url
      );
    }
    catch (FactoryConfigurationError e) {
      System.out.println("Could not locate a factory class");
    }
    catch (ParserConfigurationException e) {
      System.out.println("Could not locate a JAXP parser");
    }

  } // end main

}
```

Mostly this is fairly straightforward tree-walking code of the sort you've seen several times before. Note, however, that by default JAXP `DocumentBuilder` objects do not put any entity reference nodes in the trees they build. To get these, the expand-entity-references property must be explicitly set to false on the `DocumentBuilderFactory` that creates the `DocumentBuilder`.

Here is the output when I ran this across the DocBook source for this chapter. All of the entity references used here are internally defined references to single hard-to-type characters such as curly quotes and the em dash.

```
D:\books\XMLJAVA>java EntityLister file://D/books/XMLJava/ch11.xml
rsquo: internal entity
mdash: internal entity
hellip: internal entity
```

The Notation Interface

The `Notation` interface represents a notation declared in the DTD; it is not part of the tree. A `Notation` object has no parent and no children. The only way to access a document's notations is through the `getNotations()` method of the `DocumentType` object.

> **Note**
> Notations are very uncommon in practice. You may want to skip this section unless you discover a specific need for it.

Example 11.24 summarizes the `Notation` interface. This interface has methods to get the system ID and public ID for the notation, either of which may be null. As usual, `Notation` objects also have all the methods of the `Node` superinterface such as `getNodeName()` and `getNodeValue()`.

Example 11.24 The Notation Interface

```
package org.w3c.dom;

public interface Notation extends Node {

  public String getPublicId();
  public String getSystemId();

}
```

Example 11.25 is a simple program that lists all of the notations declared in a document's DTD. To determine whether these were actually used anywhere in the document, you would need to compare them to all of the processing instruction targets, notation type attributes, and unparsed entities to see if they matched up anywhere.

Example 11.25 Listing the Notations Declared in a DTD

```
import javax.xml.parsers.*;
import org.w3c.dom.*;
import org.xml.sax.SAXException;
import java.io.IOException;

public class NotationLister {

  // No recursion for a change. We don't need to walk the tree.
  public static void listNotations(Document doc) {

    DocumentType doctype   = doc.getDoctype();
    NamedNodeMap notations = doctype.getNotations();
    for (int i = 0; i < notations.getLength(); i++) {

      Notation notation = (Notation) notations.item(i);

      String name       = notation.getNodeName();
      String publicID   = notation.getPublicId();
      String systemID   = notation.getSystemId();

      System.out.print(name + ": ");
      if (publicID != null) System.out.print(publicID + " ");
      if (systemID != null) System.out.print(systemID + " ");
      System.out.println();

    }

  }

  public static void main(String[] args) {

    if (args.length <= 0) {
      System.out.println("Usage: java NotationLister URL");
      return;
    }
    String url = args[0];
```

```
    try {
      DocumentBuilderFactory factory
       = DocumentBuilderFactory.newInstance();
      DocumentBuilder parser = factory.newDocumentBuilder();

      // Read the document
      Document document = parser.parse(url);

      // Process the document
      listNotations(document);

    }
    catch (SAXException e) {
      System.out.println(url + " is not well-formed.");
    }
    catch (IOException e) {
      System.out.println(
       "Due to an IOException, the parser could not check " + url
      );
    }
    catch (FactoryConfigurationError e) {
      System.out.println("Could not locate a factory class");
    }
    catch (ParserConfigurationException e) {
      System.out.println("Could not locate a JAXP parser");
    }

  } // end main

}
```

DocBook is the only XML application I'm aware of that even declares any notations (and that's really only because of legacy compatibility issues with DocBook's earlier SGML incarnation). This book is written in DocBook, and so I ran `NotationLister` across one of its chapters. Here's the output:

```
D:\books\XMLJAVA>java NotationLister masterbook.xml
BMP: +//ISBN 0-7923-9432-1::Graphic Notation//NOTATION Microsoft
 Windows bitmap//EN
CGM-BINARY: ISO 8632/3//NOTATION Binary encoding//EN
CGM-CHAR: ISO 8632/2//NOTATION Character encoding//EN
```

```
CGM-CLEAR: ISO 8632/4//NOTATION Clear text encoding//EN
DITROFF: DITROFF
DVI: DVI
EPS: +//ISBN 0-201-18127-4::Adobe//NOTATION PostScript Language
 Ref. Manual//EN
EQN: EQN
FAX: -//USA-DOD//NOTATION CCITT Group 4 Facsimile Type 1
 Untiled Raster//EN
GIF: GIF
GIF87a: -//CompuServe//NOTATION Graphics Interchange Format
 87a//EN
GIF89a: -//CompuServe//NOTATION Graphics Interchange Format
 89a//EN
IGES: -//USA-DOD//NOTATION (ASME/ANSI Y14.26M-1987) Initial
 Graphics Exchange Specification//EN
JPEG: JPG
JPG: JPG
PCX: +//ISBN 0-7923-9432-1::Graphic Notation//NOTATION ZSoft PCX
 bitmap//EN
PIC: PIC
PNG: http://www.w3.org/TR/REC-png
PS: PS
SGML: ISO 8879:1986//NOTATION Standard Generalized Markup
 Language//EN
TBL: TBL
TEX: +//ISBN 0-201-13448-9::Knuth//NOTATION The TeXbook//EN
TIFF: TIFF
WMF: +//ISBN 0-7923-9432-1::Graphic Notation//NOTATION Microsoft
Windows Metafile//EN
WPG: WPG
linespecific: linespecific
```

I had to add a few line breaks to fit the output on the page, but otherwise the result would be the same given any DocBook document because the notations come from the DTD, not the instance document.

Summary

The `org.w3c.dom` package includes 13 different subclasses of `Node` that represent the various possible components of a DOM tree:

`Document`
The root of the DOM tree. Acts as a factory class for the other kinds of nodes; offers access to the root element, document type declaration, and DOM implementation.

`DocumentType`
Represents the document type declaration. Provides access to the notations and entities declared in the document's DTD.

`Element`
Represents an element, including its local name, prefixed name, namespace URI, and attributes.

`CharacterData`
A common superinterface for `Text`, `CDATASection`, and `Comment`. Provides methods to read and modify the text content of these nodes.

`Text`
Represents a text node in the DOM tree. Has a method to split a text node into two text nodes.

`Attr`
Represents an attribute of an element; not part of the tree. Has methods to get the name, value, owner element, and default status of an attribute and to change the value of an attribute (but not the name). Most of the time, the attribute-related methods in the `Element` interface are used rather than working directly with attribute nodes.

`Comment`
Represents a comment node in the DOM tree. Inherits all its methods from the superinterfaces `CharacterData` and `Node`.

`ProcessingInstruction`
Represents a processing instruction node in the DOM tree. Has methods to get the target and to get and set the data.

`CDATASection`
Represents a CDATA section node in the DOM tree. Inherits all its methods from the superinterfaces `Text`, `CharacterData`, and `Node`.

`EntityReference`
Represents an entity reference node in the DOM tree. The children of this node are formed from the replacement text of the entity. Some parsers resolve entity references without putting any entity reference nodes in the tree.

`Entity`
Represents a parsed or unparsed general entity declared in the DTD. Includes methods to get the public and system ID of the entity. The children of an `Entity` object are formed from the replacement text of the entity. `Entity` objects are only accessible through the `NamedNodeMap` returned by the `getEntities()` method in the `DocumentType` interface.

`Notation`
Represents a notation declared in the DTD. Includes methods to get the public ID and/or system ID of the notation. Only accessible through the `NamedNodeMap` returned by the `getNotations()` method in the `DocumentType` interface.

`DocumentFragment`
A placeholder for a part of a document that contains multiple sibling nodes that can be moved as a group. It differs from other nodes in that when a document fragment is inserted into a node, the children of the document fragment are placed in that node, but not the document fragment itself.

Each of these interfaces inherits the methods of the `Node` interface as well as methods providing unique functionality for that particular kind of node.

Chapter 12

The DOM Traversal Module

The examples in Chapters 9 to 11 duplicated quite a bit of tree-walking code. Some of them searched for particular information. Others modified documents in memory. What they all had in common was that they navigated a tree from the root to the deepest leaf element in document order. This is an extremely common pattern in DOM programs.

The `org.w3c.dom.traversal` package is a collection of utility interfaces that implement most of the logic needed to traverse a DOM tree. These include `NodeIterator`, `NodeFilter`, `TreeWalker`, and `DocumentTraversal`. DOM implementations are not required to support these interfaces, but many do, including the Oracle XML Parser for Java and Xerces. (Crimson does not. GNU JAXP supports `NodeIterator` but not `TreeWalker`.) By reusing these classes you can simplify your programs a great deal and save yourself a significant amount of work.

NodeIterator

The `NodeIterator` utility interface extracts a subset of the nodes in a DOM document and presents them as a list arranged in document order. In other words, the nodes appear in the order in which you would find them in a depth-first, preorder traversal of the tree. That is,

- The document node comes first.
- Parents come before their children; ancestors come before their descendants.
- Sibling nodes appear in the same order as their start-tags in the text representation of the document.

This is pretty much the order you would expect just by reading an XML document from beginning to end. As soon as you see the first character of text from a node, that node is counted.

You can iterate through this list without concerning yourself with the tree structure of the XML document. For many operations, this flatter view is more convenient than the hierarchical tree view. For example, a spell-checker can check all text nodes one at a time. An outline program can extract the headings in an XHTML document while ignoring everything else. All of this is possible by iterating though a list without having to write recursive methods.

Example 12.1 summarizes the `NodeIterator` interface. The first four getter methods simply tell you how the iterator is choosing from all of the available nodes in the document. The `nextNode()` and `previousNode()` methods move forward and backward in the list and return the requested node. Finally, the `detach()` method cleans up after the iterator when you're done with it. It's analogous to closing a stream.

Example 12.1 The NodeIterator Interface

```
package org.w3c.dom.traversal;

public interface NodeIterator {

    public Node       getRoot();
    public int        getWhatToShow();
    public NodeFilter getFilter();
    public boolean    getExpandEntityReferences();

    public Node       nextNode() throws DOMException;
    public Node       previousNode() throws DOMException;

    public void       detach();

}
```

As you see, the `NodeIterator` interface provides only the most basic methods for an iterator. Each iterator can be thought of as having a cursor, which is initially positioned before the first node in the list. The `nextNode()` method returns the node immediately following the cursor and advances the cursor one space. The `previousNode()` method returns the node immediately before the cursor and backs up the cursor one space. If the iterator is positioned at the end of the list, then `nextNode()` returns null. If the iterator is positioned at the beginning of the list, then `previousNode()` returns null. For example, given a `NodeIterator` variable named `iterator` positioned at the beginning of its list, the following code fragment prints the names of all the nodes:

```
Node node;
while ((node = iterator.nextNode()) != null) {
  System.out.println(node.getNodeName());
}
```

> **Note**
> Design pattern aficionados will have recognized this as an instance of the iterator pattern (as if the name didn't already give it away). More precisely, it's a *robust, external iterator*: Robust because the iterator still works even if its backing data structure (the `Document` object) changes underneath it. External because that client code is responsible for moving the iterator from one node to the next, rather than having the iterator move itself.

Constructing NodeIterators with DocumentTraversal

Not all DOM implementations are guaranteed to support the traversal module, although most do. You can check this with `hasFeature("traversal", "2.0")` in the `DOMImplementation` class. For example,

```
if (!impl.hasFeature("traversal", "2.0")) {
  System.err.println(
   "A DOM implementation that supports traversal is required.");
  return;
}
```

Assuming that the implementation does support traversal, the `Document` implementation class also implements the `DocumentTraversal` interface. This factory interface, shown in Example 12.2, allows you to create new `NodeIterator` and `TreeWalker` objects that traverse the nodes in that document.

Example 12.2 The DocumentTraversal Factory Interface

```
package org.w3c.dom.traversal;

public interface DocumentTraversal {

  public NodeIterator createNodeIterator(Node root,
   int whatToShow, NodeFilter filter,
   boolean entityReferenceExpansion) throws DOMException;

  public TreeWalker createTreeWalker(Node root,
   int whatToShow, NodeFilter filter,
   boolean entityReferenceExpansion) throws DOMException;

}
```

Thus, to create a `NodeIterator`, you cast the `Document` object you want to iterate over to `DocumentTraversal` and then invoke its `createNodeIterator()` method. This method takes the following four arguments:

root
The `Node` in the document from which the iterator starts. Only this node and its descendants are traversed by the iterator. This means that you can easily design iterators that iterate over a subtree of the entire document. For example, by passing in the root element, it's possible to skip everything in the document's prolog and epilog.

whatToShow
An `int` bitfield constant specifying the node types the iterator will include. These constants are

- `NodeFilter.SHOW_ELEMENT = 1`
- `NodeFilter.SHOW_ATTRIBUTE = 2`
- `NodeFilter.SHOW_TEXT = 4`
- `NodeFilter.SHOW_CDATA_SECTION = 8`
- `NodeFilter.SHOW_ENTITY_REFERENCE = 16`
- `NodeFilter.SHOW_ENTITY = 32`
- `NodeFilter.SHOW_PROCESSING_INSTRUCTION = 64`
- `NodeFilter.SHOW_DOCUMENT = 128`

- NodeFilter.SHOW_DOCUMENT_TYPE = 256
- NodeFilter.SHOW_DOCUMENT_FRAGMENT = 512
- NodeFilter.SHOW_NOTATION = 1024
- NodeFilter.SHOW_ALL = 0xFFFFFFFF

filter
A NodeFilter against which all nodes in the subtree will be compared. Only nodes that pass the filter will be let through. By implementing this interface, you can define more specific filters, such as "all elements that have xlink:type="simple" attributes" or "all text nodes that contain the word *fnord*." Alternatively, you can pass null to indicate no custom filtering.

entityReferenceExpansion
Pass true if you want the iterator to descend through the children of entity reference nodes, false otherwise. Generally, this should be set to true.

Example 11.20 demonstrated a comment reader program that recursively descended an XML tree, printing out all of the comment nodes that were found. A NodeIterator makes it possible to write the program nonrecursively. When creating the iterator, the root argument is the document node; whatToShow is NodeFilter.SHOW_COMMENT; the node filter is null; and entityReferenceExpansion is true. Example 12.3 demonstrates.

Example 12.3 Using a NodeIterator to Extract All of the Comments from a Document

```
import javax.xml.parsers.*;
import org.w3c.dom.*;
import org.w3c.dom.traversal.*;
import org.xml.sax.SAXException;
import java.io.IOException;


public class CommentIterator {

  public static void main(String[] args) {

    if (args.length <= 0) {
      System.out.println("Usage: java DOMCommentReader URL");
      return;
    }
```

```
String url = args[0];

try {
  DocumentBuilderFactory factory
   = DocumentBuilderFactory.newInstance();
  DocumentBuilder parser = factory.newDocumentBuilder();

  // Check for the traversal module
  DOMImplementation impl = parser.getDOMImplementation();
  if (!impl.hasFeature("traversal", "2.0")) {
    System.out.println(
   "A DOM implementation that supports traversal is required."
    );
    return;
  }

  // Read the document
  Document doc = parser.parse(url);

  // Create the NodeIterator
  DocumentTraversal traversable = (DocumentTraversal) doc;
  NodeIterator iterator = traversable.createNodeIterator(
   doc, NodeFilter.SHOW_COMMENT, null, true);

  // Iterate over the comments
  Node node;
  while ((node = iterator.nextNode()) != null) {
    System.out.println(node.getNodeValue());
  }

}
catch (SAXException e) {
  System.out.println(e);
  System.out.println(url + " is not well-formed.");
}
catch (IOException e) {
  System.out.println(
   "Due to an IOException, the parser could not check " + url
  );
}
catch (FactoryConfigurationError e) {
  System.out.println("Could not locate a factory class");
```

```
      }
      catch (ParserConfigurationException e) {
        System.out.println("Could not locate a JAXP parser");
      }

    } // end main

}
```

You can decide for yourself whether or not you prefer the explicit recursion and tree-walking of Example 11.20 or the hidden recursion of CommentIterator here. With a decent implementation, there shouldn't be any noticeable performance penalty, so feel free to use whichever feels more natural to you.

Liveness

Node iterators are *live*. That is, if the document changes while the program is walking the tree, then the iterator retains its state. For example, let's suppose that the program is at node C of a node iterator that's walking through nodes A, B, C, D, and E in that order. If you delete node D and then call `nextNode()`, you'll get node E. If you add node Z in between nodes B and C and then call `previousNode()`, you'll get node Z. The iterator's current position is always between two nodes (or before the first node or after the last node) but never on a node; thus, it is not invalidated by deleting the current node.

For example, the following method deletes all of the comments in its `Document` argument. When the method returns, all of the comments have been removed.

```
public static void deleteComments(Document doc) {

  // Create the NodeIterator
  DocumentTraversal traversable = (DocumentTraversal) doc;
  NodeIterator iterator = traversable.createNodeIterator(
   doc, NodeFilter.SHOW_COMMENT, null, true);

  // Iterate over the comments
  Node comment;
  while ((comment = iterator.nextNode()) != null) {
    Node parent = comment.getParentNode();
    parent.removeChild(comment);
  }

}
```

This method changes the original Document object. It does not change the XML file from which the Document object was created, unless you specifically write the changed document back out into the original file after the comments have been deleted.

Filtering by Node Type

You can combine the various flags for whatToShow with the bitwise or operator. For example, Chapter 11 used a rather convoluted recursive getText() method in the ExampleExtractor program to accumulate all of the text from both text and CDATA section nodes within an element. Example 12.4 shows how NodeIterator can accomplish this task in a much more straightforward fashion.

Example 12.4 Using a NodeIterator to Retrieve the Complete Text Content of an Element

```
import org.w3c.dom.*;
import org.w3c.dom.traversal.*;


public class TextExtractor {

  public static String getText(Node node) {

    if (node == null) return "";

    // Set up the iterator
    Document doc = node.getOwnerDocument();
    DocumentTraversal traversable = (DocumentTraversal) doc;
    int whatToShow
     = NodeFilter.SHOW_TEXT | NodeFilter.SHOW_CDATA_SECTION;
    NodeIterator iterator = traversable.createNodeIterator(node,
     whatToShow, null, true);

    // Extract the text
    StringBuffer result = new StringBuffer();
    Node current;
    while ((current = iterator.nextNode()) != null) {
      result.append(current.getNodeValue());
    }
```

```
        return result.toString();

    }

  }
```

I'll reuse this class a little later on. Something like this should definitely be in your toolbox for whenever you need to extract the text content of an element.

> **Note**
> DOM Level 3 is going to add an almost equivalent `getTextContent()` method to the `Node` interface:
>
> ```
> public String getTextContent() throws DOMException
> ```
>
> The only difference is that this method will not operate on `Document` objects, whereas `TextExtractor.getText()` will.

NodeFilter

The `whatToShow` argument allows you to iterate over only certain node types in a subtree. Suppose you want to go beyond that. For example, you may have a program that reads XHTML documents and extracts all heading elements but ignores everything else. Or perhaps you want to find all SVG content in a document, or all the `GIFT` elements whose `price` attribute has a value greater than $10.00. Or perhaps you want to find those `SKU` elements containing the ID of a product that needs to be reordered, as determined by consulting an external database. All of these tasks and many more besides can be implemented through node filters on top of a `NodeIterator` or a `TreeWalker`.

Example 12.5 summarizes the `NodeFilter` interface. You implement this interface in a class of your own devising. The `acceptNode()` method contains the custom logic that decides whether any given node passes the filter or not. This method can return one of the three named constants—`NodeFilter.FILTER_ACCEPT`, `NodeFilter.FILTER_REJECT`, or `NodeFilter.FILTER_SKIP`—to indicate what it wants to do with that node.

Example 12.5 The NodeFilter Interface

```
package org.w3c.dom.traversal;

public interface NodeFilter {

  // Constants returned by acceptNode
  public static final short FILTER_ACCEPT = 1;
  public static final short FILTER_REJECT = 2;
  public static final short FILTER_SKIP   = 3;

  // Constants for whatToShow
  public static final int SHOW_ALL                    = 0xFFFFFFFF;
  public static final int SHOW_ELEMENT                = 0x00000001;
  public static final int SHOW_ATTRIBUTE              = 0x00000002;
  public static final int SHOW_TEXT                   = 0x00000004;
  public static final int SHOW_CDATA_SECTION          = 0x00000008;
  public static final int SHOW_ENTITY_REFERENCE       = 0x00000010;
  public static final int SHOW_ENTITY                 = 0x00000020;
  public static final int SHOW_PROCESSING_INSTRUCTION
   = 0x00000040;
  public static final int SHOW_COMMENT                = 0x00000080;
  public static final int SHOW_DOCUMENT               = 0x00000100;
  public static final int SHOW_DOCUMENT_TYPE          = 0x00000200;
  public static final int SHOW_DOCUMENT_FRAGMENT      = 0x00000400;
  public static final int SHOW_NOTATION               = 0x00000800;

  public short acceptNode(Node n);

}
```

For iterators, there are really only two options for the return value of `acceptNode()`, `FILTER_ACCEPT`, and `FILTER_SKIP`. `NodeIterator` treats `FILTER_REJECT` the same as `FILTER_SKIP`. (Tree-walkers, by contrast, do make a distinction between these two.) Rejecting a node prevents it from appearing in the list, but it does not prevent the node's children and descendants from appearing. They will be tested separately.

The `NodeFilter` does not override `whatToShow`. The two work in concert. For example, `whatToShow` can limit the iterator to only elements. Then the `acceptNode()` method can confidently cast every node that is passed to it to `Element` without first checking its node type.

To configure an iterator with a filter, pass the `NodeFilter` object to the `create-NodeIterator()` method. The `NodeIterator` will then pass each potential candidate node to the `acceptNode()` method to decide whether or not to include it in the iterator.

For an example, let's revisit the `DOMSpider` program demonstrated in Example 11.6. That program needed to recurse through the entire document, looking at each and every node to see whether or not it was an element and, if it was, whether or not it had an `xlink:type` attribute with the value `simple`. We can write that program much more simply using a `NodeFilter` to find the simple XLinks and a `Node-Iterator` to walk through them. Example 12.6 demonstrates the necessary filter.

Example 12.6 An Implementation of the NodeFilter Interface

```
import org.w3c.dom.traversal.NodeFilter;
import org.w3c.dom.*;


public class XLinkFilter implements NodeFilter {

  public static String XLINK_NAMESPACE
   = "http://www.w3.org/1999/xlink";

  public short acceptNode(Node node) {

    Element candidate = (Element) node;
    String type
     = candidate.getAttributeNS(XLINK_NAMESPACE, "type");
    if (type.equals("simple")) return FILTER_ACCEPT;
    return FILTER_SKIP;

  }

}
```

The following is a `spider()` method that has been revised to take advantage of `NodeIterator` and this filter. This can replace both the `spider()` and `findLinks()` methods of the previous version. The filter replaces the `isSimpleLink()` method. The code is considerably simpler than the version in Example 11.6.

```
public void spider(String systemID) {
  currentDepth++;
```

```
try {
  if (currentDepth < maxDepth) {
    Document document = parser.parse(systemID);
    process(document, systemID);

    Vector uris = new Vector();
    // search the document for URIs,
    // store them in vector, and print them
    DocumentTraversal traversal
     = (DocumentTraversal) document;
    NodeIterator xlinks = traversal.createNodeIterator(
      document.getDocumentElement(),// start at root element
      NodeFilter.SHOW_ELEMENT,      // only see elements
      new XLinkFilter(),            // only see simple XLinks
      true                          // expand entities
    );

    Element xlink;
    while ((xlink = (Element) xlinks.nextNode()) != null) {
      String uri = xlink.getAttributeNS(XLINK_NAMESPACE,
       "href");
      if (!uri.equals("")) {
        try {
          String wholePage = absolutize(systemID, uri);
          if (!visited.contains(wholePage)
           && !uris.contains(wholePage)) {
            uris.add(wholePage);
          }
        }
        catch (MalformedURLException e) {
          // If it's not a good URL, then we can't spider it
          // anyway, so just drop it on the floor.
        }
      } // end if
    } // end while
    xlinks.detach();

    Enumeration e = uris.elements();
    while (e.hasMoreElements()) {
      String uri = (String) e.nextElement();
      visited.add(uri);
```

```
            spider(uri);
          }

        }

      }
      catch (SAXException e) {
        // Couldn't load the document,
        // probably not well-formed XML, skip it
      }
      catch (IOException e) {
        // Couldn't load the document,
        // likely network failure, skip it
      }
      finally {
        currentDepth--;
        System.out.flush();
      }

  }
```

There is, however, one feature in the earlier version that this `NodeIterator`-based variant doesn't have. The `DOMSpider` in Chapter 11 tracked `xml:base` attributes. Because the `xml:base` attributes may appear on ancestors of the XLinks rather than on the XLinks themselves, a `NodeIterator` really isn't appropriate for tracking them. The key problem is that `xml:base` has *hierarchical scope*. That is, an `xml:base` attribute only applies to the element on which it appears and its descendants. Although the filter could easily be adjusted to notice elements that have `xml:base` attributes as well as those that have `xlink:type="simple"` attributes, an iterator really can't distinguish the other elements to which any given `xml:base` attribute applies.

DOM3 will add a `getBaseURI()` method to the `Node` interface that will alleviate the need to track `xml:base` attributes manually. In fact, this will be even more effective than the manual tracking of the Chapter 11 example, because it will also notice different base URIs that arise from external entities. Revising the `spider()` method to take advantage of this requires changing only a couple of lines of code, as follows:

```
String wholePage = absolutize(xlink.getBaseURI(), uri);
```

Unfortunately, this method is not yet supported by any of the common parsers, but it should be implemented in the not too distant future.

TreeWalker

The purpose of TreeWalker is much the same as that of NodeIterator—traversing a subtree of a document rooted at a particular node and filtered by both node type and custom logic. TreeWalker differs from NodeIterator in that the traversal model is based on a tree with parents, children, and sibling nodes rather than a linear list with only previous and next nodes. Because the traversal model is very similar to what's already available in the Node interface, tree-walkers aren't as commonly used as NodeIterator. But the ability to filter the nodes that appear in the tree can be very useful on occasion.

Example 12.7 summarizes the TreeWalker interface. It has getter methods that return the configuration of the TreeWalker, methods to get and set the current node, and methods to move from the current node to its parent, first child, last child, previous sibling, next sibling, previous node, and next node. In all cases, these methods return null if there is no such node (for example, if you ask for the last child of an empty element).

Example 12.7 The TreeWalker Interface

```
package org.w3c.dom.traversal;

public interface TreeWalker {

  public Node       getRoot();
  public int        getWhatToShow();
  public NodeFilter getFilter();
  public boolean    getExpandEntityReferences();

  public Node       getCurrentNode();
  public void       setCurrentNode(Node currentNode)
   throws DOMException;
  public Node       parentNode();
  public Node       firstChild();
  public Node       lastChild();
  public Node       previousSibling();
  public Node       nextSibling();
  public Node       previousNode();
  public Node       nextNode();

}
```

A `TreeWalker` object is always positioned at one of the nodes in its subtree. It begins its existence positioned at the first node in document order. From there you can change the tree-walker's position by invoking `nextNode()`, `previousNode()`, `parentNode()`, `firstChild()`, `lastChild()`, `previousSibling()`, and `nextSibling()`. In the event that there is no parent, sibling, or child relative to the current node within the tree-walker's tree, these methods all return null. You can find out where the tree-walker is positioned with `currentNode()`.

`TreeWalker` objects are created in almost exactly the same way as `NodeIterator` objects. That is, you cast the `Document` object you want to walk to `DocumentTraversal` and invoke its `createTreeWalker()` method. The `createTreeWalker()` method takes the same four arguments and their respective meanings as the `createNodeIterator()` method: the root node of the subtree to walk, an `int` constant specifying which types of nodes to display, a custom `NodeFilter` object or null, and a boolean indicating whether or not to expand entity references.

> **Note**
> If the root node is filtered out either by `whatToShow` or by the `NodeFilter`, then the subtree being walked may not have a single root. In other words, it's more like a `DocumentFragment` than a `Document`. As long as you're cognizant of this possibility, it is not a large problem.

`TreeWalkers` are called for whenever the hierarchy matters; that is, whenever what's important is not just the node itself but also its parent and other ancestor nodes. For example, suppose you want to generate a list of examples in a DocBook document in the following format:

```
Example 1.1: A plain text document that indicates an order for 12
Birdsong Clocks, SKU 244
Example 1.2: An XML document that indicates an order for 12
Birdsong Clocks, SKU 244
Example 1.3: A document that indicates an order for 12 Birdsong
Clocks, SKU 244
...
Example 2.1: An XML document that labels elements with schema
simple types
Example 2.2: URLGrabber
Example 2.3: URLGrabberTest
...
```

To review from Chapter 11, DocBook documents are structured roughly as follows:

```
<book>
  ...
  <chapter>
    ...
    <example id="filename.java">
      <title>Some Java Program</title>
      <programlisting>import javax.xml.parsers;
        // more Java code...
      </programlisting>
    </example>
    ...
    <example id="filename.xml">
      <title>Some XML document</title>
      <programlisting><![CDATA[<?xml version="1.0"?>
<root>
  ...
</root>]]></programlisting>
     </example>
    ...
  </chapter>
  more chapters...
</book>
```

For maximum convenience, we want a `TreeWalker` that sees only `book`, `chapter`, `example`, and `title` elements. However, `title` elements should be allowed only when they represent the title of an `example`, not a `chapter`, or a `figure`, or anything else. We can set `whatToShow` to `NodeFilter.SHOW_ELEMENT` to limit the tree-walker to elements, and design a `NodeFilter` that picks out only these four elements. Example 12.8 demonstrates this filter.

Example 12.8 The ExampleFilter Class

```
import org.w3c.dom.traversal.NodeFilter;
import org.w3c.dom.*;


public class ExampleFilter implements NodeFilter {
```

```
  public short acceptNode(Node node) {

    Element candidate = (Element) node;
    String name = candidate.getNodeName();
    if (name.equals("example")) return FILTER_ACCEPT;
    else if (name.equals("chapter")) return FILTER_ACCEPT;
    else if (name.equals("book")) return FILTER_ACCEPT;
    else if (name.equals("title")) {
      // Is this the title of an example, in which case we accept
      // it, or the title of something else, in which case we
      // reject it?
      Node parent = node.getParentNode();
      if ("example".equals(parent.getNodeName())) {
        return FILTER_ACCEPT;
      }
    }
    return FILTER_SKIP;

  }

}
```

In each case when an element is rejected, `acceptNode()` returns `FILTER_SKIP`, not `FILTER_REJECT`. For `TreeWalker`, unlike `NodeIterator`, the difference is important. By returning `FILTER_SKIP`, `acceptNode()` indicates that this node should not be reported but that its children should be. If `acceptNode()` returns `FILTER_REJECT` for a node, then neither that node nor any of its descendants would be traversed.

The `TreeWalker` is simply a view of the document. It does not itself change the document or the nodes that the document contains. For example, even though the `ExampleFilter` hides all text nodes, these can still be extracted from a `title` element. Example 12.9 walks the tree and pulls out these titles using this filter.

Example 12.9 Navigating a Subtree with TreeWalker

```
import javax.xml.parsers.*;
import org.w3c.dom.*;
import org.w3c.dom.traversal.*;
import org.xml.sax.SAXException;
import java.io.IOException;
```

```
public class ExampleList {

  public static void printExampleTitles(Document doc) {

    // Create the NodeIterator
    DocumentTraversal traversable = (DocumentTraversal) doc;
    TreeWalker walker = traversable.createTreeWalker(
     doc.getDocumentElement(), NodeFilter.SHOW_ELEMENT,
     new ExampleFilter(), true);

    // The TreeWalker starts out positioned at the root
    Node chapter = walker.firstChild();
    int chapterNumber = 0;
    while (chapter != null) {
      chapterNumber++;
      Node example = walker.firstChild();
      int exampleNumber = 0;
      while (example != null) {
        exampleNumber++;
        Node title = walker.firstChild();
        String titleText = TextExtractor.getText(title);
        titleText = "Example " + chapterNumber + "."
         + exampleNumber + ": " + titleText;
        System.out.println(titleText);
        // Back up to the example
        walker.parentNode();
        example = walker.nextSibling();
      }
      // Reposition the walker on the parent chapter
      walker.parentNode();
      // Go to the next chapter
      chapter = walker.nextSibling();
    }

  }

  public static void main(String[] args) {

    if (args.length <= 0) {
      System.out.println("Usage: java ExampleList URL");
      return;
    }
```

```
    String url = args[0];

    try {
      DocumentBuilderFactory factory
       = DocumentBuilderFactory.newInstance();
      DocumentBuilder parser = factory.newDocumentBuilder();

      // Check for the traversal module
      DOMImplementation impl = parser.getDOMImplementation();
      if (!impl.hasFeature("traversal", "2.0")) {
        System.out.println(
       "A DOM implementation that supports traversal is required."
        );
        return;
      }

      // Read the document
      Document doc = parser.parse(url);
      printExampleTitles(doc);

    }
    catch (SAXException e) {
      System.out.println(url + " is not well-formed.");
    }
    catch (IOException e) {
      System.out.println(
       "Due to an IOException, the parser could not check " + url
      );
    }
    catch (FactoryConfigurationError e) {
      System.out.println("Could not locate a factory class");
    }
    catch (ParserConfigurationException e) {
      System.out.println("Could not locate a JAXP parser");
    }

  } // end main

}
```

The use of TreeWalker here and NodeIterator in TextExtractor make this task a lot simpler than it otherwise would be. Hiding all of the irrelevant parts means, among other things, that you need not worry about the complexities of example elements that appear at different depths in the tree, or about insignificant white space that may sporadically add extra text nodes where you don't expect them. The traversal package enables you to boil down a document to the minimum structure relevant to your problem.

Summary

Both NodeIterator and TreeWalker can simplify the traversal of nodes of interest in a document. NodeIterator presents nodes as a one-dimensional list. TreeWalker presents them as a tree. That difference aside, the behavior and purpose of these two interfaces is much the same.

Both NodeIterator and TreeWalker traverse a subtree of the nodes in the document. Exactly which nodes belong in this subtree depends on four factors:

- The root node of the subtree (which often is *not* the root node or root element of the document). Only this node and its descendants will be seen by the TreeNodeIterator/Walker.
- whatToShow, an int constant that contains bit flags identifying which types of nodes to include. The basic bit flags for these constants are available as public final static variables in the NodeFilter interface; for example, NodeFilter.SHOW_ELEMENT, NodeFilter.SHOW_COMMENT, and NodeFilter.SHOW_TEXT.
- A NodeFilter object whose acceptNode() method returns NodeFilter.FILTER_ACCEPT, NodeFilter.FILTER_REJECT, or NodeFilter.FILTER_SKIP for each node passed to it.
- A boolean flag that specifies whether or not to expand entity references.

Each of these is specified when the NodeIterator or TreeWalker is created by the createNodeIterator()/createTreeWalker() method in the DocumentTraversal interface. In a DOM implementation that supports the traversal module, all classes that implement the Document interface also implement the DocumentTraversal interface. This enables you to create a NodeIterator or TreeWalker over a document by casting the corresponding Document object to DocumentTraversal.

Chapter 13

Output from DOM

Traditionally, one area in which DOM has been quite weak is *serialization,* the outputting of an in-memory DOM `Document` object into a text file. In fact, it's even possible to use DOM to create `Document` objects that cannot be serialized as well-formed XML files. (For example, DOM allows an element to have attributes with the same namespace prefix but different namespace URIs.) Serialization has been left for vendor-specific classes such as Xerces' `XMLSerializer`. However, DOM Level 3 adds several classes for writing XML documents into files, onto the network, or anything else you can hook an `OutputStream` to.

Xerces Serialization

The Apache XML Project's Xerces-J includes the `org.apache.xml.serialize` package for writing DOM `Document` objects onto output streams. Although this class is bundled with Xerces, it works with any DOM2 implementation. It does not depend on the details of the Xerces implementation classes, only on the standard DOM interfaces.

The basic technique for serializing documents with `org.apache.xml.serialize` is as follows:

1. Configure an `OutputFormat` object with the serialization options you want.
2. Connect an `OutputStream` to the location where you want to store the data.

3. Use the `OutputStream` and the `OutputFormat` to construct a new `XMLSerializer` object.
4. Pass the `Document` object you want to serialize to the `XMLSerializer`'s `serialize()` method.

For example, the following code could replace the JAXP ID transform from several examples in the last few chapters:

```
try {
  OutputFormat format = new OutputFormat(document);
  XMLSerializer output = new XMLSerializer(System.out, format);
  output.serialize(document);
}
catch (IOException e) {
  System.err.println(e);
}
```

`XMLSerializer` has a number of advantages over JAXP, including maintaining the document type declaration. Furthermore, it's much more configurable.

`XMLSerializer` has several constructors. Which to choose depends on whether you want to write to an `OutputStream` or a `Writer`, and whether or not you want to provide an `OutputFormat` when you create the serializer:

```
public XMLSerializer()
public XMLSerializer (OutputFormat format)
public XMLSerializer (Writer out, OutputFormat format)
public XMLSerializer (OutputStream out, OutputFormat format)
```

Generally I recommend that you specify both the format and the stream or writer when you construct the `XMLSerializer`. That said, you can set them or change them later with these methods:

```
public void setOutputFormat (OutputFormat format)
public void setOutputByteStream (OutputStream out)
public void setOutputCharStream (Writer out)
```

You must specify either the byte stream or the char stream before you can serialize.

If you don't want to serialize the entire document, then you can pass just an `Element` or a `DocumentFragment` to the `serialize()` method:

```
public void serialize (DocumentFragment fragment)
 throws IOException
public void serialize (Document doc) throws IOException
public void serialize (Element element) throws IOException
```

There are many other methods in the `XMLSerializer` class that, for the most part, you should ignore, unless you're subclassing it.

OutputFormat

The detailed behavior of a serializer is controlled by an `OutputFormat` object. This class can configure almost any aspect of serialization, including setting the maximum line length, changing the indentation, specifying which elements have their text escaped as CDATA sections, and more. A few options even have the potential to make your documents malformed. For example, if you add an element to the list of nonescaping elements, then any reserved characters like < and & that appear in its text content will be output as themselves rather than escaped as `<` and `&`.

One of the most frequent requests for serializers is "pretty printing" data with extra line breaks and indentation. Within reasonable limits, the `OutputFormat` class can provide this. Simply pass true to `setIndenting()`, pass the number of spaces you want each level to be indented to `setIndent()`, and pass the maximum line length to `setLineWidth()`. Example 13.1 demonstrates.

Example 13.1 Using Xerces' OutputFormat Class to "Pretty Print" XML

```
import java.math.*;
import java.io.IOException;
import org.w3c.dom.*;
import javax.xml.parsers.*;
import org.apache.xml.serialize.*;

public class IndentedFibonacci {

  public static void main(String[] args) {

    try {

      // Find the implementation
```

```
      DocumentBuilderFactory factory
       = DocumentBuilderFactory.newInstance();
      factory.setNamespaceAware(true);
      DocumentBuilder builder = factory.newDocumentBuilder();
      DOMImplementation impl = builder.getDOMImplementation();

      // Create the document
      Document doc = impl.createDocument(null,
       "Fibonacci_Numbers", null);

      // Fill the document
      BigInteger low  = BigInteger.ONE;
      BigInteger high = BigInteger.ONE;

      Element root = doc.getDocumentElement();

      for (int i = 0; i < 10; i++) {
        Element number = doc.createElement("fibonacci");
        Text text = doc.createTextNode(low.toString());
        number.appendChild(text);
        root.appendChild(number);

        BigInteger temp = high;
        high = high.add(low);
        low = temp;
      }

      // Serialize the document
      OutputFormat format = new OutputFormat(doc);
      format.setLineWidth(65);
      format.setIndenting(true);
      format.setIndent(2);
      XMLSerializer serializer
       = new XMLSerializer(System.out, format);
      serializer.serialize(doc);

    }
    catch (FactoryConfigurationError e) {
      System.out.println("Could not locate a JAXP factory class");
    }
    catch (ParserConfigurationException e) {
```

```
        System.out.println(
          "Could not locate a JAXP DocumentBuilder class"
        );
      }
      catch (DOMException e) {
        System.err.println(e);
      }
      catch (IOException e) {
        System.err.println(e);
      }

    }

  }
```

When run, this program produces the following output:

```
C:\XMLJAVA>java IndentedFibonacci
<?xml version="1.0" encoding="UTF-8"?>
<Fibonacci_Numbers>
  <fibonacci>1</fibonacci>
  <fibonacci>1</fibonacci>
  <fibonacci>2</fibonacci>
  <fibonacci>3</fibonacci>
  <fibonacci>5</fibonacci>
  <fibonacci>8</fibonacci>
  <fibonacci>13</fibonacci>
  <fibonacci>21</fibonacci>
  <fibonacci>34</fibonacci>
  <fibonacci>55</fibonacci>
</Fibonacci_Numbers>
```

I think you'll agree that this looks much more attractive than the smushed together output from the bare serialization without any extra white space. *One warning, however: White space is significant in XML.* Adding this white space has changed the document. This is not the same document as existed before it was "pretty printed." For this particular application, the extra white space is insignificant, but this is not true for all XML applications.

White space is just the beginning of what the `OutputFormat` class can control. Other features include the MIME media type, the XML declaration, the system and public IDs for the document type, which elements' content should be escaped as

CDATA sections, and more. Following is a list of the properties you can control by invoking various methods on `OutputFormat`. In some cases, the default is document dependent. When it's not, the default value is given in parentheses.

Method
The method is normally set to one of three values—`xml`, `html`, or `text`—indicating the type of output that is desired. The serializer uses this value to configure itself. The default value is determined by the type of the document being serialized.

```
public void setMethod (String method)
public String getMethod()
public static String whichMethod (Document doc)
```

Media Type (Null)
This is the MIME media type for the output, such as application/xml or application/xhtml+xml. Although not included in the document itself, this may be used as part of the stream's metadata if it's written into a file system or onto an HTTP connection or some such.

```
public void setMediaType (String version)
public String getMediaType()
public static String whichMediaType (Document doc)
```

Version (1.0)
The version number used in the encoding declaration should always be "`1.0`." Do not change this.

```
public void setVersion (String version)
public String getVersion()
```

Standalone (No)
The value of the `standalone` attribute in the XML declaration. This should be true for "`yes`" and false for"`no`".

```
public void setStandalone (boolean standalone)
public boolean getStandalone()
```

Encoding (UTF-8)
The encoding specifed in the `encoding` attribute in the XML declaration and used to convert characters to bytes when serializing onto an `OutputStream`.

```
public void setEncoding (String encoding)
public String getEncoding()
```

Omit XML Declaration (False)

If true, then no XML declaration is output. If false, then an XML declaration is written.

```
public void setOmitXMLDeclaration (boolean omitXMLDeclaration)
public boolean getOmitXMLDeclaration()
```

Document Type

This specifies the system and public IDs of the external DTD subset given in the document type declaration. These values are used only if the `Document` being serialized does not contain a `DocumentType` object of its own.

```
public void setDoctype (String publicID, String systemID)
public String getDoctypePublic()
public String getDoctypeSystem()
public static String whichDoctypePublic (Document doc)
public static String whichDoctypeSystem (Document doc)
```

Omit Document Type (False)

If true, then no document type declaration is output. If false, then a document type declaration is written. If the document does not have a document type declaration and none has been set with `setDoctype()`, then no document type declaration will be written, regardless of the value of this property.

```
public void setOmitDocumentType (boolean omitDocumentType)
public boolean getDocumentType()
```

Nonescaping Elements

The elements whose text-node children should not be escaped using entity references.

```
public void setNonEscapingElements (String[] elementNames)
public String[] getNonEscapingElements (String[] elementNames)
public boolean isNonEscapingElement (String name)
```

CDATA Elements

The elements whose text content should be enclosed in a CDATA section.

```
public void setCDATAElements (String[] elementNames)
public String[] getCDATAElements (String[] elementNames)
public boolean isCDATAElement (String name)
```

Omit Comments (False)

If true, then comments in the document are not written onto the output. If false, they are written.

```
public void setOmitComments (boolean omitComments)
public boolean getOmitComments()
```

Indenting (False)
If true, then the serializer will add indents at each level and wrap lines that exceed the maximum line width. If false, it won't. The number of spaces to indent is set by the indent property, and the column to wrap at is set by the line width property.

```
public void setIndenting (boolean indenting)
public boolean getIndenting()
```

Indent (4)
The number of spaces to indent each level if indenting is true.

```
public void setIndent (int indent)
public int getIndent()
```

Line Width (72)
The maximum number of characters in a line when indenting is true. Setting this to zero turns off line wrapping completely.

```
public void setLineWidth (int width)
public int getLineWidth()
```

Line Separator (\n)
The character or characters to use for a line break. Take care to set this property only to a carriage return, a linefeed, or a carriage return/linefeed pair.

```
public void setLineSeparator (String separator)
public String getLineSeparator()
```

Example 13.2 uses these methods to create a valid MathML document encoded in ISO-8859-1 with a document type declaration, an XML declaration, no comments, a 65-character maximum line width, a two-space indent, a standalone declaration with the value yes, and the MIME media type application/xml:

Example 13.2 Using Xerces' OutputFormat Class to "Pretty Print" MathML

```
import java.math.*;
import java.io.*;
import org.w3c.dom.*;
import javax.xml.parsers.*;
import org.apache.xml.serialize.*;
```

```
public class ValidFibonacciMathML {

  public static String MATHML_NS
   = "http://www.w3.org/1998/Math/MathML";

  public static void main(String[] args) {

    try {

      DocumentBuilderFactory factory
       = DocumentBuilderFactory.newInstance();
      factory.setNamespaceAware(true);
      DocumentBuilder builder = factory.newDocumentBuilder();
      DOMImplementation impl = builder.getDOMImplementation();

      Document doc = impl.createDocument(MATHML_NS, "math", null);

      BigInteger low  = BigInteger.ONE;
      BigInteger high = BigInteger.ONE;

      Element root = doc.getDocumentElement();
      root.setAttribute("xmlns", MATHML_NS);

      for (int i = 1; i <= 10; i++) {
        Element mrow = doc.createElementNS(MATHML_NS, "mrow");

        Element mi = doc.createElementNS(MATHML_NS, "mi");
        Text function = doc.createTextNode("f(" + i + ")");
        mi.appendChild(function);

        Element mo = doc.createElementNS(MATHML_NS, "mo");
        Text equals = doc.createTextNode("=");
        mo.appendChild(equals);

        Element mn = doc.createElementNS(MATHML_NS, "mn");
        Text value = doc.createTextNode(low.toString());
        mn.appendChild(value);

        mrow.appendChild(mi);
        mrow.appendChild(mo);
        mrow.appendChild(mn);
```

```
          root.appendChild(mrow);

          BigInteger temp = high;
          high = high.add(low);
          low = temp;
        }

        OutputFormat format = new OutputFormat(doc);
        format.setLineWidth(65);
        format.setIndenting(true);
        format.setIndent(2);
        format.setEncoding("ISO-8859-1");
        format.setDoctype("-//W3C//DTD MathML 2.0//EN",
         "http://www.w3.org/TR/MathML2/dtd/mathml2.dtd");
        format.setMediaType("application/xml");
        format.setOmitComments(true);
        format.setOmitXMLDeclaration(false);
        format.setVersion("1.0");
        format.setStandalone(true);

        XMLSerializer serializer
         = new XMLSerializer(System.out, format);
        serializer.serialize(doc);

      }
      catch (FactoryConfigurationError e) {
        System.out.println("Could not locate a JAXP factory class");
      }
      catch (ParserConfigurationException e) {
        System.out.println(
          "Could not locate a JAXP DocumentBuilder class"
        );
      }
      catch (DOMException e) {
        System.err.println(e);
      }
      catch (IOException e) {
        System.err.println(e);
      }
    }
  }
```

Following is the beginning of the output that this program produces:

```
C:\XMLJAVA>java ValidFibonacciMathML
<?xml version="1.0" encoding="ISO-8859-1"?>
<!DOCTYPE math PUBLIC "-//W3C//DTD MathML 2.0//EN"
                "http://www.w3.org/TR/MathML2/dtd/mathml2.dtd">
<math xmlns="http://www.w3.org/1998/Math/MathML">
  <mrow>
    <mi>f(1)</mi>
    <mo>=</mo>
    <mn>1</mn>
  </mrow>
  <mrow>
    <mi>f(2)</mi>
    <mo>=</mo>
    <mn>1</mn>
  </mrow>
...
```

You can imagine other requests for the serializer. For example, you might want a line break after each </mrow> end-tag but no line breaks inside mrow elements. Although OutputFormat doesn't give you enough control to arrange serialization to this level of detail, you could write a custom subclass of XMLSerializer to accomplish this.

DOM Level 3

DOM Level 3 (DOM3) will finally add a standard load-and-save package, making it possible to write completely implementation-independent DOM programs. This package, org.w3c.dom.ls, is identified by the feature strings LS-Load and LS-Save. The loading part includes the DOMBuilder interface you've already encountered. The saving part is based on the DOMWriter interface. DOMWriter is more powerful than XMLSerializer. Whereas XMLSerializer is limited to outputting documents, document fragments, and elements, DOMWriter can output any kind of node at all. Furthermore, you can install a filter into a DOMWriter to control its output.

As shown by the method signatures in Example 13.3, DOMWriter can copy a Node object from memory into serialized bytes or characters. It has methods to write XML nodes onto a Java OutputStream or a String. The most common kind of node you'll write is a Document, but you also can write all of the other kinds of

Caution

This section is based on very early, bleeding-edge technology and specifications, particularly the July 25, 2002 Working Draft of the *Document Object Model (DOM) Level 3 Abstract Schemas and Load and Save Specification [http://www.w3.org/TR/2002/WD-DOM-Level-3-LS-20020725]* and Xerces-J 2.0.2. Even with Xerces-J 2.2, most of the code in this section won't even compile, much less run. Furthermore, it's virtually guaranteed that the details in this section will change before DOM3 becomes a final recommendation.

nodes as well, such as `Element`, `Attr`, and `Text`. This interface also has methods to control exactly how the output is formatted and how errors are reported.

Example 13.3 The DOM3 DOMWriter Interface

```
package org.w3c.dom.ls;

public interface DOMWriter {

  public void    setFeature(String name, boolean state)
   throws DOMException;
  public boolean canSetFeature(String name, boolean state);
  public boolean getFeature(String name) throws DOMException;

  public String  getEncoding();
  public void    setEncoding(String encoding);
  public String  getNewLine();
  public void    setNewLine(String newLine);

  public boolean writeNode(OutputStream out, Node node);
  public String writeToString(Node node) throws DOMException;

  public DOMErrorHandler getErrorHandler();
  public void setErrorHandler(DOMErrorHandler errorHandler);

  public DOMWriterFilter getFilter();
  public void setFilter(DOMWriterFilter filter);

}
```

Note
DOMWriter is not a java.io.Writer. In fact, it even prefers output streams to writers. The name is just a coincidence.

The primary purpose of this interface is to write nodes into strings or onto streams. These nodes can be complete documents or parts thereof, such as elements or text nodes. For example, the following code fragment uses the DOMWriter object writer to copy the Document object doc onto System.out and copy its root element into a String:

```
try {
  DOMWriter writer;
  // initialize the DOMWriter...
  writer.writeNode(document, System.out);
  String root =
   writer.writeToString(document.getDocumentElement());
}
catch (Exception e) {
  System.err.println(e);
}
```

DOMWriter also has several methods to configure the output. The setNewLine() method can choose the line separator used for output. The only legal values are carriage return, a line feed, or both; that is, in Java parlance, "\r", "\n", or "\r\n". You can also set this to null to indicate you want the platform's default value.

The setEncoding() method changes the character encoding used for the output. Which encodings any given serializer supports varies from implementation to implementation, but common values include UTF-8, UTF-16, and ISO-8859-1. UTF-8 is the default if a value is not supplied. For example, the following writer sets up the output for use on a Macintosh:

```
DOMWriter writer;
// initialize the DOMWriter...
writer.setNewLine("\r");
writer.setEncoding("MacRoman");
```

More detailed control of the output can be achieved by getting and setting features of the DOMWriter, as you'll see shortly.

The setErrorHandler() method can install an org.w3c.dom.DOMErrorHandler object to receive notification of any problems that arise when outputting a node such as an element that uses the same prefix for two different namespace URIs on two attributes. This is a callback interface, similar to org.xml.sax.ErrorHandler but even simpler because it doesn't use different methods for different kinds of errors. Example 13.4 demonstrates this interface. The handleError() method returns true if processing should continue after the error, or false if it shouldn't.

Example 13.4 The DOM3 DOMErrorHandler Interface

```
package org.w3c.dom;

public interface DOMErrorHandler {

  public boolean handleError(DOMError error);

}
```

In Xerces-2, the XMLSerializer class implements the DOMWriter interface. If you prefer, you can use these methods instead of the ones discussed in the last section. Example 13.5 demonstrates a complete program that builds a simple SVG document in memory and writes it into the file circle.svg in the current working directory using a \r\n line end and the UTF-16 encoding. The error handler is set to an anonymous inner class that prints error messages on System.err and returns false to indicate that processing should stop when an error is detected.

Example 13.5 Serializing with DOMWriter

```
import org.w3c.dom.*;
import org.apache.xerces.dom3.*;
import org.apache.xerces.dom3.ls.DOMWriter;
import org.apache.xml.serialize.XMLSerializer;
import java.io.IOException;
import javax.xml.parsers.*;

public class SVGCircle {

  public static void main(String[] args) {
```

```
try {
  // Find the implementation
  DocumentBuilderFactory factory
   = DocumentBuilderFactory.newInstance();
  factory.setNamespaceAware(true);
  DocumentBuilder builder = factory.newDocumentBuilder();
  DOMImplementation impl = builder.getDOMImplementation();

  // Create the document
  DocumentType svgDOCTYPE = impl.createDocumentType(
   "svg", "-//W3C//DTD SVG 1.0//EN",
   "http://www.w3.org/TR/2001/REC-SVG-20010904/DTD/svg10.dtd"
  );
  Document doc = impl.createDocument(
   "http://www.w3.org/2000/svg", "svg", svgDOCTYPE);

  // Fill the document
  Node rootElement = doc.getDocumentElement();
  Element circle = doc.createElementNS(
   "http://www.w3.org/2000/svg", "circle");
  circle.setAttribute("r", "100");
  rootElement.appendChild(circle);

  // Serialize the document onto System.out
  DOMWriter writer = new XMLSerializer();
  writer.setNewLine("\r\n");
  writer.setEncoding("UTF-16");
  writer.setErrorHandler(
    new DOMErrorHandler() {
      public boolean handleError(DOMError error) {
        System.err.println(error.getMessage());
        return false;
      }
    }
  );
  writer.writeNode(System.out, doc);

}
catch (Exception e) {
  System.err.println(e);
```

```
        }

      }

    }
```

> **Note**
> Xerces-J 2.2 currently puts the `DOMWriter` interface in the `org.apache.xerces.dom3.ls` package instead of the `org.w3c.dom.ls` package. The Xerces development team is trying to keep the experimental DOM3 classes separate from the main API until DOM3 is more stable.

Creating DOMWriters

Example 13.5 depends on Xerces-specific classes. It won't work with GNU JAXP, or the Oracle XML Parser for Java, or other parsers, even after these parsers are upgraded to support DOM3. However, you can write the code in a much more parser-independent fashion by using the `DOMImplementationLS` interface, shown in Example 13.6, to create concrete implementations of `DOMWriter`, rather than constructing the implementation classes directly. `DOMImplementationLS` is a subinterface of `DOMImplementation` that adds three methods to create new `DOMBuilders`, `DOMWriters`, and `DOMInputSources`.

Example 13.6 The DOM3 DOMImplementationLS Interface

```
package org.w3c.dom.ls;

public interface DOMImplementationLS {

  public static final short MODE_SYNCHRONOUS  = 1;
  public static final short MODE_ASYNCHRONOUS = 2;

  public DOMWriter      createDOMWriter();
  public DOMInputSource createDOMInputSource();
  public DOMBuilder     createDOMBuilder(short mode,
   String schemaType) throws DOMException;

}
```

You retrieve a concrete instance of this factory interface by using the DOM3 `DOMImplementationRegistry` factory class introduced in Chapter 10 to request a `DOMImplementation` object that supports the LS-Save feature. Then you cast that object to `DOMImplementationLS`. For example,

```
try {
  DOMImplementation impl = DOMImplementationRegistry
   .getDOMImplementation("Core 2.0 LS-Save 3.0");
  if (impl != null) {
      DOMImplementationLS implls = (DOMImplementationLS) impl;
      DOMWriter writer = implls.createDOMWriter();
      writer.writeNode(System.out, document);
  }
  else {
    System.out.println(
     "Could not find a DOM3 Save compliant parser.");
  }
}
catch (Exception e) {
  System.err.println(e);
}
```

Using this technique, it's uncomplicated to write a completely implementation-independent program to generate and serialize XML documents, as Example 13.7 demonstrates. It uses the `DOMImplementationRegistry` class to load the `DOMImplementationLS` and the `DOMWriter` class to output the final result. Otherwise, it just uses the standard DOM2 classes that you've seen in previous chapters.

Example 13.7 An Implementation-Independent DOM3 Program to Build and Serialize an XML Document

```
import org.w3c.dom.*;
import org.w3c.dom.ls.*;

public class SVGDOMCircle {

  public static void main(String[] args) {

    try {
      // Find the implementation
```

```
          DOMImplementation impl
           = DOMImplementationRegistry.getDOMImplementation(
              "Core 2.0 LS-Load 3.0 LS-Save 3.0");
          if (impl == null) {
            System.out.println(
             "Could not find a DOM3 Load-Save compliant parser.");
            return;
          }

          // Create the document
          DocumentType svgDOCTYPE = impl.createDocumentType(
           "svg", "-//W3C//DTD SVG 1.0//EN",
           "http://www.w3.org/TR/2001/REC-SVG-20010904/DTD/svg10.dtd"
          );
          Document doc = impl.createDocument(
           "http://www.w3.org/2000/svg", "svg", svgDOCTYPE);

          // Fill the document
          Node rootElement = doc.getDocumentElement();
          Element circle = doc.createElementNS(
           "http://www.w3.org/2000/svg", "circle");
          circle.setAttribute("r", "100");
          rootElement.appendChild(circle);

          // Serialize the document onto System.out
          DOMImplementationLS implls = (DOMImplementationLS) impl;
          DOMWriter writer = implls.createDOMWriter();
          writer.writeNode(System.out, doc);

        }
        catch (Exception e) {
          System.err.println(e);
        }

      }

    }
```

This program needs to test for both the LS-Load and LS-Save features because it's not absolutely guaranteed that an implementation that has one will have the other, particularly in the early days of DOM3.

Serialization Features

The default settings for the `writeNode()` and `writeToString()` methods are acceptable for most uses. Occasionally, however, you will want a little more control over the serialized form. For example, you might want the output to be "pretty printed" with extra white space added to indent the elements nicely. Or you might want the output to be in canonical form. All of this and more can be controlled by setting features in the writer before invoking the write method.

Defined features include the following:

normalize-characters, optional, default true
If true, then output text should be normalized according to the W3C Character Model. For example, the word *café* would be represented as the four-character string *c a f é* rather than the five-character string *c a f e combining_acute_accent*. Implementations are only required to support a false value for this feature.

split-cdata-sections, required, default true
If true, then CDATA sections that contain the CDATA section end delimiter `]]>` are split into pieces and the `]]>` is included in a raw text node. If false, then such CDATA sections are not split; instead, an error is reported and output stops.

entities, required, default true
If true, then entity references such as `©` are included in the output. If false, then they are not; instead, their replacement text is included.

whitespace-in-element-content, optional, default true
If true, then all white space is output. If false, then text nodes that contain only white space are deleted if the parent element's declaration from the DTD/schema does not allow #PCDATA to appear at that point.

discard-default-content, required, default true
If true, then the implementation will not write out any nodes whose presence can be inferred from the DTD or schema, for example, default attribute values. If false, then it will include them in the instance document it outputs.

canonical-form, optional, default false
If true, then the document will be written according to the rules specified by the Canonical XML specification. For example, attributes will be lexically ordered and CDATA sections will not be included. If false, then the exact output is implementation dependent.

format-pretty-print, optional, default false
If true, white space will be adjusted to "pretty print" the XML. Exactly what this means—for example, how many spaces elements are indented or what maximum line length is used—is left up to implementations.

validate, optional, default false
If true, then the document's schema is used to validate the document as it is being output. Any validation errors that are discovered are reported to the registered error handler. (Both validation and error handlers are other new features in DOM3.)

Implementations may define additional custom features, the names of which will generally begin with vendor-specific prefixes such as "apache:" or "oracle:." For portability, remember to check for the existence of such a feature with `canSetFeature()` before setting it. Otherwise, you're likely to encounter an unexpected `DOMException` when the program is run with a different parser.

For example, the following code fragment attempts to output the `Document` object `doc` onto the `OutputStream out` in canonical form. However, if the implementation of `DOMWriter` doesn't support Canonical XML, it simply outputs the document in the normal way.

```
try {
  DOMWriter writer = new XMLSerializer();
  if (writer.canSetFeature("canonical-form", true)) {
    writer.setFeature("canonical-form", true);
  }
  writer.writeNode(out, doc);
}
catch (Exception e) {
  System.err.println(e);
}
```

Filtering Output

One of the more original aspects of the `DOMWriter` API is the ability to attach filters to a writer that remove certain nodes from the output. A `DOMWriterFilter` is a subinterface of `NodeFilter` from the traversal API described in Chapter 12, and works almost exactly like it. This shouldn't be too surprising, because serializing a document is merely another tree-walking operation.

To perform output filtering, you first implement the `DOMWriterFilter` interface shown in Example 13.8. As with the `NodeFilter` superinterface, the acceptNode() method returns one of the three named constants—NodeFilter.FILTER_ACCEPT, NodeFilter.FILTER_REJECT, or NodeFilter.FILTER_SKIP—to indicate whether or not a particular node and its descendants should be output. (This method isn't listed here because it's inherited from the superinterface.)

Example 13.8 The DOMWriterFilter Interface

```
package org.w3c.dom.ls;

public interface DOMWriterFilter extends NodeFilter {

  public int getWhatToShow();

}
```

The getWhatToShow() method returns an int constant indicating which kinds of nodes are passed to this filter for processing. This is a combination of the bit constants used by NodeIterator and TreeWalker in Chapter 12: NodeFilter.SHOW_ELEMENT, NodeFilter.SHOW_TEXT, NodeFilter.SHOW_COMMENT, and so on.

Example 8.9 demonstrated a SAX filter that removed everything that wasn't in the XHTML namespace from a document. Example 13.9 is a DOMWriterFilter that accomplishes the same task.

Example 13.9 Filtering Everything That Isn't XHTML on Output

```
import org.w3c.dom.*;
import org.w3c.dom.traversal.NodeFilter;
import org.w3c.dom.ls.DOMWriterFilter;

public class XHTMLFilter implements DOMWriterFilter {

  public final static String XHTML_NAMESPACE
   = "http://www.w3.org/1999/xhtml";

  // This filter only operates on elements. Everything else
  // will be output without passing through the filter. However,
  // descendants of non-XHTML elements will not be output
  // because their ancestor elements have been rejected.
  // Note that this means we don't fully handle nested XHTML;
```

```
    // e.g., XHTML contains SVG, which contains XHTML.
    // XHTML inside SVG will not be output.
    public short getWhatToShow() {
      return NodeFilter.SHOW_ELEMENT;
    }


    public int acceptNode(Node node) {

      int type = node.getNodeType();
      if (type != Node.ELEMENT_NODE) {
        return NodeFilter.FILTER_ACCEPT;
      }

      String namespace = node.getNamespaceURI();
      if (XHTML_NAMESPACE.equals(namespace)) {
        return NodeFilter.FILTER_ACCEPT;
      }
      else {
       return NodeFilter.FILTER_SKIP;
      }

    }

  }
```

The one thing that this doesn't filter out is non-XHTML attributes. Those are written out with their elements. They are not passed to `acceptNode()`. To filter out attributes from other namespaces would require a custom `DOMWriter`. You might be able to remove them from the element nodes passed to `acceptNode()`, but this would modify the in-memory tree as well as the streamed output. Furthermore, although Java doesn't support this, the IDL code for `DOMWriter` indicates that the `Node` passed to `acceptNode()` is read only. The underlying implementation is probably not expecting `acceptNode()` to modify its argument. Doing so would be asking for corrupt data structures.

You can install a filter into a `DOMWriter` using the `setFilter()` method. Then any node the filter rejects will not be serialized. Example 13.10 uses the above `XHTMLFilter` to output pure XHTML from an input document that might contain SVG, MathML, SMIL, or other non-XHTML elements.

Example 13.10 Using a DOMWriterFilter

```
import org.w3c.dom.*;
import org.w3c.dom.ls.*;

public class XHTMLPurifier {

  public static void main(String[] args) {

    try {
      // Find the implementation
      DOMImplementation impl
       = DOMImplementationRegistry.getDOMImplementation(
          "Core 2.0 LS-Load 3.0 LS-Save 3.0");
      if (impl == null) {
        System.out.println(
         "Could not find a DOM3 Load-Save compliant parser.");
        return;
      }
      DOMImplementationLS implls = (DOMImplementationLS) impl;

      // Load the parser
      DOMBuilder parser = implls.createDOMBuilder(
       DOMImplementationLS.MODE_SYNCHRONOUS);

      // Parse the document
      Document doc = parser.parseURI(document);

      // Serialize the document onto System.out while filtering
      DOMWriter writer = implls.createDOMWriter();
      DOMWriterFilter filter = new XHTMLFilter();
      writer.setFilter(filter);
      writer.writeNode(System.out, doc);

    }
    catch (Exception e) {
      System.err.println(e);
    }
```

```
        }

    }
```

Summary

Serialization is the process of taking an in-memory DOM data structure such as a `Document` object and writing it out onto a stream as bytes or characters. DOM2 and earlier does not include any standard classes or interfaces for performing serialization. Consequently, every implementation of DOM must provide its own unique API for performing this necessary task. In Xerces, that need is filled by the `XMLSerializer` class. The `OutputFormat` class stores the various configuration options for an `XMLSerializer`, including encoding, white space added for "pretty printing," line separator, maximum line width, which elements to output using CDATA sections, and more.

DOM3 finally adds a standard set of serialization interfaces. The `DOMWriter` interface provides basic methods for serializing a `Document` object onto a stream or into a string. You can control the insignificant format of the output by setting various features, such as format-canonical and discard-default-content to either true or false. A `DOMWriterFilter` can control which nodes are output.

Part IV

JDOM

Chapter 14

JDOM

Tree-based APIs such as DOM are very useful when developers want to keep the entire document in memory at once with random access to the entire tree. Unfortunately, DOM suffers from a number of design flaws and limitations that make it less than ideal as a Java API for processing XML. These include the following:

- DOM needed to be backward compatible with the hackish, poorly thought out, unplanned object models used in third-generation web browsers.
- DOM was designed by a committee trying to reconcile differences among the object models implemented by Netscape, Microsoft, and other vendors. The DOM committee needed a solution that was at least minimally acceptable to everybody, which resulted in an API that's maximally acceptable to no one.
- DOM is a cross-language API defined in IDL. As such, it is limited to the features and classes that are available in essentially all programming languages, including not fully object-oriented scripting languages such as JavaScript and Visual Basic. It is a lowest-common-denominator API that neither takes full advantage of Java nor adheres to Java best practices, naming conventions, and coding standards.
- DOM must work for both HTML (not only XHTML, but also traditional, malformed HTML) and XML.

These four constraints made DOM a lot more clumsy and harder to use than it should have been. I'm virtually certain that if you've read Chapters 9 to 13, you've often found yourself muttering in rather colorful language about some of the more harebrained aspects of DOM. I know I certainly did as I wrote those chapters. In almost every case, the specific problem that elicits such complaints is a result of one of these four design constraints.

JDOM, on the other hand, is a tree-based API for processing XML documents with Java that threw out DOM's limitations and assumptions and started from scratch. It is designed purely for XML, purely for Java, and with no concern for backward compatibility with earlier, similar APIs. It is thus much cleaner and much simpler than DOM. Most developers find JDOM to be far more intuitive and easy to use than DOM. It's not that JDOM will enable you to do anything you can't do with DOM. However, writing the same program with JDOM will normally take you less time and have fewer bugs when finished, simply because of the greater intuitiveness of the API. In many ways, JDOM is to DOM as Java is to C++—a much improved, incompatible replacement for the earlier, more complex technology.

> **Caution**
> JDOM is still in beta at the time of this writing. This chapter is based on the most current CVS version available, which is shortly after beta-8 and somewhere before beta-9. The API has been stabilizing, and I don't foresee any major changes between now and 1.0. However, a number of the details are likely to shift. I'd definitely check the method signatures with the latest version of the JavaDoc API documentation.

What Is JDOM?

JDOM is an open source, tree-based, pure Java API for parsing, creating, manipulating, and serializing XML documents. Brett McLaughlin and Jason Hunter invented it in spring 2000. I asked Jason how it happened, and here is what he told me:

> In the early months of 2000, in a time before I knew Brett, I found myself working with XML for a contract project and growing increasingly frustrated with DOM as a way to solve my problems. My mind had an expectation for what a Java-based XML manipulation API would look like. DOM wasn't anything like it.
>
> In the spring of 2000, I attended Brett's talk on DOM and SAX at the O'Reilly Conference on Enterprise Java. I was hoping he'd share with me the DOM philosophy so I could see why reality wasn't matching my expectations. Rather than clearing things up, I found every fifth slide in his presentation was titled "Gotcha!" and listed one more thing you had to watch out for.

After his talk we sat down together on the lawn in San Jose. It was a gorgeous spring day. He was just about to release a book that was clearly destined to be a bestseller (Java and XML buzzwords in the title, what can go wrong, right elharo?). I was telling him some of what that means for a person's career, based on my experience with a popular servlets book. I used the opportunity to ask him (someone far more expert in XML than myself at the time), "Why does it have to be like this?" He thought about it, we talked about it, and ten minutes later we decided to start an open source project to create a Java-specific XML object model. It was the first alternative to DOM in the Java world.

We worked for about a month designing the early API. We each had our role to play. Brett made sure the API was consistent with XML specifications. I made sure the API was acceptable to a Java programmer who wanted to just use XML and get on with their life. We had two private betas, then a public beta 3. James Duncan Davidson was helpful during the two private betas, especially on the interfaces-versus-classes debate.

Since then numerous people have contributed to JDOM's development, including Alex Rosen, Alex Chaffee, James Duncan Davidson, Philip Nelson, Jools Enticknap, Bradley S. Huffman, and yours truly.

JDOM is open source like SAX and DOM. (Proprietary XML APIs really have not caught on.) Hunter and McLaughlin publish it under the very liberal Apache license. Essentially you can do anything you want with it except use the name "JDOM" for derivative works. It has already been forked once, resulting in James Strachan's dom4j.

dom4j

James Strachan forked JDOM in late 2000 to experiment with using interfaces built by factory methods instead of concrete classes built by constructors to represent the nodes. The result was dom4j.

dom4j has some features I like, including integrated XPath support and a generic `Node` interface that makes document navigation a lot simpler. However, my observation is that most developers find it much easier to work with class-based APIs such as JDOM than with pure interface-based APIs such as dom4j and DOM. Furthermore, classes can enforce constraints such as, "The name property of an `Element` must be a legal XML name." Interfaces can't do that. In my opinion, dom4j makes it too easy to slip out of the constraints of XML and produce a malformed document.

Like DOM, JDOM represents an XML document as a tree composed of elements, attributes, comments, processing instructions, text nodes, CDATA sections, and so forth. The entire tree is available at any time. Unlike SAX, JDOM can access any part of the tree at any time. Unlike DOM, all of the different kinds of nodes in the tree are represented by concrete classes rather than interfaces. Furthermore, there is no generic `Node` interface or class that all of the different node classes implement or extend.[1]

JDOM is written in and for Java. It consistently uses the Java coding conventions and the class library. For example, all primary JDOM classes have `equals()`, `toString()`, and `hashCode()` methods. They all implement the `Cloneable` and `Serializable` interfaces. The children of an `Element` or a `Document` object are stored in a `java.util.List`. JDOM strives to be correct—not only with respect to XML, but also with respect to Java.

JDOM does not itself include a parser. Instead it depends on a SAX parser with a custom `ContentHandler` to parse documents and build JDOM models from them. Xerces 1.4.4 is bundled with JDOM. However, it can work equally well with any SAX2 compliant parser, including Crimson, Ælfred, the Oracle XML Parser for Java, Piccolo, Xerces-2, and more. Any of these can read an XML document and feed it into JDOM. JDOM can also convert DOM `Document` objects into JDOM `Document` objects, which is useful for piping the output of existing DOM programs to the input of a JDOM program. However, if you're working with a stream of XML data read from a disk or a network, it's preferable to use SAX to produce the JDOM tree, because it avoids the overhead of building the in-memory tree twice in two different representations.

Like DOM (and unlike SAX), JDOM can build a new XML tree in memory. Data for the tree can come from a non-XML source such as a database, from literals in the Java program, or from calculations as in many of the Fibonacci number examples in this book. When creating new XML documents from scratch (rather than reading them from a parser), JDOM checks all of the data for well-formedness. For example, unlike many DOM implementations, JDOM does not allow programs to create comments whose data includes the double hyphen (`--`) or elements and attributes whose namespaces conflict in impossible ways.

Once a document has been loaded into memory, whether by creating it from scratch or by parsing it from a stream, JDOM can modify the document. A JDOM tree is fully read-write. All parts of the tree can be moved, deleted, and added to—subject to the usual restrictions of XML. (For example, you can add an attribute to an element but not to a comment.) Unlike DOM, there are no annoying read-only sections of the tree that you can't change.

Finally, when you're finished working with a document in memory, JDOM lets you serialize it back out to disk or onto a stream as a sequence of bytes. JDOM pro-

---

1. This is personally my least-favorite aspect of the JDOM design. It makes tree-walking and search operations far more cumbersome than they are in DOM.

vides numerous options to specify the encoding, indenting, line end characters, and other details of serialization. Alternately, if you don't want to convert the document to a stream, you can produce a SAX event sequence or a DOM document as output instead.

Creating XML Elements with JDOM

One of my favorite things about JDOM is that, 90 percent of the time, it works exactly the way I expect it to work. I don't have to look at the documentation because my best guess is almost always right. This is only sometimes true for SAX and almost never true for DOM. For example, suppose you wanted to create the JDOM representation of this element:

```
<fibonacci/>
```

The simplest, most obvious solution I can imagine is this:

```
Element element = new Element("fibonacci");
```

Guess what? That's exactly how you do create an element in JDOM. Compare that with the DOM approach:

```
DocumentBuilderFactory factory
 = DocumentBuilderFactory.newInstance();
DocumentBuilder builder = factory.newDocumentBuilder();
DOMImplementation impl = builder.getDOMImplementation();
Document doc = impl.createDocument(
 null, "Fibonacci_Numbers", null);
Element element = doc.createElement("fibonacci");
```

I think any sane developer would agree that JDOM is simpler, at least for this initial example.

Now suppose you want to give the element some text content like this:

```
<fibonacci>8</fibonacci>
```

Here's the first thing that occurs to me:

```
Element element = new Element("fibonacci");
element.setText("8");
```

Guess what? That works. It is exactly how JDOM fills an element with text. Unlike DOM, you don't have to create any separate text nodes. JDOM does use a `Text` class internally, but you don't need to know about that. You can just use strings.

Now suppose you want to add an attribute to the element like this:

```
<fibonacci index="6">8</fibonacci>
```

The first thing that occurs to me is this:

```
Element element = new Element("fibonacci");
element.setText("8");
element.setAttribute("index", "6");
```

Once again, the most obvious solution is the correct solution. This is a running theme in JDOM. Try the simplest thing that could possibly work, and chances are it *will* work.

> **Note**
>
> On the other hand, there are some limits to simplicity, mostly established by XML. JDOM strives to be as simple as it can be and no simpler. It does not hide the genuinely complex parts of XML. For example, it faithfully reproduces all the complexity of XML namespaces, including the parts that have occasionally been labeled "psychotic." More specifically, it allows the same prefix to map to different URIs in different parts of the document. This compares favorably with some other APIs (I'm thinking of ElectricXML here) that pretend XML is simpler than it really is. In general, if something is complex in JDOM, it's because that same something is equally complex in XML.

Of course many elements contain child elements, comments, processing instructions, and other things besides pure text. In this case, you can attach them by calling the `addContent()` method. For example, suppose you want to create this element:

```
<sequence>
  <number>3</number>
  <number>5</number>
</sequence>
```

First you need to create three Element objects, two for number elements and one for the sequence element. Then you need to add the number elements to the sequence element in the order you want them to appear. For example:

```
Element element = new Element("sequence");
Element firstNumber = new Element("number");
Element secondNumber = new Element("number");
firstNumber.setText("3");
secondNumber.setText("5");
element.addContent(firstNumber);
element.addContent(secondNumber);
```

Actually I've cheated a bit here. What this really produces is this element:

```
<sequence><number>3</number><number>5</number></sequence>
```

White space is significant in XML and thus significant in JDOM. If you want the nicely indented element, you also need to add some strings containing the appropriate white space, as follows:

```
Element element = new Element("sequence");
Element firstNumber = new Element("number");
Element secondNumber = new Element("number");
firstNumber.setText("3");
secondNumber.setText("5");
element.addContent("\n  ");
element.addContent(firstNumber);
element.addContent("\n  ");
element.addContent(secondNumber);
element.addContent("\n");
```

If you only care about the extra white space when the document is serialized, you can ask an XMLOutputter to insert it for you. I'll cover this soon.

Creating XML Documents with JDOM

Let's begin with a simple JDOM program that creates the following XML document:

```
<?xml version="1.0"?>
<GREETING>Hello JDOM!</GREETING>
```

As all documents should have root elements, we'll need to create the root GREETING element first, then use that element to create the document:

```
Element root = new Element("GREETING");
root.setText("Hello JDOM!");
Document doc = new Document(root);
```

> **Note**
> Initially the Element object is not associated with any Document. It is freestanding. This contrasts with DOM, which requires that all nodes are always part of some document. JDOM allows nodes to stand on their own if that's useful. However, JDOM does not allow a node to be part of two documents at once. Before an Element can be transferred into a new Document it must first be detached from its old document using its detach() method.

You can reorder the method calls. For example, you might want to modify the root element after it has been attached to the document, as follows:

```
Element root = new Element("GREETING");
Document doc = new Document(root);
root.setText("Hello JDOM!");
```

You can even create the Document object first by using a no-args constructor and then setting its root element, as follows:

```
Document doc = new Document();
Element root = new Element("GREETING");
root.setText("Hello JDOM!");
doc.setRootElement(root);
```

In this case, the document begins its life in a temporarily malformed state, and any attempt to do almost anything with it except set a root element or add content to the document's prolog will fail with a java.lang.IllegalStateException.

Writing XML Documents with JDOM

Once you've created a document, you're likely to want to serialize it to a network socket, a file, a string, or some other stream. JDOM's org.jdom.output.XMLOutputter class does this in a standard way. You can create an XMLOutputter object with a no-args constructor and then write a document onto an OutputStream with its output() method. For example, the following code fragment writes the Document object named doc onto System.out:

```
XMLOutputter outputter = new XMLOutputter();
try {
  outputter.output(doc, System.out);
}
catch (IOException e) {
  System.err.println(e);
}
```

Although you also can output a document onto a java.io.Writer, it's recommended that you use an OutputStream because it's generally not possible to determine the underlying encoding of a Writer and set the encoding declaration accordingly.

In addition to documents, XMLOutputter can write elements, attributes, CDATA sections, and all of the other JDOM node classes. For example, the following code fragment writes an empty element named Greeting onto System.out:

```
XMLOutputter outputter = new XMLOutputter();
try {
  Element element = new Element("Greeting");
  outputter.output(element, System.out);
}
catch (IOException e) {
  System.err.println(e);
}
```

This may be useful occasionally; but if you write anything other than a single Document or Element onto a stream, the result probably won't be a well-formed XML document.

Finally, instead of writing onto a stream or writer, you can use the outputString() methods to store an XML document or node in a String. This is often useful when passing XML data through non-XML-aware systems. For example, the following code fragment stores an empty element named Greeting in the String variable named hello:

```
XMLOutputter outputter = new XMLOutputter();
Element element = new Element("Greeting");
String hello = outputter.outputString(element);
```

Example 14.1 puts this all together with a simple program that generates the Fibonacci series in XML format.

Example 14.1 A JDOM Program That Produces an XML Document Containing Fibonacci Numbers

```
import org.jdom.*;
import org.jdom.output.XMLOutputter;
import java.math.BigInteger;
import java.io.IOException;

public class FibonacciJDOM {

  public static void main(String[] args) {

    Element root = new Element("Fibonacci_Numbers");

    BigInteger low  = BigInteger.ONE;
    BigInteger high = BigInteger.ONE;

    for (int i = 1; i <= 5; i++) {
      Element fibonacci = new Element("fibonacci");
      fibonacci.setAttribute("index", String.valueOf(i));
      fibonacci.setText(low.toString());
      root.addContent(fibonacci);

      BigInteger temp = high;
      high = high.add(low);
      low = temp;
    }

    Document doc = new Document(root);
    // serialize it onto System.out
    try {
```

```
        XMLOutputter serializer = new XMLOutputter();
        serializer.output(doc, System.out);
      }
      catch (IOException e) {
        System.err.println(e);
      }

    }

  }
```

The output is as follows:

```
D:\books\XMLJAVA\examples\14>java FibonacciJDOM
<?xml version="1.0" encoding="UTF-8"?>
<Fibonacci_Numbers><fibonacci index="1">1</fibonacci><fibonacci
index="2">1</fibonacci><fibonacci index="3">2</fibonacci>
<fibonacci index="4">3</fibonacci><fibonacci index="5">5
</fibonacci></Fibonacci_Numbers>
```

This isn't especially pretty, but there are a couple of ways to clean it up. First off you can recognize that white space is significant in XML, and by default JDOM faithfully reproduces it. Thus if you want the output to be indented, you could add strings containing line breaks and extra space in the right places. Alternatively, if you happen to know that white space is not significant in the particular XML vocabulary the program writes, then you can ask the `XMLOutputter` to format the document for you. For example, this `XMLOutputter` inserts the default line ending after elements and indents elements by two spaces per each layer of the hierarchy:

```
XMLOutputter serializer = new XMLOutputter();
serializer.setIndent("  "); // use two space indent
serializer.setNewlines(true);
serializer.output(doc, System.out);
```

Now the output looks like this:

```
<?xml version="1.0" encoding="UTF-8"?>
<Fibonacci_Numbers>
  <fibonacci index="1">1</fibonacci>
  <fibonacci index="2">1</fibonacci>
```

```
  <fibonacci index="3">2</fibonacci>
  <fibonacci index="4">3</fibonacci>
  <fibonacci index="5">5</fibonacci>
</Fibonacci_Numbers>
```

Much prettier, I think you'll agree.

You can also specify the amount of indenting to use and whether or not to add line breaks as arguments to the `XMLOutputter()` constructor, as follows:

```
XMLOutputter serializer = new XMLOutputter("  ", true);
serializer.output(doc, System.out);
```

For another example, let's revisit `FlatXMLBudget` in Example 4.2. Recall that its purpose was to read a tab-delimited file containing financial data and convert it into XML. The method that actually generated the XML was `convert()`, and it did this by writing strings onto an `OutputStream` like so:

```
public static void convert(List data, OutputStream out)
 throws IOException {

  Writer wout = new OutputStreamWriter(out, "UTF8");
  wout.write("<?xml version=\"1.0\"?>\r\n");
  wout.write("<Budget>\r\n");

  Iterator records = data.iterator();
  while (records.hasNext()) {
    wout.write("  <LineItem>\r\n");
    Map record = (Map) records.next();
    Set fields = record.entrySet();
    Iterator entries = fields.iterator();
    while (entries.hasNext()) {
      Map.Entry entry = (Map.Entry) entries.next();
      String name = (String) entry.getKey();
      String value = (String) entry.getValue();
      // some of the values contain ampersands and less than
      // signs that must be escaped
      value = escapeText(value);

      wout.write("    <" + name + ">");
      wout.write(value);
      wout.write("</" + name + ">\r\n");
    }
```

```
      wout.write("  </LineItem>\r\n");
    }
    wout.write("</Budget>\r\n");
    wout.flush();

  }
```

JDOM can make this method quite a bit simpler, as well as completely eliminate the need for the escapeText() method, since JDOM handles that internally:

```
  public static void convert(List data, OutputStream out)
   throws IOException {

    Element budget = new Element("Budget");

    Iterator records = data.iterator();
    while (records.hasNext()) {
      Element lineItem = new Element("LineItem");
      budget.addContent(lineItem);

      Map record = (Map) records.next();
      Set fields = record.entrySet();
      Iterator entries = fields.iterator();
      while (entries.hasNext()) {
        Map.Entry entry = (Map.Entry) entries.next();
        String name = (String) entry.getKey();
        String value = (String) entry.getValue();

        Element category = new Element(name);
        category.setText(value);
        lineItem.addContent(category);
      }
    }

    Document doc = new Document(budget);
    XMLOutputter outputter = new XMLOutputter("  ", true);
    outputter.output(doc, out);
    out.flush();

  }
```

The disadvantage to this approach is that even though the input is streamed, the output is not. The entire document is built and stored in memory before the first byte of output is written. This can be a problem in devices with limited memory or with large documents.

Document Type Declarations

Documents created with JDOM can have document type declarations and thus can be valid. JDOM does not offer a complete object model for DTDs, but it does allow you to point at an existing DTD or add an internal DTD subset to your documents.

Example 14.2 is a simple document type definition (DTD) for the Fibonacci number documents we've been generating.

Example 14.2 A Fibonacci DTD

```
<!ELEMENT Fibonacci_Numbers (fibonacci*)>
<!ELEMENT fibonacci (#PCDATA)>
<!ATTLIST fibonacci index CDATA #IMPLIED>
```

Let's assume that this is available at the relative URL *fibonacci.dtd*. Thus the following DOCTYPE declaration would make the document valid:

```
<!DOCTYPE Fibonacci_Numbers SYSTEM "fibonacci.dtd">
```

In JDOM, the DocType class represents document type declarations. You can create this object using a constructor that receives the root element name and system ID as arguments. For example:

```
DocType type = new DocType("Fibonacci_Numbers", "fibonacci.dtd");
```

You can either pass this DocType object as the second argument to the Document constructor, or invoke the Document class's setDocType() method.

Example 14.3 demonstrates a program that produces a completely valid document. However, JDOM does not provide any direct means to test the validity of a document, short of serializing it and passing the resulting stream through a validating parser.

Example 14.3 A JDOM Program That Produces a Valid XML Document

```
import org.jdom.*;
import org.jdom.output.XMLOutputter;
import java.math.BigInteger;
import java.io.IOException;


public class ValidFibonacci {

  public static void main(String[] args) {

    Element root = new Element("Fibonacci_Numbers");
    DocType type = new DocType("Fibonacci_Numbers",
     "fibonacci.dtd");
    Document doc = new Document(root, type);

    BigInteger low  = BigInteger.ONE;
    BigInteger high = BigInteger.ONE;

    for (int i = 1; i <= 5; i++) {
      Element fibonacci = new Element("fibonacci");
      fibonacci.setAttribute("index", String.valueOf(i));
      fibonacci.setText(low.toString());
      root.addContent(fibonacci);

      BigInteger temp = high;
      high = high.add(low);
      low = temp;
    }

    // serialize with two-space indents and extra line breaks
    try {
      XMLOutputter serializer = new XMLOutputter("  ", true);
      serializer.output(doc, System.out);
    }
    catch (IOException e) {
      System.err.println(e);
    }
```

```
    }

  }
```

Here is the output with the document type declaration in place:

```
<?xml version="1.0" encoding="UTF-8"?>
<!DOCTYPE Fibonacci_Numbers SYSTEM "fibonacci.dtd">
<Fibonacci_Numbers>
  <fibonacci index="1">1</fibonacci>
  <fibonacci index="2">1</fibonacci>
  <fibonacci index="3">2</fibonacci>
  <fibonacci index="4">3</fibonacci>
  <fibonacci index="5">5</fibonacci>
</Fibonacci_Numbers>
```

You also can specify a public ID for the external DTD subset. For example, if the public ID is `-//Elliotte Rusty Harold//Fibonacci Example//EN`, then the `DocType` object could be initialized like this:

```
DocType type = new DocType("Fibonacci_Numbers",
  "-//Elliotte Rusty Harold//Fibonacci Example//EN",
  "fibonacci.dtd");
```

You can also use the `setInternalSubset()` method to provide an internal DTD subset. As with all internal DTD subsets, this can be instead of or in addition to the external DTD subset identified by the public ID and the system ID. For example, the following code fragment uses an internal DTD subset instead of an external DTD subset.

```
Element root = new Element("Fibonacci_Numbers");

DocType type = new DocType("Fibonacci_Numbers");
String dtd = "<!ELEMENT Fibonacci_Numbers (fibonacci*)>\n";
dtd += "<!ELEMENT fibonacci (#PCDATA)>\n";
dtd += "<!ATTLIST fibonacci index CDATA #IMPLIED>\n";
type.setInternalSubset(dtd);

Document doc = new Document(root, type);
```

The document produced includes an internal DTD subset and no system or public ID:

```
<?xml version="1.0" encoding="UTF-8"
<!DOCTYPE Fibonacci_Numbers [
<!ELEMENT Fibonacci_Numbers (fibonacci*)>
<!ELEMENT fibonacci (#PCDATA)>
<!ATTLIST fibonacci index CDATA #IMPLIED>
]>
<Fibonacci_Numbers>
  <fibonacci index="1">1</fibonacci>
  ...
```

Other programs and documents might specify both an internal DTD subset and a system and public ID for the external DTD subset.

> **Note**
> DTDs and document type declarations are most important for serialization. If the document is written onto a stream and read by some other program, then that other program may take advantage of the DTD for validation or application of default attribute values and so forth. However, JDOM itself doesn't pay a lot of attention to the DTD. In fact, as far as it's concerned the various parts are all just strings. It does not, for example, apply any default attribute values indicated by either the internal or external DTD subsets. If the initial JDOM `Document` object is created by a validating parser (rather than directly in memory), then that parser will report all of the default attribute values the same as the specified attribute values. Changes made to the `DocType` of the `Document` after the document is initially parsed will not affect the rest of the `Document` content.

Namespaces

Suppose that instead of the simple custom vocabulary I've been using so far, you wanted to use the standard MathML presentation vocabulary, as shown in Example 14.4.

Example 14.4 A MathML Document Containing the First Three Fibonacci Numbers

```
<?xml version="1.0"?>
<mathml:math xmlns:mathml="http://www.w3.org/1998/Math/MathML">
  <mathml:mrow>
    <mathml:mi>f(1)</mathml:mi>
```

```
    <mathml:mo>=</mathml:mo>
    <mathml:mn>1</mathml:mn>
  </mathml:mrow>
  <mathml:mrow>
    <mathml:mi>f(2)</mathml:mi>
    <mathml:mo>=</mathml:mo>
    <mathml:mn>1</mathml:mn>
  </mathml:mrow>
  <mathml:mrow>
    <mathml:mi>f(3)</mathml:mi>
    <mathml:mo>=</mathml:mo>
    <mathml:mn>2</mathml:mn>
  </mathml:mrow>
</mathml:math>
```

The greatest difference from the previous examples is that MathML uses namespaces on all of the elements. *The basic JDOM rule about namespaces is that when an element or attribute is in a namespace, rather than specifying its full qualified name, you give its local name, its prefix, and its URI, in that order.* If the element is in the default namespace, then omit the prefix. You do not need to add attributes for the namespace declarations. The outputter will figure out reasonable places to put them when the document is serialized.

For example, the following statement creates the root `mathml:math` element:

```
Element root = new Element("math",
                           "mathml",
                           "http://www.w3.org/1998/Math/MathML");
```

Example 14.5 demonstrates a complete program that generates MathML from JDOM. The namespace has to be specified on each element. Being a child of an element in the `http://www.w3.org/1998/Math/MathML` namespace is neither sufficient nor necessary to make the element part of the `http://www.w3.org/1998/Math/MathML` namespace. Each element (and each attribute) has its own namespace URI, which is independent of the other namespace URIs in the document.

Example 14.5 A JDOM Program That Uses Namespaces

```
import org.jdom.Element;
import org.jdom.Document;
import org.jdom.output.XMLOutputter;
```

```
import java.math.BigInteger;
import java.io.IOException;

public class PrefixedFibonacci {

  public static void main(String[] args) {

    Element root = new Element("math", "mathml",
     "http://www.w3.org/1998/Math/MathML");

    BigInteger low  = BigInteger.ONE;
    BigInteger high = BigInteger.ONE;

    for (int i = 1; i <= 5; i++) {

      Element mrow = new Element("mrow", "mathml",
       "http://www.w3.org/1998/Math/MathML");

      Element mi = new Element("mi", "mathml",
       "http://www.w3.org/1998/Math/MathML");
      mi.setText("f(" + i + ")");
      mrow.addContent(mi);

      Element mo = new Element("mo", "mathml",
       "http://www.w3.org/1998/Math/MathML");
      mo.setText("=");
      mrow.addContent(mo);

      Element mn = new Element("mn", "mathml",
       "http://www.w3.org/1998/Math/MathML");
      mn.setText(low.toString());
      mrow.addContent(mn);

      BigInteger temp = high;
      high = high.add(low);
      low = temp;
      root.addContent(mrow);

    }

    Document doc = new Document(root);
```

```
      try {
        XMLOutputter serializer = new XMLOutputter("  ", true);
        serializer.output(doc, System.out);
      }
      catch (IOException e) {
        System.err.println(e);
      }

    }

  }
```

Using the default namespace is even easier. Simply specify the namespace on each element but omit the prefix. Example 14.6 demonstrates.

Example 14.6 A JDOM Program That Uses the Default Namespace

```
import org.jdom.Element;
import org.jdom.Document;
import org.jdom.output.XMLOutputter;
import java.math.BigInteger;
import java.io.IOException;

public class UnprefixedFibonacci {

  public static void main(String[] args) {

    Element root = new Element("math", "mathml",
     "http://www.w3.org/1998/Math/MathML");

    BigInteger low  = BigInteger.ONE;
    BigInteger high = BigInteger.ONE;

    for (int i = 1; i <= 5; i++) {

      Element mrow = new Element("mrow",
       "http://www.w3.org/1998/Math/MathML");

      Element mi = new Element("mi",
       "http://www.w3.org/1998/Math/MathML");
```

```
        mi.setText("f(" + i + ")");
        mrow.addContent(mi);

        Element mo = new Element("mo",
         "http://www.w3.org/1998/Math/MathML");
        mo.setText("=");
        mrow.addContent(mo);

        Element mn = new Element("mn",
         "http://www.w3.org/1998/Math/MathML");
        mn.setText(low.toString());
        mrow.addContent(mn);

        BigInteger temp = high;
        high = high.add(low);
        low = temp;
        root.addContent(mrow);

      }

      Document doc = new Document(root);
      try {
        XMLOutputter serializer = new XMLOutputter("  ", true);
        serializer.output(doc, System.out);
      }
      catch (IOException e) {
        System.err.println(e);
      }

    }

  }
```

Although these examples only use a single namespace, you are by no means limited to a single namespace per document in JDOM, any more than you are in XML. Each element can have whatever namespace it requires.

Reading XML Documents with JDOM

Naturally, JDOM can read existing XML documents from files, network sockets, strings, or anything else you can hook a stream or reader to. JDOM does not, however, include its own native parser. Instead it relies on any of a number of very fast, well-tested SAX2 parsers such as Xerces and Crimson.

The rough outline for working with an existing XML document using JDOM is as follows:

1. Construct an `org.jdom.input.SAXBuilder` object using a simple no-args constructor.
2. Invoke the builder's `build()` method to build a `Document` object from a `Reader`, `InputStream`, `URL`, `File`, or `String` containing a system ID.
3. If there's a problem reading the document, an `IOException` is thrown. If there's a problem building the document, a `JDOMException` is thrown.
4. Otherwise, navigate the document using the methods of the `Document` class, the `Element` class, and the other JDOM classes.

The `SAXBuilder` class represents the underlying XML parser. Parsing a document from a URL is straightforward. Just create a `SAXBuilder` object with the no-args constructor and pass the string form of the URL to its `build()` method. This returns a JDOM `Document` object. For example:

```
SAXBuilder parser = new SAXBuilder();
Document doc = parser.build("http://www.cafeconleche.org/");
// work with the document...
```

That's all there is to it. If you prefer, you can build the `Document` from a `java.io.File`, a `java.net.URL`, a `java.io.InputStream`, a `java.io.Reader`, or an `org.xml.sax.InputSource`.

The `build()` method throws an `IOException` if an I/O error such as a broken socket prevents the document from being read completely. It throws a `JDOMException` if the document is malformed. I/O errors aside, this is the generic superclass for most anything that can go wrong while working with JDOM. Example 14.7 demonstrates a simple program that checks XML documents for well-formedness by looking for these exceptions.

Example 14.7 A JDOM Program That Checks XML Documents for Well-Formedness

```
import org.jdom.JDOMException;
import org.jdom.input.SAXBuilder;
import java.io.IOException;

public class JDOMChecker {

  public static void main(String[] args) {

    if (args.length == 0) {
      System.out.println("Usage: java JDOMChecker URL");
      return;
    }

    SAXBuilder builder = new SAXBuilder();

    // command line should offer URIs or file names
    try {
      builder.build(args[0]);
      // If there are no well-formedness errors,
      // then no exception is thrown
      System.out.println(args[0] + " is well-formed.");
    }
    // indicates a well-formedness error
    catch (JDOMException e) {
      System.out.println(args[0] + " is not well-formed.");
      System.out.println(e.getMessage());
    }
    catch (IOException e) {
      System.out.println("Could not check " + args[0]);
      System.out.println(" because " + e.getMessage());
    }

  }

}
```

I used this program to test my Cafe con Leche web site for well-formedness. It's supposed to be well-formed XML, but I'm often sloppy. The results were informative:

```
% java JDOMChecker http://www.cafeconleche.org/
http://www.cafeconleche.org is not well formed.
Error on line 351 of document http://www.cafeconleche.org: The
element type "img" must be terminated by the matching end-tag
"</img>".
```

I fixed the problem. However, JDOM only reports the first error in a document, so it's not surprising that running the program again uncovered a second problem:

```
% java JDOMChecker http://www.cafeconleche.org/
http://www.cafeconleche.org is not well formed.
Error on line 363 of document http://www.cafeconleche.org: The
element type "input" must be terminated by the matching end-tag
"</input>".
```

Repeatedly running the program turned up several more problems in order. Once I had fixed the last one, everything finally checked out:

```
% java JDOMChecker http://www.cafeconleche.org/
http://www.cafeconleche.org is well formed.
```

Exactly which SAX parser JDOM uses to build documents depends on the local environment. By default, JDOM relies on JAXP to choose the parser class. If that fails, it picks Xerces. If you really care which parser is used, specify the fully package-qualified name of the`XMLReader` class you want as the first argument to the constructor. For example, this sets the parser as Crimson:

```
SAXBuilder parser
 = new SAXBuilder("org.apache.crimson.parser.XMLReaderImpl");
Document doc = parser.build("http://www.cafeconleche.org/");
// work with the document...
```

By default, `SAXBuilder` checks documents only for well-formedness, not for validity. If you want to validate as well, then pass the boolean `true` to the `SAXBuilder()` constructor. Then any validity errors will also cause `JDOMExceptions`. Example 14.8 demonstrates with a simple validation program.

Example 14.8 A JDOM Program That Validates XML Documents

```
import org.jdom.JDOMException;
import org.jdom.input.SAXBuilder;
import java.io.IOException;

public class JDOMValidator {

  public static void main(String[] args) {

    if (args.length == 0) {
      System.out.println("Usage: java JDOMValidator URL");
      return;
    }

    SAXBuilder builder = new SAXBuilder(true);
                                    //  ^^^^
                                    // Turn on validation

    // command line should offer URIs or file names
    try {
      builder.build(args[0]);
      // If there are no well-formedness or validity errors,
      // then no exception is thrown.
      System.out.println(args[0] + " is valid.");
    }
    // indicates a well-formedness or validity error
    catch (JDOMException e) {
      System.out.println(args[0] + " is not valid.");
      System.out.println(e.getMessage());
    }
    catch (IOException e) {
      System.out.println("Could not check " + args[0]);
      System.out.println(" because " + e.getMessage());
    }

  }

}
```

Here are the results from running this program across two documents—the first invalid (because it doesn't even have a DTD) and the second valid:

```
% java JDOMValidator http://cafeconleche.org/
http://cafeconleche.org is not valid.
Error on line 1 of document http://cafeconleche.org: Document root
element "html", must match DOCTYPE root "null".
% java JDOMValidator http://www.w3.org/TR/2000/REC-xml-
 20001006.html
http://www.w3.org/TR/2000/REC-xml-20001006.html is well formed.
```

This does assume that the default parser that JDOM picks can in fact validate, which is true of most modern parsers you're likely to encounter. If you really want to make sure, you could always ask for a known validating parser by name. For example, the following requests the Xerces `SAXParser`:

```
SAXBuilder parser
 = new SAXBuilder("org.apache.xerces.parsers.SAXParser", true);
```

Note

JDOM does not currently distinguish between validity and well-formedness errors. I'm working on a patch for this. Of course, any malformed document is de facto invalid.

Navigating JDOM Trees

Once you've parsed a document and formed a `Document` object, you'll probably want to search it to select the parts of it your program is interested in. In JDOM, most navigation takes place through the methods of the `Element` class. The complete children of each `Element` are available as a `java.util.List` returned by the `getContent()` method. Only the child elements of each `Element` are available as a `java.util.List` returned by the `getChildren()` method.[2]

Because JDOM uses the Java Collections API to manage the tree, it is simultaneously too polymorphic (everything's an object and must be cast to the right type before you can use it) and not polymorphic enough (there's no useful generic inter-

2. Yes, the terminology is a little confusing here. This is a case in which JDOM is marching out of step with the rest of the XML world. JDOM uses the word *children* to refer only to child elements.

face or superclass for navigation, such as DOM's Node class). Consequently, you're going to find yourself doing numerous tests with instanceof and casting to the determined type. This is far and away my least-favorite part of JDOM's design. Furthermore, there's no standard traversal API as there is in DOM to help you avoid reinventing the wheel every time you need to walk a tree or iterate a document. There is a Filter interface that can simplify some of the polymorphism and casting issues a little, but it still won't let you walk more than one level down the tree at a time.

Let's begin with Example 14.9, a simple program that reads a document and prints the names of the elements in that document, nicely indented to show the hierarchy. Pay special attention to the listChildren() method. This recursive method is the key to the whole program.

Example 14.9 A JDOM Program That Lists the Elements Used in a Document

```
import org.jdom.*;
import org.jdom.input.SAXBuilder;
import java.io.IOException;
import java.util.*;

public class ElementLister {

  public static void main(String[] args) {

    if (args.length == 0) {
      System.out.println("Usage: java ElementLister URL");
      return;
    }

    SAXBuilder builder = new SAXBuilder();

    try {
      Document doc = builder.build(args[0]);
      Element root = doc.getRootElement();
      listChildren(root, 0);
    }
    // indicates a well-formedness error
    catch (JDOMException e) {
      System.out.println(args[0] + " is not well-formed.");
      System.out.println(e.getMessage());
```

```
      }
      catch (IOException e) {
        System.out.println(e);
      }

    }


    public static void listChildren(Element current, int depth) {

      printSpaces(depth);
      System.out.println(current.getName());
      List children = current.getChildren();
      Iterator iterator = children.iterator();
      while (iterator.hasNext()) {
        Element child = (Element) iterator.next();
        listChildren(child, depth+1);
      }

    }

    private static void printSpaces(int n) {

      for (int i = 0; i < n; i++) {
        System.out.print(' ');
      }

    }

  }
```

The `main()` method simply parses a document and passes its root element to the `listChildren()` method along with a depth of zero. The `listChildren()` method indents a number of spaces equal to the depth in the hierarchy. Then it prints the name of the current element. Next it asks for a list of the children of that element by invoking `getChildren()`. This returns a `java.util.List` from the Java Collections API. This list is *live*. That is, any changes you make to it will be reflected in the original `Element`. However, this program does not take advantage of that. Instead, it retrieves a `java.util.Iterator` object using the `iterator()` method. Then it iterates through the list. Because each item in the list is known to be a JDOM `Element` object, each item returned by `next()` can be safely cast to

Element and passed recursively to listChildren(). Other than the knowledge that each object in the list is an Element, every step is just standard list iteration from the Java Collections API. Internally, JDOM is actually using a special package-private subclass of List—org.jdom.ContentList—but you don't need to know this. Everything you need to do can be accomplished through the documented java.util.List interface.

Following is the beginning of the output when this program is run across this chapter's source code:

```
% java ElementLister file://D/books/XMLJava/jdom.xml
chapter
 title
 caution
  para
 para
 itemizedlist
  listitem
   para
  listitem
   para
  listitem
   para
  listitem
   para
 para
 para
 caution
  para
 sect1
  title
  para
  blockquote
  ...
```

The getChildren() method only returns elements. It misses everything else completely. For instance, it doesn't report comments, processing instructions, or text nodes. To get this material, you need to use the getContent() method, which returns everything. However, this makes life a little trickier because you can no longer assume that everything in the list returned is an Element. You'll probably need to use a big tree of if (o instance of Element) { ... } else if (o instance of Text) { in order to choose the processing to perform on each member of the list. Example 14.10 demonstrates with a simple program that recursively lists all of the nodes used in the document. Elements are identified by their name. All other items are identified just by their types.

Example 14.10 A JDOM Program That Lists the Nodes Used in a Document

```
import org.jdom.*;
import org.jdom.input.SAXBuilder;
import java.io.IOException;
import java.util.*;

public class NodeLister {

  public static void main(String[] args) {

    if (args.length == 0) {
      System.out.println("Usage: java NodeLister URL");
      return;
    }

    SAXBuilder builder = new SAXBuilder();

    try {
      Document doc = builder.build(args[0]);
      listNodes(doc, 0);
    }
    // indicates a well-formedness error
    catch (JDOMException e) {
      System.out.println(args[0] + " is not well-formed.");
      System.out.println(e.getMessage());
    }
    catch (IOException e) {
      System.out.println(e);
    }

  }


  public static void listNodes(Object o, int depth) {
```

```
    printSpaces(depth);

    if (o instanceof Element) {
      Element element = (Element) o;
      System.out.println("Element: " + element.getName());
      List children = element.getContent();
      Iterator iterator = children.iterator();
      while (iterator.hasNext()) {
        Object child = iterator.next();
        listNodes(child, depth+1);
      }
    }
    else if (o instanceof Document) {
      System.out.println("Document");
      Document doc = (Document) o;
      List children = doc.getContent();
      Iterator iterator = children.iterator();
      while (iterator.hasNext()) {
        Object child = iterator.next();
        listNodes(child, depth+1);
      }
    }
    else if (o instanceof Comment) {
      System.out.println("Comment");
    }
    else if (o instanceof CDATA) {
      System.out.println("CDATA section");
      // CDATA is a subclass of Text so this test must come
      // before the test for Text.
    }
    else if (o instanceof Text) {
      System.out.println("Text");
    }
    else if (o instanceof EntityRef) {
      System.out.println("Entity reference");
    }
    else if (o instanceof ProcessingInstruction) {
      System.out.println("Processing Instruction");
    }
    else {  // This really shouldn't happen
      System.out.println("Unexpected type: " + o.getClass());
```

```
      }

    }

    private static void printSpaces(int n) {

      for (int i = 0; i < n; i++) {
        System.out.print(' ');
      }

    }

  }
```

Following is the beginning of the output when this program is run across this chapter's source code:

```
% java NodeLister file://D/books/XMLJava/jdom.xml
Document
 Element: chapter
  Text
  Element: title
   Text
  Text
  Element: caution
   Text
   Element: para
    Text
   Text
  Text
  Element: para
  ...
```

The only pieces that are missing here are the attributes and namespaces associated with each element. These are not included by either `getContent()` or `getChildren()`. If you want them, you have to ask for them explicitly using the `getAttributes()`, `getNamespace()`, `getAdditionalNamespaces()`, and related methods of the `Element` class.

In the next chapter, we'll look more closely at the classes of objects that appear when you're navigating a JDOM tree (`Element`, `Text`, `Comment`, and so on) and what you can learn from each one.

Talking to DOM Programs

JDOM is not an acronym. It does not stand for "Java Document Object Model." JDOM is not directly compatible with DOM (which is an acronym for Document Object Model). That is to say, a JDOM `Element` is not a DOM `Element`. The JDOM `Element` class does not implement the DOM `Element` interface. JDOM's `Element` class has methods that the DOM `Element` interface does not have and vice versa. You cannot pass a JDOM `Element` to a method that expects a DOM `Element` or a DOM `Element` to a method that expects a JDOM `Element`. The same is true for the JDOM `Document` class and the DOM `Document` interface, the JDOM `Attribute` class and the DOM `Attr` interface, the JDOM `ProcessingInstruction` class and the DOM `ProcessingInstruction` interface, and so forth.

That being said, JDOM does allow you to convert JDOM documents to and from DOM documents. I don't recommend this for new projects (which should pick one API or the other and stick with it), but it is useful for integrating new JDOM programs with legacy DOM code and vice versa.

If you already have a DOM `Document` object, then the `org.jdom.input.DOMBuilder` class can use it to generate the JDOM equivalent. The syntax is straightforward. Use the no-args `DOMBuilder()` constructor to create a `DOMBuilder` object, and then pass the DOM `Document` object to its `build()` method. For example, assuming that the variable `domDocument` points to an object of type `org.w3c.dom.Document`, the following code fragment will build an `org.jdom.Document` object from it:

```
DOMBuilder builder = new DOMBuilder();
org.jdom.Document jdomDocument = builder.build(domDocument);
// work with the JDOM document...
```

The original DOM object is not changed in any way. Furthermore, changes to the JDOM `Document` do not affect the DOM `Document` from which it was built. Likewise, future changes to the DOM `Document` do not affect the JDOM `Document`.

Moving in the other direction, from JDOM to DOM, the `org.jdom.output.DOMOutputter` class produces DOM `Document` objects from JDOM `Document` objects. Since this isn't really serialization, but rather than just converting from one model to another, there aren't nearly as many options to set as with `XMLOutputter`. For example, you can't add extra white space or select the encoding. (You could always do that later with a DOM serializer of some kind, if necessary.) For example:

```
DOMOutputter converter = new DOMOutputter();
org.w3c.dom.Document domDocument = converter.output(jdomDocument);
// work with the DOM document...
```

Once again, these documents are not connected after the initial creation of one from the other. Changes to one are not reflected in the other.

Talking to SAX Programs

JDOM works very well with SAX parsers. SAX is an almost-ideal event model for building a JDOM tree; and when the tree is complete, JDOM makes it easy to walk the tree, firing off SAX events as you go. Fast and memory efficient, SAX doesn't add a lot of extra overhead to JDOM programs.

Configuring SAXBuilder

When reading a file or stream through a SAX parser, you can set various properties on the parser, including the `ErrorHandler`, `EntityResolver`, `DTDHandler`, and any custom features or properties that are supported by the underlying SAX `XMLReader`. `SAXBuilder` includes several methods that delegate these configurations to the underlying `XMLReader`:

```
public void setErrorHandler (ErrorHandler errorHandler)
public void setEntityResolver (EntityResolver entityResolver)
public void setDTDHandler (DTDHandler dtdHandler)
public void setIgnoringElementContentWhitespace
 (boolean ignoreWhitespace)
public void setFeature (String name, boolean value)
public void setProperty (String name, Object value)
```

For example, suppose you want to schema validate documents before using them. This requires three additional steps beyond the norm:

1. Explicitly pick a parser class that is known to be able to schema validate, such as `org.apache.xerces.parsers.SAXParser`. (Most parsers can't schema validate.)

2. Install a SAX `ErrorHandler` that reports validity errors.
3. Set the SAX feature that turns on schema validation to true. Which feature this is depends on the parser you picked in step 1. In Xerces, it's `http://apache.org/xml/features/validation/schema`, and you also need to turn on validation using the standard SAX feature `http://xml.org/sax/features/validation`.

Example 14.11 is a simple JDOM program that uses Xerces to schema validate a URL named on the command line. This is similar to the earlier `JDOMValidator` in Example 14.8. Here, because the installed `ErrorHandler` (`BestSAXChecker` from Example 7.8) merely prints validity error messages on `System.out` and does not throw an exception, validity errors do not terminate the parse. The `Document` object is still built as long as it's well-formed, whether or not it's valid. You could of course change this behavior by using a more draconian `ErrorHandler` that did throw exceptions for validity errors.

Example 14.11 A JDOM Program That Schema Validates Documents

```
import org.jdom.JDOMException;
import org.jdom.input.SAXBuilder;
import java.io.IOException;

public class JDOMSchemaValidator {

  public static void main(String[] args) {

    if (args.length == 0) {
      System.out.println("Usage: java JDOMSchemaValidator URL");
      return;
    }

    SAXBuilder builder = new SAXBuilder(
     "org.apache.xerces.parsers.SAXParser");
    builder.setValidation(true);
    builder.setErrorHandler(new BestSAXChecker());
                               // ^^^^^^^^^^^^^^
                               // From Chapter 7
    // turn on schema support
    builder.setFeature(
```

```
  "http://apache.org/xml/features/validation/schema", true);

    // command line should offer URIs or file names
    try {
      builder.build(args[0]);
    }
    // indicates a well-formedness error
    catch (JDOMException e) {
      System.out.println(args[0] + " is not well-formed.");
      System.out.println(e.getMessage());
    }
    catch (IOException e) {
      System.out.println("Could not check " + args[0]);
      System.out.println(" because " + e.getMessage());
    }

  }

}
```

Here is the result from when I used this program to check a mildly invalid document. One error was reported.

```
% java JDOMSchemaValidator original_hotcop.xml
Error: cvc-type.3.1.3: The value '6:20' of element 'LENGTH' is
 not valid.
 at line 10, column 24
 in entity file:///D:/books/XMLJAVA/examples/14/
original_hotcop.xml
```

Caution

You should only use `setFeature()` and `setProperty()` for nonstandard features and properties like `http://apache.org/xml/features/validation/schema`. `SAXBuilder` requires certain settings of the standard features such as `http://xml.org/sax/features/namespace-prefixes` and standard properties such as `http://xml.org/sax/properties/lexical-handler` in order to work properly. If you change these, then the document may not be built correctly.

Another interesting possibility is to set a SAX filter that is applied to the document as it's read:

```
public void setXMLFilter (XMLFilter filter)
```

If you use this, the JDOM `Document` will include only the filtered content.

SAXOutputter

In addition to reading a file or stream through a SAX parser, you can also feed a JDOM document into a SAX `ContentHandler` using the `org.jdom.output.SAXOutputter` class. This class is initially configured with a `ContentHandler` and optionally an `ErrorHandler`, `DTDHandler`, `EntityResolver`, and/or `LexicalHandler`. The `output()` method walks the tree, firing off events to these handlers as it does so.

For example, suppose you've built a document in memory that happens to contain some XInclude elements, and you'd like to resolve them. JDOM does not have built-in support for XInclude. To JDOM, an XInclude element is just an element that happens to have the local name `include` and the namespace URI `http://www.w3.org/2001/XInclude`. However, GNU JAXP does include a filter that can resolve XIncludes. Unfortunately it's a SAX filter rather than a JDOM filter. Not to worry. It's straightforward to feed a JDOM document into the GNU JAXP `gnu.xml.pipeline.XIncludeFilter` using a `SAXOutputter`, as shown in Example 14.12.

Example 14.12 A JDOM Program That Passes Documents to a SAX ContentHandler

```
import org.jdom.*;
import org.jdom.input.SAXBuilder;
import org.jdom.output.SAXOutputter;
import java.io.IOException;
import gnu.xml.pipeline.*;
import org.xml.sax.SAXException;

public class XIncluder {

  public static void main(String[] args) {

    if (args.length == 0) {
      System.out.println("Usage: java XIncluder URL");
      return;
```

```
    }

    SAXBuilder builder = new SAXBuilder(
     "gnu.xml.aelfred2.XmlReader");

    // command line should offer URIs or file names
    try {
      Document doc = builder.build(args[0]);
      XIncludeFilter filter = new XIncludeFilter(
        new TextConsumer(System.out)
      );
      SAXOutputter outputter = new SAXOutputter(filter);
      outputter.setContentHandler(filter);
      outputter.setDTDHandler(filter);
      outputter.setLexicalHandler(filter);
      outputter.output(doc);
    }
    // indicates a well-formedness error
    catch (JDOMException e) {
      System.out.println(args[0] + " is not well-formed.");
      System.out.println(e.getMessage());
    }
    catch (SAXException e) {
      System.out.println(e.getMessage());
    }
    catch (IOException e) {
      System.out.println("Could not merge " + args[0]);
      System.out.println(" because " + e.getMessage());
    }

  }

}
```

Here the `XIncludeFilter` is itself hooked up to another GNU JAXP class, `TextConsumer`, which merely prints the document on a specified `OutputStream`.

Java Integration

JDOM is the most Java-centric of all the major APIs for processing XML. The JDOM developers have given a lot of thought to exactly how the JDOM classes fit into common Java systems such as the Java Collections API, Remote Method Invocation (RMI), and the I/O framework. Unlike DOM, the behavior of JDOM objects is very well defined with respect to Java operations such as cloning and serializing.

Serializing JDOM Objects

All of the major JDOM classes, such as `Element`, `Document`, and `Namespace`, implement the `java.io.Serializable` interface. This means that JDOM objects can be passed between machines using RMI and stored in files using `ObjectOutputStream` and `ObjectInputStream`. Of course just because something is possible doesn't mean it's a good idea. XML is itself a serialization format for JDOM objects, and it's a much more broadly supported one. Not as broadly known is that pure textual XML is also generally much faster and smaller than Java's binary object serialization. There is very little reason to use serialized JDOM objects instead of passing genuine XML documents back and forth.

At the time of this writing, the long-term plan for JDOM serialization is still under discussion. Although you can use object serialization to pass JDOM objects from one virtual machine to another if both have the same version of JDOM, anything beyond that is up in the air. In particular, it is highly doubtful that an object you serialize today will be able to be deserialized tomorrow in a different version of JDOM. For long-term persistence, you should absolutely use XML documents instead of serialized objects.

Synchronizing JDOM Objects

For the most part, except for a few accidental exceptions, JDOM classes are not thread safe. You cannot use a JDOM `Document`, `Element`, or other object safely in multiple threads simultaneously unless you synchronize it properly. If you build the object in one thread, and thereafter only read in from different threads (in essence, if you treat the object as if it were immutable), then you may be okay. But if you plan to write to or modify the object, you will need to synchronize your objects.

Testing Equality

All of the core JDOM classes (`Element`, `Attribute`, `ProcessingInstruction`, and so on) implement the `equals()` method. In all cases, the test is for object identity.

In other words, element1.equals(element2) if and only if element1 == element2. That is, element1 is the same element as element2. The reasoning is that order and position are significant in XML documents. Thus two nodes can't be equal unless they are in fact the same node. For example, consider the two Price elements in this XML fragment:

```
<Item>
  <Name>2002 Toyota Camry</Name>
  <Price>$10,000</Price>
</Item>
<Item>
   <Name>1976 AMC Gremlin</Name>
  <Price>$10,000</Price>
</Item>
```

The two Price elements are character-for-character identical. However, one is a very good price and the other is a very bad price because of their respective positions in the document.

This behavior is enforced by implementing the equals() method with an == test and making the method final. A typical JDOM equals() method is defined as follows:

```
public final boolean equals(Object o) {
  return (this == o);
}
```

Hash Codes

Because JDOM tests for equality based on object identity, the default hashCode() implementation inherited from java.lang.Object suffices. However, to prevent subclasses from violating this contract, the hashCode() method is implemented as a final method that calls super.hashCode(). That is, it looks like this:

```
public final int hashCode() {
   return super.hashCode();
 }
```

Thus it cannot be overridden, and subclasses cannot change its behavior.

String Representations

The JDOM toString() methods produce strings that look like these:

```
[Document:  No DOCTYPE declaration, Root is [Element: <html
 [Namespace: http://www.w3.org/1999/xhtml]/>]]
[Element: <html [Namespace: http://www.w3.org/1999/xhtml]/>]
[Attribute: xml:lang="en"]
[Text:
]
[Attribute: type="text/css"]
[Attribute: rel="stylesheet"]
[Text: Latest Version: ]
[Element: <a [Namespace: http://www.w3.org/1999/xhtml]/>]
[Attribute: href="http://www.rddl.org/"]
[Text: June 16, 2002]
```

The strings are suitable for debugging, but not for display to an end user. In particular, they are not the serialized form of the XML node that the object represents. To serialize a JDOM object onto a stream or into a String, use an XMLOutputter chained to a StringWriter. Do not use toString().

Cloning

All of the core JDOM classes implement Cloneable. Except for Namespace objects (which are immutable), all clones are deep clones. For example, cloning an element makes a copy of the element's contents as well. The clone does not have a parent, and it can be inserted into the same document or a different document.

What JDOM Doesn't Do

There is more to JDOM than what you've seen in the brief tour in this chapter. Chapter 15 will cover the capabilities of the various JDOM classes like Element and Attribute in depth, as well as take a deeper look at how these constructs are represented. However, before we take that up, it's worth taking a few minutes to note the features JDOM doesn't have, which might lead you to choose a different API instead.

First of all, JDOM cannot handle documents larger than available memory. JDOM loads the entire document tree into memory and keeps it there. JDOM is more memory efficient than some DOM implementations and less efficient than others. However, it's never going to be competitive with SAX or XMLPULL for truly humongous documents.

Second, like both DOM and SAX, JDOM presents a logical model of XML documents. It does not track every last byte of the documents it parses. For example, it cannot tell which physical entities any element came from. It treats the document as a logical whole. It cannot tell whether a character was input literally or with a character reference (a limitation it shares with DOM and SAX). It does not know the original character encoding of the document. In short, it cannot guarantee byte-for-byte faithful round-trips. Merely parsing a document with JDOM and then immediately writing it back out again may create a subtly different document, although it should still contain the same basic information.

Third, JDOM is purely about the instance document. It does not provide any real model of the DTD or schema. It cannot tell you what the type of an element is, or what its valid children are. It cannot check a `Document` object against a schema or a DTD.

Finally, JDOM does not currently provide an equivalent to the traversal package in DOM. This isn't a huge problem, because writing your own tree-walking code does not require a great deal of effort, as you'll see in the next chapter. But a standard way of doing this would be helpful.

Summary

JDOM is a pure Java API for processing XML documents. It is more complete than either SAX (which doesn't offer any standard way to write new XML documents) or DOM (which can manipulate XML documents but doesn't know how to parse or serialize them). It is also much easier to use than either SAX or DOM for most tasks. It has the convenience of a pull-based tree API with DOM and the familiarity of following standard Java conventions with SAX. However, JDOM is not SAX and it is not DOM. JDOM can transfer data to and from SAX and DOM, but it is its own API, complete unto itself.

JDOM uses concrete classes rather than interfaces. This means that you can create instances of most of the node types just by passing an argument or two to a constructor. (The notable exception is the `Namespace` class, which uses a factory method in order to implement the flyweight design pattern.) For example, to create a new `Element` object for a `number` element, you simply type

```
Element element = new Element("number");
```

Node objects need not be attached to any document; however, an object can't be part of more than one document at a time.

JDOM `Document` objects can also be created by parsing an existing file. This is done by the `SAXBuilder` class, which relies on a SAX2 parser such as Xerces. JDOM `Document` objects can also be built from existing DOM `Document` objects through the `DOMBuilder` class. Moving in the other direction, the `XMLOutputter` class can serialize a JDOM `Document` object onto a stream. The `SAXOutputter` class can feed a JDOM `Document` into a SAX `ContentHandler`, and the `DOMOutputter` class can convert a JDOM `Document` into a DOM `Document`.

Chapter 15

The JDOM Model

JDOM documents are composed of ten basic classes representing the different kinds of nodes in an XML document:

- `Document`
- `Element`
- `Attribute`
- `Text`
- `ProcessingInstruction`
- `Namespace`
- `Comment`
- `DocType`
- `EntityRef`
- `CDATA`

In JDOM, node objects can belong to a `Document`, or they can exist independently. A complete JDOM `Document` contains a list of its children, which normally includes `Comments`, `ProcessingInstructions`, possibly a single `DocType`, and one `Element` object for the root element. The remaining structure of the document is built primarily from `Element` objects, each of which contains a list of its contents, as well as separate lists of attributes and namespaces for that element.

The Document Class

JDOM's Document class, summarized in Example 15.1, represents a complete well-formed XML document. As a node, it is the root of the document tree. It enforces most of the rules XML imposes on documents. For example, it is not possible to assign two DocType objects to a single Document object because an XML document cannot have two document type declarations. The single exception to this rule is that it is possible for a Document to be temporarily rootless if it's built by the no-args constructor. In that case, however, almost anything you do with the document other than setting a root element will throw an IllegalStateException. In effect, then, this is just a temporary convenience, not a loophole that allows you to break the rules of XML.

Example 15.1 The JDOM Document Class

```
package org.jdom;

public class Document implements Serializable, Cloneable {

  protected ContentList content;
  protected DocType     docType;

  public Document()
  public Document(Element root, DocType docType)
  public Document(Element root)
  public Document(List newContent, DocType docType)
  public Document(List content)

  public boolean  hasRootElement()
  public Element  getRootElement()
  public Document setRootElement(Element rootElement)
  public Element  detachRootElement()

  public DocType  getDocType()
  public Document setDocType(DocType docType)

  public Document addContent(ProcessingInstruction pi)
  public Document addContent(Comment comment)
  public List     getContent()
  public List     getContent(Filter filter)
```

```
  public Document setContent(List newContent)
  public boolean  removeContent(ProcessingInstruction pi)
  public boolean  removeContent(Comment comment)

  // Java utility methods
  public        String  toString()
  public final boolean equals(Object o)
  public final int     hashCode()
  public        Object  clone()

}
```

As you can probably guess from the setter and getter methods, each Document object has the following three properties:

1. The root Element
2. A DocType object that represents the document type declaration
3. A List that contains the root Element and any processing instructions or comments in the prolog and epilog, in document order

The first two occasionally may be null. A document that does not have a document type declaration will have a null DocType. The root Element also may be null, but only temporarily. You can't do much of anything to a Document until you've set its root Element.

Most of the time, all you do with a Document is get the root element. From that point forward, you work exclusively with the root element and its descendants until you're ready to serialize the Document. For example,

```
Document doc = builder.build("file.xml");
Element root = doc.getRootElement();
// work with root...
```

Occasionally, you may need to hunt for a particular processing instruction in the prolog or epilog. For example, if you were writing a browser, then you would want to look for an xml-stylesheet processing instruction in the prolog by iterating through the list returned by getContent(), as follows:

```
List content = doc.getContent();
Iterator iterator = content.iterator();
while (iterator.hasNext()) {
```

```
    Object next = iterator.next();
    if (next instanceof Element) {
      // This is the root element. Thus the prolog is
      // finished.
      break;
    }
    else if (next instanceof ProcessingInstruction) {
      ProcessingInstruction candidate
       = (ProcessingInstruction) next;
      if (candidate.getTarget().equals("xml-stylesheet")) {
        // Load stylesheet...
      }
    }
  }...
```

It's uncommon, however, to pay that much attention to the contents of the prolog (and even rarer to pay attention to the epilog). Because the `addContent()`, `setContent()`, `getContent()`, and `removeContent()` methods work pretty much the same for `Document` as they do for `Element`, I'm going to defer further discussion of these to the next section.

The Element Class

The structure of an XML document is based on its elements, so it should come as no surprise that the `Element` class is one of the larger and more important classes in JDOM. Because JDOM has no generic `Node` class or interface, the `Element` class is the primary means by which a program navigates the tree to find particular content.

Each `Element` object has the following seven basic properties:

Local Name
A `String` that is initialized when the `Element` is constructed, and which can never be null or the empty string. It is accessible through the `setName()` and `getName()` methods:

```
public Element setName (String name) throws IllegalNameException
public String getName()
```

Namespace

A `Namespace` object that encapsulates both the namespace URI and an optional prefix. This can be the named constant `Namespace.NO_NAMESPACE` if the element does not have a namespace. A namespace is always set when the `Element` is constructed, but it can be changed by `setNamespace()`. It can be read by the `getNamespace()` method.

```
public Element setNamespace (Namespace namespace)
public String getNamespace()
```

Content

A `List` with no duplicates that contains all of the element's children in order. This is accessible through the `getContent()` and `setContent()` methods. The list is live; therefore, you can change the contents of the `Element` using the methods of the `List` class.

```
public Element setContent (List list) throws IllegalAddException
public List getContent()
```

In addition, you can add or remove individual nodes from the list via the `addContent()` and `removeContent()` methods.

Parent

The parent `Element` that contains this `Element`. It will be null if this is the root element, and may be null if this `Element` is not currently part of a `Document`. This is accessible through the `getParent()` method:

```
public Element getParent()
```

You can change the parent only by adding the `Element` to a new parent using the parent's `addContent()` method. This is possible only if the `Element` does not already have a parent. Before a parent can adopt a child `Element`, the child's `detach()` method must be invoked to remove it from its current parent:

```
public Element detach()
```

Owner Document

The `Document` that contains this `Element`. It will be null if this `Element` is not currently part of a `Document`. It is possible to read it through the `getDocument()` method:

```
public Document getDocument()
```

You can change it by adding the `Element` to a new document after first detaching it from its previous parent with the `detach()` method.

Attributes

A `List` containing `Attribute` objects, one for each of the element's attributes. Although JDOM stores attributes in a list for convenience, order is not significant, and is not likely to be the same as the order in which the attributes appeared in the original document. The list is accessible through the `getAttributes()` and `setAttributes()` methods:

```
public Element setAttributes (List attributes)
 throws IllegalAddException
public List getAttributes()
```

You can read and modify the items in this list via the `getAttribute()`, `getAttributeValue()`, and `setAttribute()` methods. Attributes that declare namespaces are not included in this list.

Additional Namespaces

A `List` that contains `Namespace` objects, one for each additional namespace prefix declared by the element (that is, other than those that declare the namespace of the element and the namespaces of its attributes). As with the list of attributes, order is not significant. The entire list is accessible through the `getAdditionalNamespaces()` method:

```
public List getAdditionalNamespaces()
```

You can add and remove namespaces from the list using the `addNamespaceDeclaration()`, and `removeNamespaceDeclaration()` methods:

```
public Element addNamespaceDeclaration (Namespace namespace)
public Element removeNamespaceDeclaration (Namespace namespace)
```

There are additional properties that are not independent of the above seven. For example, the prefix, namespace URI, and fully qualified name are separately readable through the `getNamespaceURI()`, `getNamespacePrefix()`, and `getQualifiedName()` convenience methods:

```
public String getNamespaceURI()
public String getNamespacePrefix()
public String getQualifiedName()
```

These simply return the relevant parts of the element's namespace and name.

All of these getter methods behave pretty much like any other getter methods. That is, they return an object of the relevant type, generally a `String`, and do not throw any exceptions. The setter methods are more unusual, however. This is one of the few areas in which JDOM does not follow standard Java conventions. Instead of returning `void`, these methods all return the `Element` object that invoked the method. That is, a.set*Foo*(b) returns a. Many other methods you naturally would expect to return void also do this. The purpose is to allow setters to be chained. For example, the following code fragment can build up an entire channel element in just a couple of statements:

```
Element channel = (new Element("channel"))
.addContent((new Element("title")).setText("Cafe con Leche"))
.addContent((new Element("link"))
 .setText("http://www.cafeconleche.org/"))
.addContent((new Element("description"))
 .setText("XML News"));
```

Caution
I must say that I personally don't find this style of code easier to write or read than the multi-statement approach. However, this is why the adder and setter methods all return the object that did the adding or setting, so I felt compelled to show it to you. But I really recommend strongly that you don't use it.

Constructors

The four public Element constructors all require you to specify a local name as a String. If the element is in a namespace, then you also need to specify the namespace URI as a String or a Namespace object. Alternatively, you can specify the prefix as a String or a piece of a Namespace object.

```
public Element (String localName) throws IllegalNameException

public Element (String localName, Namespace namespace)
 throws IllegalNameException

public Element (String localName, String namespaceURI)
 throws IllegalNameException

public Element (String localName, String prefix, String
 namespaceURI) throws IllegalNameException
```

For example, this code fragment creates four Element objects using the various constructors:

```
Element xmlRPCRoot = new Element("methodCall");
Element xhtmlRoot = new Element("html",
 "http://www.w3.org/1999/xhtml");
```

```
Element soapRoot = new Element("Envelope", "SOAP-ENV",
 "http://schemas.xmlsoap.org/soap/envelope/");
Namespace xsd = Namespace.getNamespace("xsd",
 "http://www.w3.org/2001/XMLSchema");
Element schemaRoot = new Element("schema", xsd);
```

Navigation and Search

As you learned in Chapter 14, the `getContent()` method is the fundamental means of navigating through an XML document with JDOM. This method returns a live `List` that includes all the children of an element, including comments, processing instructions, text nodes, and elements. To search deeper, you apply `getContent()` to the child elements of the current element, normally through recursion.

Example 15.2 is a simple program that walks the XML document tree, starting at the root element, and prints out the content of the various properties of each element. This is not the most interesting program in the book, but it does demonstrate all of the major getter methods and basic navigation. Pay special attention to the `process()` method, as you will need to write a method very much like this for any JDOM program that needs to search an entire XML document. It begins with an `Element` (normally the root element) and recursively applies itself to all of the child elements of the root element. The `instanceof` operator tests each object in the content list of the `Element` to determine its type and dispatch it to the right method. Here, `TreePrinter` dispatches `Element` objects to the `process()` method recursively, ignoring all other objects.

Example 15.2 Inspecting Elements

```
import org.jdom.*;
import org.jdom.input.SAXBuilder;
import java.io.IOException;
import java.util.*;

public class TreePrinter {

  // Recursively descend the tree
  public static void process(Element element) {

    inspect(element);
    List content = element.getContent();
    Iterator iterator = content.iterator();
```

```
    while (iterator.hasNext()) {
      Object o = iterator.next();
      if (o instanceof Element) {
        Element child = (Element) o;
        process(child);
      }
    }

  }

  // Print the properties of each element
  public static void inspect(Element element) {

    if (!element.isRootElement()) {
      // Print a blank line to separate it from the previous
      // element.
      System.out.println();
    }

    String qualifiedName = element.getQualifiedName();
    System.out.println(qualifiedName + ":");

    Namespace namespace = element.getNamespace();
    if (namespace != Namespace.NO_NAMESPACE) {
      String localName = element.getName();
      String uri = element.getNamespaceURI();
      String prefix = element.getNamespacePrefix();
      System.out.println("  Local name: " + localName);
      System.out.println("  Namespace URI: " + uri);
      if (!"".equals(prefix)) {
        System.out.println("  Namespace prefix: " + prefix);
      }
    }
    List attributes = element.getAttributes();
    if (!attributes.isEmpty()) {
      Iterator iterator = attributes.iterator();
      while (iterator.hasNext()) {
        Attribute attribute = (Attribute) iterator.next();
        String name = attribute.getName();
        String value = attribute.getValue();
        Namespace attributeNamespace = attribute.getNamespace();
```

```
        if (attributeNamespace == Namespace.NO_NAMESPACE) {
          System.out.println("  " + name + "=\"" + value + "\"");
        }
        else {
          String prefix = attributeNamespace.getPrefix();
          System.out.println(
           "  " + prefix + ":" + name + "=\"" + value + "\"");
        }
      }
    }

    List namespaces = element.getAdditionalNamespaces();
    if (!namespaces.isEmpty()) {
      Iterator iterator = namespaces.iterator();
      while (iterator.hasNext()) {
        Namespace additional = (Namespace) iterator.next();
        String uri = additional.getURI();
        String prefix = additional.getPrefix();
          System.out.println(
           "  xmlns:" + prefix + "=\"" + uri + "\"");
      }
    }

  }

  public static void main(String[] args) {

    if (args.length <= 0) {
      System.out.println("Usage: java TreePrinter URL");
      return;
    }

    String url = args[0];

    try {
      SAXBuilder parser = new SAXBuilder();

      // Parse the document
      Document document = parser.build(url);

      // Process the root element
      process(document.getRootElement());
```

```
    }
    catch (JDOMException e) {
      System.out.println(url + " is not well-formed.");
    }
    catch (IOException e) {
      System.out.println(
       "Due to an IOException, the parser could not encode " + url
      );
    }

  } // end main

}
```

Following is the beginning of output when I fed this chapter's XML source code into TreePrinter. DocBook doesn't use namespaces, but the XInclude elements do. The root element has some attributes, but most of the structure is based on element name alone.

```
D:\books\XMLJAVA>java TreePrinter jdom_model.xml
chapter:
  revision="20020430"
  status="rough"
  id="ch_jdom_model"
  xmlns:xinclude="http://www.w3.org/2001/XInclude"

title:

para:

para:

itemizedlist:

listitem:

para:

classname:
...
```

While in theory you could navigate and query a document using only the `List` objects returned by `getContent()`, JDOM provides many methods to simplify the process for special cases, some of which include methods that

- Return lists containing child elements only
- Return particular named child elements
- Return the complete text of an element
- Return the text of a child element
- Remove children identified by name and reference
- Return the first child of an element

Child Elements

The `Element` class has two methods (five total when you count overloaded variants separately) that operate only on the child elements of an element, not on other content such as processing intructions and text nodes. These are `getChildren()` and `removeChildren()`:

```
public List getChildren()
public List getChildren (String name)
public List getChildren (String name, Namespace namespace)
public List removeChildren (String name)
public List removeChildren (String name, Namespace namespace)
```

These methods are similar to `getContent()` and `removeContent()` except that the lists returned only contain child elements, never other kinds of children such as comments and processing instructions.[1] The `getChildren()` methods simply ignore nonelements. For example, the earlier `ElementLister` in Example 14.9 only considered elements. Consequently, it could use the `getChildren()` method instead of `getContent()`:

```
public static void process(Element element) {

  inspect(element);
  List content = element.getChildren();
  Iterator iterator = content.iterator();
  while (iterator.hasNext()) {
```

1. The name is a little misleading. An earlier beta version called these methods `getChildElements()` and `removeChildElements()`, much better names in my opinion.

```
      Object o = iterator.next();
      Element child = (Element) o;
      process(child);
    }

  }
```

This eliminates one `instanceof` check and one `if` block. This is not a huge savings, I admit; but the code is marginally more readable. However, because JDOM uses Java's `Object`-based `List` class, you still have to cast all of the items in the list that `getChildren()` returns to `Element`.

The `removeChildren()` methods remove all of the elements that match the specified name and namespace URI. If no namespace URI is given, then it removes elements with the given name in no namespace. Other content—comments, processing instructions, text, and so on—is not touched.

For example, the following method recursively descends through an element, cutting out all of the `note` elements:

```
public static void cutNotes(Element element) {

  List notes = element.getChildren("note");
  element.removeChildren(notes);
  // The element's children have changed so we have to call
  // getChildren() again
  List children = element.getChildren();
  Iterator iterator = children.iterator();
  while (iterator.hasNext()) {
    Object o = iterator.next();
    Element child = (Element) o;
    cutNotes(child);
  }

}
```

It's important to remember that when an element is removed, the entire element is removed, not just its start-tags and end-tags. Any content inside the element is lost, including, in this case, elements that aren't named `note`.

Single Children

Often you want to follow a very specific path through a document. Consider the XML-RPC request document in Example 15.3. A program that reads this is probably primarily concerned with the content of the `string` element.

Example 15.3 An XML-RPC Request Document

```
<?xml version="1.0"?>
<methodCall>
  <methodName>getQuote</methodName>
  <params>
    <param>
      <value><string>RHAT</string></value>
    </param>
  </params>
</methodCall>
```

To get the `string` element, you'll ask for the `string` child element of the `value` child element, of the `param` child element, of the `params` child element, of the root element. Rather than iterating through a list of all the child elements when there's only one of each of these, you can ask for the one you want directly using one of the `getChild()` methods:

```
public Element getChild (String name)
public Element getChild (String name, Namespace namespace)
```

For example,

```
Element root   = document.getRootElement();
Element params = root.getChild("params");
Element param  = params.getChild("param");
Element value  = param.getChild("value");
Element symbol = params.getChild("string");
```

Or, more concisely,

```
Element symbol = document.getRootElement()
                  .getChild("params")
                  .getChild("param");
                  .getChild("value")
                  .getChild("string");
```

This method has one nasty problem. It returns only the first such child. If there's more than one child element with the specified name and namespace, you still only get the first one. This is a very real possibility in many applications, including XML-RPC; therefore, you should normally prefer getChildren() unless you've used some form of schema or DTD to verify that there's exactly one of each child you address with these methods.

Similarly, you can remove a single named child element with one of the two removeChild() methods, each of which returns the removed Element, in case you want to save it for later use:

```
public Element removeChild (String name)
public Element removeChild (String name, Namespace namespace)
```

The removeChild() method shares with getChild() the problem of operating on only the first such element. However, after you've removed the first child, the second child is now the first. After you've removed that one, the original third child is now the first, and so on. Thus, there is one option that doesn't work with getChild(). You can simply call removeChild() repeatedly until it returns null, indicating that there was no further such child. For example, the following code fragment removes all of the immediate note children of the Element named element:

```
while (element.removeChild("note") != null) ;
```

However, unlike the earlier example with removeChildren(), this is not recursive and therefore will not find note elements deeper in the tree.

Getting and Setting the Text of an Element

Sometimes what you want is the text of an element. For this purpose, JDOM provides these four methods:

```
public String getText()
public String getTextTrim()
public String getTextNormalize()
public Element setText (String text)
```

The getText() method returns the PCDATA content of the element. The getTextTrim() method returns pretty much the same content, except that all leading and trailing white space has been removed. The getTextNormalize() method not only strips all leading and trailing whitespace, but also converts all runs of spaces to a single space. For example, consider this street element:

```
<street> 135  Airline  Highway </street>
```

For this element, `getText()` returns " `135  Airline  Highway` " with the white space unchanged. However, `getTextTrim()` returns "`135  Airline  Highway`," and `getTextNormalize()` returns "`135 Airline Highway`." You will need to decide at the application level which one you want.

This is trickier than you might think at first glance. For example, consider this `street` element:

```
<street>135<!-- The building doesn't actually have a number.
                 It's next door to 133 -->Airline Highway</street>
```

`getText()` returns "135Airline Highway." It ignores comments and processing instructions as if they weren't there. For the most part, that seems reasonable.

Now consider this `street` element:

```
<street>135 Airline Highway <apartment>2B</apartment></street>
```

`getText()` returns "`135 Airline Highway`." The content in the child `apartment` element is lost completely. This is really not a good thing. (I argued about this in the JDOM group, but I lost.) Before you can reliably use any of the `getText()`, `getTextTrim()`, or `getTextNormalize()` methods, you need to be very sure that the element does not have any child elements. One way to do this is to test if the number of child elements is zero before invoking the text getter. For example,

```
if (element.getChildren().size() == 0) {
   String result = element.getText();
   // work with result ...
}
else {
  // do something more complex ...
}
```

An alternative is to write your own method that recursively descends through the element, accumulating all of its text. I'll demonstrate this in the section on the `Text` Class later in this chapter.

Do not use any of these getter methods unless you have first validated the document against a DTD or schema that explicitly requires the element only to contain #PCDATA. Do not assume that you "know" that this is true in your domain without individually testing each document. Invariably, sooner or later, you will encounter a document that purports to adhere to the implicit schema, and indeed is very close to it, but does not quite match what you were assuming. Explicit validation is necessary.

The `setText()` method is a little less fraught with pitfalls. You can set the text content of any element to whatever text you desire. For example, the following code fragment sets the text of the `street` element to the string "3520 Airline Drive":

```
street.setText("3520 Airline Drive");
```

This completely wipes out any existing content the element has: child elements, descendants, comments, processing instructions, other text, and so on. If you just want to append the string to the existing text, then use the `addContent()` method instead.

Getting Child Text

One common pattern in XML documents is an element that contains only other elements, all of which contain only PCDATA, such as this `channel` element from Slashdot's RSS file:

```
<channel>
  <title>Slashdot: News for nerds, stuff that matters</title>
  <link>http://slashdot.org/</link>
  <description>News for nerds, stuff that matters</description>
</channel>
```

Given such an element, JDOM provides six convenience methods for extracting the text, the trimmed text, and the normalized text from these child elements:

```
public String getChildText (String name)
public String getChildText (String name, Namespace namespace)
public String getChildTextTrim (String name)
public String getChildTextTrim (String name,
 Namespace namespace)
public String getChildTextNormalize (String name)
public String getChildTextNormalize (String name,
 Namespace namespace)
```

For example, assuming that the `Element` object `channel` represents the just-mentioned `channel` element, this code fragment retrieves the content of the `title`, `link`, and `description` elements:

```
String title = channel.getChildText("title");
String description = channel.getChildText("description");
String link = channel.getChildText("link");
```

There are two things I really don't like about these methods. First, like the getText(), getTextTrim(), and getTextNormalize() methods, they all fail unexpectedly and silently if any of the child elements unexpectedly contain child elements. For example, the preceding code fragment fails massively if Slashdot changes its format and instead begins distributing content like this instead:

```
<channel>
  <title>
    <trademark>Slashdot</trademark>
    <trademark>News for nerds, stuff that matters</trademark>
  </title>
  <link>http://slashdot.org/</link>
  <description>
    <trademark>News for nerds, stuff that matters</trademark>
  </description>
</channel>
```

Second, these methods fail unexpectedly and silently if the any of the child elements are repeated. For example, suppose instead that the channel element has three link children, like this:

```
<channel>
  <title>Slashdot: News for nerds, stuff that matters</title>
  <link>http://slashdot.org/</link>
  <link>http://www.slashdot.org/</link>
  <link>http://slashdot.com/</link>
  <description>News for nerds, stuff that matters</description>
</channel>
```

All three methods return the text from the first link element, and neglect to inform the client program that there are more it may be interested in.

As with getText(), getTextTrim(), and getTextNormalize(), do not use any of these methods without first validating the document against a DTD or schema that explicitly requires the child elements only to contain #PCDATA and to occur exactly once each in each parent element.

Filters

You can pass an `org.jdom.filter.Filter` object to the `getContent()` method to limit the content returned by the method. This interface, shown in Example 15.4, determines whether an object can be added to, removed from, or included in a particular list. For the purposes of navigation and search, only the `matches()` method really matters. It determines whether or not any particular object is included in the `List` returned by `getContent()`. The `canAdd()` and `canRemove()` methods test whether a particular object can be added to or removed from the list. However, in the two default implementations of this class in `ElementFilter` and `ContentFilter`, both of these methods just call `matches()`.

Example 15.4 The JDOM Filter Interface

```
package org.jdom.filter;

public interface Filter {

  public boolean canAdd(Object o);
  public boolean canRemove(Object o);
  public boolean matches(Object o);

}
```

The `org.jdom.filter` package includes two implementations of this interface, `ContentFilter` (Example 15.5) and `ElementFilter` (Example 15.6). The `ContentFilter` class allows you to specify the visibility of different JDOM node types such as `ProcessingInstruction` and `Text`. The `ElementFilter` class allows you to select elements with certain names or namespaces. Finally, you can write your own custom implementations that filter according to application-specific criteria.

Example 15.5 The JDOM ContentFilter Class

```
package org.jdom.filter;

public class ContentFilter implements Filter {

  public static final int ELEMENT   = 1;
  public static final int CDATA     = 2;
  public static final int TEXT      = 4;
```

```
    public static final int COMMENT   = 8;
    public static final int PI        = 16;
    public static final int ENTITYREF = 32;
    public static final int DOCUMENT  = 64;

    protected int filterMask;

    public ContentFilter();
    public ContentFilter(boolean allVisible);
    public ContentFilter(int mask);

    public int  getFilterMask();
    public void setFilterMask(int mask);
    public void setDefaultMask();

    public void setDocumentContent();
    public void setElementContent();

    public void setElementVisible(boolean visible);
    public void setCDATAVisible(boolean visible)
    public void setTextVisible(boolean visible);
    public void setCommentVisible(boolean visible);
    public void setPIVisible(boolean visible);
    public void setEntityRefVisible(boolean visible);

    public boolean canAdd(Object o);
    public boolean canRemove(Object o);
    public boolean matches(Object o);


    public boolean equals(Object o);

}
```

For example, suppose your application only needs to concern itself with elements and text, but can completely skip all comments and processing instructions. You can simplify the code by using an appropriately configured `ContentFilter`. The most convenient approach is to construct a filter that filters out all nodes by passing false to the constructor, and then turn on only the types you want to let through, as follows:

```
// Filter out everything by default
Filter filter = new ContentFilter(false);
// Allow elements through the filter
filter.setElementVisible(true);
// Allow text nodes through the filter
filter.setTextVisible(true);
```

You'll need to pass `filter` to `getContent()` every time you call it, like so:

```
Filter filter; // set up in constructor

public static void process(Element element) {

  List children = element.getContent(filter);
  Iterator iterator = children.iterator();
  while (iterator.hasNext()) {
    Object o = iterator.next();
    if (o instanceof Element) {
      Element child = (Element) o;
      process(element);
    }
    else { // Due to filter, the only other possibility is Text
      Text text = (Text) o;
      handleText(text);
    }
  }

}
```

Generally, you will want to allow elements to pass the filter, even if you're only looking at other things like `Text`. In JDOM, recursing through the `Element` objects is the only way to search a complete tree. If you filter out the `Elements`, then you won't be able to go more than one level deep from where you start.

If you only want to select elements, you can use an `ElementFilter` instead. This can be set up to select all elements, elements with a certain name, elements in a certain namespace, or elements with a certain name in a certain namespace.

Example 15.6 The JDOM ElementFilter Class

```
package org.jdom.filter;

public class ElementFilter implements Filter {

  protected String    name;
  protected Namespace namespace;

  public ElementFilter();
  public ElementFilter(String name);
  public ElementFilter(Namespace namespace);
  public ElementFilter(String name, Namespace namespace);

  public boolean canAdd(Object o);
  public boolean canRemove(Object o);
  public boolean matches(Object o);

  public boolean equals(Object o);

}
```

For example, the following code fragment uses an `ElementFilter` to create a `List` named `content` that only contains XSLT elements:

```
Namespace xslt = Namespace.getNamespace(
                     "http://www.w3.org/1999/XSL/Transform");
Filter filter = new ElementFilter(xslt);
List content = element.getContent(filter);
```

Once again, however, this method proves to be less generally useful than the DOM equivalents, because the `getContent()` method only returns children, not all descendants. For example, you couldn't really use this to select the XSLT elements or the non-XSLT elements in a stylesheet, because each type can appear as children of the other type.

Filters also work in the `Document` class, pretty much the same way as they work in the `Element` class. For example, suppose you want to find all the processing instructions in the `Document` object `doc` outside the root element. The following code fragment creates a `List` containing those:

```
// Filter out everything by default
Filter pisOnly = new ContentFilter(false);
// Allow processing instructions through the filter
pisOnly.setPIVisible(true);
// Get the content
List pis = doc.getContent(pisOnly);
```

If you want something a little more useful, such as a filter that selects all `xml-stylesheet` processing instructions in the prolog only, then you need to write a custom implementation of `Filter`. Example 15.7 demonstrates.

Example 15.7 A Filter for xml-stylesheet Processing Instructions in the Prolog

```
import org.jdom.filter.Filter;
import org.jdom.*;
import java.util.List;

public class StylesheetFilter implements Filter {

  // This filter is read-only. Nothing can be added or removed.
  public boolean canAdd(Object o) {
    return false;
  }

  public boolean canRemove(Object o) {
    return false;
  }

  public boolean matches(Object o) {

    if (o instanceof ProcessingInstruction) {
      ProcessingInstruction pi = (ProcessingInstruction) o;
      if (pi.getTarget().equals("xml-stylesheet")) {
        // Test to see if we're outside the root element
        if (pi.getParent() == null) {
          Document doc = pi.getDocument();
          Element root = doc.getRootElement();
          List content = doc.getContent();
          if (content.indexOf(pi) < content.indexOf(root)) {
            // In prolog
```

```
                return true;
              }
            }
          }
        }
        return false;

      }

    }
```

Adding and Removing Children

You can append any legal node to an `Element` using the six-way overloaded `addContent()` methods:

```
public Element addContent (String s)
public Element addContent (Text text) throws IllegalAddException
public Element addContent (Element element)
 throws IllegalAddException
public Element addContent (ProcessingInstruction instruction)
 throws IllegalAddException
public Element addContent (EntityRef ref)
 throws IllegalAddException
public Element addContent (Comment comment)
 throws IllegalAddException
```

These methods append their argument to the child list of `Element`. Except for `addContent(String)`, they all throw an `IllegalAddException` if the argument already has a parent element. (The `addContent(String)` method is just a convenience that creates a new `Text` node behind the scenes. It does not actually add a `String` object to the content list.) All return the same `Element` object that invoked them, which allows for convenient chaining.

Each of these methods adds the new node to the end of the `Element` list. To insert a node in a different position, you'll have to retrieve the `List` object itself. For example, the following code fragment creates the same `channel` element by inserting all the child nodes in reverse order at the beginning of the list using the `add(int index, Object o)` method:

```
Element channel     = new Element("channel");
Element link        = new Element("link");
```

```
Element description = new Element("description");
Element title       = new Element("title");
title.setText("Slashdot");
link.setText("http://slashdot.org/");
description.setText("News for nerds");

List content = channel.getContent();
content.add(0, description);
content.add(0, link);
content.add(0, title);
```

There are six `removeContent()` methods that remove a node from the list, wherever it resides:

```
public Element removeContent (Text text)
public Element removeContent (CDATA cdata)
public Element removeContent (Element element)
public Element removeContent (ProcessingInstruction instruction)
public Element removeContent (EntityRef ref)
public Element removeContent (Comment comment)
```

Alternatively, you can retrieve the `List` from the `Element` with `getContent()` and remove elements by position using the list's `remove()` and `removeAll()` methods, although doing so is relatively rare. In most cases, you have or can easily obtain a reference to the specific node you want to remove. For example, the following code fragment deletes the first `link` child element of the `channel` element:

```
channel.removeContent(channel.getChild("link"));
```

There currently is no method to remove all of the content from an `Element`. Instead, just pass null to `setContent()`. That is,

```
element.setContent(null);
```

Parents and Ancestors

So far we've focused on moving down the tree using methods that return children and recursion, but JDOM can move up the tree as well.[2] As with the child-returning

2. Sideways movement, for example, getting the previous or next sibling, is noticeably lacking. For this, you normally use `List` and `Iterator`.

methods, you can only jump one level at a time; that is, you can only get the parent directly. To get other ancestor elements, you need to ask for the parent's parent, the parent of the parent's parent, and so forth, until eventually you find an element whose parent is null, which is of course the root of the tree.

Each `Element` object has zero or one parents. If the `Element` is the root element of the document (or at least the root of the tree, in the event that the `Element` is not currently part of a `Document`), then this parent is null. Otherwise, it is another `Element` object. JDOM does not consider the owner document to be the parent of the root element. The following three methods enable you to determine whether or not an `Element` object represents a root element, and what its parent and owner document are:

```
public Document getDocument()
public boolean isRootElement()
public Element getParent()
```

Unlike DOM `Elements`, JDOM `Elements` are not irrevocably tied to their owner document. An `Element` may be in no document at all (in which case `getDocument()` returns null); and it may be moved from one document to another. However, a JDOM `Element` cannot have more than one parent at a time. Before you can move an element to a different `Document` or to a different position in the same `Document`, you must first detach it from its current parent by invoking the `detach()` method:

```
public Element detach()
```

After you've called `detach()`, you are free to add the `Element` to any other `Element` or `Document`. Example 15.8 loads the XML document at *http://www.slashdot.org/slashdot.rdf*, detaches all the `link` elements from that document, and inserts them in a new `linkset` element, which it then outputs. Without the call to `detach()`, this would fail with an `IllegalAddException`.

Example 15.8 Moving Elements between Documents

```
import org.jdom.*;
import org.jdom.input.SAXBuilder;
import org.jdom.output.XMLOutputter;
import java.io.IOException;
import java.util.*;
```

```
public class Linkset {

  public static void main(String[] args) {

    String url = "http://www.slashdot.org/slashdot.rdf";

    try {
      SAXBuilder parser = new SAXBuilder();

      // Parse the document
      Document document = parser.build(url);
      Element oldRoot = document.getRootElement();
      Element newRoot = new Element("linkset");
      List content = oldRoot.getChildren();
      Iterator iterator = content.iterator();
      while (iterator.hasNext()) {
        Object next = iterator.next();
        Element element = (Element) next;
        Element link = element.getChild("link",
         Namespace.getNamespace(
         "http://my.netscape.com/rdf/simple/0.9/"));
        link.detach();
        newRoot.addContent(link);
      }

      XMLOutputter outputter = new XMLOutputter("  ", true);
      outputter.output(newRoot, System.out);
    }
    catch (JDOMException e) {
      System.out.println(url + " is not well-formed.");
    }
    catch (IOException e) {
      System.out.println(
       "Due to an IOException, the parser could not read " + url
      );
    }

  } // end main

}
```

As usual, this only affects the JDOM `Document` object in memory. It has no effect on the original document read from the remote URL.

Another natural limitation is that an element cannot be its own parent or ancestor, directly or indirectly. Trying to add an element where it would violate this restriction throws an `IllegalAddException`. You can test whether one element is an ancestor of another using the `isAncestor()` method:

```
public boolean isAncestor (Element element)
```

Attributes

The `Element` class has 13 methods that read and write the values of the various attributes of the element. Except for certain unusual cases (mostly involving attribute types), these 13 methods are all you need to handle attributes. You rarely need to concern yourself with the `Attribute` class directly.

```
public Attribute getAttribute (String name)
public Attribute getAttribute (String name, Namespace namespace)
public String getAttributeValue (String name)
public String getAttributeValue (String name, Namespace namespace)
public String getAttributeValue (String name, String default)
public String getAttributeValue (String name, Namespace namespace,
 String default)
public Element setAttributes (List attributes)
 throws IllegalAddException
public Element setAttribute (String name, String value)
 throws IllegalNameException, IllegalDataException
public Element setAttribute (String name, String value, Namespace
 namespace) throws IllegalNameException, IllegalDataException
public Element setAttribute (Attribute attribute)
 throws IllegalAddException
public boolean removeAttribute (String name, String value)
public boolean removeAttribute (String name, Namespace namespace)
public boolean removeAttribute (Attribute attribute)
```

These methods all follow the same basic rules. If an attribute is in a namespace, specify the local name and namespace to access it. If the attribute is not in a namespace, then only use the name. The setters must also specify the value to set the attribute to. The getters optionally may specify a default value used if the attribute is not found. Alternately, you can use an `Attribute` object to replace all of these. Most of the time, however, strings are more convenient.

The `getAttributeValue()` methods all return the `String` value of the attribute. If the attribute was read by a parser, then the value will be normalized according to its type. However, attributes added in memory with `setAttribute()` and its ilk will not be normalized. The setter methods all return the `Element` object itself so that the objects can be used in a chain. The remove methods all return a `boolean`—true if the attribute was removed, false if it wasn't.

As with most other constructs, JDOM checks all of the attributes you set for well-formedness and throws an exception if anything looks amiss. In particular, it verifies the following:

- The local name must be a noncolonized name.
- The value must not contain any illegal characters such as null or the byte order mark.
- The attribute must not be a namespace declaration such as `xmlns` or `xmlns:`*`prefix`* (JDOM stores these separately).

For example, suppose you want to process a RDDL document to find resources related to a particular namespace URI. Each of these is enclosed in a `rddl:resource` element like this one from the RDDL specification itself:

```
<rddl:resource xlink:type="simple"
        xlink:title="RDDL Natures"
        xlink:role="http://www.rddl.org/"
        xlink:arcrole="http://www.rddl.org/purposes#directory"
        xlink:href="http://www.rddl.org/natures"
>
<div class="resource">
<p>It is anticipated that many related-resource natures will be
   well known. A list of well-known natures may be found in the
   RDDL directory <a href=
   "http://www.rddl.org/natures">http://www.rddl.org/natures</a>.
</p>
</div>
</rddl:resource>
```

All of the information required to locate the resources is included in the attributes of the `rddl:resource` elements. The rest of the content in the document is relevant only to a browser showing the document to a human reader. Most software will want to read the `rddl:resource` elements and ignore the rest of the document. Example 15.9 is such a program. It searches a document for related resources and outputs an HTML table containing their information. The `xlink:href` attribute becomes an HTML hyperlink. The other URLs in the `xlink:role` and `xlink:arcrole` attributes are purely descriptive (like namespace URLs) and not intended to be resolved, so they're merely output as plain text.

Example 15.9 Searching for RDDL Resources

```
import org.jdom.*;
import org.jdom.input.SAXBuilder;
import org.jdom.output.XMLOutputter;
import java.util.*;
import java.io.IOException;

public class RDDLLister {

  public final static Namespace XLINK_NAMESPACE =
   Namespace.getNamespace("xl", "http://www.w3.org/1999/xlink");
  public final static String RDDL_NAMESPACE
   = "http://www.rddl.org/";

  public static void main(String[] args) {

    if (args.length <= 0) {
      System.out.println("Usage: java RDDLLister url");
      return;
    }

    SAXBuilder builder = new SAXBuilder();

    try {
      // Prepare the output document
      Element html = new Element("html");
      Element body = new Element("body");
      Element table = new Element("table");
      html.addContent(body);
      body.addContent(table);
      Document output = new Document(html);
```

```
      // Read the entire document into memory
      Document doc = builder.build(args[0]);
      Element root = doc.getRootElement();
      processElement(root, table);

      // Serialize the output document
      XMLOutputter outputter = new XMLOutputter("  ", true);
      outputter.output(output, System.out);

    }
    catch (JDOMException e) {
      System.err.println(e);
    }
    catch (IOException e) {
      System.err.println(e);
    }

  } // end main

  public static void processElement(Element input, Element output)
   {

    if (input.getName().equals("resource")
     && input.getNamespaceURI().equals(RDDL_NAMESPACE)) {

       String href = input.getAttributeValue("href",
        XLINK_NAMESPACE);
       String title = input.getAttributeValue("title",
        XLINK_NAMESPACE);
       String role  = input.getAttributeValue("role",
        XLINK_NAMESPACE);
       String arcrole = input.getAttributeValue("arcrole",
        XLINK_NAMESPACE);

       // Wrap this up in a table row
       Element tr = new Element("tr");

       Element titleCell = new Element("td");
       titleCell.setText(title);
       tr.addContent(titleCell);
```

```
          Element hrefCell = new Element("td");
          Element a = new Element("a");
          a.setAttribute("href", href);
          a.setText(href);
          hrefCell.addContent(a);
          tr.addContent(hrefCell);

          Element roleCell = new Element("td");
          roleCell.setText(role);
          tr.addContent(roleCell);

          Element arcroleCell = new Element("td");
          arcroleCell.setText(arcrole);
          tr.addContent(arcroleCell);

          output.addContent(tr);

      }

      // Recurse
      List content = input.getContent();
      Iterator iterator = content.iterator();
      while (iterator.hasNext()) {
        Object o = iterator.next();
        if (o instanceof Element) {
          processElement((Element) o, output);
        }
      } // end while

    }

  }
```

The main() method builds the general outline of a well-formed HTML document and then parses the input RDDL document in the usual fashion. It retrieves the root element with getRootElement() and then passes this root element and the table element to the processElement() method.

First processElement() checks to see if the element is a rddl:resource element. If it is, then processElement() extracts the four XLink attributes using getAttributeValue(). Each of these is then inserted in a td element, which is appended to a tr element, which is added to the table element. The setAttribute() method attaches an href attribute to the a element that defines the

HTML link. Finally, the `processElement()` method is invoked on all child elements of the current elements to find any `rddl:resource` elements that are deeper down the tree.

Following is the beginning output when I ran this program against the RDDL specification itself:

```
D:\books\XMLJAVA>java RDDLLister http://www.rddl.org
<?xml version="1.0" encoding="UTF-8"?>
<html>
  <body>
    <table>
      <tr>
        <td>RDDL Natures</td>
        <td>
          <a href="http://www.rddl.org/natures">
           http://www.rddl.org/natures</a>
        </td>
        <td>http://www.rddl.org/</td>
        <td>http://www.rddl.org/purposes#directory</td>
      </tr>
      <tr>
        <td>RDDL Purposes</td>
        <td>
          <a href="http://www.rddl.org/purposes">
           http://www.rddl.org/purposes</a>
        </td>
        <td>http://www.rddl.org/</td>
        <td>http://www.rddl.org/purposes#directory</td>
      </tr>
...
```

The Attribute Class

The `Attribute` class, shown in Example 15.10, represents an attribute of an element other than one that declares a namespace. Each attribute has these five basic properties:

Local Name
A `String` accessible through the `setName()` and `getName()` methods.

Namespace
A `Namespace` object that encapsulates both the namespace URI and the prefix. This is accessible through the `setNamespace()` and `getNamespace()` methods. For all unprefixed attributes, this is `Namespace.NO_NAMESPACE`. The prefix, URI, and fully qualified name are separately readable through the `getNamespaceURI()`, `getNamespacePrefix()`, and `getQualifiedName()` convenience methods.

Value
A `String` that contains the attribute's normalized value. This is accessible through the `getValue()` and `setValue()` methods. The unnormalized value is not available. There are also convenience methods that read the attribute value as a `double`, `float`, `long`, `int`, or `boolean`.

Parent
The `Element` that possesses this `Attribute`. This is accessible through the `getParent()` and `setParent()` methods. An `Attribute` cannot have more than one parent. Before attaching a new parent `Element`, you must first invoke `detach()` to remove the `Attribute` from its current parent.

Type
The `Attribute`'s type, as specified in the DTD. This is one of the ten named constants: `Attribute.CDATA_ATTRIBUTE`, `Attribute.ID_ATTRIBUTE`, `Attribute.IDREF_ATTRIBUTE`, `Attribute.IDREFS_ATTRIBUTE`, `Attribute.ENUMERATED_ATTRIBUTE`, and so forth. If the DTD does not specify the attribute's type, JDOM sets the type to `Attribute.UNDECLARED_ATTRIBUTE`.[3] The `getAttributeType()` and `setAttributeType()` methods access this property.

In addition, you can get the `Document` to which the `Attribute` belongs with the `getDocument()` method, although this is not truly independent of the `Element` to which the `attribute` is attached.

Example 15.10 The JDOM Attribute Class

```
package org.jdom;

public class Attribute implements Serializable, Cloneable {
```

3. In practice, SAX gets this wrong. It does not distinguish between CDATA type attributes and undeclared attributes. Thus when a SAX parser builds a JDOM `Document`, no attributes will have type `Attribute.UNDECLARED_ATTRIBUTE`.

```
public final static int UNDECLARED_ATTRIBUTE = 0;
public final static int CDATA_ATTRIBUTE      = 1;
public final static int ID_ATTRIBUTE         = 2;
public final static int IDREF_ATTRIBUTE      = 3;
public final static int IDREFS_ATTRIBUTE     = 4;
public final static int ENTITY_ATTRIBUTE     = 5;
public final static int ENTITIES_ATTRIBUTE   = 6;
public final static int NMTOKEN_ATTRIBUTE    = 7;
public final static int NMTOKENS_ATTRIBUTE   = 8;
public final static int NOTATION_ATTRIBUTE   = 9;
public final static int ENUMERATED_ATTRIBUTE = 10;

protected           String    name;
protected transient Namespace namespace;
protected           String    value;
protected           int       type;
protected           Object    parent;

protected Attribute();

public Attribute(String name, String value,
 Namespace namespace);
public Attribute(String name, String value, int type,
 Namespace namespace);
public Attribute(String name, String value);
public Attribute(String name, String value, int type);

public Document     getDocument();
public Element      getParent();
protected Attribute setParent(Element parent);
public Attribute    detach();
public String       getName();
public Attribute    setName(String name);
public String       getQualifiedName();
public String       getNamespacePrefix();
public String       getNamespaceURI();
public Namespace    getNamespace();
public Attribute    setNamespace(Namespace namespace);
public String       getValue();
public Attribute    setValue(String value);
public int          getAttributeType();
```

```
    public Attribute    setAttributeType(int type);

    public String        toString();
    public final boolean equals(Object o);
    public final int     hashCode();
    public Object        clone();

    public int     getIntValue() throws DataConversionException;
    public long    getLongValue() throws DataConversionException;
    public float   getFloatValue() throws DataConversionException;
    public double  getDoubleValue() throws DataConversionException;
    public boolean getBooleanValue() throws DataConversionException;

}
```

> **Tip**
>
> One of the key things to remember when working with attributes, whether in JDOM or any other XML technology, is that unprefixed attributes are never in any namespace. In particular,
>
> 1. Attributes are never in the default namespace.
> 2. An attribute is not in the same namespace as its parent element (except in the unusual case where it happens to have the same prefix as its parent element).

At least 90 percent of the time, you will just use the `setAttribute()`, `getAttribute()`, and `removeAttribute()` methods in the `Element` class rather than using the `Attribute` class. The only major reason to use the `Attribute` class directly is if the attribute type matters; for example, when you want to treat an ID-type attribute differently than a CDATA attribute, or a NOTATIONS attribute differently than a NMTOKENS attribute.

For example, consider attribute value normalization. When a parser reports an attribute value to the client application, it adjusts the white space according to the attribute type. Attributes of type CDATA and undeclared attributes preserve all white space. For all other attribute types, white space is trimmed from the edges, and all runs of white space are compressed to a single space. Consider this `fact` start-tag:

```
<fact source=" f21 f32   f33
 f122 f87 f893  ">
```

If the document's DTD declares that the source attribute has type IDREFS, then the parser will report its value as f21 f32 f33 f122 f87 f893. On the other hand, if the DTD declares that it has type CDATA or does not assign it a type at all, then the parser will report its value with all of the spaces and line breaks intact.

JDOM will accept whatever value the parser initially reports when the document is constructed. However, if attributes are added or their values modified later, then attributes will no longer be in normalized form. To fix this, we can write a method that searches a document for attributes whose type is something other than CDATA and normalizes their space. As usual the method is recursive:

```
public void normalizeAttributes(Element element) {

  List attributes = element.getAttributes();
  Iterator iterator = attributes.iterator();
  while (iterator.hasNext()) {
    Attribute attribute = (Attribute) iterator.next();
    int type = attribute.getAttributeType();
    if (type != Attribute.CDATA_ATTRIBUTE
     && type != Attribute.UNDECLARED_ATTRIBUTE) {
       String oldValue = attribute.getValue();
       String newValue = Text.normalizeString(oldValue);
       attribute.setValue(newValue);
    }
  }

  List content = element.getContent();
  Iterator children = content.iterator();
  while (children.hasNext()) {
    Object o = children.next();
    if (o instanceof Element) {
      Element child = (Element) o;
      normalizeAttributes(child);
    }
  }

}
```

The actual normalization is performed by the static Text.normalizeString() method from the Text class.

The Text Class

JDOM uses the Text class internally to represent text nodes. In normal usage, you don't deal with this class directly—you just use strings. The one time you may encounter it is when you use getContent() to retrieve all the children of the node, and you're iterating through the list returned. In this case, you will see Text objects.

Each Text object has a parent Element (which may be null) and a String value that holds the content of the node. This value may contain characters like < and &. If so, they will be escaped when the node is serialized. They do not need to be escaped before being inserted into a Text object.

The Text class, summarized in Example 15.11, has methods to get, set, and detach the parent Element; to get and set the text content as a String; to append more text to the node; and to get the content of the node after trimming or normalizing white space. And of course, it has the other usual Java methods such as equals(), hashCode(), and clone() that all JDOM objects possess.

Example 15.11 The JDOM Text Class

```
package org.jdom;

public class Text implements Serializable, Cloneable {

  protected String value;
  protected Object parent;

  protected Text();
  public    Text(String s);

  public String getText();
  public String getTextTrim();
  public String getTextNormalize();

  public static String normalizeString(String s);

  public Text     setText(String s);
  public void     append(String s);
  public void     append(Text text);
  public Element  getParent();
  public Document getDocument();
```

```
    protected Text  setParent(Element parent);
    public Text     detach();

    public          String  toString();
    public final int        hashCode();
    public final boolean equals(Object ob);
    public          Object  clone();

}
```

JDOM does not guarantee that each run of text is represented by a single text node. Rather, `Text` objects can be adjacent to each other, which can make it a little tricky to retrieve the complete content of an element. For example, consider this element:

```
<vendor>
  Gus's  Crawfish
</vendor>
```

Just from looking at the XML, there's no way to say whether the `Element` object representing the `vendor` element contains one `Text` object or two. Indeed, in extreme cases, it may contain three, four, or even more. If this element was read by `SAXBuilder`, then JDOM treats it as a single `Text` object. On the other hand, if a program created it or modified it in memory, then all bets are off.

In fact, this is of concern even if JDOM did not allow adjacent text nodes. For example, consider this element:

```
<vendor>
  Gus's <!-- This is my brother-in-law. My wife asked me to
       throw him some business. --> Crawfish
</vendor>
```

The text content of the `vendor` element is the same as before, but now there's no way for JDOM to represent it as a single `Text` object.

You must also consider the case in which an element contains child elements such as this one:

```
<vendor>
  Gus's <seafood>Crawfish</seafood>
</vendor>
```

To accumulate the complete text of an element, you need to iterate through its children while recursively processing any element children. This `getFullText()` method demonstrates:

```
public static String getFullText(Element element) {

  StringBuffer result = new StringBuffer();
  List content = element.getContent();
  Iterator iterator = content.iterator();
  while (iterator.hasNext()) {
    Object o = iterator.next();
    if (o instanceof Text) {
      Text t = (Text) o;
      result.append(t.getText());
    }
    else if (o instanceof Element) {
      Element child = (Element) o;
      result.append(getFullValue(child));
    }
  }

  return result.toString();

}
```

Chapter 11 demonstrated a program that encoded all the text of a document, but not its markup, in rot-13 using DOM. Let's repeat that example here, but with JDOM instead. You can compare Example 15.12 with Example 11.8 to get a good feeling for the differences between DOM and JDOM. The DOM version is significantly more complex, particularly when it comes to building the document and then serializing it.

Example 15.12 JDOM-Based Rot-13 Encoder for XML Documents

```
import org.jdom.*;
import org.jdom.output.XMLOutputter;
import org.jdom.input.SAXBuilder;
import java.io.IOException;
import java.util.*;

public class ROT13XML {
```

```
  // note use of recursion
  public static void encode(Element element) {

    List content = element.getContent();
    Iterator iterator = content.iterator();
    while (iterator.hasNext()) {
      Object o = iterator.next();
      if (o instanceof Text) {
        Text t = (Text) o;
        String cipherText = rot13(t.getText());
        t.setText(cipherText);
      }
      else if (o instanceof Element) {
        Element child = (Element) o;
        encode(child);
      }
    }

  }

  public static String rot13(String s) {

    StringBuffer out = new StringBuffer(s.length());
    for (int i = 0; i < s.length(); i++) {
      int c = s.charAt(i);
      if (c >= 'A' && c <= 'M') out.append((char) (c+13));
      else if (c >= 'N' && c <= 'Z') out.append((char) (c-13));
      else if (c >= 'a' && c <= 'm') out.append((char) (c+13));
      else if (c >= 'n' && c <= 'z') out.append((char) (c-13));
      else out.append((char) c);
    }
    return out.toString();

  }

  public static void main(String[] args) {

    if (args.length <= 0) {
      System.out.println("Usage: java ROT13XML URL");
      return;
    }
```

```
      String url = args[0];

      try {
        SAXBuilder parser = new SAXBuilder();

        // Read the document
        Document document = parser.build(url);

        // Modify the document
        ROT13XML.encode(document.getRootElement());

        // Write it out again
        XMLOutputter outputter = new XMLOutputter();
        outputter.output(document, System.out);
      }
      catch (JDOMException e) {
        System.out.println(url + " is not well-formed.");
      }
      catch (IOException e) {
        System.out.println(
         "Due to an IOException, the parser could not encode " + url
        );
      }

    } // end main

  }
```

Here is a joke encoded by this program. You'll have to run the program if you want to find out what it says. :-)

```
D:\books\XMLJAVA>java ROT13XML joke.xml
<?xml version="1.0" encoding="UTF-8"?>
<joke>
  Gur qrsvavgvba bs n yvoregnevna vf n pbafreingvir
  haqre vaqvpgzrag.
</joke>
```

The CDATA Class

The CDATA class shown in Example 15.13 is a subclass of Text with almost no functionality of its own. The only difference between CDATA and Text is that when an XMLOutputter serializes a CDATA object, it places its contents in a CDATA section rather than escaping reserved characters such as the less-than symbol with character or entity references.

Example 15.13 The JDOM CDATA Class

```
package org.jdom;

public class CDATA extends Text {

  protected CDATA() { }
  public    CDATA(String s) throws IllegalDataException;

  public Text setText(String s) throws IllegalDataException;
  public void append(String s) throws IllegalDataException;

  public String toString();

}
```

In my opinion, you really shouldn't use this class at all. The builder may (or may not) create CDATA objects when it parses a document that contains CDATA sections, but you should not create them yourself. CDATA sections are purely a convenience for human authors. They are not part of the document's Infoset. They should not be exposed as a separate item in the logical model of a document, and indeed not all parsers and APIs will report them to the client program. Even APIs like JDOM and DOM that support them do not necessarily guarantee that they'll be used where possible.

Chapter 11 already warned against using CDATA sections as a sort of pseudo-element to hide HTML in your XML documents. That warning bears repeating now. CDATA sections let you add non-well-formed text to a document, but their contents are just text like any other text. They are not a special kind of element, and a parser likely won't distinguish between the contents of the CDATA section and the surrounding text. If you have a legitimate reason for doing this, you still need to enclose the CDATA section in an actual element to provide structure that programs can detect. For example, an HTML tutorial might enclose HTML code fragments or complete documents in `example` elements, like this:

```
<example>
<![CDATA[<html>
<body>
  <h1>My First Web Page</h1>

  HTML is cool!<P>
  <hr>
  &copy; 2002 John Smith
  </body>
</html>]]>
</example>
```

This is much more flexible and much more robust than relying on CDATA sections to distinguish the examples from the main body text.

The ProcessingInstruction Class

The `ProcessingInstruction` class represents an XML processing instruction, such as `<?xml-stylesheet href="book.xsl" type="application/xml"?>` or `<?php mysql_connect("database.unc.edu", "debra", "secret"); ?>`. Each processing instruction has a target string, which must be a legal XML name; a value string, which may not contain the end-delimiter ?>; and a parent element, which may be null if the instruction is a child of a `Document` instead of an `Element`.

> **Note**
> At the time of this writing, JDOM only checks processing instruction targets for well-formedness. It does not check processing instruction data. However, checking data for the presence of illegal characters is on the TODO list.

Because so many processing instructions (but not all) have the pseudo-attribute format exemplified by `<?xml-stylesheet href="book.xsl" type="application/xml"?>`, this class also offers a second view of the instruction's data, as a map of name-value pairs. Internally, `ProcessingInstruction` always stores the string form but only stores the map form if it can successfully parse the data as pseudo-attributes. If a program uses the map-based methods such as `getValue()` and removeValue() but the actual format of the data is not pseudo-attributes, then they return null (getters). Using a setter method replaces the existing data with a pseudo-attribute. Example 15.14 summarizes the ProcessingInstruction class.

Example 15.14 The JDOM ProcessingInstruction Class

```
package org.jdom;

public class ProcessingInstruction
 implements Serializable, Cloneable {

  protected String target;
  protected String rawData;
  protected Map    mapData;
  protected Object parent;

  protected ProcessingInstruction();
  public    ProcessingInstruction(String target, Map data);
  public    ProcessingInstruction(String target, String data);

  public Element               getParent();
  public ProcessingInstruction detach();
  public Document              getDocument();

  public String getTarget();
  public String getData();
  public List   getNames();
  public String getValue(String name);

  public ProcessingInstruction setTarget(String target)
   throws IllegalTargetException;
  public ProcessingInstruction setData(String data);
  public ProcessingInstruction setData(Map data);
  public ProcessingInstruction setValue(String name,
   String value);

  public boolean removeValue(String name);

  public String        toString();
  public final boolean equals(Object ob);
```

```
  public final int      hashCode();
  public Object         clone();

}
```

For example, robots and spiders that process XML documents are supposed to recognize processing instructions in the form `<?robots index="`*yes | no*`" follow="`*yes | no*`">` to decide whether or not to index and/or follow the links in an XML document. Such a robot could use this method to decide whether to index a document it had parsed:

```
public static boolean canIndex(Document doc) {

  List content = doc.getContent();
  Iterator iterator = content.iterator();
  while (iterator.hasNext()) {
    Object o = iterator.next();
    if (o instanceof ProcessingInstruction) {
      ProcessingInstruction pi = (ProcessingInstruction) o;
      if (pi.getTarget().equals("robots")) {
        if ("no".equals(pi.getValue("index"))) return false;
      }
    }
    else if (o instanceof Element) {
      // This is the root element. The prolog is done.
      break;
    }
  }

  return true;

}
```

This method looks for the first `robots` processing instruction in the document's prolog. When it finds it, it requests the value of the `index` pseudo-attribute and returns true if it has the value yes, or returns null and false if it has the value no. If no `robots` processing instruction is present, or if it has the wrong format, then the default is to assume that indexing is permitted. A `canSpider()` method is almost identical, except that you would ask for the value of the `follow` pseudo-attribute instead.

The Comment Class

The `org.jdom.Comment` class represents an XML comment such as `<-- Remember to verify this -->`. As you can see from Example 15.15, `Comment` is a very simple class that contains some string data, the usual `getParent()` and `getDocument()` methods, and the customary Java utility methods such as `equals()` and `toString()`.

Example 15.15 The JDOM Comment Class

```
package org.jdom;

public class Comment implements Serializable, Cloneable {

  protected String text;
  protected Object parent;

  protected Comment();
  public Comment(String text);

  public Element    getParent();
  protected Comment setParent(Element parent);
  public Comment    detach();
  public Document   getDocument();
  protected Comment setDocument(Document document);
  public String     getText();
  public Comment    setText(String text);

  public       String  toString();
  public final boolean equals(Object ob);
  public final int     hashCode();
  public       Object  clone();

}
```

For example, the following code fragment adds the comment `<--An example from Chapter 15 of Processing XML with Java-->` at the top of the `Document` object doc:

```
Comment comment = new Comment(
 "An example from Chapter 15 of Processing XML with Java");
List content = doc.getContent();
content.add(0, comment);
```

As with the other JDOM node classes, JDOM does attempt to verify that any data you supply for a `Comment` is well-formed. There are really only two constraints that matter for comments:

- The comment must not contain any illegal characters such as a null or a vertical tab.
- The comment must not contain the double hyphen `--` that signals the end of the comment.

JDOM checks both of them.

There's not a lot you can do with comments, nor is there a lot you should do with them. Comments are intended purely as a convenience for human authors. Programs really shouldn't consider them or attempt to parse their contents. The only reason they're in the API at all is to support round-tripping between the document that's read and the document that's written. Thus the examples are going to be fairly simple.

Earlier in Examples 7.12 and 11.20, you saw SAX and DOM programs that printed the comments in an XML document on `System.out`. Now in Example 15.16 you can see the JDOM equivalent. The pattern is very much the same as in the DOM version, recursively descending the tree looking for objects of type `Comment`. However, the detailed classes are different.

Example 15.16 Printing Comments

```
import org.jdom.*;
import org.jdom.input.SAXBuilder;
import java.util.*;
import java.io.IOException;

public class JDOMCommentReader {

  public static void main(String[] args) {

    if (args.length <= 0) {
      System.out.println("Usage: java JDOMCommentReader url");
```

```
      return;
    }
    SAXBuilder builder = new SAXBuilder();

    try {
      // Read the entire document into memory
      Document doc = builder.build(args[0]);
      List content = doc.getContent();
      Iterator iterator = content.iterator();
      while (iterator.hasNext()) {
        Object o = iterator.next();
        if (o instanceof Comment) {
          Comment c = (Comment) o;
          System.out.println(c.getText());
          System.out.println();
        }
        else if (o instanceof Element) {
          processElement((Element) o);
        }
      }
    }
    catch (JDOMException e) {
      System.err.println(e);
    }
    catch (IOException e) {
      System.err.println(e);
    }

  } // end main

  // note use of recursion
  public static void processElement(Element element) {

    List content = element.getContent();
    Iterator iterator = content.iterator();
    while (iterator.hasNext()) {
      Object o = iterator.next();
      if (o instanceof Comment) {
        Comment c = (Comment) o;
        System.out.println(c.getText());
        System.out.println();
      }
```

```
        else if (o instanceof Element) {
          processElement((Element) o);
        }
      } // end while

    }

  }
```

Following is the result of running this program on the XLink specification:

```
% java JDOMCommentReader
http://www.w3.org/TR/2001/REC-xlink-20010627/Overview.xml

Last edited: 19 December 2000 by elm

TO DO:
- Point to the linking/style Note if it gets published in time


http://www.w3.org/TR/2000/CR-xlink-20000703/
http://www.w3.org/TR/WD-xlink-20000221
http://www.w3.org/TR/WD-xlink-20000119
http://www.w3.org/TR/WD-xlink-19991220
http://www.w3.org/1999/07/WD-xlink-19990726
http://www.w3.org/TR/1998/WD-xlink-19980303
http://www.w3.org/TR/WD-xml-link-970731
```

Namespaces

JDOM's `Namespace` class, shown in Example 15.17, represents a namespace attached to an element or an attribute. Each namespace has a URI. If the namespace is not a default namespace, then it also has a prefix. Otherwise, the prefix is the empty string.

Example 15.17 The JDOM Namespace Class

```
package org.jdom;

public final class Namespace {
```

```
  // Common namespaces
  public static final Namespace NO_NAMESPACE;
  public static final Namespace XML_NAMESPACE;

  // Factory methods
  public static Namespace getNamespace(String prefix, String uri);
  public static Namespace getNamespace(String uri);

  // Getter methods
  public String getPrefix();
  public String getURI();

  // Utility methods
  public boolean equals(Object o);
  public String toString();
  public int hashCode();

}
```

Because repeating long strings such as "`http://www.w3.org/2002/01/P3Pv1`" on each element can eat up memory very quickly, and because a typical document contains many elements in the same namespace, this class uses the flyweight design pattern. This means that the constructors are private, and you'll need to use the factory methods to create `Namespace` objects. Alternately, the `Element` and `Attribute` classes allocate or reuse the necessary `Namespace` objects automatically when you pass string forms of the namespace URIs to their constructors or `setNamespace()` methods.

For example, I try to use well-formed HTML on most of my sites, but I generally don't attach the XHTML namespace (`http://www.w3.org/1999/xhtml`) where I should. The following method forces all unqualified elements into the XHTML namespace:

```
public static void xhtmlQualify(Element element) {

  Namespace xhtml
   = Namespace.getNamespace("http://www.w3.org/1999/xhtml");

  if (element.getNamespace() == Namespace.NO_NAMESPACE) {
    element.setNamespace(xhtml);
  }
```

```
    List childElements = element.getChildren();
    Iterator iterator = childElements.iterator();
    while (iterator.hasNext()) {
      Element child = (Element) iterator.next();
      xhtmlQualify(child);
    }

}
```

This changes the `Document` object in place (but not the original file on disk or on the network). It does not create any new node objects. You could use this as a filter before passing the `Document` object to a different method that expected pure XHTML. (In practice, you'd probably also need to change all of the element names to lowercase and add a `DocType`.)

In general, you don't need to worry about exactly where the `xmlns` and `xmlns:`*`prefix`* attributes that declare namespaces are placed. Indeed JDOM won't let you add attributes with these names because it stores them separately from the other attributes. When an outputter converts a JDOM `Document` to a DOM `Document`, a SAX event sequence, or a stream of bytes, it will figure out where it needs to put namespace declarations to make everything come out right. However, some XML applications, including SOAP, XSLT, and the W3C XML Schema Language, also use namespace prefixes in attribute values and even element content. These prefixes are not necessarily used on any element or attribute names in the document, but the prefixes still need to be declared. For example, the simple XSLT stylesheet in Example 15.18 needs to declare the prefix `svg` even though it's only used in the value of the `match` attribute.

Example 15.18 An XML Document That Uses Namespace Prefixes in Attribute Values

```
<?xml version="1.0" encoding="ISO-8859-1"?>
<xsl:stylesheet version="1.0"
  xmlns:xsl="http://www.w3.org/1999/XSL/Transform"
  xmlns:svg="http://www.w3.org/2000/svg">

  <xsl:template match="svg:rect">
    <rectangle><xsl:apply-templates/></rectangle>
  </xsl:template>

</xsl:stylesheet>
```

You can add these extra namespace bindings through the `addNamespaceDeclaration()` method in the `Element` class. If necessary, you can remove one with the `removeNamespaceDeclaration()` method:

```
public Element addNamespaceDeclaration (Namespace namespace)
public Element removeNamespaceDeclaration (Namespace namespace)
```

For example, the following code fragment creates the `xsl:stylesheet` element in Example 15.18 and adds the SVG namespace declaration to it:

```
Element stylesheet = new Element(
    "stylesheet", "xsl", "http://www.w3.org/1999/XSL/Transform");
Namespace svg = Namespace.getNamespace("svg",
                                        "http://www.w3.org/2000/svg");
stylesheet.addNamespaceDeclaration(svg);
```

If you encounter a namespace prefix in character data, and you need to know what prefix it maps to, then you have to check the parent element's namespace, all of its attributes' namespaces, and all of its additional namespaces. If that doesn't give you an answer, repeat the process for the next nearest ancestor, and continue until you either find the answer or run out of ancestors. This can be a little involved, but fortunately the `Element` class provides a simple method that tells you what URI any given prefix maps to within its scope:

```
public Namespace getNamespace (String prefix)
```

Since prefixes can be remapped to different URIs in descendant elements, always check the namespace in scope from the `Attribute` or `Text` object's immediate parent.

The DocType Class

The `org.jdom.DocType` class summarized in Example 15.19 represents a document type declaration. Note that this points to and/or contains the document type definition (DTD), but it is not the same thing. JDOM does not have any representation of the DTD.

Example 15.19 The JDOM DocType Class

```
package org.jdom;

public class DocType implements Serializable, Cloneable {

  protected String   elementName;
  protected String   publicID;
  protected String   systemID;
  protected Document document;
  protected String   internalSubset;

  protected DocType();
  public DocType(String elementName, String publicID,
   String systemID);
  public DocType(String elementName, String systemID);
  public DocType(String elementName);

  public String   getElementName();
  public DocType  setElementName(String elementName);
  public String   getPublicID();
  public DocType  setPublicID(String publicID);
  public String   getSystemID();
  public DocType  setSystemID(String systemID);
  public Document getDocument();
  public void     setInternalSubset(String newData);

  public String getInternalSubset();

  public       String  toString();
  public final boolean equals(Object o);
  public final int     hashCode();
  public       Object  clone();

}
```

Each DocType object has four String properties, of which the last three may be null:

- Root element name
- Internal DTD subset

- System ID
- Public ID

For example, consider this document type declaration:

```
<!DOCTYPE chapter PUBLIC "-//OASIS//DTD DocBook XML V4.1.2//EN"
                         "docbook/docbookx.dtd">
```

It has the root element name chapter, the public ID -//OASIS//DTD DocBook XML V4.1.2//EN, and the system ID docbook/docbookx.dtd. However, its internal DTD subset is null. This code fragment constructs a DocType object representing this document type declaration and uses it to construct a new Document object:

```
DocType doctype = new DocType("chapter",
 "-//OASIS//DTD DocBook XML V4.1.2//EN", "docbook/docbookx.dtd");
Element chapter = new Element("chapter");
Document doc = new Document(chapter, doctype);
```

Note that JDOM does not require validity, only well-formedness. This means that the root element may in fact be different from what the document type declaration specifies. For example, the following is perfectly legal:

```
DocType doctype = new DocType("chapter",
 "-//OASIS//DTD DocBook XML V4.1.2//EN", "docbook/docbookx.dtd");
Element book = new Element("book");
Document doc = new Document(book, doctype);
```

This document type declaration has a root element name and an internal DTD subset, but no public ID or system ID:

```
<!DOCTYPE Fibonacci_Numbers [
  <!ELEMENT Fibonacci_Numbers (fibonacci*)>
  <!ELEMENT fibonacci (#PCDATA)>
  <!ATTLIST fibonacci index CDATA #IMPLIED>
]>
```

To set this up, you need to store the internal subset in a String and pass that to the setInternalSubset() method after the DocType object has been constructed, like so:

```
DocType doctype = new DocType("Fibonacci_Numbers");
String dtd = "<!ELEMENT Fibonacci_Numbers (fibonacci*)>\n";
dtd += "<!ELEMENT fibonacci (#PCDATA)>\n";
dtd += "<!ATTLIST fibonacci index CDATA #IMPLIED>\n";
doctype.setInternalSubset(dtd);
Element root = new Element("Fibonacci_Numbers");
Document doc = new Document(root, doctype);
```

Unlike most node classes, JDOM doesn't fully check the data used in a `DocType` object for well-formedness. It does test that the root element name is a legal XML name, and it checks that the public and system IDs adhere to the minimum constraints for these items. However, it does not check that the public ID follows the standard conventions for public identifiers; it does not check that the system ID is a legal URL; and it does not even check the characters in the internal DTD subset, much less the syntax.

As an example of this class, let's look at a program that validates XHTML 1.0 documents. XHTML validity is a little stricter than HTML validity. In particular, according to the XHTML 1.0 specification, a valid XHTML document must satisfy these four conditions:

- The document must be valid according to one of the three XHTML DTDs: strict, transitional, or frameset.
- The root element of the document must be `html`.
- This root `html` element of the document must specify the default namespace as `http://www.w3.org/1999/xhtml` using an `xmlns` attribute.
- The document must contain a DOCTYPE declaration. The public identifier for the external DTD subset must reference one of the three XHTML DTDs, using one of these three public identifiers:
  - `-//W3C//DTD XHTML 1.0 Strict//EN`
  - `-//W3C//DTD XHTML 1.0 Transitional//EN`
  - `-//W3C//DTD XHTML 1.0 Frameset//EN`

There are a few other flaky rules scattered throughout the XHTML specification, mostly involving constraints that can't be reasonably specified in a DTD, such as that an a element cannot contain another a element, but these are the major ones that define strict XHTML conformance.

Example 15.20 is similar to the earlier `JDOMValidator`. That is, it reads a URL from the command line and validates the document found at that URL against its DTD. However, it also checks the four constraints just listed. Of particular interest in this discussion is that it checks that the document type declaration is pointing to one of the three legal DTDs. This is something that pure XML validation normally doesn't tell you.

Example 15.20 Validating XHTML with the DocType Class

```
import java.io.IOException;
import org.jdom.*;
import org.jdom.input.SAXBuilder;

public class XHTMLValidator {

  public static void main(String[] args) {

    for (int i = 0; i < args.length; i++) {
      validate(args[i]);
    }

  }

  private static SAXBuilder builder = new SAXBuilder(true);
                                   /* turn on validation ^^^^ */

  // not thread safe
  public static void validate(String source) {

      Document document;
      try {
        document = builder.build(source);
      }
      catch (JDOMException e) {
        System.out.println(source
         + " is invalid XML, and thus not XHTML.");
        return;
      }
      catch (IOException e) {
        System.out.println("Could not read: " + source);
        return;
      }
```

```
// If we get this far, then the document is valid XML.
// Check to see whether the document is actually XHTML
boolean valid = true;
DocType doctype = document.getDocType();

if (doctype == null) {
  System.out.println("No DOCTYPE");
  valid = false;
}
else {
  // verify the DOCTYPE
  String name     = doctype.getElementName();
  String systemID = doctype.getSystemID();
  String publicID = doctype.getPublicID();

  if (!name.equals("html")) {
    System.out.println(
     "Incorrect root element name " + name);
    valid = false;
  }

  if (publicID == null
   || (!publicID.equals("-//W3C//DTD XHTML 1.0 Strict//EN")
    && !publicID.equals(
     "-//W3C//DTD XHTML 1.0 Transitional//EN")
    && !publicID.equals(
     "-//W3C//DTD XHTML 1.0 Frameset//EN"))) {
    valid = false;
    System.out.println(source
     + " does not seem to use an XHTML 1.0 DTD");
  }
}


// Check the namespace on the root element
Element root = document.getRootElement();
Namespace namespace = root.getNamespace();
String prefix = namespace.getPrefix();
String uri = namespace.getURI();
if (!uri.equals("http://www.w3.org/1999/xhtml")) {
  valid = false;
  System.out.println(source
```

```
            + " does not properly declare the"
            + " http://www.w3.org/1999/xhtml namespace"
            + " on the root element");
        }
        if (!prefix.equals("")) {
          valid = false;
          System.out.println(source
            + " does not use the empty prefix for XHTML");
        }

        if (valid) System.out.println(source + "is valid XHTML.");

    }

  }
```

Following is the result of running this program on the XHTML 1.0 specification:

```
D:\books\XMLJAVA>java XHTMLValidator http://www.w3.org/TR/xhtml1/
http://www.w3.org/TR/xhtml1/is valid XHTML.
```

As one would hope, it proves valid.

The EntityRef Class

The `EntityRef` class shown in Example 15.21 represents a defined entity reference such as `©` or `&chapter1;`. It is used only for entity references that the parser does not expand. Given a fully validating parser, or even just one that reads the external DTD subset, no `EntityRef` objects will normally be present in the tree.

Example 15.21 The JDOM EntityRef Class

```
package org.jdom;

public class EntityRef implements Serializable, Cloneable {

  protected String name;
  protected String publicID;
  protected String systemID;
  protected Object parent;
```

```
    protected EntityRef();

    public EntityRef(String name);
    public EntityRef(String name, String systemID);
    public EntityRef(String name, String publicID,
     String systemID);

    public EntityRef detach();

    public Document  getDocument();
    public String    getName();
    public EntityRef setName(String name);
    public Element   getParent();
    public String    getPublicID();
    public EntityRef setPublicID(String newPublicID);
    public String    getSystemID();
    public EntityRef setSystemID(String newSystemID);

    public final boolean equals(Object ob);
    public final int     hashCode();
    public       String  toString();
    public       Object  clone();

}
```

Each `EntityRef` object has these four properties:

1. The entity name
2. The public ID of the entity
3. The system ID of the entity
4. The parent `Element` of the entity

The public and system IDs will be null if the parser did not read the part of the DTD that defined the entity.

The one thing you might expect that is not available is the entity's replacement text. Unlike the `EntityReference` interface in DOM, JDOM `EntityRef` objects do not have any children. If the builder knows the replacement text of the entity, then it will insert the corresponding nodes in the tree rather than including an `EntityRef` object.

There's infrequent need to use this class directly. You can add an entity reference in place of the characters that you know are going to cause problems in your choice of encoding. On the other hand, you're probably better off just letting the XMLOutputter emit numeric character references instead. If you do choose to insert EntityRef objects into your JDOM tree, then be sure to use a DocType that either points to an external DTD subset or includes an internal DTD subset that defines your entities. JDOM will not do this for you automatically, so if you aren't careful you can produce a malformed document.

For an example, let's turn once again to XHTML. Browsers generally use non-validating parsers and tend not to read the external DTD subset by default. Thus they're likely to encounter skipped entity references. The XHTML specification states:

> If it encounters an entity reference (other than one of the predefined entities) for which the User Agent has processed no declaration (which could happen if the declaration is in the external subset which the User Agent hasn't read), the entity reference should be rendered as the characters (starting with the ampersand and ending with the semi-colon) that make up the entity reference.

Here is a simple method that assists with this requirement by converting all EntityRef objects in a tree to Text objects of the form *&name;*.

```
public static void entityRefToText(Element element) {

  List content = element.getContent();
  ListIterator iterator = content.listIterator();
  while (iterator.hasNext()) {
    Object o = iterator.next();
    if (o instanceof Element) {
      Element child = (Element) o;
      entityRefToText(child);
    }
    else if (o instanceof EntityRef) {
      EntityRef ref = (EntityRef) o;
      Text fauxRef = new Text("&");
      fauxRef.append(ref.getName());
      fauxRef.append(";");
      iterator.set(fauxRef);
    }
  }

}
```

There's one technique here you may not have seen before. Instead of a basic Iterator, I used a ListIterator. The reason is that ListIterator has an optional set() method (which JDOM does implement) that replaces the last object returned by next() with another object. That's how I replace the EntityRef with a Text.

> **Caution**
> Be sure you understand the difference here. A Text object always contains plain text, never an entity reference or a tag, even if it contains some characters such as & and < that might need to be escaped when the document is serialized. For example, invoking element.setText("<") sets the content of element to the four characters &, *l*, *t*, and *;* in that order. It does not set it to the single character <. When element is serialized, its content will be written as <.

Summary

JDOM models an XML document as a Document object that contains a List of Comment and ProcessingInstruction objects and a single Element object for the root element.

Each Element object contains a List of its children: Comment, ProcessingInstruction, Text, and other Element objects. In addition, it has separate lists of attributes and additional namespaces. The list of children is accessible through the getContent() method. Content can be appended to an element or to a document with the heavily overloaded addContent() method, or removed from the tree using the heavily overloaded removeContent() method. Other mutation operations, such as inserting a node at the beginning or in the middle of an element's children, require using the methods of java.util.List.

With the exception of Namespace, the JDOM core node classes have public constructors, and they are constructed in about the most obvious ways you can imagine. For example, to create a new Attribute object that represents the attribute revision="20020430", you would use the constructor Attribute("revision", "20020430"). Namespaces and local names are always separated in argument lists. Sometimes namespaces are provided as one or two strings containing the namespace URI and the optional prefix. At other times they're provided as a combined Namespace object. (JDOM is not perfectly consistent here.)

All of the core node classes have the getter and setter methods you would expect—for example, setTarget(), getTarget(), setData(), and getData() for ProcessingInstruction; setName(), getName(), setNamespace(), and getNamespace() for Element; and so forth. In addition there are a few common methods that show up across several classes. The `detach()` method removes a node from its parent. The `getParent()` method returns a node's parent element. And all of the JDOM nodes provide the usual Java utility methods: `equals()`, `hashCode()`, and `toString()`. Finally, all of these classes implement both `Serializable` and `Cloneable`, and all override `clone()`.

Part V

XPath/XSLT

Chapter 16

XPath

Much of the code in this book has involved navigating the tree structure of an XML document to find particular nodes. For example, the XML-RPC servlet in Example 10.13 read a client request looking for `int` elements. Such code can become quite involved and fragile if you aren't very careful. As the code walks down the tree hierarchy, loading one child after the other, a single misplaced or misnamed element may cause the program to fail. If an element isn't where it's expected to be, then the chain of method calls that gives directions to the desired elements will be broken. What's needed is a way to specify which nodes a program needs without explicitly specifying how the program navigates to those nodes.

XPath is a fourth-generation declarative language for locating nodes in XML documents. An XPath location path specifies which nodes from the document you want. It says nothing about what algorithm is used to find these nodes. You simply pass an XPath statement to a method, and the XPath engine is responsible for figuring out how to find all of the nodes that satisfy that expression. This is much more robust than writing the detailed search and navigation code yourself using DOM, SAX, or JDOM. XPath searches often succeed even when the document format is not quite what you expected. For example, a comment in the middle of a paragraph of text may break DOM code that expects to see contiguous text. XPath wouldn't be phased by this. Many XPath expressions are resistant even to much more significant alterations, such as changing the names or namespaces of ancestor elements, reordering the children of an element, or even adding or subtracting entire levels from the tree hierarchy.

In the large, using XPath in a Java program is like using SQL in a Java program. To extract information from a database, you write a SQL statement indicating what information you want, and you ask JDBC to fetch it for you. You neither know nor care how JDBC communicates with the database. Similarly with XML, you write an XPath expression to indicate what information you want from an XML document and ask the XPath engine to fetch it, without concerning yourself with the exact algorithms XPath uses to search the XML document.

Queries

XPath can be thought of as a query language like SQL. Rather than extracting information from a database, however, XPath extracts information from an XML document. An example should help make this more concrete. Consider the simple weather report document in Example 16.1.

Example 16.1 Weather Data in XML

```
<?xml version="1.0" encoding="ISO-8859-1"?>
<weather time="2002-06-06T15:35:00-05:00">
  <report latitude="41.2° N" longitude="71.6° W">
    <locality>Block Island</locality>
    <temperature units="°C">16</temperature>
    <humidity>88%</humidity>
    <dewpoint units="°C">14</dewpoint>
    <wind>
      <direction>NE</direction>
      <speed units="km/h">16.1</speed>
      <gust units="km/h">31</gust>
    </wind>
    <pressure units="hPa">1014</pressure>
    <condition>overcast</condition>
    <visibility>13 km</visibility>
  </report>
  <report latitude="34.1° N" longitude="118.4° W">
    <locality>Santa Monica</locality>
    <temperature units="°C">19</temperature>
    <humidity>79%</humidity>
    <dewpoint units="°C">16</dewpoint>
    <wind>
      <direction>WSW</direction>
```

```
      <speed units="km/h">14.5</speed>
    </wind>
    <pressure units="hPa">1010</pressure>
    <condition>hazy</condition>
    <visibility>5 km</visibility>
  </report>
</weather>
```

Here are some XPath expressions that identify particular parts of this document:

- `/weather/report` is an XPath expression that selects the two `report` elements.
- `/weather/report[1]` is an XPath expression that selects the first `report` element.
- `/weather/report/temperature` is an XPath expression that selects the two `temperature` elements.
- `/weather/report[locality="Santa Monica"]` is an XPath expression that selects the second `report` element.
- `//report[locality="Block Island"]/attribute::longitude` is an XPath expression that selects the `longitude` attribute of the first `report` element.
- `/child::weather/child::report/child::wind/child::*` is an XPath expression that selects all of the `direction`, `speed`, and `gust` elements.
- `9 * number(/weather/report[locality="Block Island"]/temperature) div 5 + 32` is an XPath expression that returns the temperature on Block Island in degrees Fahrenheit.
- `/descendant::*` is an XPath expression that selects all of the elements in the document.

Like SQL, XPath expressions are used in many different contexts, including the following:

- Dedicated query tools such as Alex Chaffee's XPath Explorer. Figure 16.1 shows this tool evaluating the expression `/weather/report/temperature` against Example 16.1.
- Native XML databases such as the Apache XML Project's XIndice and Software AG's Tamino.
- As a component of other, broader languages such as XSLT and XQuery.
- Last but certainly not least, as a search component for your own Java programs that read XML documents.

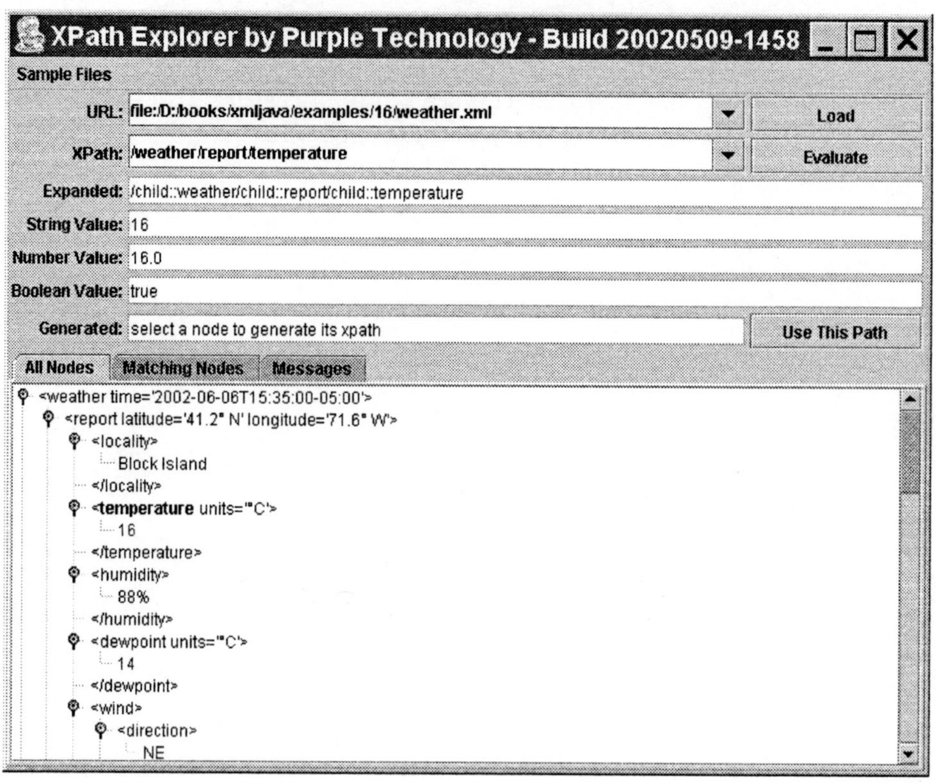

Figure 16.1 XPath Explorer

The XPath Data Model

An XPath query operates on a namespace well-formed XML document after it has been parsed into a tree structure. The particular tree model XPath uses divides each XML document into seven kinds of nodes:

Root Node
The document itself. The root node's children are the comments and processing instructions in the prolog and epilog and the root element of the document.

Element Node
An element. Its children are all of the child elements, text nodes, comments, and processing instructions that the element contains. An element also has namespaces and attributes. However, these are not child nodes.

Attribute Node
An attribute other than one that declares a namespace.

Text Node
The maximum uninterrupted run of text between tags, comments, and processing instructions. White space is included.

Processing Instruction Node
A processing instruction.

Comment Node
A comment.

Namespace Node
A namespace mapping in scope on an element.

The XPath data model does not include entity references, CDATA sections, or the document type declaration. Entity references are resolved into their component text and elements. CDATA sections are treated the same as any other text, and will be merged with any adjacent text before a text node is formed. Default attributes are applied, but otherwise the document type declaration is not considered.

In the XPath data model, each node has a string value. Furthermore, attributes, elements, processing instructions, and namespace nodes have expanded names, which are divided into a local part and a namespace URI. Table 16.1 summarizes XPath's rules for calculating names and values for its seven node types.

Table 16.1 XPath Expanded Names and String Values

Node Type	Local Name	Namespace Name	String Value
Root	None	None	The complete, ordered content of all text nodes in the document; same as the value of the root element of the document
Element	The name of the element, not including any prefix or colon	The namespace URI of the element	The complete, ordered content of all text node descendants of this element (i.e., the text that's left after all references are resolved and all other markup is stripped out)

(continued)

Table 16.1 *continued*

Node Type	Local Name	Namespace Name	String Value
Attribute	The name of the attribute, not including any prefix or colon	The namespace URI of the attribute	The normalized attribute value
Text	None	None	The complete content of the text node
Processing instruction	The target of the processing instruction	None	The processing instruction data
Comment	None	None	The text of the comment
Namespace	The prefix for the namespace	None	The absolute URI for the namespace

If an XPath function such as `local-name()` or `namespace-uri()` attempts to retrieve the value of one of these properties for a node that doesn't have that property, then it returns the empty string. An example and a diagram should help explain this. Consider the simple SOAP response document in Example 16.2.

Example 16.2 A SOAP Response Document

```
<?xml version="1.0"?>
<!-- XPath data model example -->
<SOAP-ENV:Envelope
  xmlns:SOAP-ENV="http://schemas.xmlsoap.org/soap/envelope/" />
  <SOAP-ENV:Body>
    <Quote
      xmlns="http://namespaces.cafeconleche.org/xmljava/ch2/">
      <Price currency="USD">4.12</Price>
    </Quote>
  </SOAP-ENV:Body>
</SOAP-ENV:Envelope>
```

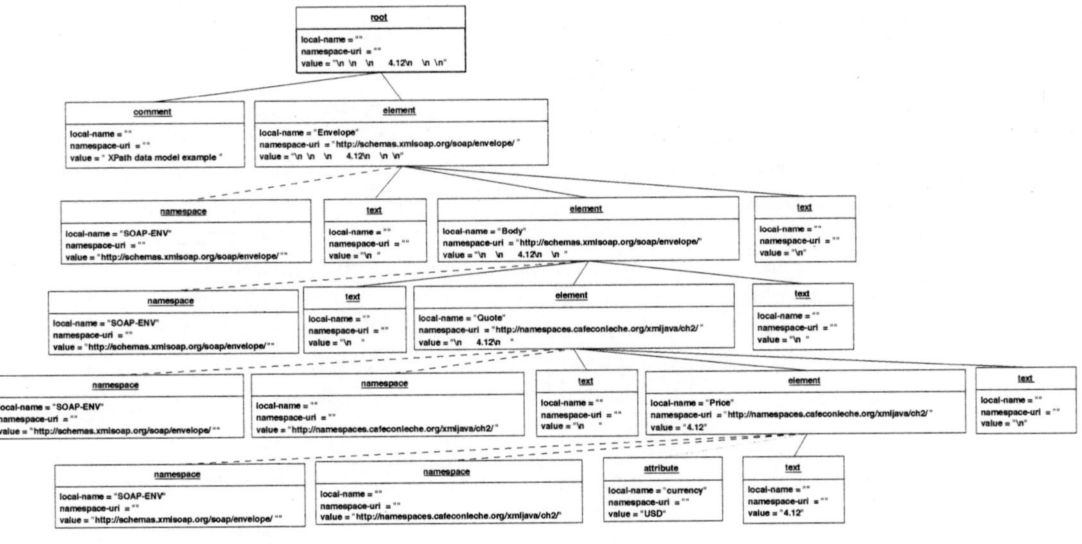

Figure 16.2 An XPath Data Model

Figure 16.2 is a UML object diagram that identifies the properties of the different XPath nodes in this document and the connections between them. Solid lines indicate a child relationship. Dashed and dotted lines indicate namespace and attribute connections, respectively. Document order runs from top to bottom and left to right (although the exact order of namespace nodes and attribute nodes attached to the same element is implementation dependent). Line breaks are indicated by `\n` in this figure. Note that white space is significant in the XPath data model.

Location Paths

Although there are many different kinds of XPath expressions, the one that's of primary use in Java programs is the *location path*. A location path selects a set of nodes from an XML document. Each location path is composed of one or more *location steps*. Each location step has an *axis*, a *node test* and, optionally, one or more *predicates*. Furthermore, each location step is evaluated with respect to a particular *context node*. A double colon (`::`) separates the axis from the node test, and each predicate is enclosed in square brackets.

Some examples will help explain these terms. Consider the simple XML-RPC request document in Example 16.3.

The Differences between the XPath and DOM Data Models

The XPath data model is similar to the DOM data model but not quite the same. The most important differences relate to the names and values of nodes. In XPath, only attributes, elements, processing instructions, and namespace nodes have names, which are divided into a local part and a namespace URI. XPath does not use pseudo-names like #document and #comment. The other big difference is that, in XPath, the value of an element or root node is the concatenation of the values of all its text node descendants, not null as it is in DOM. For example, the XPath value of `<p>Hello</p>` is the string `Hello`, and the XPath value of `<p>Hello<em>Goodbye</em></p>` is the string `HelloGoodbye`.

Other differences between the DOM and XPath data models include the following:

- XPath does not have separate nodes for CDATA sections. CDATA sections are simply merged with their surrounding text.
- XPath does not include any representation of the document type declaration.
- Each XPath text node always contains the maximum contiguous run of text. No text node is adjacent to any other text node.
- All entity references must be resolved before an XPath data model can be built. Once resolved, they are not reported separately from their contents.
- In XPath, the element that contains an attribute is the parent of that attribute, but the attribute is not a child of the element.
- Every namespace that has scope for an element or attribute is an XPath namespace node for that element or attribute. This does not refer to namespace declaration attributes, such as `xmlns:rdf="http://www.w3.org/1999/02/22-rdf-syntax-ns#"`, but rather to all elements for which a namespace mapping is defined. There are no nodes in an XPath model that directly represent namespace declaration attributes.

Example 16.3 An XML-RPC Request Document

```
<?xml version="1.0"?>
<methodCall>
  <methodName>calculateFibonacci</methodName>
  <params>
    <param>
      <value>
        <int>23</int>
      </value>
    </param>
  </params>
</methodCall>
```

Exactly how the context node for a location step is determined depends on the environment in which the location step appears. When using XPath in Java code, you normally pass the context node as an argument to the method that evaluates the expression. In XSLT the context node is normally the currently matched node in the input document. In other environments, other means are provided to choose the context node. For now, let's just pick the root `methodCall` element as the context node. Then `child::methodName` is a location step that selects a node-set containing the single `methodName` element. It moves along the child axis with the node test `methodName`. That is, it selects all the children of the context node named `methodName`. `child::params` returns a node-set that contains the single `params` element.

Location paths are not guaranteed to return a node-set that contains exactly one node (and assuming they do is a very common mistake). `child::*` returns a node-set containing two element nodes, one for the `methodName` element and one for the `params` element. The asterisk is a wildcard node test that matches any element, regardless of name.

Axes

There are 12 axes along which a location step can move. Each selects a different subset of the nodes in the document, depending on the context node. The axes are as follows:

`self`
The node itself.

`child`
All child nodes of the context node. (Attributes and namespaces are not considered to be children of the node to which they belong.)

`descendant`
All nodes completely contained inside the context node (between the end of its start-tag and the beginning of its end-tag); that is, all child nodes, plus all children of the child nodes, and all children of the children's children, and so forth. This axis is empty if the context node is not an element node or a root node.

`descendant-or-self`
All descendants of the context node and the context node itself.

`parent`
The node that most immediately contains the context node. The root node has no parent. The parent of the root element, comments, and processing

instructions in the document's prolog and epilog is the root node. The parent of every other node is an element node. The parent of a namespace or attribute node is the element node that contains it, even though namespaces and attributes aren't children of their parent elements.

`ancestor`
The root node and all element nodes that contain the context node.

`ancestor-or-self`
All ancestors of the context node and the context node itself.

`preceding`
All nonattribute, non-namespace nodes that come before the context node in document order and are not ancestors of the context node.

`preceding-sibling`
All nonattribute, non-namespace nodes that come before the context node in document order and have the same parent node.

`following`
All nonattribute, non-namespace nodes that follow the context node in document order and are not descendants of the context node.

`following-sibling`
All nonattribute, non-namespace nodes that follow the context node in document order and have the same parent node.

`attribute`
Attributes of the context node. This axis is empty if the context node is not an element node.

`namespace`
Namespaces in scope on the context node. This axis is empty if the context node is not an element node.

Consider the slightly more complex SOAP request document in Example 16.4. Let us pick the middle `Quote` element (the one whose symbol is AAPL) as the context node and move along each of the axes from there.

Example 16.4 A SOAP Request Document

```
<?xml version="1.0"?>
<!-- XPath axes example -->
<SOAP-ENV:Envelope
  xmlns:SOAP-ENV="http://schemas.xmlsoap.org/soap/envelope/"
```

```
  xmlns="http://namespaces.cafeconleche.org/xmljava/ch2/">
  <SOAP-ENV:Body>
    <Quote symbol="RHAT">
      <Price currency="USD">7.02</Price>
    </Quote>
    <Quote symbol="AAPL">
      <Price currency="USD">24.85</Price>
    </Quote>
    <Quote symbol="BAC">
      <Price currency="USD">68.59</Price>
    </Quote>
  </SOAP-ENV:Body>
</SOAP-ENV:Envelope>
```

- The self axis contains one node: the middle `Quote` element that was chosen as the context node.
- The child axis contains three nodes: a text node containing white space, an element node with the local name Price, and another text node containing only white space, in that order.[1]
- The descendant axis contains four nodes: a text node containing white space, an element node with the local name Price, a text node with the value "24.85," and another text node containing only white space, in that order.
- The descendant-or-self axis contains five nodes: an element node with the local name Quote, a text node containing white space, an element node with the local name Price, a text node with the value "24.85," and another text node containing only white space, in that order.
- The parent axis contains a single element node with the local name Body.
- The ancestor axis contains three nodes: an element node with the local name Body, an element node with the local name Envelope, and the root node, in that order.
- The ancestor-or-self axis contains four nodes: an element node with the local name Quote, an element node with the local name Body, an element node with the local name Envelope, and the root node, in that order.
- The preceding axis contains eight nodes: a text node containing only white space, another text node containing only white space, a text node

1. All of the white space counts, although there are ways to get rid of it or ignore it if you want to, as you'll see later.

containing the string 7.02, an element node named Price, another text node containing only white space, an element node named Quote, a text node containing only white space, and a comment node, in that order. Note that ancestor elements and attribute and namespace nodes are not counted along the preceding axis.

- The preceding-sibling axis contains three nodes: a text node containing white space, an element node with the name Quote and the symbol RHAT, and another text node containing only white space.
- The following axis contains eight nodes: a text node containing only white space, a `Quote` element node, a text node containing only white space, a `Price` element node, a text node containing the string 68.59, and three text nodes containing only white space. Descendants are not included in the following axis.
- The following-sibling axis contains three nodes: a text node containing white space, an element node with the name Quote and the symbol BAC, and another text node containing only white space.
- The attribute axis contains one attribute node with the name symbol and the value AAPL.
- The namespace axis contains two namespace nodes, one with the name SOAP-ENV and the value http://schemas.xmlsoap.org/soap/envelope/ and the other with an empty string name and the value http://namespaces.cafeconleche.org/xmljava/ch2/.

Generally these sets would be further subsetted via a node test. For example, if the location step `preceding::Quote` were applied to this context node, then the resulting node-set would only contain a single node, an element node named Quote.

Node Tests

The axis chooses the direction in which to move from the context node. The node test determines what kinds of nodes will be selected along that axis. The node tests are as follows:

`Name`

Any element or attribute with the specified name. If the name is prefixed, then the local name and namespace URI are compared, not the qualified names. If the name is not prefixed, then the element must be in no namespace at all. An unprefixed name in an XPath expression never matches an element in a namespace, even in the default namespace. When using XPath to search for an unprefixed element like `Quote` that is in a namespace, you have to use a prefixed name instead, such as stk:Quote. Exactly how the prefix is mapped to the namespace depends on the environment in which the XPath expression is used.

*
Along the attribute axis, the asterisk matches all attribute nodes. Along the namespace axis, the asterisk matches all namespace nodes. Along all other axes, the asterisk matches all element nodes.

prefix:*
Any element or attribute in the namespace mapped to the prefix.

comment()
Any comment.

text()
Any text node.

node()
Any node.

processing-instruction()
Any processing instruction.

processing-instruction('*target*')
Any processing instruction with the specified target.

For example, once again considering the SOAP request document in Example 16.4 and choosing the AAPL `Quote` element as the context node, consider these location steps:

- `self::*` selects one node, the middle `Quote` element that serves as the context node.
- `child::*` selects one node, an element node with the name Price and the value 24.85.
- `child::Price` selects no nodes because there are no `Price` elements in this document that are not in any namespace.
- `child::stk:Price` selects one node, an element node with the name Price and the value 24.85, provided that the prefix `stk` is bound to the `http://namespaces.cafeconleche.org/xmljava/ch2/` namespace URI in the local environment.

- `descendant::text()` selects three nodes: a text node containing white space, a text node with the value "24.85," and another text node containing only white space.
- `descendant-or-self::*` selects two nodes: an element node with the name Quote and an element node with the name Price.
- `parent::SOAP-ENV:Envelope` selects an empty node set, because the parent of the context node is not `SOAP-ENV:Envelope`.
- `ancestor::SOAP-ENV:Envelope` selects one node, the document element, assuming that the local environment maps the prefix `SOAP-ENV` to the namespace URI `http://schemas.xmlsoap.org/soap/envelope/`.
- `ancestor::SOAP-ENV:*` selects two nodes: the `SOAP-ENV:Body` element and the `SOAP-ENV:Envelope` element, again assuming that the prefixes are properly mapped.
- `ancestor-or-self::*` selects three nodes: an element node with the local name Quote, an element node with the local name Body, and an element node with the local name Envelope.
- `preceding::comment()` selects the single comment in the prolog.
- `preceding-sibling::node()` selects three nodes: a text node containing white space, an element node with the name Quote and the symbol RHAT, and another text node containing only white space, in that order.
- `following::*` selects two nodes: a `Quote` element node and a `Price` element node.
- `following-sibling::processing-instruction()` returns an empty node-set.
- `attribute::symbol` selects the attribute node with the name symbol and the value AAPL.
- `namespace::SOAP-ENV` returns a node-set containing a namespace node with name SOAP-ENV and the value http://schemas.xmlsoap.org/soap/envelope/.
- `namespace::*` returns a node-set containing two namespace nodes: one with the name SOAP-ENV and the value http://schemas.xmlsoap.org/soap/envelope/ and the other with an empty string name and the value http://namespaces.cafeconleche.org/xmljava/ch2/.

Predicates

Each location step can have zero or more predicates that further filter the node-set. A *predicate* is an XPath expression in square brackets which is evaluated for each node selected by the location step. If the predicate is true, then the node is kept in the node-set. If the predicate is false, then the node is removed from the node-set. For example, given the same SOAP request document, suppose that the context node is now the SOAP-ENV:Body element and that the stk prefix is mapped to the http://namespaces.cafeconleche.org/xmljava/ch2/ namespace URI. This location step returns a node-set containing all of the Quote elements whose price is less than ten:

```
child::stk:Quote[child::stk:Price < 10]
```

If this XPath expression were embedded in an XML document, you might need to escape the less-than sign as <. However, this is not necessary when using XPath expressions in Java programs.

There can be more than one predicate. For example, the following location step checks both that the absolute price is greater than ten and that the currency is U.S. dollars:

```
child::stk:Quote[child::stk:Price > 10][attribute::currency
 = "USD"]
```

If the predicate returns a number, then the node is kept in the set only if the number is equal to the position of the context node in the context node list. For example, the following location step selects the third Quote child of the context node but not the first or second:

```
child::stk:Quote[3]
```

If the context node has fewer than three Quote children, then this returns an empty node-set.

If the predicate returns an empty string, then the context node is deleted from the set. If the string is not empty, then the context node is not deleted. For example, this location step selects Quote elements whose symbol attribute has a value:

```
child::stk:Quote[string(attribute::symbol)]
```

This is not quite the same as selecting the Quote elements that have a symbol attribute. The following Quote element would not be matched by the above location step:

```
<Quote symbol="">
  <Price currency="USD">17.32</Price>
</Quote>
```

If the predicate returns a node-set, then the source node is kept in the returned set only if the predicate node-set is nonempty. It is deleted otherwise. For example, the following location step finds `Quote` children of the context node that have at least one `Price` child:

```
child::stk:Quote[child::stk:Price]
```

This location step finds `Quote` children of the context node that have at least one `Price` child *and* at least one `Quantity` child:

```
child::stk:Quote[child::stk:Price][child::stk:Quantity]
```

When applied to the `SOAP-ENV:Body` element in Example 16.4, this step returns an empty node-set because none of its `Quote` children have a `Quantity` child.

Compound Location Paths

The forward slash (/) combines location steps into a *location path*. The node-set selected by the first step becomes the context node-set for the second step. The node-set identified by the second step becomes the context node-set for the third step, and so on.

Continuing with Example 16.4 and still using the second `Quote` element as the context node, consider the following location paths (here I assume that the environment for the XPath expressions maps the prefix `stk` to the namespace URI `http://namespaces.cafeconleche.org/xmljava/ch2/` and the prefix `SOAP-ENV` to the namespace URI `http://schemas.xmlsoap.org/soap/envelope/`):

`child::stk:Price/attribute::currency`
This selects the `currency` attribute node `currency="USD"`

`preceding-sibling::stk:Quote/descendant::*`
This selects one node, the first `Price` element in the document.

`parent::*/child::stk:Quote`
This selects all three `Quote` element nodes in the document, including the context node itself.

parent::*/child::stk:Quote[child::stk:Price > 20]
This selects the AAPL and the BAC `Quote` element nodes, but not the RHAT `Quote` element node.

parent::*/descendant::stk:Price
This selects all three `Price` element nodes in the document.

parent::*/child::stk:Quote[attribute::symbol='BAC']/child::stk:Price
This selects the `Price` element node of the BAC `Quote` element.

parent::*/descendant::stk:Price/attribute::currency
This selects all three `currency` attribute nodes in the document.

Absolute Location Paths

So far all of the location paths have been relative to a specified context node, and I've just identified that context node in prose. When we begin discussing XPath APIs, you'll see that most methods for evaluating an XPath expression have a context node argument. But not all location paths require context nodes. In particular, a location path that begins with a forward slash (/) is an absolute path that starts at the root node of the document (not the root element but the root node).

Continuing with the same Example 16.4 and once again assuming that the environment binds the prefix `stk` to the namespace URI `http://namespaces.cafeconleche.org/xmljava/ch2/` and the prefix `SOAP-ENV` to the namespace URI `http://schemas.xmlsoap.org/soap/envelope/`, consider these location paths:

/child::SOAP-ENV:Envelope/child::SOAP-ENV:Body/child::stk:Quote/child::stk:Price
This selects all three `Price` element nodes.

/child::SOAP-ENV:Envelope/child::SOAP-ENV:Body
This selects the single `SOAP-ENV:Body` element node.

/descendant::stk:Price
This selects all three `Price` element nodes in the document.

/descendant::stk:Quote[child::stk:Price > 20]
This selects the `Quote` element nodes whose `Price` is greater than 20; that is, it selects the AAPL and the BAC `Quote` element nodes, but not the RHAT `Quote` element node.

/child::SOAP-ENV:Body
This returns an empty node-set, because the root element of the document is `SOAP-ENV:Envelope`, not `SOAP-ENV:Body`.

/descendant::*/attribute:*
This returns a node-set that contains all attribute nodes in the document.

/descendant-or-self::node()
This returns a node-set that contains all nonattribute, non-namespace nodes in the document.

/
This selects the root node of the document.

Abbreviated Location Paths

XPath location paths can use the abbreviations listed in Table 16.2 in location paths. The semantics are the same, but the syntax is a little easier to type.

Table 16.2 Abbreviated Syntax for XPath

Abbreviation	Expanded Form
Name	`child::`*Name*
@*Name*	`attribute::`*Name*
//	`/descendant-or-self::node()/`
.	`self::node()`
..	`parent::node()`

Using the abbreviated forms, the previous batch of relative XPaths from Example 16.4 that used the second `Quote` element as the context node can be rewritten as follows:

stk:Price/@currency
This selects the `currency` attribute node `currency="USD"`

preceding-sibling::stk:Quote//*
This isn't an exact abbreviation for `preceding-sibling::stk:Quote/descendant::*` (`//` expands to `/descendant-or-self::node()/`, not `/descendant::`), but the node-set selected is the same, the first `Price` element in the document.

../stk:Quote
This selects all three `Quote` element nodes in the document, including the context node itself.

..//stk:Price
This also isn't an exact abbreviation for the original expression, but again it selects the same node-set, which in this case contains all three `Price` element nodes in the document.

../stk:Quote[stk:Price > 20]
This selects the AAPL and the BAC `Quote` element nodes, but not the RHAT `Quote` element node.

../stk:Quote[@symbol='BAC']/stk:Price
This selects the `Price` child element node of the BAC `Quote` element.

..//stk:Price/@currency
This too isn't an exact abbreviation for the original expression, but once again it selects the same node-set that contains all three `currency` attribute nodes in the document.

Absolute location paths can also be abbreviated. In this case, // is especially convenient because at the start of a location path it produces a node-set containing every nonattribute, non-namespace node in the document. It is important to note, however, that it is quite inefficient in most XPath processors. If it's possible to rewrite an expression not to use // (or the unabbreviated `descendant` or `descendant-or-self` axes), then you probably should.

Following are some examples of abbreviated absolute location paths that apply to Example 16.4.

/SOAP-ENV:Envelope/SOAP-ENV:Body/stk:Quote
This selects all three `Quote` element nodes.

/SOAP-ENV:Envelope/SOAP-ENV:Body
This selects the single `SOAP-ENV:Body` element node.

//stk:Price
This selects all three `Price` element nodes in the document.

//stk:Quote[stk:Price > 20]
This selects the `Quote` element nodes whose `Price` is greater than 20; that is, it selects the AAPL and the BAC `Quote` element nodes, but not the RHAT `Quote` element node.

/stk:Price
This returns an empty node-set, because the root element of the document is `SOAP-ENV:Envelope`, not `Price`.

//@*
This returns a node-set that contains all attribute nodes in the document.

//.
This returns a node-set that contains all nonattribute, non-namespace nodes in the document.

Combining Location Paths

Occasionally it's useful to select a node-set that's built from multiple, more or less unrelated parts of an XML document. For example, you might want to select all of the `Price` elements and all of the `Quote` elements in a document. `//stk:Price` selects all of the prices. `//stk:Quote` selects all of the quotes. You can use the vertical bar, `|`, to combine these two node-sets into one, as in the following examples.

- `//stk:Price | //stk:Quote` selects all of the `Price` element nodes and all of the `Quote` element nodes in the document.
- `//@currency | //stk:Price` selects all of the `currency` attribute nodes and all of the `Price` element nodes.
- `//stk:Quote/stk:Price | //stk:Quote/stk:Quantity` selects all of the `Price` and `Quantity` child elements of all `Quote` elements.

Expressions

Not all XPath expressions are location paths. In fact, you've already seen several that weren't. The content of the square brackets in a location step predicate is a more generic form of XPath expression. Each XPath 1.0 expression returns one of these four types:

String
A sequence of zero or more Unicode characters. This is not quite the same thing as a Java `String`, which is a sequence of UTF-16 code points. A single Unicode character from outside Unicode's Basic Multilingual Plane (BMP) occupies two UTF-16 code points. XPath strings that contain characters from outside the BMP will have smaller lengths than the equivalent Java string.

Number
An IEEE 754 double. This is the same as Java's `double` primitive data type, for all intents and purposes.

Boolean
Semantically the same as Java's `boolean` type. However, XPath does allow 1 and 0 to represent true and false respectively.

Node-Set
An unordered collection of nodes from an XML document without any duplicates. Because a node-set is a mathematical set, no fundamental ordering is defined on it. On the other hand, most node-sets have a natural document order derived from the order of the nodes in the set within the input document—similar to how the set of integers {1, 4, -76, 23} is unordered. Individual elements in the set can be compared to one another and sorted if desired. In practice, most APIs use lists rather than sets to represent node-sets, and these lists are sorted in either document order or reverse document order, depending on how they were created.

Different XPath engines map these four types to different Java classes and primitive data types. For example, Jaxen uses the normal Java classes `Boolean`, `List`, `Double`, and `String`; whereas jd.xslt uses the custom types `XBoolean`, `XNodeSet`, `XNumber`, and `XString`; and DOM3 XPath uses a single `XPathResult` interface that can hold any of the four XPath types. In all cases, there are straightforward methods to convert these to the usual Java primitive types such as `boolean` and `double`. The XPath expression syntax includes literal forms for strings and numbers, as well as operators and functions for manipulating all four XPath data types.

The primary use case for XPath literals and operators is predicates. Although you can use them to perform simple arithmetic and string operations with XPath expressions, you're more likely to do complex work of this sort in the Java code. But these functions can perform some very useful operations on node-sets that would be much harder to implement in SAX, DOM, or JDOM.

Literals

XPath defines literal forms for strings and numbers. Numbers have more or less the same form as `double` literals in Java. That is, they look like `72.5`, `-72.5`, `.5321`, and so forth. XPath only uses floating point arithmetic, and so integers such as `42`, `-23`, and `0` are also number literals. However, XPath does not recognize scientific notation such as 5.5E-10 or 6.022E23.

XPath string literals are enclosed in single or double quotes. For example, `"red"` and `'red'` are different representations for the same string literal containing the word *red*. There are no boolean or node-set literals; however, the `true()` and `false()` functions sometimes substitute for the lack of boolean literals.

Operators

XPath provides the following operators for basic floating point arithmetic:

`+`	addition
`-`	subtraction
`*`	multiplication
`div`	division
`mod`	taking the remainder

All five behave the same as the equivalent operators in Java. The keywords `div` and `mod` are used in place of `/` and `%` respectively.

XPath also provides these operators for comparisons and boolean logic:

`<`	less than
`>`	greater than
`<=`	less than or equal to
`>=`	greater than or equal to
`=`	boolean equals (not an assignment statement as in Java)
`!=`	not equal to
`or`	boolean or
`and`	boolean and

In an XML context such as an XSLT stylesheet, some of these may need to be escaped with `<` or `>`. However, this is normally not necessary when using XPath in Java code. Additional arithmetic and boolean operations, such as rounding and negation, are provided by various XPath functions.

Functions

XPath defines a number of useful functions that operate on and return the four fundamental XPath data types. Some of these take variable numbers of arguments. In the list that follows, optional arguments are suffixed with a question mark. A function that has no arguments normally operates on the context node instead. For the most part, these functions are weakly typed. You can pass any of the four types in the place of an argument that is declared to be of type boolean, number, or string. XPath will convert it and use it. The exceptions are those functions that are declared to take node-sets as arguments. XPath cannot convert arguments of other types to node-sets.

None of these functions modify their arguments in any way. An object passed to any of these functions will be the same after the function returns as it was before the function was invoked. However, many of these functions return a new object, which is a variant of one of the arguments. This characteristic is necessary to make XSLT (which depends on XPath) a functional language.

Node-Set Functions

`number last()`
Returns the number of nodes in the context node list. This is the same as the position of the last node in the list.

`number position()`
Returns the position of the context node in the context node list. The first node has position 1, not 0.

`number count(node-set)`
Returns the number of nodes in the argument.

`node-set id(object)`
Returns a node-set containing the single element node with the specified ID as determined by an ID-type attribute. If no node has the specified ID, then this function returns an empty node-set. If the argument is a node-set, then it returns a node-set that contains all of the element nodes whose ID matches the string value of any of the nodes in the argument node-set.

`string local-name(node-set?)`
Returns the local name of the first node in the argument node-set, or the local name of the context node if the argument is omitted. It returns an empty string if the relevant node does not have a local name (that is, if it's a comment, root, or text node).

`string namespace-uri(node-set?)`
Returns the namespace name of the first node in the argument node-set, or the namespace name of the context node if the argument is omitted. It returns an empty string if the node is an element or attribute that is not in a namespace. It also returns an empty string if namespace names don't apply to this node (that is, if it's a comment, processing instruction, root, or text node).

`string name(node-set?)`
Returns the full, prefixed name of the first node in the argument node-set, or the name of the context node if the argument is omitted. It returns the empty string if the relevant node does not have a name (for example, if it's a comment or text node).

Boolean Functions

`boolean boolean(object)`
Converts the argument to a boolean in a fairly sensible way. NaN and 0 are false; all other numbers are true. Empty strings are false; all other strings are true. Empty node-sets are false; all other node-sets are true.

`boolean not(boolean)`
This function turns true into false and false into true.

`boolean true()`
Always returns true. It's necessary because XPath does not have any boolean literals.

`boolean false()`
Always returns false. It's necessary because XPath does not have any boolean literals.

`boolean lang(string)`
Returns true if the context node is written in the language specified by the argument. The language of the context node is determined by the currently in-scope `xml:lang` attribute. If there is no such attribute, then this function returns false.

String Functions

`string string(object?)`
Returns the string value of the argument. If the argument is a node-set, then it returns the string value of the first node in the set. If the argument is omitted, then it returns the string value of the context node.

`string concat(string, string, string...)`
Returns a string containing the concatenation of all its arguments.

`boolean starts-with(string, string)`
Returns true if the first string starts with the second string. Otherwise it returns false.

`boolean contains(string, string)`
Returns true if the first string contains the second string. Otherwise it returns false.

`string substring-before(string, string)`
Returns that part of the first string that precedes the second string. It returns the empty string if the second string is not a substring of the first string. If the second string appears multiple times in the first string, then it returns the portion of the first string before the initial appearance of the second string.

`string substring-after(string, string)`
Returns that part of the first string that follows the second string. It returns the empty string if the second string is not a substring of the first string. If the second string appears multiple times in the first string, then it returns the portion of the first string after the initial appearance of the second string.

`string substring(string, number, number?)`
Returns the substring of the first argument, beginning at the second argument and continuing for the number of characters specified by the third argument (or until the end of the string if the third argument is omitted).

`number string-length(string?)`
Returns the number of Unicode characters in the string, or the string value of the context node if the argument is omitted. This may not be the same as the number returned by the `length()` method in Java's `String` class, because XSLT counts characters and Java counts UTF-16 code points.

`string normalize-space(string?)`
Strips all leading and trailing white space from its argument, or the string value of the context node if the argument is omitted, and condenses all other runs of white space to a single space. It's very useful in XML documents where white space is used primarily for formatting.

`string translate(string, string, string)`
Replaces all characters in the first string that are found in the second string with the corresponding character from the third string.

Number Functions

`number number(object?)`
Converts its argument to a number in a reasonable way. Strings such as "23" and "42.5" are converted exactly as you would expect. Other strings are converted to NaN. Node-sets are converted by converting the string value of the first node in the set. True booleans are converted to 1; false booleans are

converted to 0. If the argument is omitted, it converts the string value of the context node to a number.

`number sum(node-set)`
Each node in the node-set is converted to a number, as if by the `number()` function. Those numbers are added together, and the sum is returned.

`number floor(number)`
Returns the largest integer less than or equal to the argument.

`number ceiling(number)`
Returns the smallest integer greater than or equal to the argument.

`number round(number)`
Returns the integer nearest to the argument.

There's more to XPath than the basics I've covered here. In particular, I haven't discussed variables or extension functions, since both of these are more important when using XPath as part of XSLT or XQuery, than when using raw XPath in combination with Java. However, this should give you the basic knowledge you need to write simple XPath expressions and include those in your programs. Now it's time to investigate the APIs that enable you to do this.

XPath Engines

There are several good open source XPath engines for Java, most distributed as part of XSLT processors. They include the following:

Saxon 6.5.x *[http://saxon.sourceforge.net]*
A very fast XSLT processor written by Michael Kay and distributed under the Mozilla Public License 1.0. This is the processor I used to generate this book. (Saxon 7.x is also available, but it's an incomplete experimental implementation of XPath 2.0, which itself likely won't be finished until sometime in 2003. Both the Saxon 6.5 API and XPath 1.0 are much more stable and bug-free.)

Xalan-J *[http://xml.apache.org/xalan-j]*
An XSLT processor used by several Apache XML projects including Cocoon. It is of course distributed under the Apache license. If you happen to work for one of those dinosaur companies with a firm policy against using free software, you can buy the same product from IBM under the name LotusXSL *[http://www.alphaworks.ibm.com/tech/LotusXSL]*.

Jaxen *[http://www.jaxen.org]*
A standalone XPath implementation that works with DOM, JDOM, dom4j, and ElectricXML.

Unfortunately, although the XPath data model and expression syntax are standardized, the API for integrating them into your Java programs is not. Each separate XPath engine does things differently. Saxon uses a custom DOM implementation that does not work with other DOM implementations such as Xerces or Crimson. Xalan-J is also based on DOM, but it only requires a generic DOM; it isn't limited to the Apache XML Project's Xerces DOM. Jaxen can work with any underlying data model, but the API still isn't portable to other XPath engines. Other implementations do something different still. This means that your code tends to become fairly closely tied to the XPath engine you choose.

To demonstrate the different APIs, let's revisit the Fibonacci SOAP client from Chapter 3. However, this time we'll use XPath to extract just the parts we want. Recall that the body of each request document contains a `calculateFibonacci` element in the `http://namespaces.cafeconleche.org/xmljava/ch3/` namespace. This element contains a single positive integer:

```
<?xml version="1.0"?>
<SOAP-ENV:Envelope
 xmlns:SOAP-ENV="http://schemas.xmlsoap.org/soap/envelope/"
 xmlns:xsi="http://www.w3.org/2001/XMLSchema-instance" >
  <SOAP-ENV:Body>
    <calculateFibonacci
      xmlns="http://namespaces.cafeconleche.org/xmljava/ch3/"
      type="xsi:positiveInteger">5</calculateFibonacci>
  </SOAP-ENV:Body>
</SOAP-ENV:Envelope>
```

The server responds with a list of Fibonacci numbers enclosed in a SOAP response envelope. For example, here is the response to a request for the first five Fibonacci numbers:

```
<?xml version="1.0"?>
<SOAP-ENV:Envelope
 xmlns:SOAP-ENV="http://schemas.xmlsoap.org/soap/envelope/" />
  <SOAP-ENV:Body>
    <Fibonacci_Numbers
      xmlns="http://namespaces.cafeconleche.org/xmljava/ch3/">
      <fibonacci index="1">1</fibonacci>
```

```
      <fibonacci index="2">1</fibonacci>
      <fibonacci index="3">2</fibonacci>
      <fibonacci index="4">3</fibonacci>
      <fibonacci index="5">5</fibonacci>
    </Fibonacci_Numbers>
  </SOAP-ENV:Body>
</SOAP-ENV:Envelope>
```

The client needs to find all of the fibonacci elements. There are many XPath expressions which will do this, the most obvious of which are

```
//fibonacci
/SOAP-ENV:Envelope/SOAP-ENV:Body/Fibonacci_Numbers/fibonacci
```

But there's a catch. *XPath expressions cannot match the default namespace.* That is, the fibonacci element in the expression is in no namespace at all. It will not match fibonacci elements in the http://namespaces.cafeconleche.org/xmljava/ch3/ namespace. So instead you have to give it a prefix, even though it doesn't have one in the original document. For example,

```
//f:fibonacci
/SOAP-ENV:Envelope/SOAP-ENV:Body/f:Fibonacci_Numbers/f:fibonacci
```

Having assigned it a prefix, you must then map that prefix to a namespace URI. Indeed you have to do this for the SOAP-ENV prefix as well, because the prefix will be used in a Java program instead of in the XML document where it was defined. Exactly how you do this varies from API to API, but generally you'll pass some collection of namespace bindings as an argument to the method that evaluates the expression, as well as the expression itself.

The second of these two location paths is more efficient in general. The // operator, and indeed any location step that uses the descendant, descendant-or-self, ancestor, or ancestor-or-self axis, will generally be slow relative to a more explicit spelling out of the hierarchy you expect. On the other hand, these axes are much more robust against unexpected changes in document structure. For example, //f:fibonacci would work even if somebody sent you an incorrect but well-formed document that left out the SOAP-ENV:Body element or used the SOAP 1.2 namespace instead of the SOAP 1.1 namespace. The more explicit path /SOAP-ENV:Envelope/SOAP-ENV:Body/f:Fibonacci_Numbers/f:fibonacci would not. Generally I recommend starting with the most robust path possible, and using the more explicit paths only if profiling proves performance to be a problem. In the latter case, I would also seriously consider checking each document I received against a schema, and rejecting it immediately if it wasn't valid.

XPath with Saxon

The Saxon 6.5 API is rather convoluted, involving more than 200 different classes in 18 different packages. Fortunately you can ignore most of these for basic XPath searching. The most common sequence of steps to search a document is

1. Use JAXP to a build a Saxon `Document` object.
2. Attach the document to a `Context` object.
3. Declare the namespaces used in the XPath expressions in a `StandaloneContext`.
4. Make an `Expression` from the `StandaloneContext` and the string form of your XPath expression.
5. Evaluate the `Expression` to return one of the four XPath data types.

Saxon requires a custom DOM that has been annotated with the information it needs. You can't just pass in a Xerces DOM or a Crimson DOM. Thus, before you use JAXP to parse the document, you have to set the *javax.xml.parsers.DocumentBuilderFactory* system property to `com.icl.saxon.om.DocumentBuilderFactoryImpl`. Because you know this at compile-time and do *not* want to allow the user to change it at runtime, use `System.setProperty()` in your code rather than passing it in on the command line. In case other parts of the program are using a different implementation, remember to save the old value and restore it when you're done. Otherwise, parsing a document with Saxon is the same as with any other parser. For example,

```
String oldFactory = System.getProperty(
 "javax.xml.parsers.DocumentBuilderFactory");
System.setProperty("javax.xml.parsers.DocumentBuilderFactory",
 "com.icl.saxon.om.DocumentBuilderFactoryImpl");
 factory.setNamespaceAware(true);

// Use the factory...

if (oldFactory != null) {
  System.setProperty(
   "javax.xml.parsers.DocumentBuilderFactory", oldFactory);
}
```

Once you've set the DocumentBuilderFactory, parse the input document as normal to produce a DOM Node or Document object. The exact type doesn't really matter because you'll immediately cast this to the Saxon implementation class com.icl.saxon.om.NodeInfo. For example,

```
DocumentBuilder builder = factory.newDocumentBuilder();
InputSource data = new InputSource(in);
 // InputSource is a SAX class
Node doc = builder.parse(data); // Node is a DOM interface
NodeInfo info = (NodeInfo) doc; // NodeInfo is a Saxon class
```

You'll notice that Saxon freely mixes classes from SAX, DOM, TrAX, JAXP, and its internal implementation. A typical Saxon program imports a lot of packages.

Before this document can be searched, you'll need to establish it as an XPath context node. Saxon uses the com.icl.saxon.Context class to represent context nodes. This is constructed with a no-args constructor. You then set its context node with the aptly named setContextNode() method, like this:

```
Context context = new Context();
context.setContextNode(info);
```

Here the root node is the context node, but you could use standard DOM methods to navigate through the tree and find another node to serve as the context node. Personally, I prefer to leave as much of the navigation work to XPath as possible.

The document we've just parsed defines its own namespace prefixes and URIs, but these may not be the same ones used in the XPath expression. In particular, any default namespaces in the document will have to be mapped to prefixes in the XPath expression. As always in XPath, the namespaces matter. The prefixes don't. There are two prefixes to map, SOAP-ENV and f. A Java program is not an XML document; therefore, these can't be mapped in the customary way with xmlns attributes. Instead they have to be added to a Saxon com.icl.saxon.expr.StandaloneContext object. Each such object needs access to the document's com.icl.saxon.om.NamePool to which the necessary namespaces can be added. This is all set up as follows:

```
DocumentInfo docInfo = info.getDocumentRoot();
NamePool pool = docInfo.getNamePool();
StandaloneContext sc = new StandaloneContext(pool);
sc.declareNamespace("SOAP-ENV",
 "http://schemas.xmlsoap.org/soap/envelope/");
```

```
sc.declareNamespace("f",
 "http://namespaces.cafeconleche.org/xmljava/ch3/");
```

That does it for the preliminaries. We're finally ready to search the document with XPath. The Saxon class that both represents and evaluates XPath expressions is `com.icl.saxon.expr.Expression`. You pass a `String` containing the XPath expression and the `StandaloneContext` object to the static `Expression.make()` factory method. This returns an `Expression` object. You then pass the `Context` object and a `boolean` specifying whether you want the result to be sorted in document order to the `enumerate()` method. This returns a `com.icl.saxon.om.NodeEnumeration`, one of Saxon's representations of node-sets. For example,

```
Expression xpath = Expression.make(
"/SOAP-ENV:Envelope/SOAP-ENV:Body/f:Fibonacci_Numbers/f:fibonacci",
 sc);
NodeEnumeration enum = xpath.enumerate(context, true);
while (enum.hasMoreElements()) {
  NodeInfo result = enum.nextElement();
  System.out.println(result.getStringValue());
}
```

The `NodeEnumeration` class is modeled after the `Enumeration` interface in the `java.util` package (but does not extend it). It allows you to iterate through the returned node-set. Each node in this set implements the Saxon `NodeInfo` interface. The `getStringValue()` method in this interface returns the XPath string value of that node.

`NodeEnumeration` is limited to a single use. That is, you cannot set it back to its beginning and iterate through a second time. If you need a persistent result, you can call `evaluateAsNodeSet()` which returns a `com.icl.saxon.expr.NodeSetValue` instead. You can then sort and enumerate this object repeatedly. For example,

```
Expression xpath = Expression.make(
"/SOAP-ENV:Envelope/SOAP-ENV:Body/f:Fibonacci_Numbers/f:fibonacci",
 sc);
NodeSetValue set = xpath.evaluateAsNodeSet(context);
set.sort();
NodeEnumeration enum = set.enumerate();
while (enum.hasMoreElements()) {
```

```
    NodeInfo result = enum.nextElement();
    System.out.println(result.getStringValue());
  }
```

Alternately, if you want the expression to return a number, string, or boolean, you can call one of these three methods instead:

```
public boolean evaluateAsBoolean (Context context)
 throws XPathException

public double evaluateAsNumber (Context context)
 throws XPathException

public String evaluateAsString (Context context)
 throws XPathException
```

If the expression returns the wrong type, then Saxon will convert the result as if by the XPath `number()`, `string()`, or `boolean()` function. The only conversion Saxon can't perform is a primitive type to a node-set. If you try to evaluate an expression that returns one of the three basic types as a node-set, then `evaluateAsNodeSet()` throws an `XPathException`.

I can now show you the complete method that takes as an argument the `InputStream` from which the response document will be read and searches out the relevant parts with XPath:

```
public static void readResponse(InputStream in)
 throws IOException, SAXException,  XPathException,
 ParserConfigurationException, TransformerException {

  String oldFactory = System.getProperty(
   "javax.xml.parsers.DocumentBuilderFactory");
  System.setProperty(
   "javax.xml.parsers.DocumentBuilderFactory",
   "com.icl.saxon.om.DocumentBuilderFactoryImpl");
  DocumentBuilderFactory factory
   = DocumentBuilderFactory.newInstance();
  factory.setNamespaceAware(true);

  DocumentBuilder builder = factory.newDocumentBuilder();

  InputSource data = new InputSource(in);
  Node doc = builder.parse(data);
  NodeInfo info = (NodeInfo) doc;
```

```
    Context context = new Context();
    context.setContextNode(info);

    NamePool pool = info.getDocumentRoot().getNamePool();
    StandaloneContext sc = new StandaloneContext(pool);
    sc.declareNamespace("SOAP",
     "http://schemas.xmlsoap.org/soap/envelope/");
    sc.declareNamespace("f",
     "http://namespaces.cafeconleche.org/xmljava/ch3/");

    Expression xpath = Expression.make(
     "/SOAP:Envelope/SOAP:Body/f:Fibonacci_Numbers/f:fibonacci",
     sc);
    NodeEnumeration enum = xpath.enumerate(context, true);
    while (enum.hasMoreElements()) {
      NodeInfo result = enum.nextElement();
      System.out.println(result.getStringValue());
    }

    // Restore the original factory
    if (oldFactory != null) {
      System.setProperty(
       "javax.xml.parsers.DocumentBuilderFactory", oldFactory);
    }

  }
```

Honestly, this is a little convoluted and perhaps more complex than the pure DOM, JDOM, or SAX equivalent. The advantage is that the code is never *more* complex than this. As the documents you're searching grow in complexity, the XPath expressions become only slightly more complex and the Java code becomes no more complex than what you see here. The more details you can defer to the declarative XPath syntax, the simpler and more robust your program will be.

XPath with Xalan

The Xalan-J XSLT processor from the Apache XML Project also includes an XPath API that's useful for navigation in DOM programs. Underneath the hood, the basic design is strikingly similar to Saxon's for two independently developed programs. However, Xalan does have one class that Saxon doesn't, which significantly simplifies life for developers: `org.apache.xpath.XPathAPI`. This class, shown in

Example 16.5, provides static methods that handle many simple use cases without lots of preliminary configuration.

Example 16.5 The Xalan XPathAPI Class

```
package org.apache.xpath;

public class XPathAPI {

  public static Node selectSingleNode(Node context, String xpath)
   throws TransformerException;
  public static Node selectSingleNode(Node context, String xpath,
   Node namespaceContextNode) throws TransformerException;
  public static NodeIterator selectNodeIterator(Node context,
   String xpath) throws TransformerException;
  public static NodeIterator selectNodeIterator(Node context,
   String xpath, Node namespaceContextNode)
   throws TransformerException;
  public static NodeList selectNodeList(Node context,
   String xpath) throws TransformerException;
  public static NodeList selectNodeList(Node context,
   String xpath, Node namespaceContextNode)
   throws TransformerException;
  public static XObject eval(Node context, String xpath)
   throws TransformerException;
  public static XObject eval(Node context, String xpath,
   Node namespaceContextNode) throws TransformerException;
  public static XObject eval(Node context, String xpath,
   PrefixResolver prefixResolver) throws TransformerException;

}
```

Each method in this class takes two or three arguments.

- The context node as a DOM `Node` object.
- The XPath expression as a `String`.
- The namespace prefix mappings as a DOM `Node` object or a Xalan `PrefixResolver` object. This can be omitted if the XPath expression does not use any namespace prefixes.

The methods differ primarily in return type. There are four possible return types:

- A single DOM `Node`
- A DOM `NodeList`
- A DOM traversal `NodeIterator`
- A Xalan `XObject`

The first three types you've encountered in previous chapters. I won't say anything more about them here except not to use the methods that only return a single `Node`. They are fragile against unexpected changes in document format.

> **Caution**
> Trust me on this one. No matter how sure you are that all of the documents you're processing contain exactly one node that matches an XPath expression, sooner or later you're going to encounter a document that is either missing the node completely or has two or more. List iteration is far more reliable than selecting a single node. If you disregard this warning and use `selectSingleNode()` anyway, then by all means use a schema to validate your document before accepting it for processing.

The `XObject` type is new. This is a class in the `org.apache.xpath.objects` package that represents the various kinds of XPath objects—string, number, boolean, and node-set—as well as a few XSLT objects—result tree fragment, unknown types, and unresolved variables. This class has a number of methods, intended mostly for use in XSLT. For XPath, all you really need are the following five methods for converting an `XObject` to a more specific type:

```
public boolean bool() throws TransformerException
public double num() throws TransformerException
public String str() throws TransformerException
public NodeIterator nodeset() throws TransformerException
public NodeList nodelist() throws TransformerException
```

The last two methods only work if the `XObject` returned by the `eval()` method is in fact a node-set. Otherwise, they throw a `TransformerException`.

For the sake of comparison, let's look at how we would use these classes to solve the Fibonacci SOAP client problem addressed earlier by Saxon.

```
public static void readResponse(InputStream in)
 throws IOException, SAXException, TransformerException,
 ParserConfigurationException {

  DocumentBuilderFactory factory
   = DocumentBuilderFactory.newInstance();
  factory.setNamespaceAware(true);
  DocumentBuilder builder = factory.newDocumentBuilder();

  InputSource data = new InputSource(in);
  Node doc = builder.parse(data);

  // set up a document purely to hold the namespace mappings
  DOMImplementation impl = builder.getDOMImplementation();
  Document namespaceHolder = impl.createDocument(
   "http://namespaces.cafeconleche.org/xmljava/ch3/",
   "f:namespaceMapping", null);
  Element root = namespaceHolder.getDocumentElement();
  root.setAttributeNS("http://www.w3.org/2000/xmlns/",
   "xmlns:SOAP",
   "http://schemas.xmlsoap.org/soap/envelope/");
  root.setAttributeNS("http://www.w3.org/2000/xmlns/", "xmlns:f",
   "http://namespaces.cafeconleche.org/xmljava/ch3/");

  NodeList results = XPathAPI.selectNodeList(doc,
   "/SOAP:Envelope/SOAP:Body/f:Fibonacci_Numbers/f:fibonacci",
   root);
  for (int i = 0; i < results.getLength(); i++) {
    Node result = results.item(i);
    XObject value = XPathAPI.eval(result, "string()");
    System.out.println(value.str());
  }

}
```

The input document is parsed in the usual way with the JAXP `DocumentBuilder` class. JAXP is also used to create a new `Element` that provides namespace bindings for the XPath expression. Alternately, I could have implemented the `org.apache.xml.utils.PrefixResolver` interface in a separate class and used that instead, but using a node is simpler.

The XPath expression, the input document, and the context node (the root element here) are passed to `XPathAPI.selectNodeList()` to find all of the matching elements. This returns a standard DOM `NodeList`, which can be iterated through in the usual way. Because the last XPath axis in the expression, child, is a forward axis, this list is sorted in document order. The string value of each node in this list is determined by calling the XPath `string()` function with the node as the context. This returns an instance of the Xalan class `XObject`, which can be converted to a Java `String` using the `str()` method. The result is printed on `System.out`.

One crucial difference you'll note between Xalan and Saxon is that at no point does Xalan require or use any specific classes from the DOM implementation. All of the DOM nodes are generic DOM nodes. Thus in theory this same code should work with any DOM2- and JAXP 1.1-compliant implementation. In practice, I've verified that it does work with Xerces and Crimson but not with GNU JAXP.

DOM Level 3 XPath

The Saxon API only works with Saxon. The Xalan API only works with Xalan. Both only work with Java. The W3C DOM Working Group is attempting to define a standard, cross-engine XPath API that can be used with many different XPath engines (as of summer 2002, this effort is just beginning and is not yet supported by any implementations). DOM Level 3 includes an optional XPath module in the `org.w3c.dom.xpath` package. The feature string "XPath" with the version "3.0" tests for the presence of this module. For example,

```
if (!impl.hasFeature("XPath", "3.0")) {
  System.err.println
   ("This DOM implementation does not support XPath");
  return;
}
```

> **Caution**
> This section is based on the March 28, 2002, working draft of the *Document Object Model (DOM) Level 3 XPath Specification [http://www.w3.org/TR/2002/WD-DOM-Level-3-XPath-20020328]*. The details are still subject to change, however.

The XPath module has two main interfaces, `XPathEvaluator` and `XPathResult`. `XPathEvaluator`, shown in Example 16.6, searches an XML document for the objects identified by an XPath expression, such as `/book/chapter/`

section[starts-with(@title, 'DOM')]. The XPath expression is passed as a Java String, and the context node is passed as a DOM Node object. The result of evaluating the expression is returned as an XPathResult, a wrapper interface for the four standard XPath data types: node-set, string, boolean, and number.

Example 16.6 The XPathEvaluator Interface

```
package org.w3c.dom.xpath;

public interface XPathEvaluator {

  public XPathResult evaluate(String expression,
   Node contextNode, XPathNSResolver resolver, short type,
   XPathResult result) throws XPathException, DOMException;

  public XPathExpression createExpression(String expression,
   XPathNSResolver resolver) throws XPathException, DOMException;
  public XPathNSResolver createNSResolver(Node nodeResolver);

}
```

In DOM implementations that support XPath, the same classes that implement org.w3c.dom.Document implement XPathEvaluator. Thus no special constructor or factory class is required. Just cast the Document object that encapsulates the document you want to query to XPathEvaluator (after checking to make sure that the implementation supports XPath with hasFeature(), of course). For example, in Chapter 5 you saw an XML-RPC server that returned Fibonacci numbers. The documents that server returned looked like this:

```
<?xml version="1.0"?>
<methodResponse>
  <params>
    <param>
      <value><double>28657</double></value>
    </param>
  </params>
</methodResponse>
```

A client for this program needs to extract the content of the `double` element, and you can use XPath to simplify this task. There are numerous XPath expressions that will retrieve the relevant node. These include

- `/methodResponse/params/param/value/double`
- `/child::methodResponse/child::params/child::param/child::value/child::double[1]`
- `/methodResponse/params/param/value/double[1]`
- `//double[1]`
- `/descendant::double[1]`

Depending on what you intend to do with the node once you have it, you might want to use one of the functions that returns the string value of the node instead. In that case, these expressions would be appropriate:

- `normalize-space(/methodResponse/params/param/value/double)`
- `normalize-space(//double[1])`
- `string(//double)`
- `normalize-space(/methodResponse)`
- `normalize-space(/)`

These are all absolute expressions that do not depend on the context node, but there are many more depending on what the context node is. For example, if the context node were set to the `methodResponse` document element, then these relative location paths and function calls would also work:

- `params/param/value/double`
- `child::params/child::param/child::value/child::double[1]`
- `.//double`
- `normalize-space(.//double[1])`
- `normalize-space(params)`
- `normalize-space(/)`

Assuming that the relevant server response has already been parsed into a DOM `Document` object named `response`, the following code will extract the desired element into an `XPathResult` object:

```
Document response;
// Initialize response object by parsing request...
String query = "/methodResponse/params/param/value/double";
if (impl.hasFeature("XPath", "3.0")) {
  XPathEvaluator evaluator = (XPathEvaluator) response;
  try {
    XPathResult index = evaluator.evaluate(query, response,
     null, XPathResult.ORDERED_NODE_ITERATOR_TYPE, null)
    // work with the result...
  }
  catch (XPathException e) {
    System.err.println(query
     + " is not a correct XPath expression");
  }
  catch (DOMException e) {
    System.err.println(e);
  }
}
```

What this builds is an `XPathResult` object, which is one step removed from the string you actually want. The `XPathResult` interface is a wrapper for the four things an XPath expression might evaluate to (double, string, boolean, or node-set). Getter methods are provided to return the relevant type from the `XPathResult`. Example 16.7 shows this interface.

Example 16.7 The XPathResult Interface

```
package org.w3c.dom.xpath;

public interface XPathResult {

  public static final short ANY_TYPE                       = 0;
  public static final short NUMBER_TYPE                    = 1;
  public static final short STRING_TYPE                    = 2;
  public static final short BOOLEAN_TYPE                   = 3;
  public static final short UNORDERED_NODE_ITERATOR_TYPE = 4;
  public static final short ORDERED_NODE_ITERATOR_TYPE   = 5;
  public static final short UNORDERED_NODE_SNAPSHOT_TYPE = 6;
  public static final short ORDERED_NODE_SNAPSHOT_TYPE   = 7;
  public static final short ANY_UNORDERED_NODE_TYPE      = 8;
```

```
    public static final short FIRST_ORDERED_NODE_TYPE       = 9;

    public short   getResultType();

    public double  getNumberValue() throws XPathException;
    public String  getStringValue() throws XPathException;
    public boolean getBooleanValue() throws XPathException;
    public Node    getSingleNodeValue() throws XPathException;

    public boolean getInvalidIteratorState();
    public int     getSnapshotLength() throws XPathException;
    public Node    iterateNext()
     throws XPathException, DOMException;
    public Node    snapshotItem(int index) throws XPathException;

}
```

Of the four `getXXXValue()` methods, only one of them will return a sensible result for any given XPath expression. The other three will throw an `XPathException` with the error code `XPathException.TYPE_ERR`. The preceding example expected only a single node as a result of evaluating the XPath location path `/methodResponse/params/param/value/double`. Consequently, the `getSingleNodeValue()` method can retrieve it:

```
Element doubleNode = (Element) index.getSingleNodeValue();
```

That this expression returns a single value is indicated by foreknowledge of the input format, not by anything intrinsic to the XPath expression. If there were more than one `double` element in the client request, then the location path would find them all.

Now we have an `Element` node, but what we really need is the complete text of that node, after accounting for possible if unlikely comments, CDATA sections, processing instructions, and other detritus that DOM presents to us. In Chapter 10, I developed a `getFullText()` utility method to account for this, and I could use it again here. But DOM XPath offers a simpler solution. The `getStringValue()` method returns the XPath value of the node-set. The *XPath value of an element node* is defined as the complete text of the node after all character references, entity references, and CDATA sections are resolved and all other markup is stripped. Thus instead of requesting a `Node`, you can ask for a `String`:

```
String value = index.getStringValue();
```

Or maybe it's not a `String` you want but a number. In this case, use `getNumberValue()`, which returns a `double`:

```
double value = index.getNumberValue();
```

The DOM3 XPath methods `getStringValue()`, `getNumberValue()`, and `getBooleanValue()` correspond to the XPath casting functions `string()`, `number()`, and `boolean()`. XPath has a number of other useful functions. For example, `normalize-space()` first converts its argument to a string as if by the `string()` function, and then strips all leading and trailing white space and converts all other runs of white space to a single space. With this function, you can use a simpler location path:

```
XPathResult index = evaluator.evaluate("normalize-space(/)",
 response, null, XPathResult.ORDERED_NODE_ITERATOR_TYPE, null)
String value = index.getStringValue();
```

In the case of an XPath expression that evaluates to a node-set, `getSingleNodeValue()` returns only the first node in the set. You can invoke `iterateNext()` and then call `getSingleNodeValue()` again to get the second node in the set. Repeat this procedure for the third node, the fourth node, and so on until `getSingleNodeValue()` returns null, indicating that there are no more nodes in the set. If the set is empty to begin with, then `getSingleNodeValue()` returns null immediately. This is how you would handle a case such as the SOAP response that returns multiple `int` elements.

Namespace Bindings

Because the SOAP request document uses namespace-qualified elements, we first need to provide some namespace bindings to use when evaluating the XPath expression. The `XPathNSResolver` interface provides the namespace bindings. Although you can implement this in any convenient class, an instance is normally created by passing a `Node` with all of the necessary bindings to the `createNSResolver()` method of the `XPathEvaluator` interface. For example, this code uses JAXP to build a very simple document whose document element binds the prefix `SOAP` to the URI `http://schemas.xmlsoap.org/soap/envelope/` and the prefix `f` to the URI `http://namespaces.cafeconleche.org/xmljava/ch3/`. Then that document element is passed to the `XPathEvaluator`'s `createNSResolver()` method to create an `XPathNSResolver` object that has the same namespace bindings as the synthetic node we created.

```
// Load JAXP
DocumentBuilderFactory factory
 = DocumentBuilderFactory.newInstance();
factory.setNamespaceAware(true);
DocumentBuilder builder = factory.newDocumentBuilder();

// Build the document
DOMImplementation impl = builder.getDOMImplementation();
Document namespaceHolder = impl.createDocument(
 "http://namespaces.cafeconleche.org/xmljava/ch3/",
 "f:namespaceMapping", null);

// Attach the namespace declaration attributes
Element root = namespaceHolder.getDocumentElement();
root.setAttributeNS("http://www.w3.org/2000/xmlns/",
 "xmlns:SOAP", "http://schemas.xmlsoap.org/soap/envelope/");
root.setAttributeNS("http://www.w3.org/2000/xmlns/",
 "xmlns:f", "http://namespaces.cafeconleche.org/xmljava/ch3/");

// Create the resolver
XPathNSResolver namespaces = evaluator.createNSResolver(root);
```

Now we're ready to repeat the earlier example, but this time using the DOM XPath API instead of the processor-specific Xalan or Saxon APIs. To relieve the tedium, I'm going to make a small shift in the pattern of the `readResponse()` method. Rather than storing the XPath search string and the namespace bindings in the source code, I'm going to move them to the separate XML document shown in Example 16.8, which can be bundled with the application and is assumed to live at the relative URL `config.xml`. (A more realistic example might store this document as a resource in the application's JAR archive.)

Example 16.8 An XML Document That Contains Namespace Bindings and an XPath Search Expression

```
<?xml version="1.0"?>
<config
search="/SOAP:Envelope/SOAP:Body/f:Fibonacci_Numbers/f:fibonacci"
 xmlns:f="http://namespaces.cafeconleche.org/xmljava/ch3/"
 xmlns:SOAP="http://schemas.xmlsoap.org/soap/envelope/"
/>
```

The program both reads the XPath expression from the search attribute of the document element and uses that element for the namespace bindings. This enables the XPath string to change independently of the source code.

Following is the configurable, DOM-XPath-based readResponse() method. Because the iterator always returns a DOM node, we have to use a second XPath evaluation on each node to take the element node's string value.

```
public static void readResponse(InputStream in)
 throws IOException, SAXException, DOMException,
 XPathException, ParserConfigurationException {

  DocumentBuilderFactory factory
   = DocumentBuilderFactory.newInstance();
  factory.setNamespaceAware(true);
  DocumentBuilder builder = factory.newDocumentBuilder();

  // Parse the server response
  InputSource data = new InputSource(in);
  Node doc = builder.parse(data);

  // Check to see that XPath is supported
  if (!impl.hasFeature("XPath", "3.0")) {
    throw new XPathException(
     "Implementation does not support XPath");
  }
  XPathEvaluator evaluator = (XPathEvaluator) doc;

  // Parse the config file
  Document config = builder.parse("config.xml");
  Element root    = config.getDocumentElement();
  String query    = root.getAttributeValue("search");
  XPathNSResolver namespaces
   = evaluator.createNSResolver(root);

  // Evaluate the expression
  XPathResult nodes = evaluator.evaluate(
   query,
   doc, namespaces, XPathResult.ORDERED_NODE_ITERATOR_TYPE,
   null);
  // work with the result...
```

```
    Node next;
    while (next = nodes.iterateNext()) {
      XPathResult stringValue = evaluator.evaluate("string()",
       next, namespaces, XPathResult.STRING_TYPE, null);
      System.out.println(stringValue.getStringValue());
    }

  }
```

Snapshots

Iterators like this one are good only for a single pass. You cannot reuse them or back up in them. Furthermore, if the `Document` object over which the iterator is traversing changes before you have finished with the iterator (for example, if a node in the iterator is deleted from the `Document` object), then `iterateNext()` throws a `DOMException` with the code INVALID_STATE_ERR.

To hold on to a more stable list that can be reused and survives document edits, request a snapshot of the node-set to be returned rather than an iterator. A snapshot is reusable and features random access through indexing. For example, using a snapshot the above code would become

```
    // Evaluate the expression
    XPathResult nodes = evaluator.evaluate(
     "/SOAP:Envelope/SOAP:Body/f:Fibonacci_Numbers/f:fibonacci",
     doc, namespaces, XPathResult.ORDERED_NODE_SNAPSHOT_TYPE,
     null);

    for (int i = 0; i < nodes.getSnapshotLength(); i++) {
      Node next = nodes.snapshotItem(i);
      XPathResult stringValue = evaluator.evaluate("string()",
       next, namespaces, XPathResult.STRING_TYPE, null);
      System.out.println(stringValue.getStringValue());
    }

  }
```

Of course, snapshots have the opposite problem: there is no guarantee that the nodes in the snapshot reflect the current state of the `Document`.

Compiled Expressions

An XPath engine that implements the DOM XPath API may need to compile the expression into some internal form rather than simply keeping it as a generic `String`. The `XPathExpression` interface, shown in Example 16.9, represents such a compiled expression.

Example 16.9 The DOM3 XPathExpression Interface

```
package org.w3c.dom.xpath;

public interface XPathExpression {

  public XPathResult evaluate(Node contextNode, short type,
   XPathResult result) throws XPathException, DOMException;

}
```

You can use the `createExpression()` method in the `XPathEvaluator` interface to compile a `String` into an `XPathExpression`:

```
public XPathExpression createExpression (String expression,
 XPathNSResolver resolver) throws XPathException
```

Then you can repeatedly invoke the same expression on different documents without needing to compile the XPath expression from a string each time. For example,

```
XPathExpression expression = evaluator.createExpression(
 "/SOAP:Envelope/SOAP:Body/f:Fibonacci_Numbers/f:fibonacci",
 namespaces);
XPathResult nodes = expression.evaluate(doc,
XPathResult.ORDERED_NODE_SNAPSHOT_TYPE, null);
```

This isn't very important for an expression that's only going to be used once or twice, but in a program that will process many documents in the same way, it can be a significant savings. Imagine, for example, an XML-RPC or SOAP server that receives thousands of requests per hour and needs to apply the same XPath expression to each request document. The exact speed that you'll gain by compiling your expressions will of course vary from implementation to implementation.

Jaxen

The *Jaxen Java XPath Engine [http://www.jaxen.org/]* is an open source, cross-API (DOM, JDOM, dom4j, and ElectricXML) XPath library for Java. Whereas DOM3 XPath attempts to be a cross-implementation, cross-language XPath API for the Document Object Model alone, Jaxen attempts to be a cross-model API for its own XPath engine. It is a Java class library that can operate on various XML object models using a standard engine rather than an API that can be offered by many different engines for one model. It allows you to pass DOM, JDOM, dom4j, and ElectricXML objects directly to XPath functions such as `position()` and `translate()`. Furthermore, whereas DOM3 XPath offers fairly rudimentary interfaces for evaluating XPath expressions in a particular document against a context node, Jaxen is a more complete object model for XPath expressions.

Jaxen's class library is large, on a par with those of Saxon and Xalan. It includes classes to represent each of XPath's functions, iterators, node tests, and axes. Fortunately, you don't need to know all of them to perform simple searches. Indeed, Jaxen's basic API is probably the simplest of the XPath APIs discussed in this chapter. The main interface you need is `XPath`, which offers four implementations in four different packages, one each for DOM, JDOM, dom4j, and ElectricXML: `org.jaxen.dom.DOMXPath`, `org.jaxen.jdom.JDOMXPath`, `org.jaxen.dom4j.Dom4jXPath`, and `org.jaxen.exml.ElectricXPath`. I'll demonstrate this API with the DOM implementation, but the patterns are much the same for the other three APIs.

The following steps search an XML document with Jaxen:

1. Construct an `XPath` object by passing a `String` that contains an XPath expression to the model-specific constructor:

   ```
   public DOMXPath (String expression) throws JaxenException

   public JDOMXPath (String expression) throws JaxenException

   public Dom4jXPath (String expression) throws JaxenException

   public ElectricXPath (String expression) throws JaxenException
   ```

2. Set the namespace bindings by calling `addNamespace()` for each namespace binding that the XPath expression uses:

   ```
   public void addNamespace (String prefix, String uri)
    throws JaxenException
   ```

   (You can skip this step if the XPath expression doesn't use any prefixed names.)

3. Invoke one of the following methods to evaluate the expression, depending on what type of result you expect or want:

```
public Object evaluate (Object context) throws JaxenException

public List selectNodes (Object context) throws JaxenException

public Object selectSingleNode (Object context)
 throws JaxenException

public String stringValueOf (Object context)
 throws JaxenException

public boolean booleanValueOf (Object context)
 throws JaxenException

public Number numberValueOf (Object context)
 throws JaxenException
```

For an example, let's rewrite the Fibonacci XML-RPC client one last time. This time, I'll use Jaxen:

```
public static void readResponse(InputStream in)
 throws IOException, SAXException, TransformerException,
 ParserConfigurationException, JaxenException {

  DocumentBuilderFactory factory
   = DocumentBuilderFactory.newInstance();
  factory.setNamespaceAware(true);
  DocumentBuilder builder = factory.newDocumentBuilder();

  InputSource data = new InputSource(in);
  Node doc = builder.parse(data);

  // There are different XPath classes in different packages
  // for the different APIs Jaxen supports
  XPath expression = new org.jaxen.dom.DOMXPath(
   "/SOAP:Envelope/SOAP:Body/f:Fibonacci_Numbers/f:fibonacci");
  expression.addNamespace("f",
   "http://namespaces.cafeconleche.org/xmljava/ch3/");
  expression.addNamespace("SOAP",
   "http://schemas.xmlsoap.org/soap/envelope/");
  Navigator navigator = expression.getNavigator();

  List results = expression.selectNodes(doc);
  Iterator iterator = results.iterator();
  while (iterator.hasNext()) {
    Node result = (Node) iterator.next();
```

```
      String value = StringFunction.evaluate(result, navigator);
      System.out.println(value);
    }

  }
```

As usual, first JAXP reads the document from the InputStream. Next a new Jaxen DOMXPath object is constructed from the String form of the XPath expression. If I were using Jaxen on top of JDOM, I would have constructed an org.jaxen.jdom.JDOMXPath object here instead. If I were using Jaxen on top of dom4j, I would have constructed an org.jaxen.dom4j.Dom4jXPath object here instead.

Once the expression is created, I immediately bind all the namespace prefixes it uses by invoking the addNamespace() method. This location path uses two different namespace prefixes, so I call addNamespace() twice. Then I get the expression's Navigator by invoking getNavigator(). In more advanced programs, you can use the Navigator class directly to move around the tree. Here, however, I just need this to pass as an argument to another method in a few lines. Finally, I pass the context node to the selectNodes() method to get a list of all nodes in that document which satisfy the location path. In this case, the context node is the document itself because the location path is an absolute path, but in other programs, you might well pass an element or some other kind of node instead.

Jaxen's selectNodes() method returns a standard java.util.List, which can be iterated through in the usual way. Because this XPath expression operated on a DOM document and returned a node-set, all of the items in the list are some form of DOM Node object. This location path only selected elements, so here they're all DOM Element objects. If the Jaxen XPath were operating on a JDOM document, then the list would contain JDOM objects. If the Jaxen XPath were operating on a dom4j document, then the list would contain dom4j objects, and so on. In most cases you'll want to cast the item in the list to some more specific type before continuing.

As the program iterates through the list, it deals with each node independently. I could use the DOM methods discussed in Chapters 9 through 13 to work with these nodes, but what I really want is to get the XPath string value of each node. This is provided by the Xpath string() function, which Jaxen represents as the org.jaxen.function.StringFunction class. The evaluate() method in this class applies the XPath string function to a specified object (here a DOM Node) in the context of a particular Jaxen Navigator. It returns the XPath string value of the object.

Jaxen's org.jaxen.function package provides Java representations for most of the functions in XPath 1.0: BooleanFunction, CeilingFunction, ConcatFunction,

> **Note**
>
> This is a little more convoluted than perhaps it needs to be because there's no XPath 1.0 way to return a list of strings. For example, `string(node-set)` returns the string value of the first node in the set rather than a list of the string values of each node in the set. That's why I have to move from XPath to DOM (where I can work with lists and sets) and back to XPath again, rather than working with a single XPath expression that returns the final result. XPath is not Turing complete. Some of the logic will need to be implemented in Java.

and so on. Each of these classes has a static `evaluate()` method that invokes the function and returns the result. The argument lists and return types of this method change from function to function as appropriate. In a few cases in which the XPath function has a variable length argument list, the Jaxen function class uses overloaded `evaluate()` methods instead. These classes and their corresponding `evaluate()` methods are

`BooleanFunction`
`public static Boolean` **`evaluate`** `(Object` *`o`*`, Navigator` *`navigator`*`)`

`CeilingFunction`
`public static Double` **`evaluate`** `(Object` *`o`*`, Navigator` *`navigator`*`)`

`ConcatFunction`
`public static String` **`evaluate`** `(List` *`list`*`, Navigator` *`navigator`*`)`

`ContainsFunction`
`public static Boolean` **`evaluate`** `(Object` *`string`*`, Object` *`match`*`, Navigator` *`navigator`*`)`

`CountFunction`
`public static Number` **`evaluate`** `(Object` *`node-set`*`)`

`FalseFunction`
`public static Boolean` **`evaluate`**`()`

`FloorFunction`
`public static Double` **`evaluate`** `(Object` *`o`*`, Navigator` *`navigator`*`)`

`IdFunction`
`public static List` **`evaluate`** `(List` *`contextNodes`*`, Object` *`arg`*`, Navigator` *`navigator`*`)`

`LastFunction`
`public static Double` **`evaluate`** `(Context` *`context`*`)`

`LocalNameFunction`
`public static String` **`evaluate`** `(List` *`node-set`*`, Navigator` *`navigator`*`)`

NameFunction
public static String **evaluate** (List *node-set*, Navigator *navigator*)

NamespaceUriFunction
public static String **evaluate** (List *node-set*, Navigator *navigator*)

NormalizeSpaceFunction
public static String **evaluate** (Object *string*, Navigator *navigator*)

NotFunction
public static Boolean **evaluate** (Object *object*, Navigator *navigator*)

NumberFunction
public static Double **evaluate** (Object *object*, Navigator *navigator*)

PositionFunction
public static Double **evaluate** (Context *context*)

RoundFunction
public static Double **evaluate** (Object *object*, Navigator *navigator*)

StartsWithFunction
public static Boolean **evaluate** (Object *string*, Object *match*, Navigator *navigator*)

StringFunction
public static String **evaluate** (Object *object*, Navigator *navigator*)

StringLengthFunction
public static Number **evaluate** (Object *object*, Navigator *navigator*)

SubstringAfterFunction
public static String **evaluate** (Object *string*, Object *match*, Navigator *navigator*)

SubstringBeforeFunction
public static String **evaluate** (Object *string*, Object *match*, Navigator *navigator*)

SubstringFunction
public static String **evaluate** (Object *string*, Object *start*, Navigator *navigator*)

public static String **evaluate** (Object *string*, Object *start*, Object *length*, Navigator *navigator*)

SumFunction
public static Double **evaluate** (Object *node-set*, Navigator *navigator*)

TranslateFunction
public static Boolean **evaluate** (Object *original*, Object *from*, Object *to*, Navigator *navigator*)

```
TrueFunction
public static Boolean evaluate()
```

Summary

XPath is a straightforward declarative language for selecting particular subsets of nodes from an XML document. Its data model is not quite the same as DOM's data model, but that's not normally a major problem. In fact, in some cases, such as taking the string value of an element, the XPath data model is likely to be a lot closer to what you want than the DOM data model.

XPath location paths are composed of one or more location steps. Each location step has an axis and a node test, and may have one or more predicates. Each location step is evaluated with respect to the context nodes determined by the previous step in the path. The axis determines the direction in which you move from the context node. The node test determines which nodes are selected along that axis, and the predicate decides which of the selected nodes are retained in the set.

A location path is actually just one kind of the more generic XPath expressions. In addition to node-sets, XPath expressions can return doubles, strings, and booleans, which are pretty much the same as the Java types of the same name, with a few minor differences you normally don't have to worry about. XPath offers the usual arithmetic and relational operators for working with these data types, as well as a library of more than two dozen useful functions.

Most XSLT processors have APIs that allow you to search XML documents with XPath expressions. The two most popular are Saxon and Xalan. Saxon's API requires a custom DOM, whereas Xalan can work with pretty much any complete and correct DOM implementation.

DOM Level 3 XPath is a developing standard for using XPath in DOM programs that can be implemented across different processors, although as yet it isn't implemented by any. It provides a reasonably simple API for saying, "Here's a document, a context node, and a location path. Find me all the nodes from the document that match."

Jaxen is a somewhat more ambitious cross-model effort to model XPath expressions themselves rather than just treating them as opaque strings. For example, Jaxen provides Java classes that represent all of the different XPath functions, enabling you to pass Java objects such as a `Node` or an `Element` directly to XPath functions such as `normalize-space()` or `namespace-uri()`. More important, Jaxen works across different XML object models including not just DOM, but also JDOM, dom4j, and ElectricXML.

Chapter 17

XSLT

Extensible Stylesheet Language Transformations (XSLT) is provably *Turing complete*. That is, given enough memory, an XSLT stylesheet can perform any calculation a program written in any other language can perform. Note, however, that XSLT is not designed as a general-purpose programming language, and attempting to use it as one inevitably causes pain (especially if you're accustomed to procedural languages like Java instead of functional languages like Scheme). Instead, XSLT is designed as a templating language. Used in this manner, it is extremely flexible, powerful, and easy to use. But you do have to recognize what it is and is not good for. You could calculate Fibonacci numbers in XSLT, but Java will do a much better job of that. You could write a Java program to convert DocBook documents to XHTML, but XSLT will make the task much easier. Use the right tool for the right job. Fortunately, you can combine XSLT stylesheets with Java programs so that each tool can be applied to the parts of the job for which it's appropriate.

XSL Transformations

XSLT is a transformation language. An XSLT stylesheet describes how documents in one format are converted to documents in another format. Both input and output documents are represented by the XPath data model. XPath expressions select nodes from the input document for further processing. Templates that contain XSLT instructions are applied to the selected nodes to generate new nodes, which are added to the output document. The final document can be identical to the input document, a little different, or a lot different. Most of the time it's somewhere in the middle.

XSLT is based on the notion of templates. An XSLT stylesheet contains semi-independent templates for each element or other node that will be processed. An XSLT processor parses the stylesheet and an input document. Then it compares the nodes in the input document to the templates in the stylesheet. When it finds a match, it instantiates the template and adds the result to the output tree.

The biggest difference between XSLT and traditional programming languages is that the input document drives the flow of the program, rather than the stylesheet controlling it explicitly. When designing an XSLT stylesheet, you concentrate on which input constructs map to which output constructs rather than on how or when the processor reads the input and generates the output.

In some sense, XSLT is a push model like SAX rather than a pull model like DOM. This approach is initially uncomfortable for programmers accustomed to more procedural languages, but it has the advantage of being much more robust against unexpected changes in the structure of the input data. An XSLT transform rarely fails completely just because an expected element is missing or misplaced, or because an unexpected, invalid element is encountered.

> **Tip**
>
> If you are concerned about the exact structure of the input data and want to respond differently if it's not precisely correct (for example, if an XML-RPC server should respond to a malformed request with a fault document rather than a best guess), then validate the documents with a DTD or a schema before transforming them. XSLT doesn't provide the means to do this, but you can implement this in Java in a separate layer before deciding whether to pass the input document to the XSLT processor for transformation.

Template Rules

An XSLT stylesheet contains examples of what belongs in the output document—roughly one example for each significantly different construct that exists in the input documents. It also contains instructions that tell the XSLT processor how to convert input nodes into the example output nodes. The XSLT processor uses those examples and instructions to convert nodes in the input documents to nodes in the output document.

Examples and instructions are written as *template rules*. Each template rule has a *pattern* and a *template*. The template rule is represented by an `xsl:template` element. The customary prefix `xsl` is bound to the namespace URI `http://www.w3.org/1999/XSL/Transform`, and as usual the prefix can change as long as the URI remains the same. The pattern, a limited form of an XPath expression, is stored in this element's `match` attribute. The contents of the `xsl:template` element form the template. For example, the following is a template rule that matches `methodCall` elements and responds with a template consisting of a single `methodResponse` element:

```
<xsl:template match="methodCall">
  <methodResponse>
    <params>
      <param>
        <value><string>Hello</string></value>
      </param>
    </params>
  </methodResponse>
</xsl:template>
```

Stylesheets

A complete XSLT stylesheet is a well-formed XML document. The root element of this document is `xsl:stylesheet`, which has a `version` attribute with the value 1.0. In practice, stylesheets normally contain multiple template rules to match different kinds of input nodes, but for now Example 17.1 shows one that contains just one template rule.

Example 17.1 An XSLT Stylesheet for XML-RPC Request Documents

```
<?xml version="1.0" encoding="ISO-8859-1"?>
<xsl:stylesheet version="1.0"
  xmlns:xsl="http://www.w3.org/1999/XSL/Transform">

  <xsl:template match="methodCall">
    <methodResponse>
      <params>
        <param>
          <value><string>Hello</string></value>
        </param>
      </params>
    </methodResponse>
  </xsl:template>

</xsl:stylesheet>
```

Applying this stylesheet to any XML-RPC request document produces the following result:

```
<?xml version="1.0" encoding="utf-8"?><methodResponse><params>
<param><value><string>Hello</string></value></param></params>
</methodResponse>
```

The template in Example 17.1's template rule consists exclusively of *literal result elements* and *literal data* that are copied directly to the output document from the stylesheet. It also contains some white-space-only text nodes, but by default an XSLT processor strips these out.[1]

A template can also contain XSLT instructions that copy data from the input document to the output document, or create new data algorithmically.

Taking the Value of a Node

Perhaps the most common XSLT instruction is `xsl:value-of`. This returns the XPath string value of an object selected by an XPath expression. For example, the value of an element is the concatenation of all the character data but none of the markup contained between the element's start-tag and end-tag. Each `xsl:value-of` element has a `select` attribute whose value contains an XPath expression. This XPath expression identifies the object to take the value of. For example, this `xsl:value-of` element takes the value of the root `methodCall` element:

```
<xsl:value-of select="/methodCall" />
```

This `xsl:value-of` element takes the value of the root `int` element further down the tree:

```
<xsl:value-of select="/methodCall/params/value/int" />
```

This `xsl:value-of` element uses a relative location path. It calculates the string value of the `int` child of the `value` child of the `params` child of the context node (normally the node matched by the containing template):

```
<xsl:value-of select="params/value/int" />
```

---

1. You can keep the white space by adding an `xml:space="preserve"` attribute to the `xsl:template` element if you want.

The `xsl:value-of` element can calculate the value of any of the four XPath data types (number, boolean, string, and node-set). For example, this expression calculates the value of e times π:

```
<xsl:value-of select="2.71828 * 3.141592" />
```

In fact, you can use absolutely any legal XPath expression in the `select` attribute. This `xsl:value-of` element multiplies the number in the `int` element by ten and returns it:

```
<xsl:value-of select="10 * params/value/int" />
```

In all cases, the value of an object is the XPath string value that the XPath `string()` function would return.

When `xsl:value-of` is used in a template, the context node is a node matched by the template and for which the template is being instantiated. The template in Example 17.2 copies the string value of the `value` element in the input document to the `string` element in the output document.

Example 17.2 An XSLT Stylesheet That Echoes XML-RPC Requests

```
<?xml version="1.0" encoding="ISO-8859-1"?>
<xsl:stylesheet version="1.0"
  xmlns:xsl="http://www.w3.org/1999/XSL/Transform">

<xsl:template match="methodCall" xml:space="preserve">
<methodResponse>
  <params>
    <param>
      <value>
        <string>
          <xsl:value-of select="params/param/value" />
        </string>
      </value>
    </param>
  </params>
</methodResponse>
</xsl:template>

</xsl:stylesheet>
```

When this stylesheet is applied to the XML document in Example 17.3, the result is the XML document shown in Example 17.4. There are a number of GUI, command line, and server side programs that will do this, though our interest is going to be in integrating XSLT stylesheets into Java programs so I'm going to omit the details of exactly how this takes place for the moment. I'll pick it up again in the next section.

Example 17.3 An XML-RPC Request Document

```
<?xml version="1.0"?>
<methodCall>
  <methodName>calculateFibonacci</methodName>
  <params>
    <param>
      <value><int>10</int></value>
    </param>
  </params>
</methodCall>
```

Example 17.4 An XML-RPC Response Document

```
<?xml version="1.0" encoding="utf-8"?>
<methodResponse>
  <params>
    <param>
      <value>
        <string>
          10
        </string>
      </value>
    </param>
  </params>
</methodResponse>
```

The white space in the output is a little prettier here than in the last example, because I used an `xml:space="preserve"` attribute in the stylesheet. More important, the content of the `string` element has now been copied from the input document. The output is a combination of literal result data from the stylesheet and information read from the transformed XML document.

Applying Templates

Probably the single most important XSLT instruction is the one that tells the processor to continue processing other nodes in the input document and instantiate their matching templates. This instruction is the `xsl:apply-templates` element. Its `select` attribute contains an XPath expression that identifies the nodes to apply templates to. The currently matched node is the context node for this expression. For example, the following template matches `methodCall` elements. However, rather than outputting a fixed response, it generates a `methodResponse` element whose contents are formed by instantiating the template for each `params` child element in turn:

```
<xsl:template match="methodCall">
  <methodResponse>
    <xsl:apply-templates select="child::params"/>
  </methodResponse>
</xsl:template>
```

The complete output this template rule generates depends on what the template rule for the `params` element does. That template rule may further apply templates to its own `param` children, like this:

```
<xsl:template match="params">
  <params>
    <xsl:apply-templates select="child::param"/>
  </params>
</xsl:template>
```

The `param` template rule may apply templates to its `value` child, like this:

```
<xsl:template match="param">
  <param>
    <xsl:apply-templates select="child::value"/>
  </param>
</xsl:template>
```

The `value` template rule may apply templates to all of its child elements whatever their type, by using the * wildcard:

```
<xsl:template match="value">
  <value>
```

```
    <xsl:apply-templates select="child::*"/>
  </value>
</xsl:template>
```

Finally, one template rule may take the value of all the possible children of `value`, by using the union operator `|`:

```
<xsl:template match="int | i4 | string | boolean | double
 | dateTime.iso8601 | base64 | struct">
  <string>
    <xsl:value-of select="."/>
  </string>
</xsl:template>
```

This example descended straight down the expected tree, and mostly copied the existing markup. However, XSLT is a lot more flexible and can move in many different directions at any point. Templates can skip nodes, move to preceding or following siblings, reprocess previously processed nodes, or move along any of the axes defined in XPath.

The Default Template Rules

XSLT defines default template rules that are used when no explicit rule matches a node. The first such rule applies to the root node and to element nodes. It simply applies templates to the children of that node but does not specifically generate any output:

```
<xsl:template match="*|/">
  <xsl:apply-templates/>
</xsl:template>
```

This allows the XSLT processor to walk the tree from top to bottom by default, unless told to do something else by other templates. Any explicit templates override the default templates.

The second default rule applies to text and attribute nodes. It copies the value of each of these nodes into the output tree:

```
<xsl:template match="text()|@*">
  <xsl:value-of select="."/>
</xsl:template>
```

Together, these rules have the effect of copying the text contents of an element or document to the output, but deleting the markup structure. Of course you can change this behavior by overriding the built-in template rules with your own template rules.

Selection

Adding XPath predicates to match patterns and select expressions offers much of the if-then functionality you need. For the times when that's not quite enough, you can take advantage of the `xsl:if` and `xsl:choose` elements.

xsl:if

The `xsl:if` instruction enables the stylesheet to decide whether or not to do something. It contains a template. If the XPath expression in the `test` attribute evaluates to true, then the template is instantiated and added to the result tree. If the XPath expression evaluates to false, then it isn't. If the XPath expression evaluates to something that isn't a boolean, then it is converted to true or false using the XPath `boolean()` function described in Chapter 16. That is, 0 and NaN are false; all other numbers are true. Empty strings and node-sets are false; nonempty strings and node-sets are true.

For example, when evaluating an XML-RPC request, you might want to check that the request document indeed adheres to the specification, or at least that it's close enough for what you need it for. This requires checking that the root element is `methodCall`, that the root element has exactly one `methodName` child and one `params` child, and so forth. Following is an XPath expression that checks for various violations of XML-RPC syntax. (Remember that according to XPath, empty node-sets are false, and nonempty node-sets are true.)

```
count(/methodCall/methodName) != 1
 or count(/methodCall/params) != 1
 or not(/methodCall/params/param/value)
```

I could check considerably more than this, but this suffices for an example. Now we can use this XPath expression in an `xsl:if` test inside the template for the root node. If the test succeeds (that is, if the request document is incorrect), then the `xsl:message` instruction terminates the processing:

```
<xsl:template match="/">
  <xsl:if test="count(/methodCall/methodName) != 1
                or count(/methodCall/params) != 1
                or not(/methodCall/params/param/value)">
```

```
      <xsl:message terminate="yes">
        The request document is invalid.
      </xsl:message>
    </xsl:if>
    <xsl:apply-templates select="child::methodCall"/>
  </xsl:template>
```

The exact behavior of the xsl:message instruction is processor dependent. The message might be delivered by printing it on System.out, writing it into a log file, or popping up a dialog box. Soon, you'll see how to generate a fault document instead.

There is no xsl:else or xsl:else-if instruction. To choose from multiple alternatives, use the xsl:choose instruction instead.

xsl:choose

The xsl:choose instruction selects from multiple alternative templates. It contains one or more xsl:when elements, each of which contains a test attribute and a template. The first xsl:when element whose test attribute evaluates to true is instantiated. The others are ignored. There may also be an optional final xsl:otherwise element whose template is instantiated only if all the xsl:when elements are false.

For example, when an XML-RPC request is well-formed but syntactically incorrect, the server should respond with a fault document. This template tests for a number of possible problems with an XML-RPC request and processes the request only if none of the problems arise. Otherwise it emits an error message:

```
<xsl:template match="/">
  <xsl:choose>
    <xsl:when test="not(/methodCall/methodName)">
       Missing methodName
    </xsl:when>
    <xsl:when test="count(/methodCall/methodName) &gt; 1">
      Multiple methodNames
    </xsl:when>
    <xsl:when test="count(/methodCall/params) &gt; 1">
       Multiple params elements
    </xsl:when>
    <xsl:otherwise>
      <xsl:apply-templates select="child::methodCall"/>
    </xsl:otherwise>
  </xsl:choose>
</xsl:template>
```

XSLT does not have any real exception handling or error reporting mechanism. In the worst case, the processor simply gives up and prints an error message on the console. This template, like every other template, is instantiated to create a node-set. The nodes contained in that set will depend on which conditions are true. If there is an error condition, then this set will contain a single text node with the contents, "Missing methodName," "Multiple methodNames," or "Multiple params elements." Otherwise it will contain whatever nodes are created by applying templates to the `methodCall` child element. In either case, a node-set is returned that is inserted into the output document.

Calling Templates by Name

There is a second way in which a template can be instantiated. As well as matching a node in the input document, a template can be called by name using the `xsl:call-template` element. Parameters can be passed to such templates, and templates can even be called recursively. Indeed, it is recursion that makes XSLT Turing complete.

For example, here's a template named `faultResponse` that generates a complete XML-RPC fault document when invoked:

```
<xsl:template name="faultResponse">
  <methodResponse>
    <fault>
      <value>
        <struct>
          <member>
            <name>faultCode</name>
            <value><int>0</int></value>
          </member>
          <member>
            <name>faultString</name>
            <value><string>Invalid request document</string></value>
          </member>
        </struct>
      </value>
    </fault>
  </methodResponse>
</xsl:template>
```

The `xsl:call-template` element applies a named template to the context node. For example, earlier in this chapter you saw a root node template that terminated the processing if it detected an invalid document. Now it can call the fault template instead:

```
<xsl:template match="/">
  <xsl:choose>
    <xsl:when test="count(/methodCall/methodName) != 1
                 or count(/methodCall/params) != 1
                 or not(/methodCall/params/param/value)">
      <xsl:call-template name="faultResponse"/>
    </xsl:when>
    <xsl:otherwise>
      <xsl:apply-templates select="child::methodCall"/>
    </xsl:otherwise>
  </xsl:choose>
</xsl:template>
```

Named templates can factor out common code that's used in multiple places through top-down design, just as a complicated algorithm in a Java program may be broken into multiple methods rather than being kept as one large monolithic method. Indeed some large stylesheets, including the DocBook XSL stylesheets that produced this book, do use named templates for this purpose. However, named templates become even more important when you add parameters and recursion to the mix.

Passing Parameters to Templates

Each template rule can have any number of parameters represented as `xsl:param` elements. These appear inside the `xsl:template` element before the template itself. Each `xsl:param` element has a `name` attribute and an optional `select` attribute. The `select` attribute provides a default value for that parameter when the template is invoked but can be overridden. If the `select` attribute is omitted, then the default value for the parameter is set by the contents of the `xsl:param` element. (For a non-overridable variable, you can use a local `xsl:variable` element instead.)

For example, the parameters in the following fault template specify the fault code and the fault string. The default fault code is 0. The default fault string is `Unspecified Error`.

```
<xsl:template name="faultResponse">
  <xsl:param name="err_code" select="0"/>
  <xsl:param name="err_message">Unspecified Error</xsl:param>
  <methodResponse>
    <fault>
```

```
        <value>
          <struct>
            <member>
              <name>faultCode</name>
              <value>
                <int><xsl:value-of select="$err_code"/></int>
              </value>
            </member>
            <member>
              <name>faultString</name>
              <value>
                <string>
                  <xsl:value-of select="$err_message"/>
                </string>
              </value>
            </member>
          </struct>
        </value>
      </fault>
    </methodResponse>
  </xsl:template>
```

XSLT is weakly typed. There is no `type` attribute on the `xsl:param` element. You can pass in pretty much any object as the value of one of these parameters. If you use such a variable in a place where an item of that type can't be used and can't be converted to the right type, then the processor will stop and report an error.

The `xsl:call-template` element can provide values for each of the named parameters using `xsl:with-param` child elements, or it can accept the default values specified by the `xsl:param` elements. For example, the following template rule for the root node uses different error codes and messages for different problems:

```
<xsl:template match="/">
  <xsl:choose>
    <xsl:when test="not(/methodCall/methodName)">
      <xsl:call-template name="faultResponse">
        <xsl:with-param name="err_code" select="1" />
        <xsl:with-param name="err_message">
          Missing methodName
        </xsl:with-param>
      </xsl:call-template>
    </xsl:when>
```

```
      <xsl:when test="count(/methodCall/methodName) &gt; 1">
        <xsl:call-template name="faultResponse">
          <xsl:with-param name="err_code" select="1" />
          <xsl:with-param name="err_message">
            Multiple method names
          </xsl:with-param>
        </xsl:call-template>
      </xsl:when>
      <xsl:when test="count(/methodCall/params) &gt; 1">
        <xsl:call-template name="faultResponse">
          <xsl:with-param name="err_code" select="2" />
          <xsl:with-param name="err_message">
            Multiple params elements
          </xsl:with-param>
        </xsl:call-template>
      </xsl:when>
    <!-- etc. -->
      <xsl:otherwise>
        <xsl:apply-templates select="child::methodCall"/>
      </xsl:otherwise>
    </xsl:choose>
  </xsl:template>
```

I'm not sure I would always recommend this approach for validation. Most of the time, writing a schema is easier, but this technique can verify things a schema can't. For example, it could test that a `value` element contains either an ASCII string or a type element such as `int`, but not a type element and an ASCII string.

Recursion

The ability for a template to call itself (recursion) is the final ingredient of a fully Turing-complete language. For example, here's a template that implements the factorial function:

```
<xsl:template name="factorial">
  <xsl:param name="arg" select="0"/>
  <xsl:param name="return_value" select="1"/>
  <xsl:choose>
    <xsl:when test="$arg = 0">
      <xsl:value-of select="$return_value"/>
    </xsl:when>
    <xsl:when test="$arg &gt; 0">
```

```
          <xsl:call-template name="factorial">
            <xsl:with-param name="arg" select="$arg - 1"/>
            <xsl:with-param name="return_value"
                            select="$return_value * $arg"/>
          </xsl:call-template>
        </xsl:when>
        <xsl:when
          test="$arg &lt; 0">Error: function undefined!</xsl:when>
      </xsl:choose>
    </xsl:template>
```

The factorial template has two arguments, `$arg` and `$return_value`. `$arg` is the number whose factorial the client wants, and must be passed as a parameter the first time this template is invoked. `$return_value` is initially 1. When `$arg` reaches zero, the template returns `$return_value`. However, if `$arg` is not 0, the template decrements `$arg` by 1, multiplies `$return_value` by the current value of `$arg`, and calls itself again.

Functional languages such as XSLT neither allow variables to change their values nor permit side effects. This can seem a little strange to programmers accustomed to imperative languages like Java. The key is to remember that almost any task a loop performs in Java, recursion performs in XSLT. For example, consider the most basic CS101 problem, printing out the integers from 1 to 10. In Java it's a simple `for` loop:

```
for (int i=1; i <= 10; i++) {
  System.out.print(i);
}
```

In XSLT you'd use recursion in this fashion:

```
<xsl:template name="CS101">
  <xsl:param name="index" select="1"/>
  <xsl:if test="$index &lt;= 10">
    <xsl:value-of select="$index"/>
    <xsl:call-template name="CS101">
      <xsl:with-param name="index" select="$index + 1"/>
    </xsl:call-template>
  </xsl:if>
</xsl:template>
```

Similar recursive techniques can be used for other looping operations such as sums, averages, sorting, and more. Neither iteration nor recursion is mathematically better or fundamentally faster than the other. They produce the same results in the end.

> **Note**
>
> The XSLT solution is more complex and less obvious than the Java equivalent, but that has more to do with XSLT's XML syntax than with recursion itself. In Java the same operation could be written recursively like this:
>
> ```
> public void fakeLoop(int i) {
>   System.out.print(i);
>   if (i < 10) fakeLoop(i++);
> }
> ```
>
> In fact, it has been proven that, given sufficient memory, any recursive algorithm can be transformed into an iterative one and vice versa.

Let's look at a more complex example. Example 17.5 is a simple XSLT stylesheet that reads input XML-RPC requests in the form of Example 17.3 and converts them into output XML-RPC responses.

Example 17.5 An XSLT Stylesheet That Calculates Fibonacci Numbers

```
<?xml version="1.0" encoding="ISO-8859-1"?>
<xsl:stylesheet version="1.0"
  xmlns:xsl="http://www.w3.org/1999/XSL/Transform">

  <xsl:template match="/">
    <xsl:choose>
      <!-- Basic sanity check on the input -->
      <xsl:when
        test="count(methodCall/params/param/value/int) = 1">
        <xsl:apply-templates select="child::methodCall"/>
      </xsl:when>
      <xsl:otherwise>
        <!-- Sanity check failed -->
        <xsl:call-template name="faultResponse"/>
      </xsl:otherwise>
    </xsl:choose>
  </xsl:template>
```

```
<xsl:template match="methodCall">
  <methodResponse>
    <params>
      <param>
        <value>
          <xsl:apply-templates
            select="params/param/value/int"/>
        </value>
      </param>
    </params>
  </methodResponse>
</xsl:template>

<xsl:template match="int">
  <int>
    <xsl:call-template name="calculateFibonacci">
      <xsl:with-param name="index" select="number(.)"/>
    </xsl:call-template>
  </int>
</xsl:template>

<xsl:template name="calculateFibonacci">
  <xsl:param name="index"/>
  <xsl:param name="low"  select="1"/>
  <xsl:param name="high" select="1"/>
  <xsl:choose>
    <xsl:when test="$index &lt;= 1">
      <xsl:value-of select="$low"/>
    </xsl:when>
    <xsl:otherwise>
      <xsl:call-template name="calculateFibonacci">
        <xsl:with-param name="index" select="$index - 1"/>
        <xsl:with-param name="low"   select="$high"/>
        <xsl:with-param name="high"  select="$high + $low"/>
      </xsl:call-template>
    </xsl:otherwise>
  </xsl:choose>
</xsl:template>

<xsl:template name="faultResponse">
```

```
      <xsl:param name="err_code"    select="0" />
      <xsl:param name="err_message" select="'Unspecified Error'"/>
      <methodResponse>
        <fault>
          <value>
            <struct>
              <member>
                <name>faultCode</name>
                <value>
                  <int><xsl:value-of select="$err_code"/></int>
                </value>
              </member>
              <member>
                <name>faultString</name>
                <value>
                  <string>
                    <xsl:value-of select="$err_message"/>
                  </string>
                </value>
              </member>
            </struct>
          </value>
        </fault>
      </methodResponse>
    </xsl:template>

  </xsl:stylesheet>
```

Although XSLT is Turing complete in a theoretical sense, in practical use it is missing a lot of the functionality you'd expect from a modern programming language, such as mathematical functions, I/O, and network access. To actually use this stylesheet as an XML-RPC server, we need to wrap it up in a Java program that can provide all this.

TrAX

TrAX, the Transformations API for XML, is a Java API for performing XSLT transforms. It is sufficiently parser independent that it can work with many different XSLT processors, including Xalan and Saxon. It is sufficiently model independent that it can transform to and from XML streams, SAX event sequences, and DOM and JDOM trees.

TrAX is a standard part of JAXP and bundled with Java 1.4 and later. Furthermore, most current XSLT processors written in Java support TrAX, including Xalan-J 2.x, jd.xslt, LotusXSL, and Saxon. The specific implementation included with Java 1.4 is Xalan-J 2.2D10.

> **Note**
> Annoyingly, the Xalan-J classes included in Java 1.4 are zipped into the `rt.jar` archive, so it's hard to replace them with a less buggy release version of Xalan. It can be done, but you have to put the `xalan.jar` file in your `$JAVA_HOME/lib/endorsed` directory rather than in the normal `jre/lib/ext directory`. The exact location of `$JAVA_HOME` varies from system to system, but it's probably something like `C:\j2sdk1.4.0` on Windows. None of this is an issue with Java 1.3 and earlier, which don't bundle these classes. On these systems, you just need to install whatever JAR files your XSLT engine vendor provides in the usual locations, the same as you would any other third-party library.

There are four main classes and interfaces in TrAX that you need to use, all in the `javax.xml.transforms` package:

`Transformer`
The class that represents the stylesheet. It transforms a `Source` into a `Result`.

`TransformerFactory`
The class that represents the XSLT processor. This is a factory class that reads a stylesheet to produce a new `Transformer`.

`Source`
The interface that represents the input XML document to be transformed, whether presented as a DOM tree, an `InputStream`, or a SAX event sequence.

`Result`
The interface that represents the XML document produced by the transformation, whether generated as a DOM tree, an `OutputStream`, or a SAX event sequence.

To transform an input document into an output document, follow these steps:

1. Load the `TransformerFactory` with the static `TransformerFactory.newInstance()` factory method.
2. Form a `Source` object from the XSLT stylesheet.

3. Pass this `Source` object to the factory's `newTransformer()` factory method to build a `Transformer` object.
4. Build a `Source` object from the input XML document you wish to transform.
5. Build a `Result` object for the target of the transformation.
6. Pass both the source and the result to the `Transformer` object's `transform()` method.

Steps 4 through 6 can be repeated for as many different input documents as you want. You can reuse the same `Transformer` object repeatedly in series, but you can't use it in multiple threads in parallel.

For example, suppose you want to use the Fibonacci stylesheet in Example 17.5 to implement a simple XML-RPC server. The request document will arrive on an `InputStream` named `in` and will be returned on an `OutputStream` named `out`. Therefore, we'll use `javax.xml.transform.stream.StreamSource` as the `Source` for the input document and `javax.xml.transform.stream.StreamResult` as the `Result` for the output document. We will assume that the stylesheet itself lives at the relative URL *FibonacciXMLRPC.xsl*, and that it is also loaded into a `javax.xml.transform.stream.StreamSource`. The following code fragment performs that transform:

```
try {
  TransformerFactory xformFactory
   = TransformerFactory.newInstance();
  Source xsl = new StreamSource("FibonacciXMLRPC.xsl");
  Transformer stylesheet = xformFactory.newTransformer(xsl);

  Source request  = new StreamSource(in);
  Result response = new StreamResult(out);
  stylesheet.transform(request, response);
}
catch (TransformerException e) {
  System.err.println(e);
}
```

Thread Safety

Neither `TransformerFactory` nor `Transformer` is guaranteed to be thread safe. If your program is multithreaded, then the simplest solution is to give each separate thread its own `TransformerFactory` and `Transformer` objects. This can be expensive, especially if you frequently reuse the same large stylesheet, because it will need to be read from disk or the network and parsed every time you create a new `Transformer` object. There is also likely to be some overhead in building the processor's internal representation of an XSLT stylesheet from the parsed XML tree.

An alternative is to ask the `TransformerFactory` to build a `Templates` object. The `Templates` class represents the parsed stylesheet, and you can ask the `Templates` class to give you as many separate `Transformer` objects as you need. Each of these can be created very quickly by copying the processor's in-memory data structures rather than by reparsing the entire stylesheet from disk or the network. The `Templates` class itself can be used safely across multiple threads.

For example, you might begin loading and compiling the stylesheet, like this:

```
TransformerFactory xformFactory
 = TransformerFactory.newInstance();
Source xsl = new StreamSource("FibonacciXMLRPC.xsl");
Templates stylesheet = xformFactory.newTemplates(xsl);
```

Then later in a loop, you would repeatedly load documents and transform them like this:

```
while (true) {
  InputStream  in    = getNextDocument();
  OutputStream out   = getNextTarget();
  Source request     = new StreamSource(in);
  Result response    = new StreamResult(out);
  Transformer transform = templates.newTransformer();
  transformer.transform(request, response);
}
```

The thread-unsafe `Transformer` object is local to the `while` loop; therefore, references to it don't escape into other threads. This prevents the `transform()` method from being called concurrently. The `Templates` object may be shared among multiple threads. It is thread safe, so this isn't a problem. Furthermore, all of the time-consuming work is done when the `Templates` object is created. Calling `templates.newTransformer()` is very quick by comparison.

This technique is particularly important in server environments in which the transform may be applied to thousands of different input documents, with potentially dozens being processed in parallel in separate threads. Example 17.6 demonstrates with yet another variation of the Fibonacci XML-RPC servlet. This is the first variation that does not implement the `SingleThreadModel` interface. It can safely run in multiple threads simultaneously.

Example 17.6 A Servlet That Uses TrAX and XSLT to Respond to XML-RPC Requests

```
import java.io.*;
import javax.servlet.*;
import javax.servlet.http.*;
import javax.xml.transform.*;
import javax.xml.transform.stream.*;


public class FibonacciXMLRPCXSLServlet extends HttpServlet {

  private Templates stylesheet;

  // Load the stylesheet
  public void init() throws ServletException {

    try {
      TransformerFactory xformFactory
       = TransformerFactory.newInstance();
      Source source    = new StreamSource("FibonacciXMLRPC.xsl");
      this.stylesheet = xformFactory.newTemplates(source);
    }
    catch (TransformerException e) {
      throw new ServletException(
       "Could not load the stylesheet", e);
    }

  }

  // Respond to an XML-RPC request
  public void doPost(HttpServletRequest servletRequest,
   HttpServletResponse servletResponse)
   throws ServletException, IOException {

   servletResponse.setContentType("text/xml; charset=UTF-8");

    try {
      InputStream in  = servletRequest.getInputStream();
      Source source   = new StreamSource(in);
      PrintWriter out = servletResponse.getWriter();
```

```
      Result result   = new StreamResult(out);
      Transformer transformer = stylesheet.newTransformer();
      transformer.transform(source, result);
      servletResponse.flushBuffer();
      out.flush();
      out.println();
    }
    catch (TransformerException e) {
      // If we get an exception at this point, it's too late to
      // switch over to an XML-RPC fault.
      throw new ServletException(e);
    }

  }

}
```

The `init()` method simply loads the stylesheet that will transform requests into responses. The `doPost()` method reads the request and returns the response. The `Source` is a `StreamSource`. The result is a `StreamResult`.

I'm not sure I would recommend this as the proper design for a servlet of this nature. The XSLT transform comes with a lot of overhead. At the least, I would definitely recommend doing the math in Java, as XSLT is not optimized for this sort of work. Still, I'm quite impressed with the simplicity and robustness of this code. The thread safety is just the first benefit. Shifting the XML generation into an XSLT document makes the whole program a lot more modular. It's easy to change the expected input or output format without even recompiling the servlet.

Locating Transformers

The *javax.xml.transform.TransformerFactory* Java system property determines which XSLT engine TrAX uses. Its value is the fully qualified name of the implementation of the abstract `javax.xml.transform.TransformerFactory` class. Possible values of this property include

- Saxon 6.x: `com.icl.saxon.TransformerFactoryImpl`
- Saxon 7.x: `net.sf.saxon.TransformerFactoryImpl`
- Xalan: `org.apache.xalan.processor.TransformerFactoryImpl`
- jd.xslt: `jd.xml.xslt.trax.TransformerFactoryImpl`
- Oracle: `oracle.xml.jaxp.JXSAXTransformerFactory`

This property can be set in all the usual ways in which a Java system property can be set. TrAX picks from them in the following order:

1. Invoking `System.setProperty` `"javax.xml.transform.TransformerFactory", "classname")`.
2. The value specified at the command line using the `-Djavax.xml.transform.TransformerFactory=classname` option to the `java` interpreter.
3. The class named in the `lib/jaxp.properties` properties file in the JRE directory, in a line like this one:

   ```
   javax.xml.parsers.DocumentBuilderFactory=classname
   ```

4. The class named in the `META-INF/services/javax.xml.transform.TransformerFactory` file in the JAR archives available to the runtime.
5. Finally, if all of the preceding options fail, `TransformerFactory.newInstance()` returns a default implementation. In Sun's JDK 1.4, this is Xalan 2.2d10.

The xml-stylesheet Processing Instruction

XML documents may contain an `xml-stylesheet` processing instruction in their prologs that specifies the stylesheet to apply to the XML document. At a minimum, this has an `href` pseudo-attribute specifying the location of the stylesheet to apply, and a `type` pseudo-attribute specifying the MIME media type of the stylesheet. For XSLT stylesheets, the proper type is application/xml. For example, this `xml-stylesheet` processing instruction indicates the XSLT stylesheet found at the relative URL *docbook-xsl-1.50.0/fo/docbook.xsl*:

```
<?xml-stylesheet href="docbook-xsl-1.50.0/fo/docbook.xsl"
                 type="application/xml"?>
```

This processing instruction is a hint. It is only a hint. Programs are not required to use the stylesheet that the document indicates. They are free to choose a different transform, multiple transforms, or no transform at all. Indeed, the purpose of this processing instruction is primarily browser display. Programs doing something other than loading the document into a browser for a human to read will likely want to use their own XSLT transforms for their own purposes.

> **Note**
>
> Contrary to what some other books will tell you, there is no such MIME media type as `text/xsl`, nor is it correct to use it as the value of the `type` pseudo-attribute. This alleged type is a figment of Microsoft's imagination. It has never been registered with the Internet Assigned Numbers Authority (IANA) as MIME types must be. It is not endorsed by the relevant W3C specifications for XSLT and attaching stylesheets to XML documents, and it is unlikely to be in the future.
>
> Official registration of an XSLT specific-media-type application/xml+xslt has begun, and this type may be used in the future to distinguish XSLT stylesheets from other kinds of XML documents. However, the registration has not been completed at the time of this writing.

In addition to the required `href` and `type` pseudo-attributes, the `xml-stylesheet` processing instruction can have up to four other optional pseudo-attributes:

`alternate`
`no` if this stylesheet is the primary stylesheet for the document; `yes` if it isn't. The default is `no`.

`media`
A string indicating in which kinds of environments this stylesheet should be used. Possible values include `screen` (the default), `tty`, `tv`, `projection`, `handheld`, `print`, `braille`, `aural`, and `all`.

`charset`
The character encoding of the stylesheet; for example, `ISO-8859-1`, `UTF-8`, or `SJIS`.

`title`
A name for the stylesheet.

For example, the following `xml-stylesheet` processing instructions point at two different XSLT stylesheets, one intended for print and found at the relative URL *docbook-xsl-1.50.0/fo/docbook.xsl*, and the other intended for on-screen display and found at *docbook-xsl-1.50.0/html/docbook.xsl*. Each is the primary stylesheet for its media.

```
<?xml-stylesheet href="docbook-xsl-1.50.0/fo/docbook.xsl"
                 type="application/xml"
                 media="print"
                 title="XSL-FO"
```

```
                  encoding="UTF-8"
                  alternate="no"?>
<?xml-stylesheet href="docbook-xsl-1.50.0/html/docbook.xsl"
                  type="application/xml"
                  media="screen"
                  title="HTML"
                  encoding="UTF-8"
                  alternate="no"?>
```

The `TransformerFactory` class has a `getAssociatedStylesheet()` method that loads the stylesheet indicated by such a processing instruction:

```
public abstract Source getAssociatedStylesheet (Source
 xmlDocument, String media, String title, String charset)
 throws TransformerConfigurationException
```

This method reads the XML document indicated by the first argument, and looks in its prolog for the stylesheet that matches the criteria given in the other three arguments. If any of these are null, it ignores that criterion. The method then loads the stylesheet matching the criteria into a JAXP `Source` object and returns it. You can use the `TransformerFactory.newTransformer()` object to convert this `Source` into a `Transformer` object. For example, the following code fragment attempts to transform the document read from the `InputStream in` according to an `xml-stylesheet` processing instruction for print media found in that document's prolog. The title and encoding of the stylesheet are not considered, and thus are set to null.

```
// The InputStream in contains the XML document to be transformed
try {
  Source inputDocument = new StreamSource(in);
  TransformerFactory xformFactory
   = TransformerFactory.newInstance();
  Source xsl = xformFactory.getAssociatedStyleSheet(
   inputDocument, "print", null, null);
  Transformer stylesheet = xformFactory.newTransformer(xsl);

  Result outputDocument = new StreamResult(out);
  stylesheet.transform(inputDocument, outputDocument);
}
catch (TransformerConfigurationException e) {
  System.err.println(
   "Problem with the xml-stylesheet processing instruction");
}
```

```
catch (TransformerException e) {
  System.err.println("Problem with the stylesheet");
}
```

A `TransformerConfigurationException` is thrown if there is no `xml-stylesheet` processing instruction that points to an XSLT stylesheet matching the specified criteria.

Features

Not all XSLT processors support exactly the same set of capabilities, even within the limits defined by XSLT 1.0. For example, some processors can only transform DOM trees, whereas others may require a sequence of SAX events, and still others may only be able to work with raw streams of text. TrAX uses URI-named features to indicate which of the TrAX classes any given implementation supports. It defines eight standard features as unresolvable URL strings, each of which is also available as a named constant in the relevant TrAX class:

- `StreamSource.FEATURE`: `http://javax.xml.transform.stream.StreamSource/feature`
- `StreamResult.FEATURE`: `http://javax.xml.transform.stream.StreamResult/feature`
- `DOMSource.FEATURE`: `http://javax.xml.transform.dom.DOMSource/feature`
- `DOMResult.FEATURE`: `http://javax.xml.transform.dom.DOMResult/feature`
- `SAXSource.FEATURE`: `http://javax.xml.transform.dom.SAXSource/feature`
- `SAXResult.FEATURE`: `http://javax.xml.transform.dom.SAXResult/feature`
- `SAXTransformerFactory.FEATURE`: `http://javax.xml.transform.sax.SAXTransformerFactory/feature`
- `SAXTransformerFactory.FEATURE_XMLFILTER`: `http://javax.xml.transform.sax.SAXTransformerFactory/feature/xmlfilter`

It's possible to test the boolean values of these features for the current XSLT engine with the `getFeature()` method in the `TransformerFactory` class:

```
public abstract boolean getFeature (String Name)
```

Note
These URLs are just identifiers like namespace URLs. They do not need to be and indeed cannot be resolved. A system does not need to be connected to the Internet to use a transformer that supports these features.

There's no corresponding `setFeature()` method, because a TrAX feature reflects the nature of the underlying parser. Unlike a SAX feature, it is not something you can just turn on or off with a switch. A processor either supports DOM input or it doesn't. A processor either supports SAX output or it doesn't, and so on.

Example 17.7 is a simple program that tests an XSLT processor's support for the standard JAXP 1.1 features.

Example 17.7 Testing the Availability of TrAX Features

```
import javax.xml.transform.*;
import javax.xml.transform.dom.*;
import javax.xml.transform.stream.*;
import javax.xml.transform.sax.*;

public class TrAXFeatureTester {

  public static void main(String[] args) {

    TransformerFactory xformFactory
     = TransformerFactory.newInstance();

    String name = xformFactory.getClass().getName();

    if (xformFactory.getFeature(DOMResult.FEATURE)) {
      System.out.println(name + " supports DOM output.");
    }
    else {
      System.out.println(name + " does not support DOM output.");
    }
    if (xformFactory.getFeature(DOMSource.FEATURE)) {
      System.out.println(name + " supports DOM input.");
    }
    else {
      System.out.println(name + " does not support DOM input.");
    }
```

```
    if (xformFactory.getFeature(SAXResult.FEATURE)) {
      System.out.println(name + " supports SAX output.");
    }
    else {
      System.out.println(name + " does not support SAX output.");
    }
    if (xformFactory.getFeature(SAXSource.FEATURE)) {
      System.out.println(name + " supports SAX input.");
    }
    else {
      System.out.println(name + " does not support SAX input.");
    }

    if (xformFactory.getFeature(StreamResult.FEATURE)) {
      System.out.println(name + " supports stream output.");
    }
    else {
      System.out.println(name
       + " does not support stream output.");
    }
    if (xformFactory.getFeature(StreamSource.FEATURE)) {
      System.out.println(name + " supports stream input.");
    }
    else {
      System.out.println(name
       + " does not support stream input.");
    }

    if (xformFactory.getFeature(SAXTransformerFactory.FEATURE)) {
      System.out.println(name + " returns SAXTransformerFactory "
       + "objects from TransformerFactory.newInstance().");
    }
    else {
      System.out.println(name
       + " does not use SAXTransformerFactory.");
    }
    if
(xformFactory.getFeature(SAXTransformerFactory.FEATURE_XMLFILTER)){
      System.out.println(
       name + " supports the newXMLFilter() methods.");
    }
```

```
      else {
        System.out.println(
         name + " does not support the newXMLFilter() methods.");
      }

    }

  }
```

Following are the results of running this program against Saxon 6.5.1:

```
C:\XMLJAVA>java -Djavax.xml.transform.TransformerFactory=
com.icl.saxon.TransformerFactoryImpl TrAXFeatureTester
com.icl.saxon.TransformerFactoryImpl supports DOM output.
com.icl.saxon.TransformerFactoryImpl supports DOM input.
com.icl.saxon.TransformerFactoryImpl supports SAX output.
com.icl.saxon.TransformerFactoryImpl supports SAX input.
com.icl.saxon.TransformerFactoryImpl supports stream output.
com.icl.saxon.TransformerFactoryImpl supports stream input.
com.icl.saxon.TransformerFactoryImpl returns
 SAXTransformerFactory objects from
 TransformerFactory.newInstance().
com.icl.saxon.TransformerFactoryImpl supports the newXMLFilter()
 methods.
```

As you can see, Saxon supports all eight features. Xalan also supports all eight features.

XSLT Processor Attributes

Some XSLT processors provide nonstandard, custom *attributes* that control their behavior. Like features, these are also named via URIs. For example, Xalan-J 2.3 defines the following three attributes:

`http://apache.org/xalan/features/optimize`
By default, Xalan rewrites stylesheets in an attempt to optimize them (similar to the behavior of an optimizing compiler for Java or other languages). This can confuse tools that need direct access to the stylesheet, such as XSLT profilers and debuggers. If you're using such a tool with Xalan, you should set this attribute to false.

`http://apache.org/xalan/features/incremental`
Setting this to true allows Xalan to begin producing output before it has finished processing the entire input document. This may cause problems if an error is detected late in the process, but it shouldn't be a big problem in fully debugged and tested environments.

`http://apache.org/xalan/features/source_location`
Setting this to true tells Xalan to provide a JAXP `SourceLocator` that a program can use to determine the location (line numbers, column numbers, system IDs, and public IDs) of individual nodes during the transform. It engenders a substantial performance hit, so it's turned off by default.

Other processors define their own attributes. Although TrAX is designed as a generic API, it does let you access such custom features with these two methods:

```
public abstract void setAttribute (String name, Object value)
 throws IllegalArgumentException

public abstract Object getAttribute (String name)
 throws IllegalArgumentException
```

For example, the following code tries to turn on incremental output:

```
TransformerFactory xformFactory
 = TransformerFactory.newInstance();
try {
  xformFactory.setAttribute(
   "http://apache.org/xalan/features/incremental", Boolean.TRUE);
}
catch (IllegalArgumentException e) {
  // This XSLT processor does not support the
  // http://apache.org/xalan/features/incremental attribute,
  // but we can still use the processor anyway
}
```

If you're using any processor except Xalan-J 2.x., this will not exactly fail but it won't exactly succeed either. Using nonstandard attributes may limit the portability of your programs. However, most attributes (and all of the Xalan attributes) merely adjust how the processor achieves its result; they do not change the final result in any way.

URI Resolution

An XSLT stylesheet can use the `document()` function to load additional source documents for processing. It can also import or include additional stylesheets with the `xsl:import` and `xsl:include` instructions. In all three cases, the document to load is identified by a URI.

Normally a `Transformer` simply loads the document at that URL. However, by using a `URIResolver`, you can redirect the request to a proxy server, to local copies, or to previously cached copies. This interface, summarized in Example 17.8, returns `Source` objects for a specified URL and an optional base. It is similar in intent to SAX's `EntityResolver` except that `EntityResolver` is based on public and system IDs, whereas this interface is based on URLs and base URLs.

Example 17.8 The TrAX URIResolver Interface

```
package javax.xml.transform;

public interface URIResolver {

  public Source resolve(String href, String base)
   throws TransformerException;

}
```

The `resolve()` method should return a `Source` object if it successfully resolves the URL. Otherwise it should return null to indicate that the default URL resolution mechanism should be used. Example 17.9 is a simple `URIResolver` implementation that looks for a gzipped version of a document (that is, a file name that ends with `.gz`). If it finds one, it uses the `java.util.zip.GZIPInputStream` class to build a `StreamSource` from the gzipped document. Otherwise, it returns null, and the usual methods for resolving URLs are followed.

Example 17.9 A URIResolver Class

```
import javax.xml.transform.*;
import javax.xml.transform.stream.StreamSource;
import java.util.zip.GZIPInputStream;
import java.net.URL;
import java.io.InputStream;
```

```
public class GZipURIResolver implements URIResolver {

  public Source resolve(String href, String base) {

    try {
      href = href + ".gz";
      URL context = new URL(base);
      URL u = new URL(context, href);
      InputStream in = u.openStream();
      GZIPInputStream gin = new GZIPInputStream(in);
      return new StreamSource(gin, u.toString());
    }
    catch (Exception e) {
      // If anything goes wrong, just return null and let
      // the default resolver try.
    }
    return null;
  }

}
```

The following two methods in `TransformerFactory` set and get the `URIResolver` that the `Transformer` objects it creates will use to resolve URIs:

```
public abstract void setURIResolver (URIResolver resolver)
public abstract URIResolver getURIResolver()
```

For example,

```
URIResolver resolver = new GZipURIResolver();
factory.setURIResolver(resolver);
```

Error Handling

XSLT transformations can fail for any of several reasons, including the following:

- The stylesheet is syntactically incorrect.
- The source document is malformed.
- Some external resource that the processor needs to load, such as a document referenced by the `document()` function or the `.class` file that implements an extension function, is unavailable.

By default, any such problems are reported by printing them on System.err. You also can provide more sophisticated error handling, reporting, and logging by implementing the ErrorListener interface. This interface, shown in Example 17.10, is modeled after SAX's ErrorHandler interface. Indeed, aside from all of the arguments being TransformerExceptions instead of SAXExceptions, it's almost identical.

Example 17.10 The TrAX ErrorListener Interface

```
package javax.xml.transform;

public interface ErrorListener {

  public void warning(TransformerException exception)
   throws TransformerException;
  public void error(TransformerException exception)
   throws TransformerException;
  public void fatalError(TransformerException exception)
   throws TransformerException;

}
```

Example 17.11 demonstrates with a simple class that uses the java.util.logging package, introduced in Java 1.4 to report errors rather than printing them on System.err. Each exception is logged to a Logger specified in the constructor. Unfortunately, the Logging API doesn't really have separate categories for fatal and nonfatal errors, so I just classify them both as "severe."[2]

Example 17.11 An ErrorListener That Uses the Logging API

```
import javax.xml.transform.*;
import java.util.logging.*;

public class LoggingErrorListener implements ErrorListener {
```

2. You could define a custom subclass of Level that did differentiate fatal and nonfatal errors, but because this is not a book about the Logging API, I leave that as an exercise for the reader.

```
  private Logger logger;

  public LoggingErrorListener(Logger logger) {
    this.logger = logger;
  }

  public void warning(TransformerException exception) {

    logger.log(Level.WARNING, exception.getMessage(), exception);

    // Don't throw an exception and stop the processor
    // just for a warning; but do log the problem
  }

  public void error(TransformerException exception)
   throws TransformerException {

    logger.log(Level.SEVERE, exception.getMessage(), exception);
    // XSLT is not as draconian as XML. There are numerous errors
    // which the processor may but does not have to recover from;
    // e.g., multiple templates that match a node with the same
    // priority. I do not want to allow that, so I throw this
    // exception here.
    throw exception;

  }

  public void fatalError(TransformerException exception)
   throws TransformerException {

    logger.log(Level.SEVERE, exception.getMessage(), exception);

    // This is an error which the processor cannot recover from;
    // e.g., a malformed stylesheet or input document,
    // so I must throw this exception here.
    throw exception;

  }

}
```

The following two methods appear in both `TransformerFactory` and `Transformer`. They enable you to set and get the `ErrorListener` to which the object will report problems.

```
public abstract void setErrorListener (ErrorListener listener)
 throws IllegalArgumentException

public abstract ErrorListener getErrorListener()
```

An `ErrorListener` registered with a `Transformer` will report errors with the transformation. An `ErrorListener` registered with a `TransformerFactory` will report errors with the factory's attempts to create new `Transformer` objects. For example, the following code fragment installs separate `LoggingErrorListeners` on the `TransformerFactory`, as well as the `Transformer` object it creates, which will record messages in two different logs.

```
TransformerFactory factory = TransformerFactory.newInstance();
Logger factoryLogger
 = Logger.getLogger("com.macfaq.trax.factory");
ErrorListener factoryListener
 = new LoggingErrorListener(factoryLogger);
factory.setErrorListener(factoryListener);
Source source = new StreamSource("FibonacciXMLRPC.xsl");
Transformer stylesheet = factory.newTransformer(source);
Logger transformerLogger
 = Logger.getLogger("com.macfaq.trax.transformer");
ErrorListener transformerListener
 = new LoggingErrorListener(transformerLogger);
stylesheet.setErrorListener(transformerListener);
```

Passing Parameters to Stylesheets

Top-level `xsl:param` and `xsl:variable` elements both define variables by binding a name to a value. This variable can be de-referenced elsewhere in the stylesheet using the form `$name`. Once set, the value of an XSLT variable is fixed and cannot be changed. There is an exception, however: if the variable is defined with a top-level `xsl:param` element instead of an `xsl:variable` element, then the default value can be changed before the transformation begins.

For example, the DocBook XSL stylesheets I used to generate this book have a number of parameters that set various formatting options. I used these settings:

```
<xsl:param name="fop.extensions">1</xsl:param>
<xsl:param name="page.width.portrait">7.375in</xsl:param>
<xsl:param name="page.height.portrait">9.25in</xsl:param>
<xsl:param name="page.margin.top">0.5in</xsl:param>
<xsl:param name="page.margin.bottom">0.5in</xsl:param>
<xsl:param name="region.before.extent">0.5in</xsl:param>
<xsl:param name="body.margin.top">0.5in</xsl:param>
<xsl:param name="page.margin.outer">1.0in</xsl:param>
<xsl:param name="page.margin.inner">1.0in</xsl:param>
<xsl:param name="body.font.family">Times</xsl:param>
<xsl:param name="variablelist.as.blocks" select="1"/>
<xsl:param name="generate.section.toc.level" select="1"/>
<xsl:param name="generate.component.toc" select="0"/>
```

You can change the initial (and thus final) value of any parameter inside your Java code using these three methods of the `Transformer` class:

```
public abstract void setParameter (String name, Object value)
public abstract Object getParameter (String name)
public abstract void clearParameters()
```

The `setParameter()` method provides a value for a parameter that overrides any value used in the stylesheet itself. The processor is responsible for converting the Java object type passed to a reasonable XSLT equivalent. This should work well enough for `String`, `Integer`, `Double`, and `Boolean`, as well as for DOM types such as `Node` and `NodeList`. I wouldn't rely on it for anything more complex, such as a `File` or a `Frame`.

The `getParameter()` method returns the value of a parameter previously set by Java. It will not return any value from the stylesheet itself, even if it has not been overridden by the Java code. Finally, the `clearParameters()` method eliminates all Java mappings of parameters, so that those variables are returned to whatever value is specified in the stylesheet.

For example, in Java the preceding list of parameters for the DocBook stylesheets could be set with a JAXP `Transformer` object, like this:

```
transformer.setParameter("fop.extensions", "1");
transformer.setParameter("page.width.portrait", "7.375in");
transformer.setParameter("page.height.portrait", "9.25in");
transformer.setParameter("page.margin.top", "0.5in");
transformer.setParameter("region.before.extent", "0.5in");
transformer.setParameter("body.margin.top", "0.5in");
```

```
transformer.setParameter("page.margin.bottom", "0.5in");
transformer.setParameter("page.margin.outer", "1.0in");
transformer.setParameter("page.margin.inner", "1.0in");
transformer.setParameter("body.font.family", "Times");
transformer.setParameter("variablelist.as.blocks", "1");
transformer.setParameter("generate.section.toc.level", "1");
transformer.setParameter("generate.component.toc", "0");
```

Here I used strings for all of the values, but in a few cases I could have used a `Number` of some kind instead.

Output Properties

XSLT is defined in terms of a transformation from one tree to a different tree, all of which takes place in memory. The actual conversion of that tree to a stream of bytes or a file is an optional step. If that step is taken, the `xsl:output` instruction controls the details of serialization. For example, it can specify XML, HTML, or plain text output. It can specify the encoding of the output, what the document type declaration points to, whether the elements should be indented, what the value of the standalone declaration is, where CDATA sections should be used, and more. For example, adding this `xsl:output` element to a stylesheet would produce plain text output instead of XML:

```
<xsl:output
  method="text"
  encoding="US-ASCII"
  media-type="text/plain"
/>
```

This `xsl:output` element asks for "pretty-printed" XML:

```
<xsl:output
  method="xml"
  encoding="UTF-16"
  indent="yes"
  media-type="text/xml"
  standalone="yes"
/>
```

In all, there are ten attributes of the `xsl:output` element that control serialization of the result tree:

method="*xml | html | text*"
The output method. `xml` is the default. `html` uses classic HTML syntax, such as <hr> instead of <hr />. `text` outputs plain text but no markup.

version="`1.0`"
The version number used in the XML declaration. Currently, this should always have the value `1.0`.

encoding="*UTF-8 | UTF-16 | ISO-8859-1 | ...*"
The encoding used for the output and in the encoding declaration of the output document.

omit-xml-declaration="*yes | no*"
yes if the XML declaration should be omitted, no otherwise (that is, no if the XML declaration should be included, yes if it shouldn't be). The default is no.

standalone="*yes | no*"
The value of the `standalone` attribute for the XML declaration: either yes or no.

doctype-public="*public ID*"
The public identifier used in the DOCTYPE declaration.

doctype-system="*URI*"
The URL used as a system identifier in the DOCTYPE declaration.

cdata-section-elements="*element_name_1 element_name_2 ...*"
A white-space-separated list of the qualified names of the elements whose content should be output as a CDATA section.

indent="*yes | no*"
yes if extra white space should be added to "pretty print" the result, no otherwise. The default is no.

media-type="*text/xml | text/html | text/plain | application/xml...* "
The MIME media type of the output, such as text/html, application/xml, or application/xml+svg.

Note
All of these output properties are at the discretion of the XSLT processor. The processor is not required to serialize the result tree at all, much less to serialize it with extra white space, a document type declaration, and so forth. In particular, I have encountered XSLT processors that only partially support `indent="yes."`

You can also control these output properties from inside your Java programs using these four methods in the Transformer class. You can set them either one by one or as a group with the java.util.Properties class.

```
public abstract void setOutputProperties (Properties outputFormat)
 throws IllegalArgumentException

public abstract Properties getOutputProperties()

public abstract void setOutputProperty (String name, String value)
 throws IllegalArgumentException

public abstract String getOutputProperty (String name)
```

The keys and values for these properties are simply the string names established by the XSLT 1.0 specification. For convenience, the javax.xml.transform.OutputKeys class in Example 17.12 provides named constants for all of the property names.

Example 17.12 The TrAX OutputKeys Class

```
package javax.xml.transform;

public class OutputKeys {

  private OutputKeys() {}

  public static final String METHOD = "method";
  public static final String VERSION = "version";
  public static final String ENCODING = "encoding";
  public static final String OMIT_XML_DECLARATION
   = "omit-xml-declaration";
  public static final String STANDALONE = "standalone";
  public static final String DOCTYPE_PUBLIC = "doctype-public";
  public static final String DOCTYPE_SYSTEM = "doctype-system";
  public static final String CDATA_SECTION_ELEMENTS
   = "cdata-section-elements";
  public static final String INDENT = "indent";
  public static final String MEDIA_TYPE = "media-type";

}
```

For example, the following Java code fragment has the same effect as the preceding `xsl:output` element:

```
transformer.setOutputProperty(OutputKeys.METHOD, "xml");
transformer.setOutputProperty(OutputKeys.ENCODING, "UTF-16");
transformer.setOutputProperty(OutputKeys.INDENT, "yes");
transformer.setOutputProperty(OutputKeys.MEDIA_TYPE, "text/xml");
transformer.setOutputProperty(OutputKeys.STANDALONE, "yes");
```

In the event of a conflict between what the Java code requests (with output properties requests) and what the stylesheet requests (with an `xsl:output` element), the ones specified in the Java code take precedence.

Sources and Results

The `Source` and `Result` interfaces abstract out the API dependent details of how an XML document is represented. You can construct sources from DOM nodes, SAX event sequences, and raw streams. You can target the result of a transform at a DOM `Node`, a SAX `ContentHandler`, or a stream-based target such as an `OutputStream`, `Writer`, `File`, or `String`. Other models may provide their own implementations of these interfaces. For example, JDOM has an `org.jdom.transform` package that includes a `JDOMSource` and `JDOMResult` class.

In fact, these different models have very little in common, other than that they all hold an XML document. Consequently, the `Source` and `Result` interfaces don't themselves provide a lot of the functionality you need, just methods to get the system and public IDs of the document. Everything else is deferred to the implementations. In fact, XSLT engines generally need to work directly with the subclasses rather than with the generic superclasses; and not all engines are able to process all three kinds of sources and targets. Polymorphism just doesn't work very well here.

> **Note**
> It is important to set at least the system IDs of your sources, because some parts of the stylesheet may rely on this. In particular, if any of your `xsl:import` or `xsl:include` elements or `document()` functions contain relative URLs, then they will be resolved relative to the URL of the stylesheet source.

DOMSource and DOMResult

A `DOMSource` is a wrapper around a DOM `Node`. The `DOMSource` class, shown in Example 17.13, provides methods to set and get the node that serves as the root of the transform, as well as the system and public IDs of that node.

Example 17.13 The TrAX DOMSource Class

```
package javax.xml.transform.dom;

public class DOMSource implements Source {

  public static final String FEATURE =
    "http://javax.xml.transform.dom.DOMSource/feature";

  public DOMSource() {}
  public DOMSource(Node node);
  public DOMSource(Node node, String systemID);

  public void   setNode(Node node);
  public Node   getNode();
  public void   setSystemId(String baseID);
  public String getSystemId();

}
```

In theory, you should be able to convert any DOM `Node` object into a `DOMSource` and transform it. In practice, transforming document nodes is all that is truly reliable. (It's not even clear that the XSLT processing model applies to anything that isn't a complete document.) In my tests, Xalan-J could transform all of the nodes I threw at it. However, Saxon could only transform `Document` objects and `Element` objects that were part of a document tree.

A `DOMResult` is a wrapper around a DOM `Document`, `DocumentFragment`, or `Element Node` to which the output of the transform will be appended. The `DOMResult` class, shown in Example 17.14, provides constructors and methods to set and get the node that serves as the root of the transform, as well as the system and public IDs of that node.

Example 17.14 The TrAX DOMResult Class

```
package javax.xml.transform.dom;

public class DOMResult implements Result {

  public static final String FEATURE =
  "http://javax.xml.transform.dom.DOMResult/feature";
```

```
  public DOMResult();
  public DOMResult(Node node);
  public DOMResult(Node node, String systemID);

  public void setNode(Node node);
  public Node getNode();
  public void setSystemId(String systemId);
  public String getSystemId();

}
```

If you specify a `Node` for the result, either via the constructor or by calling `setNode()`, then the output of the transform will be appended to that node's children. Otherwise, the transform output will be appended to a new `Document` or `DocumentFragment` `Node`. The `getNode()` method returns this `Node`.

SAXSource and SAXResult

The `SAXSource` class, shown in Example 17.15, provides input to the XSLT processor that an `XMLReader` reads from a SAX `InputSource`.

Example 17.15 The TrAX SAXSource Class

```
package javax.xml.transform.sax;

public class SAXSource implements Source {

  public static final String FEATURE =
   "http://javax.xml.transform.sax.SAXSource/feature";

  public SAXSource();
  public SAXSource(XMLReader reader, InputSource inputSource);
  public SAXSource(InputSource inputSource);

  public void        setXMLReader(XMLReader reader);
  public XMLReader   getXMLReader();
  public void        setInputSource(InputSource inputSource);
  public InputSource getInputSource();
  public void        setSystemId(String systemID);
  public String      getSystemId();
```

```
  public static InputSource sourceToInputSource(Source source);

}
```

The `SAXResult` class, shown in Example 17.16, receives output from the XSLT processor as a stream of SAX events fired at a specified `ContentHandler` and optional `LexicalHandler`.

Example 17.16 The TrAX SAXResult Class

```
package javax.xml.transform.sax;

public class SAXResult implements Result

  public static final String FEATURE =
   "http://javax.xml.transform.sax.SAXResult/feature";

  public SAXResult();
  public SAXResult(ContentHandler handler);

  public void           setHandler(ContentHandler handler);
  public ContentHandler getHandler();
  public void           setLexicalHandler(LexicalHandler handler);
  public LexicalHandler getLexicalHandler();
  public void           setSystemId(String systemId);
  public String         getSystemId();

}
```

StreamSource and StreamResult

The `StreamSource` and `StreamResult` classes are used as sources and targets for transforms from sequences of bytes and characters. These include streams, readers, writers, strings, and files. What unifies these is that none of them know they contain an XML document. Indeed, on input they may not always contain an XML document, in which case an exception will be thrown as soon as you attempt to build a `Transformer` or a `Templates` object from the `StreamSource`.

The `StreamSource` class, shown in Example 17.17, provides constructors and methods to get and set the actual source of data.

Example 17.17 The TrAX StreamSource Class

```
package javax.xml.transform.stream;

public class StreamSource implements Source {

  public static final String FEATURE =
   "http://javax.xml.transform.stream.StreamSource/feature";

  public StreamSource();
  public StreamSource(InputStream inputStream);
  public StreamSource(InputStream inputStream, String systemID);
  public StreamSource(Reader reader);
  public StreamSource(Reader reader, String systemID);
  public StreamSource(String systemID);
  public StreamSource(File f);

  public void        setInputStream(InputStream inputStream);
  public InputStream getInputStream();
  public void        setReader(Reader reader);
  public Reader      getReader();
  public void        setPublicId(String publicID);
  public String      getPublicId();
  public void        setSystemId(String systemID);
  public String      getSystemId();
  public void        setSystemId(File f);

}
```

Avoid specifying both an `InputStream` and a `Reader`. If both of these are specified, then which one the processor reads from is implementation dependent. If neither an `InputStream` nor a `Reader` is available, then the processor will attempt to open a connection to the URI specified by the system ID. Be sure to set the system ID even if you do specify an `InputStream` or a `Reader`, because this will be needed to resolve relative URLs that appear inside the stylesheet and input document.

The `StreamResult` class, shown in Example 17.18, provides constructors and methods to get and set the actual target of the data.

Example 17.18 The TrAX StreamResult Class

```
package javax.xml.transform.stream;

public class StreamResult implements Result

  public static final String FEATURE =
   "http://javax.xml.transform.stream.StreamResult/feature";

  public StreamResult() {}
  public StreamResult(OutputStream outputStream);
  public StreamResult(Writer writer);
  public StreamResult(String systemID);
  public StreamResult(File f);

  public void         setOutputStream(OutputStream outputStream);
  public OutputStream getOutputStream();
  public void         setWriter(Writer writer);
  public Writer       getWriter();
  public void         setSystemId(String systemID);
  public void         setSystemId(File f);
  public String       getSystemId();

}
```

Be sure to specify the system ID URL and only one of the other identifiers (`File`, `OutputStream`, `Writer`, or `String`). If you specify more than one possible target, then which one the processor chooses is implementation dependent.

Extending XSLT with Java

TrAX enables you to integrate XSLT code with Java programs. Most XSLT processors written in Java also let you go the other way, integrating Java code with XSLT stylesheets. The most common reason to do this is to provide access to operating system functionality that XSLT doesn't offer, such as querying a database, listing the files in a directory, or asking the user for more information with a dialog box. You can also use Java when you simply find it easier to implement some complex algorithm in imperative Java rather than in functional XSLT. For example, although you can do complicated string search and replace in XSLT, I guarantee you it will be about a thousand times easier in Java, especially with a good regular expression library. And finally, even though it might be relatively easy to implement a function in pure XSLT, you may choose to write it in Java anyway purely for performance reasons. This is especially true for mathematical functions such as factorial and Fibonacci numbers. XSLT optimizers are not nearly as mature or as reliable as Java optimizers, and they mostly focus on optimizing XPath search and evaluation on node-sets rather than on mathematical operations on numbers.

XSLT defines two mechanisms for integrating Java code into stylesheets—extension functions and extension elements. These are invoked in exactly the same way as built-in functions and elements such as `document()` and `xsl:template`. However, rather than being provided by the processor, they're written in Java. Furthermore, they have names in some non-XSLT namespace. The exact way such functions and elements are linked with the processor varies from processor to processor.

Regardless of which XSLT processor you're using, there are two basic parts to writing and using extension functions and elements:

1. Binding the extensions to the stylesheet. This is done via namespaces, class names, and the Java class path.
2. Mapping the five XSLT types (number, boolean, string, node-set, and result tree fragment) to Java types, and vice versa.

Extension Functions

Example 17.19 is a simple extension function that calculates Fibonacci numbers. It is a faster alternative to the earlier recursive template. The entire class is in the `com.macfaq.math` package. When writing extension functions and elements, you really have to use proper Java package naming and set up your class path appropriately.

Example 17.19 A Java Class That Calculates Fibonacci Numbers

```
package com.macfaq.math;

import java.math.BigInteger;

public class FibonacciNumber {

  public static BigInteger calculate(int n) {
```

```
        if (n <= 0) {
          throw new IllegalArgumentException(
           "Fibonacci numbers are only defined for positive integers"
          );
        }
        BigInteger low  = BigInteger.ONE;
        BigInteger high = BigInteger.ONE;

        for (int i = 3; i <= n; i++) {
          BigInteger temp = high;
          high = high.add(low);
          low = temp;
        }

        return high;

      }

    }
```

Notice that there's nothing about XSLT in this example. This is just like any other Java class. On the Java side, all that's needed to make it accessible to the XSLT processor is to compile it and install the `.class` file in the proper place in the processor's class path.

If the extension function throws an exception, as `calculate()` might if it's passed a negative number as an argument, then the XSLT processing will halt. XSLT has no way to catch and respond to exceptions thrown by extension functions. Consequently, if you want to handle them, you'll need to do so in the Java code. After catching the exception, you'll want to return something. Possibilities include

- A `String` that contains an error message
- A `NodeList` that contains a fault document
- An integer error code

This may not be the same type you normally return, so you'll probably need to declare that the method returns `Object` in order to gain the additional flexibility. For example, the following method returns an error message inside a `String` instead of throwing an exception:

```
public static Object calculate(int n) {

  if (n <= 0) {
   return
    "Fibonacci numbers are only defined for positive integers";
  }
  BigInteger low  = BigInteger.ONE;
  BigInteger high = BigInteger.ONE;

  for (int i = 3; i <= n; i++) {
    BigInteger temp = high;
    high = high.add(low);
    low = temp;
  }

  return high;

}
```

This method returns -1 (an illegal value for a Fibonacci number) instead of throwing an exception:

```
public static BigInteger calculate(int n) {

  if (n <= 0) return new BigInteger("-1");
  BigInteger low  = BigInteger.ONE;
  BigInteger high = BigInteger.ONE;

  for (int i = 3; i <= n; i++) {
    BigInteger temp = high;
    high = high.add(low);
    low = temp;
  }

  return high;

}
```

It would be up to the stylesheet to check for the error code before using the result, and handle such a situation appropriately. In this example, that might require calling the extension function before any output is generated, storing the result in a variable, and deciding whether to output a successful response or a fault document based on the value of that variable. Waiting until the template for the `int` element is activated would be too late, because by that point, substantial parts of a successful response document already have been generated.

Now we need a stylesheet that uses this function to calculate Fibonacci numbers instead of the XSLT template. The details at this point are somewhat processor specific, so I will cover the two most popular—Saxon and Xalan. As you'll see, there are quite a few points of similarity between them (although I think Saxon's approach is the cleaner of the two). Most other processors are likely to use something similar.

> **Tip**
>
> Before spending a lot of time writing your own extension functions, check to see if the EXSLT library *[http://www.exslt.org/]* already has the extension function you need. EXSLT provides many useful extension functions and elements for working with dates and times, functions, math, strings, regular expressions, sets, and more. This library has been ported to many different processors in many platforms and languages. I used some of the date functions in the stylesheets for this book.

Extension Functions in Saxon

Saxon allows you to bind any Java class to a namespace prefix. The trick is to use the custom URI scheme `java` followed by a colon and the fully package-qualified name of the class. For example, the following attribute binds the namespace prefix `fib` to the `com.macfaq.math.FibonacciNumber` class:

```
xmlns:fib="java:com.macfaq.math.FibonacciNumber"
```

As long as this mapping is in scope, you can invoke any static function in the `com.macfaq.math.FibonacciNumber` class by using the prefix `fib` and the name of the method. For example, the old template for the `int` element could be replaced by this one:

```
<xsl:template match="int"
              xmlns:fib="java:com.macfaq.math.FibonacciNumber">
  <int>
    <xsl:value-of select="fib:calculate(number(.))"/>
  </int>
</xsl:template>
```

Here the `number()` function converts the value of the context node to an XSLT number. Then the processor looks for a static method named `calculate()` in the

Java class mapped to the `fib` prefix that takes a single argument. It finds one, invokes it, and inserts the return value into the result tree.

XSLT is much more weakly typed than Java, and this can be useful when writing extension functions. Saxon will only invoke methods that have the right name and the right number of arguments; however, it will often convert the types of arguments and return values as necessary to make a function fit. In this case, the `calculate()` method expects to receive an `int`, but an XSLT number is really more like a Java `double`. In this case, because Saxon can't find a matching method that takes a `double`, it truncates the fractional part of the `double` to get an `int` and invokes the method that takes an `int`. This is a conversion that Java itself would not do without an explicit cast.

Working in the opposite direction, the `calculate()` method returns a `BigInteger`, which is not equivalent to any of XSLT's types. Thus Saxon converts it to a string using its `toString()` method before inserting it into the result tree. Other more recognizable return types may be converted differently. For example, `void` is converted to an empty node-set, and primitive number types such as `int` and `double` are converted to XSLT numbers, as are type wrapper classes such as `Integer` and `Double`. A DOM `NodeList` is converted to an XPath node-set; however, the nodes in the list must all be created by Saxon's own DOM implementation. You can't use third-party DOM implementations such as Xerces or GNU JAXP in a Saxon extension function.

> **Tip**
>
> Normally, namespace mappings for extension functions and elements are relevant only in the stylesheet. Nonetheless, they often have an annoying habit of popping up in the output document. If you know that an extension element or function prefix will not be used in the output document (and 99 percent of the time you do know exactly this), then you can add an `exclude-result-prefixes` attribute to the stylesheet root element that contains a list of the namespace prefixes whose declarations should not be copied into the output document. For example,
>
> ```
> <xsl:stylesheet version="1.0"
>   xmlns:xsl="http://www.w3.org/1999/XSL/Transform"
>   xmlns:fib="java:com.macfaq.math.FibonacciNumber"
>   xmlns:saxon="http://icl.com/saxon"
>   exclude-result-prefixes="fib saxon">
> ```

Instance Methods and Constructors in Saxon

XSLT is not an object-oriented language. Static methods fit much more neatly into its structures than do objects and instance methods. If I'm writing a method just for XSLT, I'll normally make it static, if at all possible. However, Saxon can use instance methods as extension functions too. As before, the fully package-qualified class name must be bound to a namespace prefix. The constructor for the class can be called using the special local function name new(). For example, the following template retrieves the current time using the Java Date class:

```
<xsl:template name="currentTime"
              xmlns:date="java:java.util.Date">
  <xsl:value-of select="date:new()"/>
</xsl:template>
```

date:new() in XSLT is basically the same thing as new Date() in Java. When the Date constructor is invoked with no arguments, Java initializes the resulting Date object to the current time. You can also pass arguments to constructors, just like you can to static methods.

The object that the new() function returns is normally assigned to a variable. You can pass this variable to other extension functions as an argument. To invoke instance methods on that object, pass the variable that points to the object whose instance method you're invoking as the first argument to the instance method. This causes the normal first argument to get pushed over to become the second argument, the second argument to become the third, and so on. For example, the following template uses the GregorianCalendar class to get today's date. First it uses the static getInstance() method to return a GregorianCalendar object initialized to the current time. Then it passes the appropriate integer constants to the get() instance method to retrieve the month, day, and year. It produces the current date in the form 2002-3-26.

```
<xsl:template name="today"
              xmlns:cal="java:java.util.GregorianCalendar">
  <xsl:variable name="rightNow" select="cal:getInstance()" />
  <!-- The Calendar class uses zero-based months;
       i.e., January is month 0, February is month 1, and
       so on. We have to add one to get the customary month
       number. -->
  <xsl:variable name="month" select="cal:get($rightNow, 2) + 1" />
  <xsl:variable name="day" select="cal:get($rightNow, 5)" />
  <xsl:variable name="year" select="cal:get($rightNow, 1)" />
  <xsl:value-of
   select="$year" />-<xsl:value-of
   select="$month" />-<xsl:value-of
   select="$day" />
</xsl:template>
```

Note

If I were writing this in Java rather than in XSLT, the code would look like this:

```
Calendar rightNow = Calendar.getInstance();
// Months are zero-based; i.e., January is month 0, February
// is month 1, and so on. We have to add one to get the
// customary month number.
String month = rightNow.get(Calendar.MONTH) + 1;
String date  = rightNow.get(Calendar.DATE);
String year  = rightNow.get(Calendar.YEAR);
String result = year + "-" + month + "-" + date;
```

However, Saxon doesn't support extension *fields*, so XSLT must use the actual constant key values instead of the named constants.

If you absolutely must use the value of a field (for example, because a method expects an instance of the type-safe enum pattern instead of an `int` constant), you can always write an extension function whose sole purpose is to return the relevant field.

Extension Functions in Xalan

Xalan's extension function mechanism is a little more complicated and a little more powerful than Saxon's, but not a great deal more. Xalan offers somewhat greater access to the XSLT context inside extension functions if you need it, and has some additional shortcuts for mapping Java classes to namespace prefixes. Most important, it allows extension functions to work with any compliant DOM2 implementation, rather than requiring its own custom DOM.

Xalan uses the custom URI scheme `xalan` to bind namespace prefixes to classes. To bind a Java class to a namespace prefix in Xalan, you add an attribute of the form `xmlns:`*`prefix`*`="xalan://`*`packagename.classname`*`"` to the root element of the stylesheet or some other ancestor element. For example, the following attribute binds the namespace prefix `fib` to the `com.macfaq.math.FibonacciNumber` class:

```
xmlns:fib="xalan://com.macfaq.math.FibonacciNumber"
```

As long as this mapping is in scope, you can invoke any static function in the `com.macfaq.math.FibonacciNumber` class by using the prefix `fib` and the name of the method. For example, the pure XSLT template for the `int` element could be replaced by this one:

```
<xsl:template match="int"
   xmlns:fib="xalan://com.macfaq.math.FibonacciNumber">
  <int>
    <xsl:value-of select="fib:calculate(number(.))"/>
  </int>
</xsl:template>
```

Xalan also allows you to define a namespace prefix for the entire Java class library by associating it with the URI `http://xml.apache.org/xslt/java`. The function calls must then use fully qualified class names. For example, the following template uses the prefix `java` to identify extension functions:

```
<xsl:template match="int"
    xmlns:java="http://xml.apache.org/xslt/java">
  <int>
    <xsl:value-of select=
     "java:com.macfaq.math.FibonacciNumber.calculate(number(.))"
    />
  </int>
</xsl:template>
```

This form is convenient if your stylesheets use many different classes. It of course is not limited to classes you write yourself. It works equally well for classes from the standard library and third-party libraries. For example, following is a random template that uses Java's `Math.random()` method:

```
<xsl:template name="random"
              xmlns:java="http://xml.apache.org/xslt/java">
  <xsl:value-of select="java:java.lang.Math.random()" />
</xsl:template>
```

Constructors and Instance Methods in Xalan

Xalan can use instance methods as extension functions too. The `new()` function invokes the constructor for the class and can take whatever arguments the constructor requires. For example, the following template retrieves the current time using the Java `Date` class:

```
<xsl:template name="currentTime"
              xmlns:java="http://xml.apache.org/xslt/java">
  <xsl:value-of select="java:java.util.Date.new()"/>
</xsl:template>
```

If the prefix is bound to a specific class, you can omit the class name. For example,

```
<xsl:template name="currentTime"
              xmlns:date="xalan://java.util.Date">
  <xsl:value-of select="date:new()"/>
</xsl:template>
```

The object the new() function returns can be assigned to an XSLT variable, which then can be passed as an argument to other extension functions or used to invoke instance methods on the object. As in Saxon, to invoke an instance method you pass the object whose method you're invoking as the first argument to the method. For example, following is the Xalan version of the GregorianCalendar template that produces the current date in the form 2002-3-26.

```
<xsl:template name="today"
              xmlns:cal="xalan://java.util.GregorianCalendar">
  <xsl:variable name="rightNow" select="cal:getInstance()" />
   <!-- The GregorianCalendar class counts months from zero
        so we have to add one to get the customary number -->
<xsl:variable name="month" select="cal:get($rightNow, 2) + 1" />
<xsl:variable name="day" select="cal:get($rightNow, 5) + 1" />
  <xsl:variable name="year" select="cal:get($rightNow, 1)" />
  <xsl:value-of
   select="$year" />-<xsl:value-of
   select="$month" />-<xsl:value-of
   select="$day" />
</xsl:template>
```

Like Saxon, Xalan does not permit access to fields in a class, so once again it's necessary to use the actual values instead of the named constants for the arguments to the get() method.

Exceptions thrown by extension functions have the same results in Xalan as in Saxon; that is, the XSLT processing halts, possibly in the middle of transforming a document. Once again, it's probably a good idea to design your extension functions so that they handle all probable exceptions internally and always return a sensible result.

Type Conversion in Xalan

Xalan converts method arguments and return types between Java and XSLT types in a mostly intuitive way. Table 17.1 lists the conversions from XSLT's five types to Java types in order of preference:

Table 17.1 Xalan Conversions from XSLT to Java

XSLT Type	Java Types, in Decreasing Order of Preference
Node-set	`org.w3c.dom.traversal.NodeIterator, org.w3c.dom.NodeList, org.w3c.dom.Node, String, Object, char, double, float, long, int, short, byte, boolean`
String	`String, Object, char, double, float, long, int, short, byte, boolean`
Boolean	`boolean, Boolean, Object, String`
Number	`double, Double, float, long, int, short, char, byte, boolean, String, Object`
Result tree fragment	`org.w3c.dom.traversal.NodeIterator, org.w3c.dom.NodeList, org.w3c.dom.Node, String, Object, char, double, float, long, int, short, byte, boolean`

Working in the reverse direction from Java to XSLT, the conversions are fairly obvious. Table 17.2 summarizes them. In addition to the ones listed here, other object types will normally be converted to a string using their `toString()` method if they're actually de-referenced somewhere in the stylesheet. However, their original type will be maintained when they're passed back to another extension function.

Table 17.2 Xalan Conversions from Java to XSLT

Java Type	Xalan XSLT Type
`org.w3c.dom.traversal.NodeIterator`	Node-set
`org.apache.xml.dtm.DTM`	Node-set
`org.apache.xml.dtm.DTMAxisIterator`	Node-set
`org.apache.xml.dtm.DTMIterator`	Node-set
`org.w3c.dom.Node` and its subtypes (`Element`, `Attr`, etc.)	Node-set
`org.w3c.dom.DocumentFragment`	Result tree fragment
`String`	String
`Boolean`	Boolean
`Number` and its subclasses (`Double`, `Integer`, etc.)	Number

Java Type	Xalan XSLT Type
`double`	Number
`float`	Number
`int`	Number
`long`	Number
`short`	Number
`byte`	Number
`char`	Object
`boolean`	Boolean
`null`	Empty string
`void`	Empty string

Expression Context in Xalan

There is one thing Xalan extension functions can do that Saxon extension functions can't do. A Xalan extension function can receive the current XSLT context as an argument. This provides information about the context node, the context node position, the context node list, and variable bindings. Admittedly, needing to know this information inside an extension function is rare. Most operations that consider the current context are more easily implemented in XSLT than in Java. Nonetheless, if you need to know this for some reason, you can declare that the initial argument to your function has type `org.apache.xalan.extensions.ExpressionContext`; for example,

```
public static Node findMaximum (ExpressionContext context)
```

You do not need to pass an argument of this type explicitly. Xalan will create an `ExpressionContext` object for you and pass it to the method automatically. Furthermore, Xalan will always pick a method that takes an `ExpressionContext` over one that does not.

This Xalan-J `ExpressionContext` interface, shown in Example 17.20, provides methods to get the context and the context node list, convert the context node into either its string or number value (as defined by the XPath `string()` and `number()` functions), and to get the XPath object bound to a known variable or parameter.

Example 17.20 The Xalan ExpressionContext Interface

```
package org.apache.xalan.extensions;

public interface ExpressionContext {

  public Node         getContextNode();
  public NodeIterator getContextNodes();
  public double       toNumber(Node n);
  public String       toString(Node n);
  public XObject      getVariableOrParam(
   org.apache.xml.utils.QName qualifiedName)
   throws javax.xml.transform.TransformerException;

}
```

Extension Elements

An extension element is much like an extension function. In the stylesheet, however, it appears as an entire element such as `<saxon:script/>` or `<redirect:write />` rather than as a mere function in an XPath expression contained in a `select` or `test` attribute. Any value it returns is placed directly in the result tree.

For example, suppose you wanted to define a `fibonacci` element like this one:

```
<fib:fibonacci xmlns:fib="java:com.macfaq.math.FibonacciNumber">
  10
</fib:fibonacci>
```

When processed, this element would be replaced by the specified Fibonacci number.

The first question is how the XSLT processor should recognize this as an extension element. After all, `fib:fibonacci` looks just like a literal result element that should be copied verbatim. The answer is that the `xsl:stylesheet` root element (or some other ancestor element) should have an `extension-element-prefixes` attribute containing a white-space-separated list of namespace prefixes that identify extension elements. For example, the following stylesheet uses the `saxon` and `fib` prefixes for extension elements:

```
<xsl:stylesheet version="1.0"
  xmlns:xsl="http://www.w3.org/1999/XSL/Transform"
  xmlns:saxon="http://icl.com/saxon"
```

```
  xmlns:fib="java:com.macfaq.math.FibonacciNumber"
  extension-element-prefixes="saxon fib">

  <!- - ... - ->

</xsl:stylesheet>
```

Because you can't be sure which extension elements are likely to be available across processors, it's customary to include one or more `xsl:fallback` elements as children of each extension element. Each such element contains a template that is instantiated if and only if the parent extension element can't be found. Example 17.21 demonstrates a stylesheet that attempts to use the `fib:fibonacci` extension element. If that element cannot be found, then a pure XSLT solution is used instead.

Example 17.21 A Stylesheet That Uses an Extension Element

```
<?xml version="1.0" encoding="ISO-8859-1"?>
<xsl:stylesheet version="1.0"
  xmlns:xsl="http://www.w3.org/1999/XSL/Transform"
  xmlns:fib="http://namespaces.cafeconleche.org/fibonacci"
  extension-element-prefixes="fib">

  <!-- I deleted the validation code from this stylesheet to
       save space, but it would be easy to add back in
       for production use. -->

  <xsl:template match="/methodCall">
    <methodResponse>
      <params>
        <param>
          <value>
            <xsl:apply-templates select="params/param/value" />
          </value>
        </param>
      </params>
    </methodResponse>
  </xsl:template>

  <xsl:template match="value">
    <int>
```

```
          <fib:fibonacci>
            <xsl:value-of select="number(.)"/>
            <xsl:fallback>
              <!-- This template will be called only if the
                   fib:fibonacci code can't be loaded. -->
              <xsl:call-template name="calculateFibonacci">
                <xsl:with-param name="index" select="number(.)" />
              </xsl:call-template>
            </xsl:fallback>
          </fib:fibonacci>
        </int>
      </xsl:template>

      <xsl:template name="calculateFibonacci">
        <xsl:param name="index"/>
        <xsl:param name="low"  select="1"/>
        <xsl:param name="high" select="1"/>
        <xsl:choose>
          <xsl:when test="$index &lt;= 1">
            <xsl:value-of select="$low"/>
          </xsl:when>
          <xsl:otherwise>
            <xsl:call-template name="calculateFibonacci">
              <xsl:with-param name="index" select="$index - 1"/>
              <xsl:with-param name="low"   select="$high"/>
              <xsl:with-param name="high"  select="$high + $low"/>
            </xsl:call-template>
          </xsl:otherwise>
        </xsl:choose>
      </xsl:template>

    </xsl:stylesheet>
```

Alternately, you can pass the namespace-qualified name of the extension element to the `element-available()` function to figure out whether or not the extension is available. For example,

```
    <xsl:template match="value">
      <int>
        <xsl:choose>
```

```
        <xsl:when test="element-available('fib:fibonacci')">
          <fib:fibonacci>
            <xsl:value-of select="number(.)"/>
          </fib:fibonacci>
        </xsl:when>
        <xsl:otherwise>
          <xsl:call-template name="calculateFibonacci">
            <xsl:with-param name="index" select="number(.)" />
          </xsl:call-template>
        </xsl:otherwise>
      </xsl:choose>
    </int>
  </xsl:template>
```

From this point on, the exact details of how to code the extension element in Java are implementation dependent. Consult the documentation for your XSLT processor to learn how to write an extension element and install it. You will not be able to use preexisting methods and classes as extension elements; rather, you will need to custom code extension elements to fit in with the processor's own code.

> **Caution**
> Writing an extension element is much more complex than writing an extension function. It requires intimate knowledge of and interaction with the XSLT processor. If at all possible, it's advisable to use an extension function, perhaps one that returns a node-set, instead of an extension element.

Summary

XSLT is a template-driven environment for defining transformations between one XML document format and another. An XSLT stylesheet contains template rules that are matched against nodes in the input document. When a match is detected, the rule's template is instantiated and the result is added to the result tree. XSLT is itself an XML application that contains numerous elements for specifying exactly which nodes are matched when and what output is generated as a result.

XSLT is also a Turing-complete, functional programming language. Templates can be called by name and can be called recursively. Parameters can be passed to templates. XSLT is not as convenient to program in as traditional languages such as Java, but in its problem domain this approach works extremely well.

TrAX is a standard API for XSLT processors that is part of Java 1.4 and later and is bundled with most current XSLT processors for Java, including Saxon, Xalan, and jd.xslt. TrAX follows the abstract-factory design pattern. A `TransformerFactory` object creates `Transformer` objects from stylesheets. The `Transformer` objects transform XML documents in a variety of representations according to the instructions in their stylesheets. Both XSLT stylesheets and input XML documents are initially wrapped by a `Source` object. The target for output is wrapped by a `Result` object. TrAX includes a number of standard source and result implementations for different models, including SAX, DOM, and streams.

In addition to integrating XSLT into your Java programs, you can integrate Java into your XSLT stylesheets through extension elements and functions. The `extension-element-prefixes` attribute specifies which namespace prefixes are mapped to extension elements. The namespace URIs are used to find the necessary `.class` files in the processor's class path. The `element-available()` and `function-available()` functions and the `xsl:fallback` element test for the presence of extension functions and elements, enabling you to write portable stylesheets that work with or without the extensions. Once you've set this up, you can use the extension elements and functions just like standard XSLT elements and functions.

Part VI

Appendixes

Appendix

XML API Quick Reference

This appendix provides complete signatures for the documented public packages, classes, methods, and fields in the various APIs you might use to process XML with Java, including

- SAX 2.0
- DOM Level 2
- JAXP 1.1
- TrAX
- JDOM
- XMLPULL 1.0.8

SAX

SAX, the Simple API for XML, is an event-driven API that, rather than modeling the document, models the parser and the client application that receives information from the parser. It's suitable for documents that are fairly local—that is, situations in which processing one piece of the document does not depend heavily on content from other pieces of the document. It is extremely fast, and far and away the most memory efficient of the various XML APIs. It is the only API that can easily handle documents in the multi-gigabyte range.

SAX is divided into three packages:

- `org.xml.sax`: the core classes and interfaces that all SAX parsers and most SAX programs use
- `org.xml.sax.helpers`: factory classes for loading instances of the core SAX interfaces, as well as some implementations of those interfaces
- `org.xml.sax.ext`: optional extensions to SAX, which not all parsers provide

org.xml.sax

The `org.xml.sax` package contains the core classes and interfaces that represent the parser, the client application, the input document, and more. It also contains a number of classes from SAX1 that can be safely ignored in modern applications.

AttributeList

The `AttributeList` interface was used in SAX1 to pass attribute sets to the `startElement()` method of `DocumentHandler`. It is now deprecated and should not be used.

```
package org.xml.sax;

public interface AttributeList  {

  public int    getLength();
  public String getName(int i);
  public String getType(int i);
  public String getValue(int i);
  public String getType(String name);
  public String getValue(String name);

}
```

Attributes

The `Attributes` interface is used to pass attribute sets to the `startElement()` method of `ContentHandler` Although list-like, indexed access is supported for convenience, there is absolutely no guarantee that the attributes will be stored in the list in the order they appear in the start-tag. Indeed, in practice it's more likely than not that they won't be. If the attribute is declared to have any type other than CDATA (for example, ID, NMTOKENS, or enumerated) and the parser has read the DTD, then the reported value is normalized; that is, leading and trailing white space is trimmed, and runs of white space are converted to single space. The unnormalized value will not be available. Undeclared attributes are not normalized.

```
package org.xml.sax;

public interface Attributes {

  public int    getLength();
  public String getURI(int index);
  public String getLocalName(int index);
  public String getQName(int index);
  public String getType(int index);
  public String getValue(int index);
  public int    getIndex(String uri, String localName);
  public int    getIndex(String qualifiedName);
  public String getType(String uri, String localName);
  public String getType(String qualifiedName);
  public String getValue(String uri, String localName);
  public String getValue(String qualifiedName);

}
```

ContentHandler

`ContentHandler` is the basic callback interface a client application implements in order to receive information from the parser. Client applications register an instance of this interface with the parser using the `setContentHandler()` method in `XMLReader`. The parser will invoke the methods in that object in the same order that the corresponding markup and text appears in the original document.

> **Note**
> This interface has no relation to the moribund `java.net.ContentHandler`. But because the name does conflict, don't import `java.net.*` in a class that uses `org.xml.sax.ContentHandler`. Just import the classes you actually use.

```
package org.xml.sax;

public interface ContentHandler {

  public void setDocumentLocator(Locator locator);
  public void startDocument()
   throws SAXException;
```

```
    public void endDocument()
     throws SAXException;
    public void startPrefixMapping(String prefix, String uri)
     throws SAXException;
    public void endPrefixMapping(String prefix)
     throws SAXException;
    public void startElement(String namespaceURI, String localName,
     String qualifiedName, Attributes atts) throws SAXException;
    public void endElement(String namespaceURI, String localName,
     String qualifiedName) throws SAXException;
    public void characters(char[] text, int start, int length)
     throws SAXException;
    public void ignorableWhitespace(char[] space, int start,
     int length) throws SAXException;
    public void processingInstruction(String target, String data)
     throws SAXException;
    public void skippedEntity(String name) throws SAXException;

}
```

DocumentHandler

DocumentHandler is the SAX1 equivalent of ContentHandler. It is now deprecated and should not be used.

```
package org.xml.sax;

public interface DocumentHandler  {

  public void setDocumentLocator(Locator locator);
  public void startDocument() throws SAXException;
  public void endDocument() throws SAXException;
  public void startElement(String name, AttributeList atts)
   throws SAXException;
  public void endElement(String name) throws SAXException;
  public void characters(char[] text, int start, int length)
   throws SAXException;
  public void ignorableWhitespace(char[] space, int start,
   int length) throws SAXException;
  public void processingInstruction(String target, String data)
   throws SAXException;

}
```

DTDHandler

`DTDHandler` is a callback interface that a client application can implement and register with the `XMLReader` using the `setDTDHandler()` method if it wishes to receive information from the parser about notations and unparsed entities declared in the DTD. These methods will be called sometime after `startDocument()` and again sometime before the `startElement()` method for the root element. You'll generally store the information in some data structure such as a `Map` so that you can refer back to it when you encounter an attribute with type NOTATION or ENTITY.

```
package org.xml.sax;

public interface DTDHandler {

  public void notationDecl(String name, String publicID,
   String systemID) throws SAXException;
  public void unparsedEntityDecl(String name, String publicID,
   String systemID, String notationName) throws SAXException;

}
```

EntityResolver

A client program can implement the `EntityResolver` interface to substitute different sources for entities referenced in the main document by public or system ID. A specific instance of `EntityResolver` is registered with the parser by passing it to the `setEntityResolver()` method in `XMLReader`. If `resolveEntity()` cannot locate a requested entity, then it should return null, to tell the parser to use its default entity resolution mechanism.

```
package org.xml.sax;

public interface EntityResolver {

  public InputSource resolveEntity(String publicID,
   String systemID) throws SAXException, IOException;

}
```

ErrorHandler

`ErrorHandler` is a callback interface that parsers use to report the three levels of errors that may be encountered while parsing an XML document: a fatal well-formedness error, a nonfatal error such as a validity violation, and a warning.

Parsers normally stop parsing the current document after reporting a fatal error. That is, the parser calls `endDocument()` and the `parse()` method returns. If you want the same behavior from a nonfatal error, then rethrow the exception from inside the `error()` method. You install a specific instance of this interface by passing it to the `setErrorHandler()` method in `XMLReader`.

```
package org.xml.sax;

public interface ErrorHandler  {

  public void warning(SAXParseException ex) throws SAXException;
  public void error(SAXParseException ex) throws SAXException;
  public void fatalError(SAXParseException ex)
   throws SAXException;

}
```

HandlerBase

`HandlerBase` is the SAX1 equivalent of `DefaultHandler`—that is, an adapter class that provides do-nothing implementations of the SAX1 callback interfaces. It is now deprecated and should not be used.

```
package org.xml.sax;

public class HandlerBase implements EntityResolver,
 DTDHandler, DocumentHandler, ErrorHandler {

  public HandlerBase();

  // EntityResolver methods
  public InputSource resolveEntity(String publicID,
   String systemID) throws SAXException;

  // DTDHandler methods
  public void notationDecl(String name, String publicID,
   String systemID);
  public void unparsedEntityDecl(String name, String publicID,
   String systemID, String notationName);

  // DocumentHandler methods
  public void setDocumentLocator(Locator locator);
```

```
  public void startDocument() throws SAXException;
  public void endDocument() throws SAXException;
  public void startElement(String name, AttributeList attributes)
   throws SAXException;
  public void endElement(String name) throws SAXException;
  public void characters(char[] text, int start, int length)
   throws SAXException;
  public void ignorableWhitespace(char[] space, int start,
   int length) throws SAXException;
  public void processingInstruction(String target, String data)
   throws SAXException;

  // ErrorHandler methods
  public void warning(SAXParseException ex) throws SAXException;
  public void error(SAXParseException ex) throws SAXException;
  public void fatalError(SAXParseException ex)
   throws SAXException;

}
```

InputSource

InputSource is a wrapper for the many things that may contain an XML document, including URLs, InputStreams, and Readers. An InputSource should be configured with a system ID URL and either an InputStream or a Reader.

```
package org.xml.sax;

public class InputSource  {

  public InputSource();
  public InputSource(String systemID);
  public InputSource(InputStream byteStream);
  public InputSource(Reader characterStream);

  public void        setPublicId(String publicID);
  public String      getPublicId();
  public void        setSystemId(String url);
  public String      getSystemId();
  public void        setByteStream(InputStream in);
  public InputStream getByteStream();
  public void        setEncoding(String encoding);
```

```
    public String       getEncoding();
    public void         setCharacterStream(Reader in);
    public Reader       getCharacterStream();

}
```

Remember always to set the system ID for an InputSource. If nothing else is set, then the parser will read the document from that URL. You also may set either the byte stream or the character stream, in which case that will be used to read the document. If you set both the byte stream and the character stream, then the parser will read from the character stream.

Locator

Many parsers pass a Locator object to the setLocator() method of ContentHandler before they call startDocument(). If a parser does this (and it's not required to), then client applications can use that Locator object to determine in which entity at which line and column a particular event occurs. The location information returned is not guaranteed to be perfectly accurate, but it's normally close enough to help in debugging.

```
package org.xml.sax;

public interface Locator {

  public String getPublicId();
  public String getSystemId();
  public int    getLineNumber();
  public int    getColumnNumber();

}
```

Parser

Parser is the SAX1 class that represents an XML parser. Modern programs should use SAX2's XMLReader instead.

```
package org.xml.sax;

public interface Parser {

  public void setLocale(Locale locale) throws SAXException;
  public void setEntityResolver(EntityResolver resolver);
```

```
    public void setDTDHandler(DTDHandler handler);
    public void setDocumentHandler(DocumentHandler handler);
    public void setErrorHandler(ErrorHandler handler);

    public void parse(InputSource source)
     throws SAXException, IOException;
    public void parse(String systemID)
     throws SAXException, IOException;

  }
```

XMLFilter

XMLFilter is an XMLReader that receives its content from another XMLReader rather than directly from a parsed document. Thus it has the opportunity to modify, log, replace, or otherwise manipulate the content that the parser sends. Most of the time, it is much easier to write a filter by subclassing the org.xml.sax.helpers.XMLFilterImpl class rather than by implementing this interface directly.

```
package org.xml.sax;

public interface XMLFilter implements XMLReader {

  public void       setParent(XMLReader parent);
  public XMLReader getParent();

}
```

XMLReader

XMLReader is SAX2's representation of an XML parser. It has methods to get and set features and properties, to configure the parser with the various handler classes, and to parse documents from an InputSource or a URL.

```
package org.xml.sax;

public interface XMLReader  {

  public boolean getFeature(String name)
   throws SAXNotRecognizedException, SAXNotSupportedException;
  public void    setFeature(String name, boolean value)
   throws SAXNotRecognizedException, SAXNotSupportedException;
  public Object  getProperty(String name)
   throws SAXNotRecognizedException, SAXNotSupportedException;
```

```
    public void    setProperty(String name, Object value)
     throws SAXNotRecognizedException, SAXNotSupportedException;

    public void          setEntityResolver(EntityResolver resolver);
    public EntityResolver getEntityResolver();
    public void           setDTDHandler(DTDHandler handler);
    public DTDHandler     getDTDHandler();
    public void           setContentHandler(ContentHandler handler);
    public ContentHandler getContentHandler();
    public void           setErrorHandler(ErrorHandler handler);
    public ErrorHandler   getErrorHandler();

    public void parse(InputSource input)
     throws IOException, SAXException;
    public void parse(String systemID)
     throws IOException, SAXException;

}
```

Exceptions and Errors

All SAX exceptions are checked exceptions and all are derived from `org.xml.sax.SAXException`. In addition, a few methods that perform input/output can throw an `IOException`.

SAXException

`SAXException` is the generic checked exception for just about anything that can go wrong while parsing an XML document aside from an I/O error. Often a more specific subclass of `SAXException` will be thrown instead, even if the method is only declared to throw `SAXException`. The `SAXException` class predates Java 1.4 by a couple of years; therefore, it uses its own `getException()` method to report the nested exception that caused the `SAXException` (if such exists), rather than the `getCause()` method introduced in Java 1.4.

```
package org.xml.sax;

public class SAXException extends Exception {

  public SAXException(String message);
  public SAXException(Exception ex);
  public SAXException(String message, Exception ex);
```

```
    public String    getMessage();
    public Exception getException();
    public String    toString();

}
```

SAXNotRecognizedException

A `SAXNotRecognizedException` signals that the parser does not support the feature or property you're trying to set; for example, you're trying to turn on validation for a nonvalidating parser.

```
package org.xml.sax;

public class SAXNotRecognizedException extends SAXException {

  public SAXNotRecognizedException(String message);

}
```

SAXNotSupportedException

A `SAXNotSupportedException` indicates one of two things. Either the parser cannot set a feature or property to the requested value (for example, you're trying to set the value of the *http://xml.org/sax/properties/lexical-handler* property to an object that does not implement `LexicalHandler`), or it cannot set that feature or property at this point in time (for example, you're trying to turn on validation when the parser is halfway through the document).

```
package org.xml.sax;

public class SAXNotSupportedException extends SAXException {

  public SAXNotSupportedException(String message);

}
```

SAXParseException

A `SAXParseException` normally indicates a well-formedness error. In `ErrorHandler` it is also used to indicate validity errors, other nonfatal errors, and warnings. It normally provides line and column numbers locating the position of the error in the XML document that caused the exception. However, sometimes these are set to -1 if the error occurs very early in the document or if the parser can't determine exactly where the problem is.

```
package org.xml.sax;

public class SAXParseException extends SAXException {

  public SAXParseException(String message, Locator locator);
  public SAXParseException(String message, Locator locator,
   Exception e);
  public SAXParseException(String message, String publicID,
   String systemID, int lineNumber, int columnNumber);
  public SAXParseException(String message, String publicID,
   String systemID, int lineNumber, int columnNumber,
   Exception e);

  public String getPublicId();
  public String getSystemId();
  public int    getLineNumber();
  public int    getColumnNumber();

}
```

org.xml.sax.ext

The `org.xml.sax.ext` package contains optional extensions to SAX that parsers are not required to implement. In practice, the major parsers do implement the `DeclHandler` and `LexicalHandler` callback interfaces from this package.

DeclHandler

`DeclHandler` is a callback interface that client applications can implement and register with the parser in order to receive notification of element, attribute, and parsed entity declarations. Parsers are not required to provide this information, but most validating parsers do. If a `LexicalHandler` is also installed, then all calls to these methods occur in between the calls to `startDTD()` and `endDTD()`.

A `DeclHandler` is installed in an `XMLReader` as the value of the `http://xml.org/sax/properties/declaration-handler` property with the `setProperty()` method. Parsers that do not provide declaration events will throw a `SAXNotRecognizedException` when you do this.

```
package org.xml.sax.ext;

public interface DeclHandler  {
```

```
  public void elementDecl(String name, String model)
   throws SAXException;
  public void attributeDecl(String elementName,
   String attributeName, String type, String valueDefault,
   String value) throws SAXException;
  public void internalEntityDecl(String name, String value)
   throws SAXException;
  public void externalEntityDecl(String name, String publicID,
   String systemID) throws SAXException;

}
```

LexicalHandler

`LexicalHandler` is a callback interface that client applications can implement and register with the parser in order to receive notification of lexical information such as comments, parsed entities, and CDATA section boundaries. Parsers are not required to provide lexical information, but most do. In normal usage, this interface is not uncommon. Excessive reliance on it often indicates a poorly designed XML application.

A `LexicalHandler` is installed in an `XMLReader` as the value of the `http://xml.org/sax/properties/lexical-handler` property with the `setProperty()` method. Parsers that do not provide lexical events will throw a `SAXNotRecognizedException` when you do this.

```
package org.xml.sax.ext;

public interface LexicalHandler  {

  public void startDTD(String name, String publicID,
   String systemID) throws SAXException;
  public void endDTD() throws SAXException;
  public void startEntity(String name) throws SAXException;
  public void endEntity(String name) throws SAXException;
  public void startCDATA() throws SAXException;
  public void endCDATA() throws SAXException;
  public void comment(char[] text, int start, int length)
   throws SAXException;

}
```

org.xml.sax.helpers

The `org.xml.sax.helpers` package contains classes that may assist with many SAX tasks but are not necessarily required. The ones that client developers will find most useful are the factory classes for locating `XMLReaders`, but there are also classes that provide minimal implementations of several SAX interfaces, such as `Attributes` that can be useful when writing filters.

AttributeListImpl

The legacy `AttributeListImpl` class is a SAX1 class that parser vendors may (or may not) use to implement the `AttributesList` interface. There's little to no need for this in SAX2.

```
package org.xml.sax.helpers;

public class AttributeListImpl implements AttributeList {

  public AttributeListImpl();
  public AttributeListImpl(AttributeList atts);

  public int    getLength();
  public String getName(int i);
  public String getType(int i);
  public String getValue(int i);
  public String getType(String name);
  public String getValue(String name);

  public void   setAttributeList(AttributeList atts);
  public void   addAttribute(String name, String type,
   String value);
  public void   removeAttribute(String name);
  public void   clear();

}
```

AttributesImpl

`AttributesImpl` is a class that parser vendors may (or may not) use to implement the `Attributes` interface. It can also be useful for taking persistent snapshots of `Attributes` objects and modifying `Attributes` lists in filters.

```
package org.xml.sax.helpers;
```

```
public class AttributesImpl implements Attributes {

  public AttributesImpl();
  public AttributesImpl(Attributes atts);

  public int    getLength();
  public String getURI(int index);
  public String getLocalName(int index);
  public String getQName(int index);
  public String getType(int index);
  public String getValue(int index);
  public void   removeAttribute(int index);
  public void   setURI(int index, String uri);
  public void   setLocalName(int index, String localName);
  public void   setQName(int index, String qualifiedName);
  public void   setType(int index, String type);
  public void   setValue(int index, String value);

  public int    getIndex(String uri, String localName);
  public int    getIndex(String qualifiedName);
  public String getType(String uri, String localName);
  public String getType(String qualifiedName);
  public String getValue(String uri, String localName);
  public String getValue(String qualifiedName);

  public void   clear();
  public void   setAttributes(Attributes atts);
  public void   addAttribute(String uri, String localName,
   String qualifiedName, String type, String value);
  public void   setAttribute(int index, String uri,
   String localName, String qualifiedName, String type,
   String value);

}
```

DefaultHandler

`DefaultHandler` is an adapter class that implements the four required SAX2 callback interfaces—`EntityResolver`, `DTDHandler`, `ContentHandler`, and `ErrorHandler`—with do-nothing implementations of all of their methods. It's often more convenient to subclass this class rather than implement those interfaces directly.

```
package org.xml.sax.helpers;

public class DefaultHandler implements EntityResolver,
 DTDHandler, ContentHandler, ErrorHandler {

  public DefaultHandler();

  // EntityResolver methods
  public InputSource resolveEntity(String publicID,
   String systemID) throws SAXException;

  // DTDHandler methods
  public void notationDecl(String name, String publicID,
   String systemID) throws SAXException;
  public void unparsedEntityDecl(String name, String publicID,
   String systemID, String notationName) throws SAXException;

  // ContentHandler methods
  public void setDocumentLocator(Locator locator);
  public void startDocument() throws SAXException;
  public void endDocument() throws SAXException;
  public void startPrefixMapping(String prefix, String uri)
   throws SAXException;
  public void endPrefixMapping(String prefix)
   throws SAXException;
  public void startElement(String uri, String localName,
   String qualifiedName, Attributes attributes)
   throws SAXException;
  public void endElement(String uri, String localName,
   String qualifiedName) throws SAXException;
  public void characters(char[] text, int start, int length)
   throws SAXException;
  public void ignorableWhitespace(char[] space, int start,
   int length) throws SAXException;
  public void processingInstruction(String target, String data)
   throws SAXException;
  public void skippedEntity(String name) throws SAXException;

  // ErrorHandler methods
  public void warning(SAXParseException e) throws SAXException;
  public void error(SAXParseException e) throws SAXException;
```

```
    public void fatalError(SAXParseException e) throws SAXException;

  }
```

LocatorImpl

LocatorImpl is a class that parser vendors may implement to help them provide the optional Locator interface. There's little reason for most developers to use it, although occasionally it may be useful if you want to provide pseudo-location information from a filter or nonparser-based XMLReader, or if you want to take a persistent snapshot of location information at some point in the parse process.

```
package org.xml.sax.helpers;

public class LocatorImpl implements Locator {

  public LocatorImpl();
  public LocatorImpl(Locator locator);

  public String getPublicId();
  public String getSystemId();
  public int    getLineNumber();
  public int    getColumnNumber();

  public void setPublicId(String publicID);
  public void setSystemId(String systemID);
  public void setLineNumber(int lineNumber);
  public void setColumnNumber(int columnNumber);

}
```

NamespaceSupport

The NamespaceSupport class provides a stack for storing namespace-prefix-to-URI mappings. It's useful when a program needs to resolve namespace prefixes that occur in attribute values and element content. You can reuse a NamespaceSupport object for multiple documents, but if you do so, you need to call reset() in between documents (typically in startDocument()).

```
package org.xml.sax.helpers;

public class NamespaceSupport  {
```

```
  public static final String XMLNS;

  public NamespaceSupport();

  public void        reset();
  public void        pushContext();
  public void        popContext();
  public boolean     declarePrefix(String prefix, String uri);
  public String[]    processName(String qualifiedName,
   String parts, boolean isAttribute);

  public String      getURI(String prefix);
  public Enumeration getPrefixes();
  public String      getPrefix(String uri);
  public Enumeration getPrefixes(String uri);
  public Enumeration getDeclaredPrefixes();

}
```

ParserAdapter

ParserAdapter uses the adapter design pattern to convert SAX1 Parser objects into SAX2 XMLReader objects. Given the large number of high-quality, native SAX2 parsers now available, there's little reason to use this class anymore.

```
package org.xml.sax.helpers;

public class ParserAdapter implements XMLReader, DocumentHandler {

  public ParserAdapter() throws SAXException;
  public ParserAdapter(Parser parser);

  // XMLReader methods
  public void setFeature(String name, boolean state)
   throws SAXNotRecognizedException, SAXNotSupportedException;
  public boolean getFeature(String name)
   throws SAXNotRecognizedException, SAXNotSupportedException;
  public void setProperty(String name, Object value)
   throws SAXNotRecognizedException, SAXNotSupportedException;
  public Object getProperty(String name)
   throws SAXNotRecognizedException, SAXNotSupportedException;
  public void setEntityResolver(EntityResolver resolver);
```

```
    public EntityResolver getEntityResolver();
    public void setDTDHandler(DTDHandler handler);
    public DTDHandler getDTDHandler();
    public void setContentHandler(ContentHandler handler);
    public ContentHandler getContentHandler();
    public void setErrorHandler(ErrorHandler handler);
    public ErrorHandler getErrorHandler();

    public void parse(String systemID)
     throws IOException, SAXException;
    public void parse(InputSource input)
     throws IOException, SAXException;

    // DocumentHandler methods
    public void setDocumentLocator(Locator locator);
    public void startDocument() throws SAXException;
    public void endDocument() throws SAXException;
    public void startElement(String qualifiedName,
     AttributeList qAtts) throws SAXException;
    public void endElement(String qualifiedName)
     throws SAXException;
    public void characters(char[] text, int start, int length)
     throws SAXException;
    public void ignorableWhitespace(char[] space, int start,
     int length) throws SAXException;
    public void processingInstruction(String target, String data)
     throws SAXException;

  }
```

ParserFactory

ParserFactory is a factory class used to create implementation-specific instances of the SAX1 Parser class. The *org.xml.sax.parser* Java system property determines its default implementation. ParserFactory is now deprecated like the rest of SAX1 and should no longer be used.

```
  package org.xml.sax.helpers;

  public class ParserFactory {
```

```
    public static Parser makeParser()
     throws ClassNotFoundException, IllegalAccessException,
            InstantiationException, NullPointerException,
            ClassCastException;
    public static Parser makeParser(String className)
     throws ClassNotFoundException, IllegalAccessException,
            InstantiationException, ClassCastException;

}
```

XMLFilterImpl

Although there is a more generic XMLFilter interface, XMLFilterImpl is the class you should actually subclass to implement SAX filters. The parent XMLReader is the object from which the filter will receive its information. By default, all of the methods in this class simply delegate to the parent's equivalent methods or objects, but you can override any or all of them to perform the filtering.

```
package org.xml.sax.helpers;

public class XMLFilterImpl
 implements XMLFilter, EntityResolver, DTDHandler,
            ContentHandler, ErrorHandler {

  public XMLFilterImpl();
  public XMLFilterImpl(XMLReader parent);

  public void      setParent(XMLReader parent);
  public XMLReader getParent();

  // XMLReader methods
  public void           setFeature(String name, boolean state)
   throws SAXNotRecognizedException, SAXNotSupportedException;
  public boolean        getFeature(String name)
   throws SAXNotRecognizedException, SAXNotSupportedException;
  public void           setProperty(String name, Object value)
   throws SAXNotRecognizedException, SAXNotSupportedException;
  public Object         getProperty(String name)
   throws SAXNotRecognizedException, SAXNotSupportedException;
  public void          setEntityResolver(EntityResolver resolver);
  public EntityResolver getEntityResolver();
  public void           setDTDHandler(DTDHandler handler);
```

```
public DTDHandler      getDTDHandler();
public void           setContentHandler(ContentHandler handler);
public ContentHandler getContentHandler();
public void           setErrorHandler(ErrorHandler handler);
public ErrorHandler   getErrorHandler();

public void           parse(InputSource input)
 throws SAXException, IOException;
public void           parse(String systemID)
 throws SAXException, IOException;

// EntityResolver methods
public InputSource resolveEntity(String publicID,
 String systemID) throws SAXException, IOException;

// DTDHandler methods
public void notationDecl(String name, String publicID,
 String systemID) throws SAXException;
public void unparsedEntityDecl(String name, String publicID,
 String systemID, String notationName) throws SAXException;

// ContentHandler methods
public void setDocumentLocator(Locator locator);
public void startDocument() throws SAXException;
public void endDocument() throws SAXException;
public void startPrefixMapping(String prefix, String uri)
 throws SAXException;
public void endPrefixMapping(String prefix)
 throws SAXException;
public void startElement(String uri, String localName,
 String qualifiedName, Attributes atts) throws SAXException;
public void endElement(String uri, String localName,
 String qualifiedName) throws SAXException;
public void characters(char[] text, int start, int length)
 throws SAXException;
public void ignorableWhitespace(char[] space, int start,
 int length) throws SAXException;
public void processingInstruction(String target, String data)
 throws SAXException;
public void skippedEntity(String name) throws SAXException;
```

```
  // ErrorHandler methods
  public void warning(SAXParseException e) throws SAXException;
  public void error(SAXParseException e) throws SAXException;
  public void fatalError(SAXParseException e)
   throws SAXException;

}
```

XMLReaderAdapter

XMLReaderAdapter uses the adapter design pattern to convert SAX2 XMLReader objects into SAX1 Parser objects for compatibility with legacy code.

```
package org.xml.sax.helpers;

public class XMLReaderAdapter implements Parser, ContentHandler {

  public XMLReaderAdapter() throws SAXException;
  public XMLReaderAdapter(XMLReader xmlReader);

  // Parser methods
  public void setLocale(Locale locale) throws SAXException;
  public void setEntityResolver(EntityResolver resolver);
  public void setDTDHandler(DTDHandler handler);
  public void setDocumentHandler(DocumentHandler handler);
  public void setErrorHandler(ErrorHandler handler);

  public void parse(String systemID)
   throws IOException, SAXException;
  public void parse(InputSource input)
   throws IOException, SAXException;

  // ContentHandler methods
  public void setDocumentLocator(Locator locator);
  public void startDocument() throws SAXException;
  public void endDocument() throws SAXException;
  public void startPrefixMapping(String prefix, String uri);
  public void endPrefixMapping(String prefix);
  public void startElement(String uri, String localName,
   String qualifiedName, Attributes atts) throws SAXException;
  public void endElement(String uri, String localName,
   String qualifiedName) throws SAXException;
```

```
  public void characters(char[] text, int start, int length)
   throws SAXException;
  public void ignorableWhitespace(char[] space, int start,
   int length) throws SAXException;
  public void processingInstruction(String target, String data)
   throws SAXException;
  public void skippedEntity(String name) throws SAXException;

}
```

XMLReaderFactory

`XMLReaderFactory` is a factory class used to create implementation-specific instances of `XMLReader`. The *org.xml.sax.driver* Java system property determines the default implementation.

```
package org.xml.sax.helpers;

public final class XMLReaderFactory  {

  public static XMLReader createXMLReader() throws SAXException;
  public static XMLReader createXMLReader(String className)
   throws SAXException;

}
```

DOM

The Document Object Model defines a tree-based representation of XML documents. The `org.w3c.dom` package contains the basic node classes that represent the different components which make up the tree. The `org.w3c.dom.traversal` package includes some useful utility classes for navigating, searching, and querying the tree.

DOM Level 2, the version described here, is incomplete. It does not define how a `DOMImplementation` is loaded, how a document is parsed, or how a document is serialized. For the moment, JAXP provides a stopgap solution. Eventually, DOM3 will fill in these holes, but because it was far from complete at the time of this writing, this appendix covers DOM2 exclusively.

The DOM Data Model

Table A.1 summarizes the DOM data model with the name, value, parent, and possible children for each kind of node.

Table A.1 DOM2 Node Properties

Node Type	Name	Value	Parent	Children
Document	#document	Null	Null	Comment, processing instruction, zero or one document type, one element
Document type	Root element name specified by the DOCTYPE declaration	Null	Document	None
Element	Prefixed name	Null	Element, document, or document fragment	Comment, processing instruction, text, element, entity reference, CDATA section
Text	#text	Text of the node	Element, attr, entity, or entity reference	None
Attr	Prefixed name	Normalized attribute value	Element	Text, entity reference
Comment	#comment	Text of comment	Element, document, or document fragment	None

Node Type	Name	Value	Parent	Children
Processing instruction	Target	Data	Element, document, or document fragment	None
Entity reference	Name	Null	Element or document fragment	Comment, processing instruction, text, element, entity reference, CDATA section
Entity	Entity name	Null	Null	Comment, processing instruction, text, element, entity reference, CDATA section
CDATA section	#cdata-section	Text of the section	Element, entity, or entity reference	None
Notation	Notation name	Null	Null	None
Document fragment	#document-fragment	Null	Null	Comment, processing instruction, text, element, entity reference, CDATA section

One thing to keep in mind is the parts of the XML document that are not exposed in this data model:

- The XML declaration, including the version, standalone, and encoding declarations. These will be added as properties of the document node in DOM3, but current parsers do not provide them.

- Most information from the DTD and/or schema is not provided including element and attribute types and content models. DOM3 will add some of this.
- Any white space outside the root element.
- Whether or not each character was provided by a character reference. Parsers may provide information about entity references but are not required to do so.

A DOM program cannot manipulate any of these constructs. It cannot, for example, read in an XML document and then write it out again in the same encoding as in the original document, because it doesn't know what encoding the original document used. It cannot treat `$var` differently than `$var`, because it doesn't know which was originally written.

org.w3c.dom

The `org.w3c.dom` package contains the core interfaces that are used to form DOM documents. `Node` is the common superinterface that all of these node types share. In addition, this package contains a few data structures used to hold collections of DOM nodes and one exception class.

Attr

The `Attr` interface represents an attribute node. Its node properties are defined as follows:

Node name	The full name of the attribute, including a prefix and a colon if the attribute is in a namespace
Node value	The attribute's normalized value
Local name	The local part of the attribute's name
Namespace URI	The namespace URI of the attribute, or null if the attribute does not have a prefix
Namespace prefix	The namespace prefix of the attribute, or null if the attribute is not in a namespace

`Attr` objects are not part of the tree, and they have neither parents nor siblings. `getParentNode()`, `getPreviousSibling()`, and `getNextSibling()` all return null when invoked on an `Attr` object. `Attr` objects do have children (`Text` and `EntityReference` objects), but it's generally best to ignore this and simply use the `getValue()` method to read the value of an attribute.

```
package org.w3c.dom;

public interface Attr extends Node {

  public String  getName();
  public boolean getSpecified();
  public String  getValue();
  public void    setValue(String value) throws DOMException;
  public Element getOwnerElement();

}
```

CDATASection

The `CDATASection` interface represents a CDATA section. DOM parsers are not required to use this interface to report CDATA sections. They may just use `Text` objects to report the content of CDATA sections. Do not write code that depends on recognizing CDATA sections in text. The node properties of `CDATASection` are defined as follows:

Node name	`#cdata-section`
Node value	The text of the CDATA section
Local name	null
Namespace URI	null
Namespace prefix	null

```
package org.w3c.dom;

public interface CDATASection extends Text {

}
```

CharacterData

The `CharacterData` interface is the generic superinterface for nodes composed of plain text: `Comment`, `Text`, and `CDATASection`. All actual instances of `CharacterData` should be instances of one of these subinterfaces. The node properties depend on the specific subinterface.

```
package org.w3c.dom;

public interface CharacterData extends Node {

  public String getData() throws DOMException;
  public void   setData(String data) throws DOMException;
  public int    getLength();
  public String substringData(int offset, int count)
   throws DOMException;
  public void   appendData(String s) throws DOMException;
  public void   insertData(int offset, String s)
   throws DOMException;
  public void   deleteData(int offset, int count)
   throws DOMException;
  public void   replaceData(int offset, int count, String s)
   throws DOMException;

}
```

Comment

The `Comment` interface represents a comment node. It inherits all of its methods from the `CharacterData` and `Node` superinterfaces. Its node properties are defined as follows:

Node name	`#comment`
Node value	The text of the comment, not including `<--`and `-->`
Local name	null
Namespace URI	null
Namespace prefix	null

```
package org.w3c.dom;

public interface Comment extends CharacterData {

}
```

Document

The `Document` interface represents the root node of the tree. It also serves as an abstract factory to create the other kinds of nodes (element, attribute, comment, and so on) that will be stored in the tree. Its node properties are defined as follows:

Node name	`#document`
Node value	null
Local name	null
Namespace URI	null
Namespace prefix	null

```
package org.w3c.dom;

public interface Document extends Node {

  public DocumentType          getDoctype();
  public DOMImplementation     getImplementation();
  public Element               getDocumentElement();

  public Element               createElement(String tagName)
   throws DOMException;
  public Element               createElementNS(
   String namespaceURI, String qualifiedName) throws DOMException;
  public Attr                  createAttribute(String name)
   throws DOMException;
  public Attr                  createAttributeNS(
   String namespaceURI, String qualifiedName) throws DOMException;
  public DocumentFragment      createDocumentFragment();
  public Text                  createTextNode(String data);
  public Comment               createComment(String data);
  public CDATASection          createCDATASection(String data)
   throws DOMException;
```

```
  public ProcessingInstruction createProcessingInstruction(
   String target, String data) throws DOMException;
  public EntityReference       createEntityReference(String name)
   throws DOMException;

  public NodeList getElementsByTagName(String tagName);
  public Node     importNode(Node importedNode, boolean deep)
   throws DOMException;
  public NodeList getElementsByTagNameNS(String namespaceURI,
   String localName);
  public Element  getElementById(String id);

}
```

DocumentFragment

The `DocumentFragment` interface is used to hold lists of element, text, comment, CDATA section, and processing instruction nodes when those nodes do not have a parent. It's convenient for cutting and pasting or inserting and moving fragments of an XML document that don't necessarily contain a single element.

The node properties of `DocumentFragment` are defined as follows:

Node name	`#document-fragment`
Node value	null
Local name	null
Namespace URI	null
Namespace prefix	null

```
package org.w3c.dom;

public interface DocumentFragment extends Node {

}
```

This interface is for advanced use only. DOM trees created by a parser won't contain any `DocumentFragment` objects, and adding a `DocumentFragment` to a `Document` actually adds the contents of the fragment instead.

DocumentType

The `DocumentType` interface represents a document type declaration. It contains the root element name it declares, the system ID and public ID for the external DTD subset, and the complete internal DTD subset as a `String`. It also contains lists of the notations and general entities declared in the DTD. Otherwise it contains no information from the DTD. The node properties of a `DocumentType` object are defined as follows:

Node name	declared root element name
Node value	null
Local name	null
Namespace URI	null
Namespace prefix	null

```
package org.w3c.dom;

public interface DocumentType extends Node {

  public String getName();
  public String getPublicId();
  public String getSystemId();
  public String getInternalSubset();

  public NamedNodeMap getEntities();
  public NamedNodeMap getNotations();


}
```

In DOM2, the entire `DocumentType` object is read-only. No part of it can be modified. Furthermore, a `Document` object's `DocumentType` cannot be changed after the `Document` object is created. This restriction is lifted in DOM3.

DOM2 does not provide any representation of the document type definition (DTD) as distinguished from the document type declaration.

DOMImplementation

DOMImplementation is an abstract factory used to create new Document and DocumentType objects. The javax.xml.parsers.DocumentBuilder class can create new DOMImplementation objects.

```
package org.w3c.dom;

public interface DOMImplementation {

  public DocumentType createDocumentType(String qualifiedName,
   String publicID, String systemID) throws DOMException;
  public Document     createDocument(String namespaceURI,
   String qualifiedName, DocumentType doctype)
    throws DOMException;

  public boolean hasFeature(String feature, String version);

}
```

Element

The Element interface represents an element node. The most important methods for this interface are inherited from the Node superinterface. Its node properties are defined as follows:

Node name	The qualified name of the element, possibly including a prefix and a colon
Node value	null
Local name	The local part of the element name
Namespace URI	The namespace URI of the element, or null if this element is not in a namespace
Namespace prefix	The namespace prefix of the element, or null if this element is in the default namespace or no namespace at all

```
package org.w3c.dom;

public interface Element extends Node {
```

```
    public String   getTagName();
    public NodeList getElementsByTagNameNS(String namespaceURI,
     String localName);
    public NodeList getElementsByTagName(String name);

    public String  getAttribute(String name);
    public void    setAttribute(String name, String value)
     throws DOMException;
    public void    removeAttribute(String name)
     throws DOMException;
    public Attr    getAttributeNode(String name);
    public Attr    setAttributeNode(Attr newAttr)
     throws DOMException;
    public Attr    removeAttributeNode(Attr oldAttr)
     throws DOMException;
    public String  getAttributeNS(String namespaceURI,
     String localName);
    public void    setAttributeNS(String namespaceURI,
     String qualifiedName, String value) throws DOMException;
    public void    removeAttributeNS(String namespaceURI,
     String localName) throws DOMException;
    public Attr    getAttributeNodeNS(String namespaceURI,
     String localName);
    public Attr    setAttributeNodeNS(Attr newAttr)
     throws DOMException;
    public boolean hasAttribute(String name);
    public boolean hasAttributeNS(String namespaceURI,
     String localName);

}
```

Entity
The `Entity` interface represents an entity node. It does not appear directly in the tree; instead, an `EntityReference` node appears in the tree. The name of the `EntityReference` identifies a member of the document's entities map, which is accessible through the `DocumentType` interface. If the `Entity` object represents a parsed entity and the parser resolved the entity, then this node will have children that represent its replacement text. All aspects of the `Entity` object, including all of its children, are read-only. They cannot be modified or changed in any way.

The node properties of `Entity` are defined as follows:

Node name	The name of the entity
Node value	null
Local name	null
Namespace URI	null
Namespace prefix	null

```
package org.w3c.dom;

public interface Entity extends Node {

  public String getPublicId();
  public String getSystemId();
  public String getNotationName();

}
```

Because `Entity` objects are not part of the tree, they have neither parents nor siblings. `getParentNode()`, `getPreviousSibling()`, and `getNextSibling()` all return null when invoked on an `Entity` object.

EntityReference

The `EntityReference` interface represents a parsed entity reference that appears in the document tree. Parsers are not required to use this class. Some parsers silently resolve all entity references to their replacement text. If a parser does not resolve external entity references, then it must include `EntityReference` objects instead, although the only information available from these objects will be the name. A parser that does resolve external entity references and chooses to include `EntityReference` objects anyway will also set the children of this node, so as to represent the entity's replacement text. In this case, you can use the methods inherited from the `Node` superinterface to walk the entity's tree. Note, however, that all of these children and their descendants are completely read-only, and you will not be able to change them in any way. If you need to modify them, you must first clone each of the `EntityReference` children, and then replace the `EntityReference` with the cloned children.

`EntityReference` objects are never used for the five predefined entity references (`<`, `>`, `&`, `"`, and `'`,) or for character references such as ` ` or ` `.

The node properties of `EntityReference` are defined as follows:

Node name	The name of the entity
Node value	null
Local name	null
Namespace URI	null
Namespace prefix	null

```
package org.w3c.dom;

public interface EntityReference extends Node {

}
```

NamedNodeMap

DOM uses `NamedNodeMap` data structures to hold unordered sets of attributes, notations, and entities. You can iterate through a map using `item()` and `getLength()`. The first item in the map is at index 0. Note that the particular order the implementation chooses is not significant or even reproducible.

```
package org.w3c.dom;

public interface NamedNodeMap  {

  public Node getNamedItem(String name);
  public Node setNamedItem(Node node) throws DOMException;
  public Node removeNamedItem(String name) throws DOMException;
  public Node item(int index);
  public int  getLength();
  public Node getNamedItemNS(String namespaceURI,
   String localName);
  public Node setNamedItemNS(Node node) throws DOMException;
  public Node removeNamedItemNS(String namespaceURI,
   String localName) throws DOMException;

}
```

NamedNodeMaps are *live*. That is, adding an item to the map or removing an item from the map will add it to or remove it from whatever construct produced the map in the first place.

Node

Node is the key superinterface for almost all of the other classes in the org.w3c.dom package. It is the primary means by which you navigate, search, query, and occasionally even update an XML document with DOM.

```
package org.w3c.dom;

public interface Node {

  // Node type constants
  public static final short ELEMENT_NODE;
  public static final short ATTRIBUTE_NODE;
  public static final short TEXT_NODE;
  public static final short CDATA_SECTION_NODE;
  public static final short ENTITY_REFERENCE_NODE;
  public static final short ENTITY_NODE;
  public static final short PROCESSING_INSTRUCTION_NODE;
  public static final short COMMENT_NODE;
  public static final short DOCUMENT_NODE;
  public static final short DOCUMENT_TYPE_NODE;
  public static final short DOCUMENT_FRAGMENT_NODE;
  public static final short NOTATION_NODE;

  // Basic getter methods
  public String   getNodeName();
  public String   getNodeValue() throws DOMException;
  public void     setNodeValue(String value) throws DOMException;
  public short    getNodeType();
  public String   getNamespaceURI();
  public String   getPrefix();
  public void     setPrefix(String prefix) throws DOMException;
  public String   getLocalName();

  // Navigation methods
  public Node     getParentNode();
  public boolean  hasChildNodes();
  public NodeList getChildNodes();
  public Node     getFirstChild();
```

```
  public Node     getLastChild();
  public Node     getPreviousSibling();
  public Node     getNextSibling();
  public Document getOwnerDocument();

  // Attribute methods
  public boolean      hasAttributes();
  public NamedNodeMap getAttributes();

  // Tree modification methods
  public Node     insertBefore(Node newChild, Node refChild)
   throws DOMException;
  public Node     replaceChild(Node newChild, Node oldChild)
   throws DOMException;
  public Node     removeChild(Node oldChild) throws DOMException;
  public Node     appendChild(Node newChild) throws DOMException;

  // Utility methods
  public Node     cloneNode(boolean deep);
  public void     normalize();
  public boolean  isSupported(String feature, String version);

}
```

NodeList

`NodeList` is the basic DOM list type. Its most common use is for lists of children of an `Element` or `Document`. The index of the first item in the list is 0, as with Java arrays.

The actual data structure used to implement the list can vary from implementation to implementation, but one constant is that the lists are *live*. In other words, if a node is deleted or moved from its parent, then it is also deleted from all lists that were built from the children of that parent. Similarly, if a new node is added to some node, then it is also added to all lists that point to the children of that node.

```
package org.w3c.dom;

public interface NodeList  {

  public Node item(int index);
  public int  getLength();

}
```

Notation

The `Notation` interface represents a notation declared in the document's DTD. It does not have a position in the tree. The complete list of notations in the document is accessible through the `getNotations()` method of the `DocumentType` interface. Both this list and the individual `Notation` objects are read-only.

The node properties of `Notation` are defined as follows:

Node name	Notation name
Node value	null
Local name	null
Namespace URI	null
Namespace prefix	null

```
package org.w3c.dom;

public interface Notation extends Node {

  public String getPublicId();
  public String getSystemId();

}
```

ProcessingInstruction

The `ProcessingInstruction` interface represents a processing instruction node. Its node properties are defined as follows:

Node name	The target
Node value	The data
Local name	null
Namespace URI	null
Namespace prefix	null

```
package org.w3c.dom;

public interface ProcessingInstruction extends Node {

  public String getTarget();
  public String getData();
  public void   setData(String data) throws DOMException;

}
```

Text

The Text interface represents a text node. It can contain any characters that are legal in XML text, including characters such as the less-than sign and ampersand that may need to be escaped when the document is serialized. When a parser reads an XML document and builds a DOM tree, each Text object will contain the longest-possible contiguous run of text. However, DOM does not maintain this constraint as the document is manipulated in memory. Its node properties are defined as follows:

Node name	#text
Node value	The text of the node
Local name	null
Namespace URI	null
Namespace prefix	null

The Text interface declares only one method of its own, splitText(). Most of its functionality is inherited from the superinterfaces CharacterData and Node.

```
package org.w3c.dom;

public interface Text extends CharacterData {

  public Text splitText(int offset) throws DOMException;

}
```

Exceptions and Errors

DOM2 defines only one exception class, `DOMException`. This is a runtime exception used for almost anything that can go wrong while constructing or manipulating a DOM `Document`. The details are provided by a short field, `code`, which is set to any of several named constants.

```
package org.w3c.dom;

public class DOMException extends RuntimeException {

  public short code;

  public static final short INDEX_SIZE_ERR;
  public static final short DOMSTRING_SIZE_ERR;
  public static final short HIERARCHY_REQUEST_ERR;
  public static final short WRONG_DOCUMENT_ERR;
  public static final short INVALID_CHARACTER_ERR;
  public static final short NO_DATA_ALLOWED_ERR;
  public static final short NO_MODIFICATION_ALLOWED_ERR;
  public static final short NOT_FOUND_ERR;
  public static final short NOT_SUPPORTED_ERR;
  public static final short INUSE_ATTRIBUTE_ERR;
  public static final short INVALID_STATE_ERR;
  public static final short SYNTAX_ERR;
  public static final short INVALID_MODIFICATION_ERR;
  public static final short NAMESPACE_ERR;
  public static final short INVALID_ACCESS_ERR;

  public DOMException(short code, String message);

}
```

org.w3c.dom.traversal

The DOM traversal API in the `org.w3c.dom.traversal` package provides some convenience classes for navigating and searching an XML document. The most useful aspect of this class is the capability to get lists and trees that contain the kinds of nodes that you're interested in while ignoring everything else.

DocumentTraversal

DocumentTraversal is a factory interface for creating new NodeIterator and TreeWalker objects that present a filtered view of the content of an element or a document. (You can filter other kinds of nodes, too, but there's not much point to this if they don't have any children.)

In implementations that support the traversal API (which can be determined by invoking the hasFeature("Traversal", "2.0") method in the Document or DOMImplementation classes) all objects that implement Document also implement DocumentTraversal. That is, to create a DocumentTraversal object, just cast a Document to DocumentTraversal.

```
package org.w3c.dom.traversal;

public interface DocumentTraversal  {

  public NodeIterator createNodeIterator(Node root,
   int whatToShow, NodeFilter filter, boolean expandEntities)
   throws DOMException;
  public TreeWalker createTreeWalker(Node root, int whatToShow,
   NodeFilter filter, boolean expandEntities)
   throws DOMException;

}
```

NodeFilter

The NodeFilter interface is used by NodeIterators and TreeWalkers to determine which nodes are included in the view of the document that they present to the client. Each node in the subtree will be passed to the filter's acceptNode() method. This returns one of the three named constants:

NodeFilter.FILTER_ACCEPT	Include the node.
NodeFilter.FILTER_REJECT	Do not include the node or any of its descendants when tree-walking; do not include the node but do include its descendants when iterating.
NodeFilter.FILTER_SKIP	Do not include the node but do include its children if they pass the filter individually.

In addition, this class has 13 named constants that can be combined with the bitwise operators and passed to `createNodeIterator()` and `createTreeWalker()` to specify which kinds of nodes should be included in their views.

```
package org.w3c.dom.traversal;

public interface NodeFilter  {

  public static final short FILTER_ACCEPT;
  public static final short FILTER_REJECT;
  public static final short FILTER_SKIP;

  public static final int SHOW_ALL;
  public static final int SHOW_ELEMENT;
  public static final int SHOW_ATTRIBUTE;
  public static final int SHOW_TEXT;
  public static final int SHOW_CDATA_SECTION;
  public static final int SHOW_ENTITY_REFERENCE;
  public static final int SHOW_ENTITY;
  public static final int SHOW_PROCESSING_INSTRUCTION;
  public static final int SHOW_COMMENT;
  public static final int SHOW_DOCUMENT;
  public static final int SHOW_DOCUMENT_TYPE;
  public static final int SHOW_DOCUMENT_FRAGMENT;
  public static final int SHOW_NOTATION;

  public short acceptNode(Node node);

}
```

NodeIterator

The `NodeIterator` interface presents a subset of nodes from the document as a list in document order. The list is *live;* that is, changes to the document are reflected in the list.

```
package org.w3c.dom.traversal;

public interface NodeIterator  {

  public Node       nextNode() throws DOMException;
  public Node       previousNode() throws DOMException;
```

```
    public Node       getRoot();
    public int        getWhatToShow();
    public NodeFilter getFilter();
    public boolean    getExpandEntityReferences();

    public void       detach();

  }
```

TreeWalker

The TreeWalker interface presents a subset of nodes from the document as a tree. Walking the TreeWalker is much like walking a full Document or Element, except that many of the node's descendants in which you aren't interested can be filtered out so they don't get in your way. The tree is *live;* that is, changes to the document are reflected in the tree.

```
package org.w3c.dom.traversal;

public interface TreeWalker  {

  public Node parentNode();
  public Node firstChild();
  public Node lastChild();
  public Node previousSibling();
  public Node nextSibling();
  public Node previousNode();
  public Node nextNode();

  public Node       getRoot();
  public int        getWhatToShow();
  public NodeFilter getFilter();
  public boolean    getExpandEntityReferences();
  public Node       getCurrentNode();
  public void       setCurrentNode(Node node)
   throws DOMException;

}
```

JAXP

JAXP, the Java API for XML Processing, is a fairly complete set of APIs for processing XML with Java. It is bundled with Java 1.4 and later, and available as a separate extension for Java 1.2 and later. (All pieces except TrAX should run in Java 1.1 and later.) JAXP is supported by most current XML parsers for Java, including Crimson, Ælfred, Xerces, Piccolo, and the Oracle XML Parser for Java. JAXP incorporates SAX and DOM by reference. In addition, it adds the Transformations API for XML (TrAX) and some factory classes for locating a parser and building new documents in memory. This section covers those factory classes, all of which are in the `javax.xml.parsers` package.

As well as adopting DOM and SAX into the core Java API, JAXP adds a few factory classes to fill some holes in these APIs and to enable Java programmers to write completely parser-independent code.

javax.xml.parsers

The one major innovation in JAXP not based on previous standards is a series of abstract factory classes in the `javax.xml.parsers` package. These enable a Java program to obtain a DOM parser, a SAX1 `Parser`, or a `DOMImplementation` in a parser-independent fashion. The SAX1 factories are now obsolete, but the DOM factories remain quite useful.

DocumentBuilder

The `DocumentBuilder` class is an abstract factory used to create new DOM `Document` and `DOMImplementation` objects. As well as creating new instances from scratch, `DocumentBuilder` can read a document from an `InputStream`, `Reader`, `File`, SAX `InputSource`, or URI.

```
package javax.xml.parsers;

public abstract class DocumentBuilder  {

  protected DocumentBuilder();

  public Document          newDocument();
  public DOMImplementation getDOMImplementation();

  public Document parse(InputStream in)
   throws SAXException, IOException;
  public Document parse(InputStream in, String systemID)
   throws SAXException, IOException;
```

```
  public Document parse(String uri)
   throws SAXException, IOException;
  public Document parse(File f)
   throws SAXException, IOException;
  public Document parse(InputSource in)
   throws SAXException, IOException;

  public boolean  isNamespaceAware();
  public boolean  isValidating();
  public void     setEntityResolver(EntityResolver resolver);
  public void     setErrorHandler(ErrorHandler handler);

}
```

DocumentBuilderFactory

The `DocumentBuilderFactory` class is an abstract factory used to create new `DocumentBuilder` objects. You should always call `setNamespaceAware(true)` before calling `newInstance(true)`.

```
package javax.xml.parsers;

public abstract class DocumentBuilderFactory  {

  protected DocumentBuilderFactory();

  public static DocumentBuilderFactory newInstance()
   throws FactoryConfigurationError;
  public DocumentBuilder newDocumentBuilder()
   throws ParserConfigurationException;

  public void    setNamespaceAware(boolean awareness);
  public void    setValidating(boolean validating);
  public void    setIgnoringElementContentWhitespace(
   boolean ignoreWhitespace);
  public void    setExpandEntityReferences(
   boolean expandEntities);
  public void    setIgnoringComments(boolean ignoreComments);
  public void    setCoalescing(boolean coalescing);
  public boolean isNamespaceAware();
  public boolean isValidating();
  public boolean isIgnoringElementContentWhitespace();
```

```
    public boolean isExpandEntityReferences();
    public boolean isIgnoringComments();
    public boolean isCoalescing();
    public void    setAttribute(String name, Object value)
     throws IllegalArgumentException;
    public Object  getAttribute(String name)
     throws IllegalArgumentException;

}
```

The various vendors provide different implementations of this abstract class. Java chooses the one to use based on the following conditions in order of preference:

1. The value of the *javax.xml.parsers.DocumentBuilderFactory* Java system property
2. The value of the *javax.xml.parsers.DocumentBuilderFactory* property specified in the `lib/jaxp.properties` properties file in the JRE directory
3. The first value found in a `META-INF/services/javax.xml.parsers.DocumentBuilderFactory` file in the JAR files available to the runtime
4. The platform default (`org.apache.crimson.jaxp.DocumentBuilderFactoryImpl` in Sun's JDK 1.4)

SAXParser

`SAXParser` is an obsolete class for locating SAX1 parsers and parsing documents. It's been replaced by the `org.xml.sax.helpers.XMLReaderFactory` class in SAX2.

```
package javax.xml.parsers;

public abstract class SAXParser  {

  protected SAXParser();

  public void parse(InputStream in, HandlerBase handler)
   throws SAXException, IOException;
  public void parse(InputStream in, HandlerBase handler,
   String systemID) throws SAXException, IOException;
```

```
  public void parse(InputStream in, DefaultHandler handler)
   throws SAXException, IOException;
  public void parse(InputStream in, DefaultHandler handler,
   String systemID) throws SAXException, IOException;
  public void parse(String uri, HandlerBase handler)
   throws SAXException, IOException;
  public void parse(String uri, DefaultHandler handler)
   throws SAXException, IOException;
  public void parse(File f, HandlerBase handler)
   throws SAXException, IOException;
  public void parse(File f, DefaultHandler handler)
   throws SAXException, IOException;
  public void parse(InputSource in, HandlerBase handler)
   throws SAXException, IOException;
  public void parse(InputSource in, DefaultHandler handler)
   throws SAXException, IOException;

  public Parser    getParser() throws SAXException;
  public XMLReader getXMLReader() throws SAXException;
  public boolean   isNamespaceAware();
  public boolean   isValidating();
  public void      setProperty(String name, Object value)
   throws SAXNotRecognizedException, SAXNotSupportedException;
  public Object    getProperty(String name)
   throws SAXNotRecognizedException, SAXNotSupportedException;

}
```

SAXParserFactory

SAXParserFactory is an obsolete class for building and configuring SAXParser objects in an implementation-independent fashion. The concrete subclass to load is read from the *javax.xml.parsers.SAXParserFactory* Java system property. This class has been replaced by the org.xml.sax.helpers.XMLReaderFactory class in SAX2, and there's little reason to use it anymore.

```
package javax.xml.parsers;

public abstract class SAXParserFactory  {

  protected SAXParserFactory();
```

```
  public static SAXParserFactory newInstance()
   throws FactoryConfigurationError;

  public SAXParser newSAXParser()
   throws ParserConfigurationException, SAXException;
  public void       setNamespaceAware(boolean awareness);
  public void       setValidating(boolean validating);
  public boolean    isNamespaceAware();
  public boolean    isValidating();
  public void       setFeature(String name, boolean value)
   throws ParserConfigurationException,
          SAXNotRecognizedException, SAXNotSupportedException;
  public boolean    getFeature(String name)
   throws ParserConfigurationException,
          SAXNotRecognizedException, SAXNotSupportedException;

}
```

Exceptions and Errors

The javax.xml.parsers package includes one error and one exception, to represent the things that can go wrong when loading a parser or a DOM implementation. Either one is normally a symptom of class path problems.

FactoryConfigurationError

A FactoryConfigurationError signals that Java is unable to load and instantiate the concrete factory class. This is normally a symptom of class path problems.

```
package javax.xml.parsers;

public class FactoryConfigurationError extends Error {

  public FactoryConfigurationError();
  public FactoryConfigurationError(String message);
  public FactoryConfigurationError(Exception e);
  public FactoryConfigurationError(Exception e, String message);

  public String    getMessage();
  public Exception getException();

}
```

ParserConfigurationException

A `ParserConfigurationException` signals that a factory is unable to load and instantiate a parser class.

```
package javax.xml.parsers;

public class ParserConfigurationException extends Exception {

  public ParserConfigurationException();
  public ParserConfigurationException(String message);

}
```

TrAX

The Transformations API for XML (TrAX) integrates XSLT processing into Java in a manner that is independent of both the specific XSLT processor and the document model. It works equally well with DOM, JDOM, SAX, and raw streams. Indeed, identity transforms can be used to transform one into the other.

javax.xml.transform

The `javax.xml.transform` package includes the base interfaces and abstract classes that provide abstract representations of both source and result XML documents and of the transformation itself. The subpackages specialize the sources and results for particular document models and APIs.

ErrorListener

`ErrorListener` is a callback interface that `Transformers` use to report problems which occur during a transformation. There are three levels of errors: fatal errors that prevent the transformation from continuing, recoverable errors, and warnings. If a `Transformer` does not have an `ErrorListener`, then it prints error messages on `System.err`.

```
package javax.xml.transform;

public interface ErrorListener  {

  public void warning(TransformerException exception)
   throws TransformerException;
```

```
    public void error(TransformerException exception)
     throws TransformerException;
    public void fatalError(TransformerException exception)
     throws TransformerException;

}
```

OutputKeys

The OutputKeys class defines named constants for serialization parameters that are normally set by an xsl:output element in an XSLT stylesheet. In TrAX, these are used as the name arguments to the setOutputProperty() and getOutputProperty() methods of the Transformer class.

```
package javax.xml.transform;

public class OutputKeys {

  public static final String METHOD = "method";
  public static final String VERSION = "version";
  public static final String ENCODING = "encoding";
  public static final String OMIT_XML_DECLARATION
   = "omit-xml-declaration";
  public static final String STANDALONE = "standalone";
  public static final String DOCTYPE_PUBLIC = "doctype-public";
  public static final String DOCTYPE_SYSTEM = "doctype-system";
  public static final String CDATA_SECTION_ELEMENTS
   = "cdata-section-elements";
  public static final String INDENT = "indent";
  public static final String MEDIA_TYPE = "media-type";

}
```

Result

The Result interface is a generic container for an XML document that will be produced by a transformation. Concrete classes implement this interface for SAX event sequences, DOM nodes, streams, and more.

```
package javax.xml.transform;

public interface Result {
```

```
    public static final String PI_DISABLE_OUTPUT_ESCAPING;
    public static final String PI_ENABLE_OUTPUT_ESCAPING;

    public void   setSystemId(String url);
    public String getSystemId();

}
```

Source

The Source interface is a generic container for existing XML documents that will be used in a transformation as either the input document or the stylesheet. Concrete classes implement this interface for SAX event sequences, DOM nodes, streams, and more.

```
package javax.xml.transform;

public interface Source  {

  public void   setSystemId(String systemID);
  public String getSystemId();

}
```

SourceLocator

SourceLocator objects are used by the various kinds of TransformerException to indicate where in which file the problem that caused the exception lies.

```
package javax.xml.transform;

public interface SourceLocator  {

  public String getPublicId();
  public String getSystemId();
  public int    getLineNumber();
  public int    getColumnNumber();

}
```

Templates

`Templates` is a thread-safe class that represents a compiled stylesheet. It can quickly create new `Transformer` objects without having to reread and reparse the original stylesheet. It's particularly useful when you want to use the same stylesheet in multiple threads.

```
package javax.xml.transform;

public interface Templates {

  public Transformer newTransformer()
   throws TransformerConfigurationException;

  public Properties  getOutputProperties();

}
```

Transformer

`Transformer` is the class that represents a compiled stylesheet. It transforms `Source` objects into `Result` objects. A single `Transformer` can transform multiple input documents in sequence but not in parallel.

```
package javax.xml.transform;

public abstract class Transformer  {

  protected Transformer();

  public void transform(Source input, Result output)
   throws TransformerException;

  public void          setParameter(String name, Object value);
  public Object        getParameter(String name);
  public void          clearParameters();
  public void          setURIResolver(URIResolver resolver);
  public URIResolver   getURIResolver();
  public void          setOutputProperties
   (Properties serialization) throws IllegalArgumentException;
  public Properties    getOutputProperties();
  public void          setOutputProperty(String name,
   String value) throws IllegalArgumentException;
```

```
    public String         getOutputProperty(String name)
     throws IllegalArgumentException;
    public void           setErrorListener(ErrorListener listener)
     throws IllegalArgumentException;
    public ErrorListener getErrorListener();

}
```

TransformerFactory

TransformerFactory is an abstract factory that creates new Transformer and Templates objects. The concrete subclass that newInstance()instantiates is specified by the *javax.xml.transform.TransformerFactory* Java system property. If this class is not set, a platform-dependent default class is chosen.

```
package javax.xml.transform;

public abstract class TransformerFactory  {

  protected TransformerFactory();

  public static TransformerFactory newInstance()
   throws TransformerFactoryConfigurationError;

  public Transformer newTransformer(Source source)
   throws TransformerConfigurationException;
  public Transformer newTransformer()
   throws TransformerConfigurationException;
  public Templates   newTemplates(Source source)
   throws TransformerConfigurationException;

  public Source        getAssociatedStylesheet(Source source,
   String media, String title, String charset)
   throws TransformerConfigurationException;
  public void          setURIResolver(URIResolver resolver);
  public URIResolver   getURIResolver();
  public boolean       getFeature(String name);
  public void          setAttribute(String name, Object value)
   throws IllegalArgumentException;
  public Object        getAttribute(String name)
   throws IllegalArgumentException;
```

```
    public void          setErrorListener(ErrorListener listener)
     throws IllegalArgumentException;
    public ErrorListener getErrorListener();

}
```

URIResolver

The XSLT processor passes any URLs encountered in the stylesheet's `xsl:import` or `xsl:include` elements or referenced by the `document()` function to its `URIResolver` in order to give the program a chance to substitute a different resource. Returning null indicates that the default resolution mechanism should be used. The pattern is very similar to that of the SAX `EntityResolver` class. You can specify a `URIResolver` object by passing it to the `setURIResolver()` method of either `Transformer` or `TransformerFactory`.

```
package javax.xml.transform;

public interface URIResolver  {

  public Source resolve(String href, String base)
   throws TransformerException;

}
```

Exceptions and Errors

TrAX includes several exceptions and errors for signaling problems that occur during a transformation. Most TrAX methods wrap all checked exceptions that occur during processing in one of the TrAX exception classes. For example, the `transform()` method does not throw an `IOException` if the network connection goes down while it's reading a remote input document. Instead it throws a `TransformerException`.

TransformerConfigurationException

A `TransformerConfigurationException` is a checked exception thrown when an attempt to create a new `Transformer` or `Templates` object fails. The usual reason is a syntax error in the stylesheet or an `IOException` that prevents the stylesheet from being read completely.

```
package javax.xml.transform;

public class TransformerConfigurationException
 extends TransformerException {
```

```
    public TransformerConfigurationException();
    public TransformerConfigurationException(String message);
    public TransformerConfigurationException(Throwable t);
    public TransformerConfigurationException(String message,
     Throwable t);
    public TransformerConfigurationException(String message,
     SourceLocator locator);
    public TransformerConfigurationException(String message,
     SourceLocator locator, Throwable t);

}
```

TransformerException

`TransformerException` is a checked exception that signals a problem which occurred during an attempted transformation. Possible causes include malformed input documents, and `IOExceptions` that prevent either the input document from being read or the output document from being written.

```
package javax.xml.transform;

public class TransformerException extends Exception {

  public TransformerException(String message);
  public TransformerException(Throwable t);
  public TransformerException(String message, Throwable t);
  public TransformerException(String message,
   SourceLocator locator);
  public TransformerException(String message,
   SourceLocator locator, Throwable t);

  public SourceLocator getLocator();
  public void          setLocator(SourceLocator location);
  public Throwable     getException();
  public Throwable     getCause();
  public Throwable     initCause(Throwable cause);
  public String        getMessageAndLocation();
  public String        getLocationAsString();
  public void          printStackTrace();
  public void          printStackTrace(PrintStream s);
  public void          printStackTrace(PrintWriter s);

}
```

TransformerFactoryConfigurationError

A `TransformerFactoryConfigurationError` indicates a problem with the `TransformerFactory`. The most common cause is that the specific concrete subclass of `TransformerFactory` indicated by the *javax.xml.transform.TransformerFactory* system property could not be found in the local class path. Unlike most errors, it's not a bad idea to catch this and handle it appropriately.

```
package javax.xml.transform;

public class TransformerFactoryConfigurationError extends Error {

  public TransformerFactoryConfigurationError();
  public TransformerFactoryConfigurationError(String message);
  public TransformerFactoryConfigurationError(Exception e);
  public TransformerFactoryConfigurationError(Exception e,
   String message);

  public String    getMessage();
  public Exception getException();

}
```

javax.xml.transform.stream

The `javax.xml.transform.stream` package contains classes that wrap streams as either input to a transformation or output from a transformation. Supported streams include files, `InputStreams` and `OutputStreams`, `Readers` and `Writers`, files, and URLs.

StreamResult

A `StreamResult` directs the output of an XSLT transformation onto an `OutputStream`, `Writer`, URL, file, or other sink of bytes or characters.

```
package javax.xml.transform.stream;

public class StreamResult implements Result {

  public static final String FEATURE;

  public StreamResult();
  public StreamResult(OutputStream out);
  public StreamResult(Writer writer);
```

```
  public StreamResult(String systemID);
  public StreamResult(File f);

  public void         setOutputStream(OutputStream out);
  public OutputStream getOutputStream();
  public void         setWriter(Writer out);
  public Writer       getWriter();
  public void         setSystemId(String url);
  public void         setSystemId(File f);
  public String       getSystemId();

}
```

If possible, use an `OutputStream` or a `File` instead of a `Writer` so that TrAX can determine where it might need to emit a character reference instead of the actual character. If you specify more than one of these three possibilities, then the one to which the processor writes will be implementation dependent.

StreamSource

A `StreamSource` provides input to an XSLT processor from an `InputStream`, `Reader`, URL, file, or other source of bytes or characters.

```
package javax.xml.transform.stream;

public class StreamSource implements Source {

  public static final String FEATURE;

  public StreamSource();
  public StreamSource(InputStream in);
  public StreamSource(InputStream in, String systemID);
  public StreamSource(Reader in);
  public StreamSource(Reader in, String systemID);
  public StreamSource(String url);
  public StreamSource(File f);

  public void         setInputStream(InputStream in);
  public InputStream  getInputStream();
  public void         set Reader(Reader in);
  public Reader       get Reader();
  public void         setPublicId(String publicID);
```

```
    public String     getPublicId();
    public void       setSystemId(String url);
    public String     getSystemId();
    public void       setSystemId(File f);

}
```

Always specify a system ID URL when creating a `StreamSource`. This is needed for resolving relative URLs that occur in the document. If you also specify an `InputStream`, `File`, or `Reader`, then that actual content will be read from that source instead of the URL. If you specify more than one of these three possibilities, then the one from which the processor reads will be implementation dependent.

javax.xml.transform.dom

The `javax.xml.transform.dom` package contains the classes needed to hook up DOM `Node` objects to TrAX transformations.

DOMLocator

The `DOMLocator` interface allows a `Transformer` reading from a `DOMSource` to report the actual DOM `Node` where an error occurred. To use this, you'll need to cast the `SourceLocator` returned by the `getLocator()` method in `Transformer` to `DOMLocator`. (Naturally this will fail if the original source was not a `DOMSource`.)

```
package javax.xml.transform.dom;

public interface DOMLocator extends SourceLocator {

  public Node getOriginatingNode();

}
```

DOMResult

A `DOMResult` uses the output of an XSLT transformation to create a new DOM `Document` or `DocumentFragment` object.

```
package javax.xml.transform.dom;

public class DOMResult implements Result {

  public static final String FEATURE;
```

```
    public DOMResult();
    public DOMResult(Node node);
    public DOMResult(Node node, String systemID);

    public void   setNode(Node node);
    public Node   getNode();
    public void   setSystemId(String url);
    public String getSystemId();

  }
```

DOMSource

A `DOMSource` provides input to an XSLT processor from a DOM `Node` object. In practice, only DOM `Document` objects can be transformed reliably, not arbitrary types of nodes.

```
  package javax.xml.transform.dom;

  public class DOMSource implements Source {

    public static final String FEATURE;

    public DOMSource();
    public DOMSource(Node node);
    public DOMSource(Node node, String systemID);

    public void   setNode(Node node);
    public Node   getNode();
    public void   setSystemId(String url);
    public String getSystemId();

  }
```

javax.xml.transform.sax

The `javax.xml.transform.sax` package contains the classes needed to hook up SAX event sequences (normally represented as `ContentHandlers`) to TrAX transformations.

SAXResult

A SAXResult passes the output of an XSLT transformation into a SAX ContentHandler (and optionally into a LexicalHandler). This allows you to post-process the output of a transform with a SAX program.

```
package javax.xml.transform.sax;

public class SAXResult implements Result {

  public static final String FEATURE;

  public SAXResult();
  public SAXResult(ContentHandler handler);

  public void           setHandler(ContentHandler handler);
  public ContentHandler getHandler();
  public void           setLexicalHandler(LexicalHandler handler);
  public LexicalHandler getLexicalHandler();
  public void           setSystemId(String systemID);
  public String         getSystemId();

}
```

SAXSource

A SAXSource provides input to an XSLT processor from a SAX event sequence. This is especially useful when you want to apply a SAX filter to a document before transforming it.

```
package javax.xml.transform.sax;

public class SAXSource implements Source {

  public static final String FEATURE;

  public SAXSource();
  public SAXSource(XMLReader reader, InputSource input);
  public SAXSource(InputSource input);

  public void        setXMLReader(XMLReader reader);
  public XMLReader   getXMLReader();
  public void        setInputSource(InputSource input);
  public InputSource getInputSource();
```

```
    public void         setSystemId(String url);
    public String       getSystemId();

    public static InputSource sourceToInputSource(Source source);

  }
```

SAXTransformerFactory

The SAXTransformerFactory class enables you to create Transformer and Templates objects that apply a SAX filter to the source document before transforming it.

```
  package javax.xml.transform.sax;

  public abstract class SAXTransformerFactory
   extends TransformerFactory {

    public static final String FEATURE;
    public static final String FEATURE_XMLFILTER;

    protected SAXTransformerFactory();

    public TransformerHandler newTransformerHandler(Source source)
     throws TransformerConfigurationException;
    public TransformerHandler newTransformerHandler(
     Templates templates) throws TransformerConfigurationException;
    public TransformerHandler newTransformerHandler()
     throws TransformerConfigurationException;
    public TemplatesHandler   newTemplatesHandler()
     throws TransformerConfigurationException;
    public XMLFilter          newXMLFilter(Source source)
     throws TransformerConfigurationException;
    public XMLFilter          newXMLFilter(Templates templates)
     throws TransformerConfigurationException;

  }
```

TemplatesHandler

TemplatesHandler is a ContentHandler that builds a Templates object from a SAX event sequence that reads a stylesheet. Client applications do not normally need to use this class directly.

```
package javax.xml.transform.sax;

public interface TemplatesHandler extends ContentHandler {

  public Templates getTemplates();
  public void      setSystemId(String url);
  public String    getSystemId();

}
```

TransformerHandler

`TransformerHandler` objects receive SAX events from a transformation and convert them into output. Client applications do not normally need to use this class directly.

```
package javax.xml.transform.sax;

public interface TransformerHandler
 extends ContentHandler, LexicalHandler, DTDHandler {

  public void        setResult(Result result)
   throws IllegalArgumentException;
  public void        setSystemId(String url);
  public String      getSystemId();
  public Transformer getTransformer();

}
```

JDOM

JDOM is an open source, pure Java API for reading, writing, and manipulating XML documents. This section provides complete signatures for the documented, public parts of JDOM, with the single exception of the `org.jdom.adapters` package, which is really intended only for internal use in JDOM.

org.jdom

The `org.jdom` package contains the core classes that JDOM uses to model the XML tree, one class per node type, as well as some generically useful classes such as `Verifier` and `JDOMException`.

> **Caution**
> JDOM is not finished at the time of this writing. This appendix is based on an early development release of JDOM beta 9, current as of May 17, 2002. I expect some of the details here to change before JDOM is released. (In fact, I'm actively lobbying for a few changes.)

Attribute

The `Attribute` class represents an attribute node. Each attribute has a local name, a namespace (which may be null), a string value, a type, and a parent `Element`. Attribute types are represented by the named `int` constants in this class.

```
package org.jdom;

public class Attribute implements Serializable, Cloneable {

  public static final int UNDECLARED_ATTRIBUTE;
  public static final int CDATA_ATTRIBUTE;
  public static final int ID_ATTRIBUTE;
  public static final int IDREF_ATTRIBUTE;
  public static final int IDREFS_ATTRIBUTE;
  public static final int ENTITY_ATTRIBUTE;
  public static final int ENTITIES_ATTRIBUTE;
  public static final int NMTOKEN_ATTRIBUTE;
  public static final int NMTOKENS_ATTRIBUTE;
  public static final int NOTATION_ATTRIBUTE;
  public static final int ENUMERATED_ATTRIBUTE;

  protected String    name;
  protected Namespace namespace;
  protected String    value;
  protected int       type;
  protected Object    parent;

  protected Attribute();
  public    Attribute(
   String name, String value, Namespace namespace)
   throws IllegalNameException, IllegalDataException;
  public    Attribute(
   String name, String value, int type, Namespace namespace)
   throws IllegalNameException, IllegalDataException;
```

```
public    Attribute(String name, String value)
 throws IllegalNameException, IllegalDataException;
public    Attribute(String name, String value, int type)
 throws IllegalNameException, IllegalDataException;

public    Element   getParent();
protected Attribute setParent(Element parent);
public    Document  getDocument();
public    Attribute detach();
public    String    getName();
public    Attribute setName(String name)
 throws IllegalNameException;
public    String    getQualifiedName();
public    String    getNamespacePrefix();
public    String    getNamespaceURI();
public    Namespace getNamespace();
public    Attribute setNamespace(Namespace namespace)
 throws IllegalNameException;
public    String    getValue();
public    Attribute setValue(String value);
public    int       getAttributeType();
public    Attribute setAttributeType(int type)
 throws IllegalDataException;

// Java utility methods
public       String  toString();
public final boolean equals(Object o);
public final int     hashCode();
public       Object  clone();

// Convenience methods for converting the value to various
// primitive types
public int     getIntValue() throws DataConversionException;
public long    getLongValue() throws DataConversionException;
public float   getFloatValue() throws DataConversionException;
public double  getDoubleValue() throws DataConversionException;
public boolean getBooleanValue()
 throws DataConversionException;

}
```

CDATA

The CDATA class is a subclass of Text (from which it inherits most of its functionality) that represents a CDATA section. The only real difference between this class and Text is that an XMLOutputter will use a CDATA section to write out the contents of a CDATA object rather than escaping characters such as the less-than sign with entity and character references.

```
package org.jdom;

public class CDATA extends Text {

  protected CDATA();
  public    CDATA(String s);

  public Text setText(String s) throws IllegalDataException;
  public void append(String s) throws IllegalDataException;

  public String toString();

}
```

Comment

The Comment class represents a comment node. Each Comment object contains the text of the comment, a parent Element (which will be null if this comment is in the prolog or epilog), and an owner Document.

```
package org.jdom;

public class Comment implements Serializable, Cloneable {

  protected String text;
  protected Object parent;

  protected Comment();
  public    Comment(String text) throws IllegalDataException;

  public    Element  getParent();
  protected Comment  setParent(Element parent);
  public    Comment  detach();
  public    Document getDocument();
  protected Comment  setDocument(Document document);
```

```
  public    String   getText();
  public    Comment  setText(String text)
   throws IllegalDataException;

  // Java utility methods
  public       String  toString();
  public final boolean equals(Object o);
  public final int     hashCode();
  public       Object  clone();

}
```

DocType

The `DocType` class represents a document type declaration. Each `DocType` object contains the declared root element name, the public ID and the system ID (both of which may be null), the owner document, and a `String` containing the internal DTD subset.

```
package org.jdom;

public class DocType implements Serializable, Cloneable {

  protected String   elementName;
  protected String   publicID;
  protected String   systemID;
  protected Document document;
  protected String   internalSubset;

  protected DocType();
  public    DocType(String elementName, String publicID,
   String systemID)
   throws IllegalNameException, IllegalDataException;
  public    DocType(String elementName, String systemID)
   throws IllegalNameException;
  public    DocType(String elementName)
   throws IllegalNameException;

  public    String   getElementName();
  public    DocType  setElementName(String elementName)
   throws IllegalNameException;
```

```
public    String   getPublicID();
public    DocType  setPublicID(String publicID)
 throws IllegalDataException;;
public    String   getSystemID();
public    DocType  setSystemID(String url);
public    Document getDocument();
protected DocType  setDocument(Document document);
public    void     setInternalSubset(String declarations);
public    String   getInternalSubset();

// Java utility methods
public       String  toString();
public final boolean equals(Object o);
public final int     hashCode();
public       Object  clone();

}
```

Document

The Document class represents a complete document and serves as the root of the JDOM tree. Each Document object contains a list of its content and the document's DocType (if it has one). Each Document should have exactly one Element in its content list. However, documents may be temporarily rootless. Almost anything you do to such a Document other than setting the root element will throw an IllegalStateException.

```
package org.jdom;

public class Document implements Serializable, Cloneable {

  protected ContentList content;
  protected DocType     docType;

  public Document();
  public Document(Element rootElement, DocType docType)
   throws IllegalAddException;
  public Document(Element rootElement);
  public Document(List newContent, DocType docType)
   throws IllegalAddException;
  public Document(List content) throws IllegalAddException;
```

```
  public boolean  hasRootElement();
  public Element  getRootElement() throws IllegalStateException;
  public Document setRootElement(Element rootElement);
  public Element  detachRootElement();
  public DocType  getDocType();
  public Document setDocType(DocType docType)
   throws IllegalAddException;
  public Document addContent(ProcessingInstruction pi);
  public Document addContent(Comment comment);
  public List     getContent();
  public List     getContent(Filter filter);
  public Document setContent(List newContent)
   throws IllegalAddException;
  public boolean  removeContent(ProcessingInstruction pi);
  public boolean  removeContent(Comment comment);

  // Java utility methods
  public       String  toString();
  public final boolean equals(Object o);
  public final int     hashCode();
  public       Object  clone();

}
```

Element

The Element class represents a complete element. Each element has a local name, a namespace (which may be null), a parent Element (which is null if this is the root element or not currently part of a document), a list of its children, a list of its attributes, and a list of any namespace prefixes declared on the element that are not used by the element or one of its attributes.

```
package org.jdom;

public class Element implements Serializable, Cloneable {

  protected String        name;
  protected Namespace     namespace;
  protected List          additionalNamespaces;
  protected Object        parent;
  protected AttributeList attributes;
  protected ContentList   content;
```

```
protected Element();
public    Element(String name, Namespace namespace)
 throws IllegalNameException;
public    Element(String name) throws IllegalNameException;
public    Element(String name, String uri)
 throws IllegalNameException;
public    Element(String name, String prefix, String uri)
 throws IllegalNameException;

public    String    getName();
public    Element   setName(String name)
 throws IllegalNameException;
public    Namespace getNamespace();
public    Element   setNamespace(Namespace namespace);
public    String    getNamespacePrefix();
public    String    getNamespaceURI();
public    Namespace getNamespace(String prefix);
public    String    getQualifiedName();
public    void      addNamespaceDeclaration(
 Namespace additional);
public    void      removeNamespaceDeclaration(
 Namespace additionalNamespace);
public    List      getAdditionalNamespaces();

public    Element   getParent();
protected Element   setParent(Element parent);
public    Element   detach();
public    boolean   isRootElement();
protected Element   setDocument(Document document);
public    Document  getDocument();
public    boolean   isAncestor(Element element);

public    String    getText();
public    Element   setText(String text);
public    String    getTextTrim();
public    String    getTextNormalize();

public    String    getChildText(String name);
public    String    getChildTextTrim(String name);
public    String    getChildTextNormalize(String name);
public    String    getChildText(String name, Namespace ns);
```

```
public    String    getChildTextTrim(String name,
 Namespace namespace);
public    String    getChildTextNormalize(String name,
 Namespace namespace);

public    List      getContent();
public    List      getContent(Filter filter);
public    Element   setContent(List newContent)
 throws IllegalAddException;
public    List      getChildren();
public    List      getChildren(String name);
public    List      getChildren(String name, Namespace ns);
public    Element   getChild(String name, Namespace ns);
public    Element   getChild(String name);
public    Element   addContent(String s)
 throws IllegalAddException;
public    Element   addContent(Text text)
 throws IllegalAddException;
public    Element   addContent(Element element)
 throws IllegalAddException;
public    Element   addContent(ProcessingInstruction pi)
 throws IllegalAddException;
public    Element   addContent(EntityRef ref)
 throws IllegalAddException;
public    Element   addContent(Comment comment)
 throws IllegalAddException;
public    boolean   removeChild(String name);
public    boolean   removeChild(String name, Namespace ns);
public    boolean   removeChildren(String name);
public    boolean   removeChildren(String name, Namespace ns);
public    boolean   removeContent(Element element);
public    boolean   removeContent(ProcessingInstruction pi);
public    boolean   removeContent(Comment comment);
public    boolean   removeContent(Text text);
public    boolean   removeContent(EntityRef entity);

// Attribute methods
public    List      getAttributes();
public    Attribute getAttribute(String name);
public    Attribute getAttribute(String name, Namespace ns);
public    String    getAttributeValue(String name);
```

```
  public    String    getAttributeValue(String name,
   Namespace ns, String def);
  public    String    getAttributeValue(String name, String def);
  public    String    getAttributeValue(String name,
   Namespace ns);
  public    Element   setAttributes(List newAttributes)
   throws IllegalAddException;
  public    Element   setAttribute(String name, String value)
   throws IllegalNameException, IllegalDataException;
  public    Element   setAttribute(String name, String value,
   Namespace ns)
   throws IllegalNameException, IllegalDataException;
  public    Element   setAttribute(Attribute attribute);
  public    boolean   removeAttribute(String name);
  public    boolean   removeAttribute(String name, Namespace ns);
  public    boolean   removeAttribute(Attribute attribute);

  // Java utility methods
  public        String  toString();
  public final boolean equals(Object o);
  public final int     hashCode();
  public        Object  clone();

}
```

EntityRef

The `EntityRef` class represents an unexpanded entity reference, such as might be produced by a nonvalidating parser that does not read the external DTD subset. Entity references for which the replacement text is known are not included as `EntityRef` objects. Instead their replacement text is parsed and included.

```
package org.jdom;

public class EntityRef implements Serializable, Cloneable {

  protected String name;
  protected String publicID;
  protected String systemID;
  protected Object parent;

  protected EntityRef();
  public    EntityRef(String name);
```

```
  public    EntityRef(String name, String systemID);
  public    EntityRef(String name, String publicID,
   String systemID);

  public    String    getName();
  public    EntityRef setName(String name)
   throws IllegalNameException;
  public    String    getPublicID();
  public    String    getSystemID();
  public    EntityRef setPublicID(String newPublicID)
   throws IllegalDataException;
  public    EntityRef setSystemID(String url)
   throws IllegalDataException;
  public    Document  getDocument();
  public    Element   getParent();
  public    EntityRef detach();
  protected EntityRef setParent(Element parent);

  // Java utility methods
  public       String  toString();
  public final boolean equals(Object o);
  public final int     hashCode();
  public       Object  clone();

}
```

Namespace

The Namespace class encapsulates a namespace URI and possibly a prefix. It uses the flyweight design pattern, so that twenty different elements in the same namespace share only one Namespace object between them.

```
package org.jdom;

public final class Namespace  {

  // empty string
  public static final Namespace NO_NAMESPACE;

  // http://www.w3.org/XML/1998/namespace
  public static final Namespace XML_NAMESPACE;
```

```
    // The constructor is private

    // Factory methods
    public static Namespace getNamespace(String prefix, String uri)
     throws IllegalNameException;
    public static Namespace getNamespace(String uri)
     throws IllegalNameException;

    public String getPrefix();
    public String getURI();

    // Java utility methods
    public       String  toString();
    public final boolean equals(Object o);
    public final int     hashCode();

  }
```

ProcessingInstruction

The `ProcessingInstruction` class represents a complete processing instruction. Each `ProcessingInstruction` has a target, data, a parent `Element` (which will be null if this instruction is in the prolog or epilog), and an owner `Document`. If the data is stored in pseudo-attributes, then there's also a map containing the pseudo-attributes separated into names and values. Not all processing instructions can be represented in this format, however.

```
package org.jdom;

public class ProcessingInstruction
 implements Serializable, Cloneable {

  protected String target;
  protected String rawData;
  protected Map    mapData;
  protected Object parent;

  protected ProcessingInstruction();
  public    ProcessingInstruction(String target, Map data)
   throws IllegalTargetException;
  public    ProcessingInstruction(String target, String data)
   throws IllegalTargetException;
```

```
  public    ProcessingInstruction setTarget(String newTarget)
   throws IllegalTargetException;
  public    String                getTarget();
  public    Element               getParent();
  protected ProcessingInstruction setParent(Element parent);
  public    ProcessingInstruction detach();
  public    Document              getDocument();
  protected ProcessingInstruction setDocument(Document document);
  public    String                getData();
  public    ProcessingInstruction setData(String data);

  public    ProcessingInstruction setData(Map data);
  public    List                  getNames();
  public    String                getValue(String name);
  public    ProcessingInstruction setValue(String name,
   String value);
  public    boolean               removeValue(String name);

  // Java utility methods
  public       String  toString();
  public final boolean equals(Object o);
  public final int     hashCode();
  public       Object  clone();

}
```

Text

The Text class represents a text node. In general, Text objects are not guaranteed to contain the maximum possible contiguous run of text, although this will be true of documents created by a SAXBuilder and not modified since. In common usage, you can ignore this class and use strings instead.

```
package org.jdom;

public class Text implements Serializable, Cloneable {

  protected String value;
  protected Object parent;

  protected Text();
  public    Text(String s) throws IllegalDataException;
```

```
  public String   getText();
  public String   getTextTrim();
  public String   getTextNormalize();
  public Text     setText(String s) throws IllegalDataException;
  public void     append(String s) throws IllegalDataException;
  public void     append(Text text) throws IllegalDataException;

  public Element  getParent();
  public Document getDocument();
  protected Text  setParent(Element parent);
  public Text     detach();

  public static String normalizeString(String s);

  // Java utility methods
  public       String  toString();
  public final boolean equals(Object o);
  public final int     hashCode();
  public       Object  clone();

}
```

Verifier

`Verifier` is a utility class the other JDOM classes rely on to decide whether or not particular strings are acceptable for particular purposes. For example, `TimeLimit` is a legal element name, but `Time Limit` is not. You will seldom need to use this class directly. If you do, then note that all of the various check methods return null if the argument passes the test and a nonempty string containing an error message if the test fails.

```
package org.jdom;

public final class Verifier  {

  public static String checkElementName(String name);
  public static String checkAttributeName(String name);
  public static String checkCharacterData(String text);
  public static String checkCDATASection(String data);
  public static String checkNamespacePrefix(String prefix);
  public static String checkNamespaceURI(String uri);
  public static String checkNamespaceCollision(
   Namespace namespace, Namespace other);
```

```
  public static String checkNamespaceCollision(
   Attribute attribute, Element element);
  public static String checkNamespaceCollision(
   Namespace namespace, Element element);
  public static String checkNamespaceCollision(
   Namespace namespace, Attribute attribute);
  public static String checkNamespaceCollision(
   Namespace namespace, List list);
  public static String checkProcessingInstructionTarget(
   String target);
  public static String checkCommentData(String data);
  public static String checkPublicID(String publicID);
  public static String checkSystemLiteral(String systemID);
  public static String checkXMLName(String name);

  public static boolean isXMLCharacter(char c);
  public static boolean isXMLNameCharacter(char c);
  public static boolean isXMLNameStartCharacter(char c);
  public static boolean isXMLLetterOrDigit(char c);
  public static boolean isXMLLetter(char c);
  public static boolean isXMLCombiningChar(char c);
  public static boolean isXMLExtender(char c);
  public static boolean isXMLDigit(char c);

}
```

Exceptions and Errors

JDOM defines a number of unique exceptions. `JDOMException` is the basic superclass for most checked exceptions that JDOM methods can throw. A few methods in the input and output packages also throw standard `IOExceptions`. Finally, JDOM provides several subclasses of `IllegalArgumentException` (a runtime exception) that are thrown when a program attempts to set XML constructs such as element names to illegal values.

DataConversionException

`DataConversionException` is thrown by the five `getInt/Long/Float/Double/BooleanValue()` methods in `Attribute` when the attribute value cannot be parsed as the requested type. This is a checked exception.

```
package org.jdom;

public class DataConversionException extends JDOMException {
```

```
  public DataConversionException(String message, String type);

}
```

IllegalAddException

`IllegalAddException` is thrown when code attempts to add a node where it doesn't belong. This could be because the new child already has a parent or because the new child can never be placed where you're trying to fit it (for example, adding `Text` object as a child of a `Document`). This is a runtime exception.

```
package org.jdom;

public class IllegalAddException
 extends IllegalArgumentException {

  public IllegalAddException(Element base, Attribute added,
   String reason);
  public IllegalAddException(Element base, Element added,
   String reason);
  public IllegalAddException(Document base, Element added,
   String reason);
  public IllegalAddException(Element base,
   ProcessingInstruction added, String reason);
  public IllegalAddException(Document base,
   ProcessingInstruction added, String reason);
  public IllegalAddException(Element base, Comment added,
   String reason);
  public IllegalAddException(Element base, CDATA added,
   String reason);
  public IllegalAddException(Element base, Text added,
   String reason);
  public IllegalAddException(Document base, Comment added,
   String reason);
  public IllegalAddException(Element base, EntityRef added,
   String reason);
  public IllegalAddException(Element base, Namespace added,
   String reason);
  public IllegalAddException(Document base, DocType added,
   String reason);
  public IllegalAddException(String reason);

}
```

IllegalDataException

An `IllegalDataException` is thrown when code attempts to set some text content to a string that does not satisfy XML well-formedness rules. Exactly what these rules are depends on context. For example, a comment cannot contain the two-hyphen string `--`. No content can include the ASCII vertical tab or bell characters, and so forth. The `data` argument contains the illegal text. This is a runtime exception.

```
package org.jdom;

public class IllegalDataException
 extends IllegalArgumentException {

  public IllegalDataException(String data, String construct,
   String reason);
  public IllegalDataException(String data, String construct);

}
```

IllegalNameException

An `IllegalNameException` is thrown when code attempts to set the name of an attribute, element, or entity reference to a string that is not a namespace well-formed XML name. This is a runtime exception.

```
package org.jdom;

public class IllegalNameException
 extends IllegalArgumentException {

  public IllegalNameException(String name, String construct,
   String reason);
  public IllegalNameException(String name, String construct);

}
```

IllegalTargetException

An `IllegalTargetException` is thrown when code attempts to set the target of a processing instruction to a string that is not a legal XML name. This is a runtime exception.

```
package org.jdom;

public class IllegalTargetException
 extends IllegalArgumentException {

  public IllegalTargetException(String target,
   String reason);
  public IllegalTargetException(String target);

}
```

JDOMException

`JDOMException` is the common superclass for the different kinds of checked exceptions that may be thrown while working with JDOM.

```
package org.jdom;

public class JDOMException extends Exception {

  protected Throwable cause;

  public JDOMException();
  public JDOMException(String message);
  public JDOMException(String message, Throwable cause);

  public Throwable initCause(Throwable cause);
  public Throwable getCause();
  public String    getMessage();
  public void      printStackTrace();
  public void      printStackTrace(PrintStream out);
  public void      printStackTrace(PrintWriter out);

}
```

org.jdom.filter

JDOM uses the filter package internally to ensure that client code doesn't do silly things such as adding a `java.io.InputStream` to an `Element`'s children, or slightly less silly but still illegal things such as adding a `Text` object to a `Document`'s children. You can also use filters in your own code to simplify navigation and search in XML documents.

ContentFilter

ContentFilter is the basic filter that allows you to specify what kinds of nodes you want to pass the filter. The actual filter is stored as an int mask. The individual node types are integral powers of two that set exactly one bit in the mask. As usual with bit masks, you can combine the different fields with the bitwise or operator |.

```
package org.jdom.filter;

public class ContentFilter implements Filter {

  public static final int ELEMENT;
  public static final int CDATA;
  public static final int TEXT;
  public static final int COMMENT;
  public static final int PI;
  public static final int ENTITYREF;
  public static final int DOCUMENT;

  protected int filterMask;

  public ContentFilter();
  public ContentFilter(boolean allVisible);
  public ContentFilter(int mask);

  public int  getFilterMask();
  public void setFilterMask(int mask);
  public void setDefaultMask();

  public void setDocumentContent();
  public void setElementContent();
  public void setElementVisible(boolean visible);
  public void setCDATAVisible(boolean visible);
  public void setTextVisible(boolean visible);
  public void setCommentVisible(boolean visible);
  public void setPIVisible(boolean visible);
  public void setEntityRefVisible(boolean visible);

  public boolean canAdd(Object o);
  public boolean canRemove(Object o);
  public boolean matches(Object o);
```

```
    public boolean equals(Object o);

  }
```

ElementFilter

The ElementFilter class enables you to define filters that pass only elements with a certain name, or a certain namespace, or a certain name in a certain namespace.

> **Note**
> It is likely that the behavior of the ElementFilter(String *name*) constructor will be changed to create a filter that selects elements with that name and no namespace rather than elements with that name in any namespace.

```
package org.jdom.filter;

public class ElementFilter implements Filter {

  protected String name;
  protected Namespace namespace;

  public ElementFilter();
  public ElementFilter(String name);
  public ElementFilter(Namespace namespace);
  public ElementFilter(String name, Namespace namespace);

  public boolean canAdd(Object o);
  public boolean canRemove(Object o);
  public boolean matches(Object o);
  public boolean equals(Object o);

}
```

Filter

The Filter interface identifies the child nodes that should appear in a JDOM list. Node objects for which matches() returns false are filtered out of the list.

```
package org.jdom.filter;

public interface Filter {
```

```
  public boolean canAdd(Object o);
  public boolean canRemove(Object o);
  public boolean matches(Object o);

}
```

> **Caution**
> The canAdd() and canRemove() methods are likely to be deprecated and then removed in the near future.

org.jdom.input

The `org.jdom.input` class contains classes involved with building JDOM objects from other formats such as XML files, DOM `Document` objects, and such.

BuilderErrorHandler

The `BuilderErrorHandler` class reports errors that occur during SAX parsing. By default it rethrows the exception to halt parsing for errors and fatal errors and ignores warnings. You seldom need to interact with this class directly.

```
package org.jdom.input;

public class BuilderErrorHandler
 implements org.xml.sax.ErrorHandler {

  public BuilderErrorHandler();

  public void warning(SAXParseException exception)
   throws SAXException;
  public void error(SAXParseException exception)
   throws SAXException;
  public void fatalError(SAXParseException exception)
   throws SAXException;

}
```

DefaultJDOMFactory

The `DefaultJDOMFactory` class is used by `SAXBuilder` and `DOMBuilder` to create standard, undecorated JDOM trees. You rarely need to use this class directly.

```
package org.jdom.input;

public class DefaultJDOMFactory implements JDOMFactory {

  public DefaultJDOMFactory();

  public Attribute             attribute(String name,
   String value, Namespace namespace)
   throws IllegalNameException, IllegalDataException;
  public Attribute             attribute(String name,
   String value, int type, Namespace namespace)
   throws IllegalNameException, IllegalDataException;
  public Attribute             attribute(String name,
   String value) throws IllegalNameException, IllegalDataException;
  public Attribute             attribute(String name,
   String value, int type)
   throws IllegalNameException, IllegalDataException;
  public CDATA                 cdata(String text)
   throws IllegalDataException;
  public Text                  text(String text)
   throws IllegalDataException;
  public Comment               comment(String text)
   throws IllegalDataException;
  public DocType               docType(String elementName,
   String publicID, String systemID)
   throws IllegalNameException, IllegalDataException;
  public DocType               docType(String elementName,
   String systemID) throws IllegalNameException,
    IllegalDataException;
  public DocType               docType(String elementName)
   throws IllegalNameException;
  public Document              document(Element rootElement,
   DocType docType) IllegalAddException;
  public Document              document(Element rootElement)
   throws IllegalAddException;
  public Element               element(String name,
   Namespace namespace) throws IllegalNameException;
  public Element               element(String name)
   throws IllegalNameException;
  public Element               element(String name, String uri)
   throws IllegalNameException;
```

```
  public Element                    element(String name,
   String prefix, String uri) throws IllegalNameException;
  public ProcessingInstruction processingInstruction(
   String target, Map data) throws IllegalTargetException;
  public ProcessingInstruction processingInstruction(
   String target, String data) throws IllegalTargetException;
  public EntityRef                  entityRef(String name)
   throws IllegalNameException;
  public EntityRef                  entityRef(String name,
   String publicID, String systemID)
   throws IllegalNameException, IllegalTargetException;

}
```

DOMBuilder

The `DOMBuilder` class converts DOM `org.w3c.dom.Document` objects into `org.jdom.Document` objects and DOM `org.w3c.dom.Element` objects into `org.jdom.Element` objects. It's useful when interoperating with DOM programs and libraries.

```
package org.jdom.input;

public class DOMBuilder  {

  public DOMBuilder();
  public DOMBuilder(String adapterClass);

  public void setFactory(JDOMFactory factory);

  public Document build(org.w3c.dom.Document domDocument)
   throws IllegalDataException;
  public Element  build(org.w3c.dom.Element  domElement)
   throws IllegalDataException;

}
```

JDOMFactory

`DOMBuilder` and `SAXBuilder` rely on a `JDOMFactory` to build node objects. You can implement this class in order to have the builder objects build subclasses of your own devising rather than the standard JDOM classes. This interface is for advanced use, and then only when subclassing the standard `org.jdom` classes.

```
package org.jdom.input;

public interface JDOMFactory  {

  public Attribute               attribute(String name,
   String value, Namespace namespace);
  public Attribute               attribute(String name,
   String value, int type, Namespace namespace);
  public Attribute               attribute(String name,
   String value);
  public Attribute               attribute(String name,
   String value, int type);
  public CDATA                   cdata(String text);
  public Text                    text(String text);
  public Comment                 comment(String text);
  public DocType                 docType(String elementName,
   String publicID, String systemID);
  public DocType                 docType(String elementName,
   String systemID);
  public DocType                 docType(String elementName);
  public Document                document(Element rootElement,
   DocType docType);
  public Document                document(Element rootElement);
  public Element                 element(String name,
   Namespace namespace);
  public Element                 element(String name);
  public Element                 element(String name, String uri);
  public Element                 element(String name,
   String prefix, String uri);
  public ProcessingInstruction processingInstruction(
   String target, Map data);
  public ProcessingInstruction processingInstruction(
   String target, String data);
  public EntityRef               entityRef(String name);
  public EntityRef               entityRef(String name,
   String publicID, String systemID);

}
```

SAXBuilder

SAXBuilder is the preferred means of parsing XML documents into JDOM. It relies on an underlying SAX parser, but it is agnostic about which parser is used.

```
package org.jdom.input;

public class SAXBuilder  {

  protected JDOMFactory factory;

  public SAXBuilder();
  public SAXBuilder(boolean validate);
  public SAXBuilder(String saxDriverClass);
  public SAXBuilder(String saxDriverClass, boolean validate);

  public void setFactory(JDOMFactory factory);
  public void setValidation(boolean validate);
  public void setErrorHandler(ErrorHandler errorHandler);
  public void setEntityResolver(EntityResolver entityResolver);
  public void setDTDHandler(DTDHandler dtdHandler);
  public void setXMLFilter(XMLFilter xmlFilter);
  public void setIgnoringElementContentWhitespace(
   boolean ignoringWhite);
  public void setFeature(String name, boolean value);
  public void setProperty(String name, Object value);
  public void setExpandEntities(boolean expand);

  public Document build(InputSource in)
   throws JDOMException, IOException;
  public Document build(InputStream in)
   throws JDOMException, IOException;
  public Document build(File file)
   throws JDOMException, IOException;
  public Document build(URL url)
   throws JDOMException, IOException;
  public Document build(InputStream in, String systemID)
   throws JDOMException, IOException;
  public Document build(Reader characterStream)
   throws JDOMException, IOException;
  public Document build(Reader characterStream, String SystemID)
   throws JDOMException, IOException;
```

```
    public Document build(String systemID)
     throws JDOMException, IOException;

    protected SAXHandler createContentHandler();
    protected void       configureContentHandler(
     SAXHandler contentHandler);
    protected XMLReader  createParser() throws JDOMException;
    protected void       configureParser(XMLReader parser,
     SAXHandler contentHandler) throws JDOMException;
    protected URL        fileToURL(File f)
     throws MalformedURLException;

  }
```

SAXHandler

SAXBuilder uses SAXHandler to receive information from the underlying SAX parser. It's extremely rare that you need to use this class yourself.

```
package org.jdom.input;

public class SAXHandler extends DefaultHandler
 implements LexicalHandler, DeclHandler, DTDHandler {

  protected Stack      stack;
  protected boolean    atRoot;
  protected boolean    inDTD;
  protected boolean    inInternalSubset;
  protected boolean    previousCDATA;
  protected boolean    inCDATA;
  protected boolean    suppress;
  protected LinkedList declaredNamespaces;
  protected LinkedList availableNamespaces;

  public SAXHandler();
  public SAXHandler(JDOMFactory factory);

  public Document    getDocument();
  public JDOMFactory getFactory();
  public Locator     getDocumentLocator();

  public void    setExpandEntities(boolean expand);
```

```
public boolean getExpandEntities();
public void    setIgnoringElementContentWhitespace(
 boolean ignoringWhite);
public boolean getIgnoringElementContentWhitespace();

// DeclHandler methods
public void    externalEntityDecl(String name,
 String publicID, String systemID)
 throws SAXException;
public void    attributeDecl(String elementName,
 String attributeName, String type, String valueDefault,
  String value) throws SAXException;
public void    elementDecl(String name, String model)
 throws SAXException;
public void    internalEntityDecl(String name, String value)
 throws SAXException;

// ContentHandler methods
public void setDocumentLocator(Locator locator);
public void startPrefixMapping(String prefix, String uri)
 throws SAXException;
public void endPrefixMapping(String prefix) throws SAXException;
public void startElement(String namespaceURI, String localName,
 String qualifiedName, Attributes atts)
  throws SAXException;
public void characters(char ch, int start, int length)
 throws SAXException;
public void ignorableWhitespace(char ch, int start, int length)
 throws SAXException;
public void skippedEntity(String name) throws SAXException;
public void processingInstruction(String target, String data)
 throws SAXException;
public void endElement(String namespaceURI, String localName,
 String qualifiedName) throws SAXException;

// LexicalHandler methods
public void startDTD(String name, String publicID,
 String systemID) throws SAXException;
public void endDTD() throws SAXException;
public void startEntity(String name) throws SAXException;
public void endEntity(String name) throws SAXException;
```

```
  public void startCDATA() throws SAXException;
  public void endCDATA() throws SAXException;
  public void comment(char ch, int start, int length)
   throws SAXException;

  // DTDHandler methods
  public void notationDecl(String name, String publicID,
   String systemID) throws SAXException;
  public void unparsedEntityDecl(String name, String publicID,
   String systemID, String notationName) throws SAXException;

  // Internal methods
  protected void    flushCharacters() throws SAXException;
  protected void    appendExternalId(String publicID,
   String systemID);
  protected Element getCurrentElement() throws SAXException;

}
```

org.jdom.output

The `org.jdom.output` package is responsible for converting JDOM `Document` objects into other forms, such as files, streams of text, DOM `Document` objects, and SAX event sequences.

DOMOutputter

The `DOMOutputter` class converts a JDOM `Document` object to a DOM `Document` object.

```
package org.jdom.output;

public class DOMOutputter  {

  public DOMOutputter();
  public DOMOutputter(String adapterClass);

  public org.w3c.dom.Document output(Document document)
   throws JDOMException;

  protected org.w3c.dom.Element output(Element element,
   org.w3c.dom.Document factory, NamespaceStack namespaces)
   throws JDOMException;
```

```
  protected org.w3c.dom.Attr    output(Attribute attribute,
   org.w3c.dom.Document factory) throws JDOMException;

}
```

SAXOutputter

The SAXOutputter class walks a JDOM Document tree while firing events at a SAX ContentHandler.

```
package org.jdom.output;

public class SAXOutputter  {

  public SAXOutputter();
  public SAXOutputter(ContentHandler contentHandler);
  public SAXOutputter(ContentHandler contentHandler,
   ErrorHandler errorHandler, DTDHandler dtdHandler,
   EntityResolver entityResolver);
  public SAXOutputter(ContentHandler contentHandler,
   ErrorHandler errorHandler, DTDHandler dtdHandler,
   EntityResolver entityResolver, LexicalHandler lexicalHandler);

  public void              setContentHandler(
   ContentHandler contentHandler);
  public ContentHandler getContentHandler();
  public void              setErrorHandler(
   ErrorHandler errorHandler);
  public ErrorHandler    getErrorHandler();
  public void              setDTDHandler(DTDHandler dtdHandler);
  public DTDHandler      getDTDHandler();
  public void              setEntityResolver(
   EntityResolver entityResolver);
  public EntityResolver getEntityResolver();
  public void              setLexicalHandler(
   LexicalHandler lexicalHandler);
  public LexicalHandler getLexicalHandler();
  public void              setDeclHandler(DeclHandler declHandler);
  public DeclHandler     getDeclHandler();

  public void     setReportNamespaceDeclarations(
   boolean declareNamespaces);
```

```
  public void    setReportDTDEvents(boolean reportDtdEvents);
  public void    setFeature(String name, boolean value)
   throws SAXNotRecognizedException, SAXNotSupportedException;
  public boolean getFeature(String name)
   throws SAXNotRecognizedException, SAXNotSupportedException;
  public void    setProperty(String name, Object value)
   throws SAXNotRecognizedException, SAXNotSupportedException;
  public Object  getProperty(String name)
   throws SAXNotRecognizedException, SAXNotSupportedException;

  public void output(Document document) throws JDOMException;

  protected XMLReader createParser() throws Exception;

}
```

XMLOutputter

The `XMLOutputter` class writes a JDOM `Document` onto an `OutputStream` or `Writer` or into a `String`. Using an `OutputStream` is preferable to using a `Writer` because it allows JDOM to more accurately determine which characters need to be escaped.

```
package org.jdom.output;

public class XMLOutputter implements Cloneable {

  public XMLOutputter();
  public XMLOutputter(String indent);
  public XMLOutputter(String indent, boolean newlines);
  public XMLOutputter(String indent, boolean newlines,
   String encoding);
  public XMLOutputter(XMLOutputter that);

  public void setLineSeparator(String separator);
  public void setNewlines(boolean newlines);
  public void setEncoding(String encoding);
  public void setOmitEncoding(boolean omitEncoding);
  public void setOmitDeclaration(boolean omitDeclaration);
  public void setExpandEmptyElements(boolean expandEmpties);
  public void setTrimAllWhite(boolean trimAllWhite);
  public void setTextTrim(boolean textTrim);
```

```
public void setTextNormalize(boolean textNormalize);
public void setIndent(String indent);

public void output(Document doc, OutputStream out)
 throws IOException;
public void output(DocType doctype, OutputStream out)
 throws IOException;
public void output(Element element, OutputStream out)
 throws IOException;
public void outputElementContent(Element element,
 OutputStream out) throws IOException;
public void output(List list, OutputStream out)
 throws IOException;
public void output(CDATA cdata, OutputStream out)
 throws IOException;
public void output(Text text, OutputStream out)
 throws IOException;
public void output(Comment comment, OutputStream out)
 throws IOException;
public void output(ProcessingInstruction pi, OutputStream out)
 throws IOException;
public void output(EntityRef entity, OutputStream out)
 throws IOException;

public void output(Document doc, Writer out)
 throws IOException;
public void output(DocType doctype, Writer out)
 throws IOException;
public void output(Element element, Writer out)
 throws IOException;
public void outputElementContent(Element element, Writer out)
 throws IOException;
public void output(List list, Writer out)
 throws IOException;
public void output(CDATA cdata, Writer out)
 throws IOException;
public void output(Text text, Writer out)
 throws IOException;
public void output(Comment comment, Writer out)
 throws IOException;
public void output(ProcessingInstruction pi, Writer out)
 throws IOException;
```

```
public void output(EntityRef entity, Writer out)
 throws IOException;

public String outputString(Document doc);
public String outputString(DocType doctype);
public String outputString(Element element);
public String outputString(List list);
public String outputString(CDATA cdata);
public String outputString(Text text);
public String outputString(String s);
public String outputString(Comment comment);
public String outputString(ProcessingInstruction pi);
public String outputString(EntityRef entity);

public String escapeAttributeEntities(String s);
public String escapeElementEntities(String s);

public int parseArgs(String args, int i);

protected Writer makeWriter(OutputStream out)
 throws UnsupportedEncodingException;
protected Writer makeWriter(OutputStream out, String enc)
 throws UnsupportedEncodingException;

protected void printDeclaration(Document doc, Writer out,
 String encoding) throws IOException;
protected void printDocType(DocType docType, Writer out)
 throws IOException;
protected void printComment(Comment comment, Writer out)
 throws IOException;
protected void printProcessingInstruction(
 ProcessingInstruction pi, Writer out) throws IOException;
protected void printEntityRef(EntityRef entity, Writer out)
 throws IOException;
protected void printCDATA(CDATA cdata, Writer out)
 throws IOException;
protected void printText(Text text, Writer out)
 throws IOException;
protected void printString(String s, Writer out)
 throws IOException;
protected void printElement(Element element, Writer out,
 int level,
```

```
    XMLOutputter.NamespaceStack namespaces) throws IOException;
   protected void printContentRange(List content, int start,
    int end, Writer out, int level, XMLOutputter.NamespaceStack
     namespaces) throws IOException;
   protected void printTextRange(List content, int start, int end,
    Writer out) throws IOException;
   protected void printAttributes(List attributes, Element parent,
    Writer out, XMLOutputter.NamespaceStack namespaces)
    throws IOException;
   protected void newline(Writer out) throws IOException;
   protected void indent(Writer out, int level)
    throws IOException;

   protected XMLOutputter.NamespaceStack createNamespaceStack();

   public Object clone();
   public String toString();

 }
```

XMLOutputter.NamespaceStack

The inner class `NamespaceStack` is used by `XMLOutputter` to keep track of which namespaces are in scope at any given point, and thus do not need to be redeclared. You only need to use this class if you're subclassing `XMLOutputter`.

```
package org.jdom.output;

protected class XMLOutputter.NamespaceStack
 extends NamespaceStack {

  protected XMLOutputter.NamespaceStack();

 }
```

org.jdom.transform

The `org.jdom.transform` package enables JDOM programs to interface with TrAX-based XSLT processors by providing JDOM implementations of the TrAX `Source` and `Result` interfaces.

JDOMResult

JDOMResult is useful as an output for TrAX transformations that produce JDOM Documents.

```
package org.jdom.transform;

public class JDOMResult extends SAXResult {

  public static final String JDOM_FEATURE;

  public JDOMResult();

  public void        setDocument(Document document);
  public Document    getDocument();
  public void        setFactory(JDOMFactory factory);
  public JDOMFactory getFactory();
  public void        setHandler(ContentHandler handler);
  public void        setLexicalHandler(LexicalHandler handler);

}
```

JDOMSource

JDOMSource is useful as an input for TrAX transformations that transform JDOM Documents.

```
package org.jdom.transform;

public class JDOMSource extends SAXSource {

  public static final String JDOM_FEATURE;

  public JDOMSource(Document source);

  public void      setDocument(Document source);
  public Document  getDocument();
  public void      setInputSource(InputSource inputSource)
   throws UnsupportedOperationException;
  public void      setXMLReader(XMLReader reader)
   throws UnsupportedOperationException;
  public XMLReader getXMLReader();

}
```

org.jdom.xpath

The `org.jdom.xpath` package provides a simple interface for XPath evaluation of JDOM `Documents`. Jaxen is the underlying implementation.

XPath

The `XPath` class allows you to evaluate XPath expressions relative to JDOM node objects.

```
package org.jdom.xpath;

public abstract class XPath implements Serializable {

  protected XPath(String expr) throws JDOMException;

  public static XPath newInstance(String path)
   throws JDOMException;

  public List   selectNodes(Object context)
   throws JDOMException;
  public Object selectSingleNode(Object context)
   throws JDOMException;
  public String valueOf(Object context) throws JDOMException;
  public Number numberValueOf(Object context)
   throws JDOMException;
  public void   setVariable(String name, Object value)
   throws IllegalArgumentException;
  public String getXPath();

  public static List   selectNodes(Object context, String path)
   throws JDOMException;
  public static Object selectSingleNode(Object context,
   String path) throws JDOMException;

}
```

XMLPULL

XMLPULL is the newest and perhaps the simplest API discussed in this book. It includes only one package, which contains one factory class, one interface representing the parser, and one exception. A pull parser works in streaming mode like a SAX parser. However, it waits for the client program to request the next event rather than pushing it to it. This section is based on version 1.0.8 of XMLPULL.

org.xmlpull.v1

The `org.xmlpull.v1` package includes all three parts of the XMLPULL API: `XmlPullParser`, `XmlPullParserFactory`, and `XmlPullParserException`.

XmlPullParser

The `XmlPullParser` interface represents the parser. It contains constant fields that represent type codes and features. It declares methods to get and set features and properties, to retrieve the next token from the parser, and to extract the data from that token.

```
package org.xmlpull.v1;

public interface XmlPullParser  {

  public static final String   NO_NAMESPACE;

  public static final int      START_DOCUMENT;
  public static final int      END_DOCUMENT;
  public static final int      START_TAG;
  public static final int      END_TAG;
  public static final int      TEXT;
  public static final byte     CDSECT;
  public static final byte     ENTITY_REF;
  public static final byte     IGNORABLE_WHITESPACE;
  public static final byte     PROCESSING_INSTRUCTION;
  public static final int      COMMENT;
  public static final int      DOCDECL;
  public static final String[] TYPES;

  public static final String FEATURE_PROCESS_NAMESPACES;
  public static final String FEATURE_REPORT_NAMESPACE_ATTRIBUTES;
  public static final String FEATURE_PROCESS_DOCDECL;
  public static final String FEATURE_VALIDATION;

  public void    setFeature(String name, boolean state)
   throws XmlPullParserException;
  public boolean getFeature(String name);
```

```
public void    setProperty(String name, Object value)
 throws XmlPullParserException;
public Object  getProperty(String name);
public void    setInput(Reader in)
 throws XmlPullParserException;
public void    setInput(InputStream in, String encoding)
 throws XmlPullParserException;
public String  getInputEncoding();
public void    defineEntityReplacementText(String entityName,
 String replacementText) throws XmlPullParserException;

public int     getNamespaceCount(int depth)
 throws XmlPullParserException;
public String  getNamespacePrefix(int position)
 throws XmlPullParserException;
public String  getNamespaceUri(int position)
 throws XmlPullParserException;
public String  getNamespace(String prefix);
public int     getDepth();
public String  getPositionDescription();
public int     getLineNumber();
public int     getColumnNumber();
public boolean isWhitespace() throws XmlPullParserException;
public String  getText();
public char[]  getTextCharacters(int holderForStartAndLength);
public String  getNamespace();
public String  getName();
public String  getPrefix();
public boolean isEmptyElementTag()
 throws XmlPullParserException;
public int     getAttributeCount();
public String  getAttributeNamespace(int index);
public String  getAttributeName(int index);
public String  getAttributePrefix(int index);
public String  getAttributeType(int index);
public boolean isAttributeDefault(int index);
public String  getAttributeValue(int index);
public String  getAttributeValue(String namespace,
 String name);
public int     getEventType()
 throws XmlPullParserException;
```

```
  public int     next()
   throws XmlPullParserException, IOException;
  public int     nextToken()
   throws XmlPullParserException, IOException;
  public void    require(int type, String namespace, String name)
   throws XmlPullParserException, IOException;
  public String  nextText()
   throws XmlPullParserException, IOException;
  public int     nextTag()
   throws XmlPullParserException, IOException;

}
```

XmlPullParserFactory

The `XmlPullParserFactory` class creates and configures new `XmlPullParser` objects in an implementation-independent fashion.

```
package org.xmlpull.v1;

public class XmlPullParserFactory  {

  public static final String PROPERTY_NAME;

  protected Vector    parserClasses;
  protected String    parserClassesLocation;
  protected Hashtable features;

  protected XmlPullParserFactory();

  public void    setFeature(String name, boolean state)
   throws XmlPullParserException;
  public boolean getFeature(String name);
  public void    setNamespaceAware(boolean awareness);
  public boolean isNamespaceAware();
  public void    setValidating(boolean validating);
  public boolean isValidating();

  public XmlPullParser newPullParser()
   throws XmlPullParserException;

  public static XmlPullParserFactory newInstance()
   throws XmlPullParserException;
```

```
  public static XmlPullParserFactory newInstance(
   String classNames, Class context)
   throws XmlPullParserException;

}
```

Exceptions and Errors

XMLPULL includes a single exception class, `XmlPullParserException`, which represents the various things that can go wrong while parsing an XML document. In addition, a few methods that perform I/O can throw an `IOException`.

XmlPullParserException

An `XmlPullParserException` indicates that something has gone wrong during a parse. This may be a well-formedness error in the document, such as an unclosed element or a programming error in the code.

```
package org.xmlpull.v1;

public class XmlPullParserException extends Exception {

  protected Throwable detail;
  protected int       row;
  protected int       column;

  public XmlPullParserException(String message);
  public XmlPullParserException(String message,
   XmlPullParser parser, Throwable detail);

  public Throwable getDetail();
  public int       getLineNumber();
  public int       getColumnNumber();
  public void      printStackTrace();

}
```

Appendix B

SOAP 1.1 Schemas

This appendix contains the complete, official schema for SOAP 1.1. This schema is organized in two documents, the envelope schema from *http://schemas.xml-soap.org/soap/envelope/* and the encoding schema from *http://schemas.xml-soap.org/soap/encoding/*. The envelope schema declares the SOAP complex types—`SOAP-ENV:Envelope`, `SOAP-ENV:header`, `SOAP-ENV:Body`, and so on—that define the basic structure of a SOAP document. The encoding schema declares the data types used in a SOAP document—`SOAP-ENC:int`, `SOAP-ENC:NMTOKENS`, `SOAP-ENC:gYear`, `SOAP-ENC:Array`, and so on.

Both of these schemas are Copyright © 2001 by Martin Gudgin. They are derived from the official SOAP 1.2 schemas and are subject to the fairly lenient W3C Software Licensing terms reprinted in the section entitled "W3C® Software Notice and License" at the end of this appendix. The white space has been cleaned up a little to fit everything within the margins of the page. Otherwise these are exactly as published at *schemas.xmlsoap.org*.

The SOAP 1.1 Envelope Schema

```
<?xml version='1.0' encoding='UTF-8' ?>

<!-- Schema for the SOAP/1.1 envelope
```

```
This schema has been produced using W3C's SOAP Version 1.2 schema
found at:

     http://www.w3.org/2001/06/soap-envelope

     Copyright 2001 Martin Gudgin, Developmentor.

Changes made are the following:
- reverted namespace to http://schemas.xmlsoap.org/soap/envelope/
- reverted mustUnderstand to only allow 0 and 1 as lexical values

Original copyright:

Copyright 2001 W3C (Massachusetts Institute of Technology,
Institut National de Recherche en Informatique et en Automatique,
Keio University). All Rights Reserved.
http://www.w3.org/Consortium/Legal/

This document is governed by the W3C Software License [1] as
described in the FAQ [2].

[1]http://www.w3.org/Consortium/Legal/copyright-software-19980720
[2]http://www.w3.org/Consortium/Legal/IPR-FAQ-20000620.html#DTD
-->
<xs:schema xmlns:xs="http://www.w3.org/2001/XMLSchema"
           xmlns:tns="http://schemas.xmlsoap.org/soap/envelope/"
    targetNamespace="http://schemas.xmlsoap.org/soap/envelope/" >


  <!-- Envelope, header and body -->
  <xs:element name="Envelope" type="tns:Envelope" />
  <xs:complexType name="Envelope" >
    <xs:sequence>
      <xs:element ref="tns:Header" minOccurs="0" />
      <xs:element ref="tns:Body" minOccurs="1" />
      <xs:any namespace="##other" minOccurs="0"
              maxOccurs="unbounded" processContents="lax" />
    </xs:sequence>
    <xs:anyAttribute namespace="##other" processContents="lax" />
  </xs:complexType>
```

```
<xs:element name="Header" type="tns:Header" />
<xs:complexType name="Header" >
  <xs:sequence>
    <xs:any namespace="##other" minOccurs="0"
            maxOccurs="unbounded" processContents="lax" />
  </xs:sequence>
  <xs:anyAttribute namespace="##other" processContents="lax" />
</xs:complexType>

<xs:element name="Body" type="tns:Body" />
<xs:complexType name="Body" >
  <xs:sequence>
    <xs:any namespace="##any" minOccurs="0"
            maxOccurs="unbounded" processContents="lax" />
  </xs:sequence>
  <xs:anyAttribute namespace="##any" processContents="lax" >
        <xs:annotation>
          <xs:documentation>
                Prose in the spec does not specify that
                attributes are allowed on the Body element
          </xs:documentation>
        </xs:annotation>
  </xs:anyAttribute>
</xs:complexType>


<!-- Global Attributes.  The following attributes are intended
     to be usable via qualified attribute names on any complex
     type referencing them.  -->
<xs:attribute name="mustUnderstand" default="0" >
   <xs:simpleType>
   <xs:restriction base='xs:boolean'>
        <xs:pattern value='0|1' />
      </xs:restriction>
 </xs:simpleType>
</xs:attribute>
<xs:attribute name="actor" type="xs:anyURI" />

<xs:simpleType name="encodingStyle" >
  <xs:annotation>
        <xs:documentation>
```

```
      'encodingStyle' indicates any canonicalization conventions
      followed in the contents of the containing element.  For
      example, the value
      'http://schemas.xmlsoap.org/soap/encoding/' indicates the
      pattern described in SOAP specification
          </xs:documentation>
        </xs:annotation>
    <xs:list itemType="xs:anyURI" />
  </xs:simpleType>

  <xs:attributeGroup name="encodingStyle" >
    <xs:attribute name="encodingStyle" type="tns:encodingStyle"/>
  </xs:attributeGroup>

  <xs:complexType name="Fault" final="extension" >
    <xs:annotation>
          <xs:documentation>
            Fault reporting structure
          </xs:documentation>
        </xs:annotation>
    <xs:sequence>
      <xs:element name="faultcode" type="xs:QName" />
      <xs:element name="faultstring" type="xs:string" />
      <xs:element name="faultactor" type="xs:anyURI"
                  minOccurs="0" />
    <xs:element name="detail" type="tns:detail" minOccurs="0"/>
    </xs:sequence>
  </xs:complexType>

  <xs:complexType name="detail">
    <xs:sequence>
      <xs:any namespace="##any" minOccurs="0"
              maxOccurs="unbounded" processContents="lax" />
    </xs:sequence>
    <xs:anyAttribute namespace="##any" processContents="lax" />
  </xs:complexType>

</xs:schema>
```

The SOAP 1.1 Encoding Schema

```
<?xml version='1.0' encoding='UTF-8' ?>

<!-- Schema for the SOAP/1.1 encoding

This schema has been produced using W3C's SOAP Version 1.2 schema
found at:

     http://www.w3.org/2001/06/soap-encoding

     Copyright 2001 Martin Gudgin, Developmentor.
         http://www.develop.co.uk

Changes made are the following:
- reverted namespace to http://schemas.xmlsoap.org/soap/encoding/
- reverted root to only allow 0 and 1 as lexical values

     Original copyright:

Copyright 2001 W3C (Massachusetts Institute of Technology,
Institut National de Recherche en Informatique et en Automatique,
Keio University). All Rights Reserved.
http://www.w3.org/Consortium/Legal/

     This document is governed by the W3C Software License [1] as
     described in the FAQ [2].

[1]http://www.w3.org/Consortium/Legal/copyright-software-19980720
[2]http://www.w3.org/Consortium/Legal/IPR-FAQ-20000620.html#DTD
-->
<xs:schema xmlns:xs="http://www.w3.org/2001/XMLSchema"
           xmlns:tns="http://schemas.xmlsoap.org/soap/encoding/"
    targetNamespace="http://schemas.xmlsoap.org/soap/encoding/" >

  <xs:attribute name="root" default="0" >
    <xs:annotation>
      <xs:documentation>
           'root' can be used to distinguish serialization
         roots from other elements that are present in a
```

```
        serialization but are not roots of a serialized
        value graph
      </xs:documentation>
    </xs:annotation>
    <xs:simpleType>
      <xs:restriction base='xs:boolean'>
           <xs:pattern value='0|1' />
         </xs:restriction>
    </xs:simpleType>
  </xs:attribute>

  <xs:attributeGroup name="commonAttributes" >
    <xs:annotation>
          <xs:documentation>
            Attributes common to all elements that function as
        accessors or represent independent (multi-ref) values.
        The href attribute is intended to be used in a manner
        like CONREF.  That is, the element content should be
        empty iff the href attribute appears
          </xs:documentation>
        </xs:annotation>
    <xs:attribute name="id" type="xs:ID" />
    <xs:attribute name="href" type="xs:anyURI" />
    <xs:anyAttribute namespace="##other" processContents="lax" />
  </xs:attributeGroup>

  <!-- Global Attributes.  The following attributes are intended
       to be usable via qualified attribute names on any complex
       type referencing them. -->

  <!-- Array attributes. Needed to give the type and dimensions
       of an array's contents, and the offset for
       partially-transmitted arrays. -->

  <xs:simpleType name="arrayCoordinate" >
    <xs:restriction base="xs:string" />
  </xs:simpleType>

  <xs:attribute name="arrayType" type="xs:string" />
  <xs:attribute name="offset" type="tns:arrayCoordinate" />
```

```
<xs:attributeGroup name="arrayAttributes" >
  <xs:attribute ref="tns:arrayType" />
  <xs:attribute ref="tns:offset" />
</xs:attributeGroup>

<xs:attribute name="position" type="tns:arrayCoordinate" />

<xs:attributeGroup name="arrayMemberAttributes" >
  <xs:attribute ref="tns:position" />
</xs:attributeGroup>

<xs:group name="Array" >
  <xs:sequence>
    <xs:any namespace="##any" minOccurs="0"
            maxOccurs="unbounded" processContents="lax" />
      </xs:sequence>
</xs:group>

<xs:element name="Array" type="tns:Array" />
<xs:complexType name="Array" >
  <xs:annotation>
        <xs:documentation>
  'Array' is a complex type for accessors identified by position
        </xs:documentation>
      </xs:annotation>
  <xs:group ref="tns:Array" minOccurs="0" />
  <xs:attributeGroup ref="tns:arrayAttributes" />
  <xs:attributeGroup ref="tns:commonAttributes" />
</xs:complexType>

<!-- 'Struct' is a complex type for accessors identified by
     name. Constraint: No element may be have the same name as
     any other, nor may any element have a maxOccurs > 1. -->

<xs:element name="Struct" type="tns:Struct" />

<xs:group name="Struct" >
  <xs:sequence>
    <xs:any namespace="##any" minOccurs="0"
            maxOccurs="unbounded" processContents="lax" />
```

```
      </xs:sequence>
  </xs:group>

  <xs:complexType name="Struct" >
    <xs:group ref="tns:Struct" minOccurs="0" />
    <xs:attributeGroup ref="tns:commonAttributes"/>
  </xs:complexType>

  <!-- 'Base64' can be used to serialize binary data using base64
       encoding as defined in RFC2045 but without the MIME line
       length limitation. -->

  <xs:simpleType name="base64" >
    <xs:restriction base="xs:base64Binary" />
  </xs:simpleType>

 <!-- Element declarations corresponding to each of the simple
      types in the XML Schemas Specification. -->

  <xs:element name="duration" type="tns:duration" />
  <xs:complexType name="duration" >
    <xs:simpleContent>
      <xs:extension base="xs:duration" >
        <xs:attributeGroup ref="tns:commonAttributes" />
      </xs:extension>
    </xs:simpleContent>
  </xs:complexType>

  <xs:element name="dateTime" type="tns:dateTime" />
  <xs:complexType name="dateTime" >
    <xs:simpleContent>
      <xs:extension base="xs:dateTime" >
        <xs:attributeGroup ref="tns:commonAttributes" />
      </xs:extension>
    </xs:simpleContent>
  </xs:complexType>


  <xs:element name="NOTATION" type="tns:NOTATION" />
  <xs:complexType name="NOTATION" >
    <xs:simpleContent>
```

```
      <xs:extension base="xs:QName" >
        <xs:attributeGroup ref="tns:commonAttributes" />
      </xs:extension>
    </xs:simpleContent>
  </xs:complexType>


  <xs:element name="time" type="tns:time" />
  <xs:complexType name="time" >
    <xs:simpleContent>
      <xs:extension base="xs:time" >
        <xs:attributeGroup ref="tns:commonAttributes" />
      </xs:extension>
    </xs:simpleContent>
  </xs:complexType>

  <xs:element name="date" type="tns:date" />
  <xs:complexType name="date" >
    <xs:simpleContent>
      <xs:extension base="xs:date" >
        <xs:attributeGroup ref="tns:commonAttributes" />
      </xs:extension>
    </xs:simpleContent>
  </xs:complexType>

  <xs:element name="gYearMonth" type="tns:gYearMonth" />
  <xs:complexType name="gYearMonth" >
    <xs:simpleContent>
      <xs:extension base="xs:gYearMonth" >
        <xs:attributeGroup ref="tns:commonAttributes" />
      </xs:extension>
    </xs:simpleContent>
  </xs:complexType>

  <xs:element name="gYear" type="tns:gYear" />
  <xs:complexType name="gYear" >
    <xs:simpleContent>
      <xs:extension base="xs:gYear" >
        <xs:attributeGroup ref="tns:commonAttributes" />
      </xs:extension>
    </xs:simpleContent>
  </xs:complexType>
```

```
<xs:element name="gMonthDay" type="tns:gMonthDay" />
<xs:complexType name="gMonthDay" >
  <xs:simpleContent>
    <xs:extension base="xs:gMonthDay" >
      <xs:attributeGroup ref="tns:commonAttributes" />
    </xs:extension>
  </xs:simpleContent>
</xs:complexType>

<xs:element name="gDay" type="tns:gDay" />
<xs:complexType name="gDay" >
  <xs:simpleContent>
    <xs:extension base="xs:gDay" >
      <xs:attributeGroup ref="tns:commonAttributes" />
    </xs:extension>
  </xs:simpleContent>
</xs:complexType>

<xs:element name="gMonth" type="tns:gMonth" />
<xs:complexType name="gMonth" >
  <xs:simpleContent>
    <xs:extension base="xs:gMonth" >
      <xs:attributeGroup ref="tns:commonAttributes" />
    </xs:extension>
  </xs:simpleContent>
</xs:complexType>

<xs:element name="boolean" type="tns:boolean" />
<xs:complexType name="boolean" >
  <xs:simpleContent>
    <xs:extension base="xs:boolean" >
      <xs:attributeGroup ref="tns:commonAttributes" />
    </xs:extension>
  </xs:simpleContent>
</xs:complexType>

<xs:element name="base64Binary" type="tns:base64Binary" />
<xs:complexType name="base64Binary" >
  <xs:simpleContent>
    <xs:extension base="xs:base64Binary" >
      <xs:attributeGroup ref="tns:commonAttributes" />
```

```
    </xs:extension>
  </xs:simpleContent>
</xs:complexType>

<xs:element name="hexBinary" type="tns:hexBinary" />
<xs:complexType name="hexBinary" >
  <xs:simpleContent>
   <xs:extension base="xs:hexBinary" >
     <xs:attributeGroup ref="tns:commonAttributes" />
   </xs:extension>
  </xs:simpleContent>
</xs:complexType>

<xs:element name="float" type="tns:float" />
<xs:complexType name="float" >
  <xs:simpleContent>
    <xs:extension base="xs:float" >
      <xs:attributeGroup ref="tns:commonAttributes" />
    </xs:extension>
  </xs:simpleContent>
</xs:complexType>

<xs:element name="double" type="tns:double" />
<xs:complexType name="double" >
  <xs:simpleContent>
    <xs:extension base="xs:double" >
      <xs:attributeGroup ref="tns:commonAttributes" />
    </xs:extension>
  </xs:simpleContent>
</xs:complexType>

<xs:element name="anyURI" type="tns:anyURI" />
<xs:complexType name="anyURI" >
  <xs:simpleContent>
    <xs:extension base="xs:anyURI" >
      <xs:attributeGroup ref="tns:commonAttributes" />
    </xs:extension>
  </xs:simpleContent>
</xs:complexType>
```

```
<xs:element name="QName" type="tns:QName" />
<xs:complexType name="QName" >
  <xs:simpleContent>
    <xs:extension base="xs:QName" >
      <xs:attributeGroup ref="tns:commonAttributes" />
    </xs:extension>
  </xs:simpleContent>
</xs:complexType>


<xs:element name="string" type="tns:string" />
<xs:complexType name="string" >
  <xs:simpleContent>
    <xs:extension base="xs:string" >
      <xs:attributeGroup ref="tns:commonAttributes" />
    </xs:extension>
  </xs:simpleContent>
</xs:complexType>

<xs:element name="normalizedString"
            type="tns:normalizedString" />
<xs:complexType name="normalizedString" >
  <xs:simpleContent>
    <xs:extension base="xs:normalizedString" >
      <xs:attributeGroup ref="tns:commonAttributes" />
    </xs:extension>
  </xs:simpleContent>
</xs:complexType>

<xs:element name="token" type="tns:token" />
<xs:complexType name="token" >
  <xs:simpleContent>
    <xs:extension base="xs:token" >
      <xs:attributeGroup ref="tns:commonAttributes" />
    </xs:extension>
  </xs:simpleContent>
</xs:complexType>

<xs:element name="language" type="tns:language" />
<xs:complexType name="language" >
  <xs:simpleContent>
```

```
      <xs:extension base="xs:language" >
        <xs:attributeGroup ref="tns:commonAttributes" />
      </xs:extension>
    </xs:simpleContent>
  </xs:complexType>

  <xs:element name="Name" type="tns:Name" />
  <xs:complexType name="Name" >
    <xs:simpleContent>
      <xs:extension base="xs:Name" >
        <xs:attributeGroup ref="tns:commonAttributes" />
      </xs:extension>
    </xs:simpleContent>
  </xs:complexType>

  <xs:element name="NMTOKEN" type="tns:NMTOKEN" />
  <xs:complexType name="NMTOKEN" >
    <xs:simpleContent>
      <xs:extension base="xs:NMTOKEN" >
        <xs:attributeGroup ref="tns:commonAttributes" />
      </xs:extension>
    </xs:simpleContent>
  </xs:complexType>

  <xs:element name="NCName" type="tns:NCName" />
  <xs:complexType name="NCName" >
    <xs:simpleContent>
      <xs:extension base="xs:NCName" >
        <xs:attributeGroup ref="tns:commonAttributes" />
      </xs:extension>
    </xs:simpleContent>
  </xs:complexType>

  <xs:element name="NMTOKENS" type="tns:NMTOKENS" />
  <xs:complexType name="NMTOKENS" >
    <xs:simpleContent>
      <xs:extension base="xs:NMTOKENS" >
        <xs:attributeGroup ref="tns:commonAttributes" />
      </xs:extension>
    </xs:simpleContent>
  </xs:complexType>
```

```
<xs:element name="ID" type="tns:ID" />
<xs:complexType name="ID" >
  <xs:simpleContent>
    <xs:extension base="xs:ID" >
      <xs:attributeGroup ref="tns:commonAttributes" />
    </xs:extension>
  </xs:simpleContent>
</xs:complexType>

<xs:element name="IDREF" type="tns:IDREF" />
<xs:complexType name="IDREF" >
  <xs:simpleContent>
    <xs:extension base="xs:IDREF" >
      <xs:attributeGroup ref="tns:commonAttributes" />
    </xs:extension>
  </xs:simpleContent>
</xs:complexType>

<xs:element name="ENTITY" type="tns:ENTITY" />
<xs:complexType name="ENTITY" >
  <xs:simpleContent>
    <xs:extension base="xs:ENTITY" >
      <xs:attributeGroup ref="tns:commonAttributes" />
    </xs:extension>
  </xs:simpleContent>
</xs:complexType>

<xs:element name="IDREFS" type="tns:IDREFS" />
<xs:complexType name="IDREFS" >
  <xs:simpleContent>
    <xs:extension base="xs:IDREFS" >
      <xs:attributeGroup ref="tns:commonAttributes" />
    </xs:extension>
  </xs:simpleContent>
</xs:complexType>

<xs:element name="ENTITIES" type="tns:ENTITIES" />
<xs:complexType name="ENTITIES" >
  <xs:simpleContent>
    <xs:extension base="xs:ENTITIES" >
      <xs:attributeGroup ref="tns:commonAttributes" />
```

```
      </xs:extension>
    </xs:simpleContent>
  </xs:complexType>

  <xs:element name="decimal" type="tns:decimal" />
  <xs:complexType name="decimal" >
    <xs:simpleContent>
      <xs:extension base="xs:decimal" >
        <xs:attributeGroup ref="tns:commonAttributes" />
      </xs:extension>
    </xs:simpleContent>
  </xs:complexType>

  <xs:element name="integer" type="tns:integer" />
  <xs:complexType name="integer" >
    <xs:simpleContent>
      <xs:extension base="xs:integer" >
        <xs:attributeGroup ref="tns:commonAttributes" />
      </xs:extension>
    </xs:simpleContent>
  </xs:complexType>

  <xs:element name="nonPositiveInteger"
              type="tns:nonPositiveInteger" />
  <xs:complexType name="nonPositiveInteger" >
    <xs:simpleContent>
      <xs:extension base="xs:nonPositiveInteger" >
        <xs:attributeGroup ref="tns:commonAttributes" />
      </xs:extension>
    </xs:simpleContent>
  </xs:complexType>

  <xs:element name="negativeInteger" type="tns:negativeInteger"/>
  <xs:complexType name="negativeInteger" >
    <xs:simpleContent>
      <xs:extension base="xs:negativeInteger" >
        <xs:attributeGroup ref="tns:commonAttributes" />
      </xs:extension>
    </xs:simpleContent>
  </xs:complexType>
```

```
<xs:element name="long" type="tns:long" />
<xs:complexType name="long" >
  <xs:simpleContent>
    <xs:extension base="xs:long" >
      <xs:attributeGroup ref="tns:commonAttributes" />
    </xs:extension>
  </xs:simpleContent>
</xs:complexType>

<xs:element name="int" type="tns:int" />
<xs:complexType name="int" >
  <xs:simpleContent>
    <xs:extension base="xs:int" >
      <xs:attributeGroup ref="tns:commonAttributes" />
    </xs:extension>
  </xs:simpleContent>
</xs:complexType>

<xs:element name="short" type="tns:short" />
<xs:complexType name="short" >
  <xs:simpleContent>
    <xs:extension base="xs:short" >
      <xs:attributeGroup ref="tns:commonAttributes" />
    </xs:extension>
  </xs:simpleContent>
</xs:complexType>

<xs:element name="byte" type="tns:byte" />
<xs:complexType name="byte" >
  <xs:simpleContent>
    <xs:extension base="xs:byte" >
      <xs:attributeGroup ref="tns:commonAttributes" />
    </xs:extension>
  </xs:simpleContent>
</xs:complexType>

<xs:element name="nonNegativeInteger"
            type="tns:nonNegativeInteger" />
<xs:complexType name="nonNegativeInteger" >
  <xs:simpleContent>
    <xs:extension base="xs:nonNegativeInteger" >
```

```
      <xs:attributeGroup ref="tns:commonAttributes" />
    </xs:extension>
  </xs:simpleContent>
</xs:complexType>

<xs:element name="unsignedLong" type="tns:unsignedLong" />
<xs:complexType name="unsignedLong" >
  <xs:simpleContent>
    <xs:extension base="xs:unsignedLong" >
      <xs:attributeGroup ref="tns:commonAttributes" />
    </xs:extension>
  </xs:simpleContent>
</xs:complexType>

<xs:element name="unsignedInt" type="tns:unsignedInt" />
<xs:complexType name="unsignedInt" >
  <xs:simpleContent>
    <xs:extension base="xs:unsignedInt" >
      <xs:attributeGroup ref="tns:commonAttributes" />
    </xs:extension>
  </xs:simpleContent>
</xs:complexType>

<xs:element name="unsignedShort" type="tns:unsignedShort" />
<xs:complexType name="unsignedShort" >
  <xs:simpleContent>
    <xs:extension base="xs:unsignedShort" >
      <xs:attributeGroup ref="tns:commonAttributes" />
    </xs:extension>
  </xs:simpleContent>
</xs:complexType>

<xs:element name="unsignedByte" type="tns:unsignedByte" />
<xs:complexType name="unsignedByte" >
  <xs:simpleContent>
    <xs:extension base="xs:unsignedByte" >
      <xs:attributeGroup ref="tns:commonAttributes" />
    </xs:extension>
  </xs:simpleContent>
</xs:complexType>
```

```
  <xs:element name="positiveInteger" type="tns:positiveInteger"/>
  <xs:complexType name="positiveInteger" >
    <xs:simpleContent>
      <xs:extension base="xs:positiveInteger" >
        <xs:attributeGroup ref="tns:commonAttributes" />
      </xs:extension>
    </xs:simpleContent>
  </xs:complexType>

  <xs:element name="anyType" />
</xs:schema>
```

W3C Software Notice and License

Copyright © 1994–2001 World Wide Web Consortium *[http://www.w3.org/]*, (Massachusetts Institute of Technology *[http://www.lcs.mit.edu/]*, Institut National de Recherche en Informatique et en Automatique *[http://www.inria.fr/]*, Keio University *[http://www.keio.ac.jp/]*). All Rights Reserved. http://www.w3.org/Consortium/Legal/

This W3C work (including software, documents, or other related items) is being provided by the copyright holders under the following license. By obtaining, using and/or copying this work, you (the licensee) agree that you have read, understood, and will comply with the following terms and conditions:

Permission to use, copy, modify, and distribute this software and its documentation, with or without modification, for any purpose and without fee or royalty is hereby granted, provided that you include the following on ALL copies of the software and documentation or portions thereof, including modifications, that you make:

1. The full text of this NOTICE in a location viewable to users of the redistributed or derivative work.
2. Any pre-existing intellectual property disclaimers, notices, or terms and conditions. If none exist, a short notice of the following form (hypertext is preferred, text is permitted) should be used within the body of any redistributed or derivative code: "Copyright © [$date-of-software] World Wide Web Consortium *[http://www.w3.org/]*, (Massachusetts Institute of Technology *[http://www.lcs.mit.edu/]*, Institut National de Recherche en Informatique et en Automatique *[http://www.inria.fr/]*, Keio University *[http://*

Appendix C

Recommended Reading

Books

In all likelihood, this is neither the first book you'll read on the subject of XML and Java, nor the last. The following books were useful to me while writing this book, and they may be helpful to you, too.

Callaway, D. R. 2001. *Inside Servlets, Second Edition*. Reading, MA.: Addison-Wesley. ISBN 0-201-70906-6.

Harold, E. R. 1999. *Java I/O.* Cambridge, MA: O'Reilly & Associates. ISBN 1-56592-485-1.

———. 2001. *XML Bible.* 2d edition. New York: Hungry Minds. ISBN 0-7645-4760-7.

———. 2001. *XML Bible.* Gold edition. New York: Hungry Minds. ISBN 0-7645-4819-0.

Harold, E. R., and W. S. Means. 2002. *XML in a Nutshell.* 2d edition. Cambridge: O'Reilly & Associates. ISBN 0-5960-0292-0.

Walsh, N., and L. Muellner. 2002. *DocBook: The Definitive Guide [http://www.docbook.org/tdg/en/]*. Cambridge, MA: O'Reilly & Associates.

Specifications

What follows are the official specifications for the technologies discussed in this book, such as DOM, SAX, and XML. I would not in general recommend these as the first place to look to figure out how to do something, but when you need to know exactly why something has failed, these are the canonical sources.

Biron, P. V., and Ashok Malhotra, eds. 2001. *XML Schema Part 2: Datatypes. [http://www.w3.org/TR/2001/REC-xmlschema-2-20010502/]* World Wide Web Consortium, 2 May.

Box, D., D. Ehnebuske, G. Kakivaya, A. Layman, N. Mendelsohn, H. F. Nielsen, S. Thatte, and D. Winer. 2000. *Simple Object Access Protocol (SOAP) 1.1. [http://www.w3.org/TR/2000/NOTE-SOAP-20000508]* World Wide Web Consortium, 8 May.

Bray, T., D. Hollander, and A. Layman, eds. 1999. *Namespaces in XML. [http://www.w3.org/TR/1999/REC-xml-names-19990114]* World Wide Web Consortium, 14 January.

Bray, T., J. Paoli, C. M. Sperberg-McQueen, and E. Maler, eds. 2000. *Extensible Markup Language (XML) 1.0. 2d edition. [http://www.w3.org/TR/2000/REC-xml-20001006]*. World Wide Web Consortium, 6 October.

Clark, J. 1999. *XSL Transformations (XSLT) Version 1.0. [http://www.w3.org/TR/1999/REC-xslt-19991116]* World Wide Web Consortium, 16 November.

Clark, J., and S. DeRose, eds. 1999. *XML Path Language (XPath) Version 1.0. [http://www.w3.org/TR/1999/REC-xpath-19991116]* World Wide Web Consortium, 16 November.

Cowan, J., and R. Tobin, eds. 2001. *XML Information Set. [http://www.w3.org/TR/2001/REC-xml-infoset-20011024]* World Wide Web Consortium, 24 October.

DeRose, S., E. Maler, and D. Orchard, eds. 2001. *XML Linking Language (XLink) Version 1.0. [http://www.w3.org/TR/2000/REC-xlink-20010627/]* World Wide Web Consortium, 27 June.

Fallside, D. C., ed. 2001. *XML Schema Part 0: Primer. [http://www.w3.org/TR/2001/REC-xmlschema-0-20010502/]* W3C XML Schema Working Group, World Wide Web Consortium, 2 May.

Hunter, J., and B. McLaughlin. *JDOM. [http://www.jdom.org/]*.

Kesselman, J., J. Robie, M. Champion, P. Sharpe, V. Apparao, and L. Wood, eds. 2000. *Document Object Model (DOM) Level 2 Traversal and Range Specification Version 1.0. [http://www.w3.org/TR/2000/REC-DOM-Level-2-Traversal-Range-20001113]* W3C DOM Working Group, World Wide Web Consortium, 13 November.

Le Hors, A., and L. Cable, eds. 2000. *Document Object Model (DOM) Level 2 Views Specification Version 1.0. [http://www.w3.org/TR/2000/REC-DOM-Level-2-Views-20001113]* World Wide Web Consortium, 13 November.

Le Hors, A., P. Le Hégaret, and L. Wood, eds. 2000. *Document Object Model (DOM) Level 2 Core Specification Core Version 1.0. [http://www.w3.org/TR/2000/REC-DOM-Level-2-20001113]* World Wide Web Consortium, 3 November.

Le Hors, A., P. Le Hégaret, and L. Wood, eds. 2002. *Document Object Model (DOM) Level 3 Core Specification. [http://www.w3.org/TR/2002/WD-DOM-Level-3-Core-20020409]* World Wide Web Consortium, 9 April.

Megginson, D., and D. Brownell. *SAX. [http://www.saxproject.org/]*.

Pixley, T., ed. 2000. *Document Object Model (DOM) Level 2 Events Specification Version 1.0. [http://www.w3.org/TR/2000/REC-DOM-Level-2-Events-20001113]* World Wide Web Consortium, 13 November.

Thompson, H. S., D. Beech, M. Maloney, and N. Mendelson, eds. 2001. *XML Schema Part 1: Structures. [http://www.w3.org/TR/2001/REC-xmlschema-1-20010502/]* World Wide Web Consortium, 2 May.

Whitmer, R., ed. 2002. *Document Object Model (DOM) Level 3 XPath Specification. [http://www.w3.org/TR-2002/WD-DOM-Level-3-XPath-20020328]* World Wide Web Consortium, 28 March.

Wilson C., P. Le Hégaret, and V. Apparao, eds. *Document Object Model (DOM) Level 2 Style Specification Version 1.0. [http://www.w3.org/TR/2000/REC-DOM-Level-2-Style-2000113]* World Wide Web Consortium, 13 November.

Winer, D. 1999. *XML-RPC Specification. [http://www.xml-rpc.com/]* UserLand Software, 12 December.

Index

D

E

Q

R

S

X

Z

I wrote this book in XML from start to finish. The specific XML application used was DocBook 4.2.0; I use the jEdit text editor on Windows and Linux to write. XInclude was used to merge the individual chapters and examples. I used Michael Kay's Saxon XSLT processor and Norm Walsh's XSL stylesheets for Docbook 1.52.2 to produce the HTML and XSL-FO output. I used FOP 0.20.4 to convert the XSL-FO files to PDFs. Stratford Publishing Services pulled the DocBook source files into Adobe FrameMaker 7.0 for typesetting. The text of this book is set in 10.5 point Berkeley on a 13-point lead. The code is set in Lucida Sans LDX. The display text is set in Stone Sans.

—Elliotte Rusty Harold